T0398185

Representation and Effectiveness in Latin American Democracies

Legislatures, the judiciary and civil society are important actors in representative democracies. In what ways and how well do they represent? How effectively do they carry out their institutional and social roles? Both questions refer to the key dimensions of democracy analyzed in this book: representativeness and effectiveness, respectively. While they have been developed separately in scholarly work on institutions and regimes, there is little work considering them simultaneously, and focusing on their interaction. Using quantitative and/or qualitative methods, contributions from top scholars in the field of legislatures, the judiciary and civil society examine these two concepts and their relationships in four Latin American countries: Argentina, Brazil, Chile and Mexico.

The chapters engage in a larger set of theoretical debates about different approaches to representation in each sphere. In doing so, they also debate how effectively these spheres carry out their roles in each country: whether Congress is institutionalized, its accountability and its performance as a lawmaker; whether the judicial system is independent, carries out oversight and protects citizen rights; and the role of civil society in a representative democracy.

Representation and Effectiveness in Latin American Democracies is a timely and welcome contribution to the to the growing debate about the quality of democracy in Latin America, and the developing world more generally.

Moira B. MacKinnon is a Post-Doctoral Fellow at the Center for Inter-American Policy and Research (CIPR) at Tulane University. She is a political and historical sociologist whose area of special interest is political institutions in Latin America, in particular Congress and political parties in the South Cone.

Ludovico Feoli is the director of the Center for Inter-American Policy and Research (CIPR) and a Research Associate Professor in the Stone Center for Latin American Studies and the Department of Political Science at Tulane University. His research interests include the political economy of market reforms in Latin America, institutions and institutional change, and the quality of governance.

Routledge Studies in Latin American Politics

Representation and Effectiveness in Latin American Democracies

Congress, Judiciary and Civil Society

**Edited by Moira B. MacKinnon
and Ludovico Feoli**

Routledge
Taylor & Francis Group

NEW YORK AND LONDON

First published 2013
by Routledge
711 Third Avenue, New York, NY 10017

Simultaneously published in the UK
by Routledge
2 Park Square, Milton Park, Abingdon, Oxfordshire OX14 4RN

First issued in paperback 2015

*Routledge is an imprint of the Taylor & Francis Group,
an informa business*

Library of Congress Cataloging-in-Publication Data
Representation and effectiveness in Latin American democracies : congress,
    judiciary and civil society / edited by Moira B. MacKinnon and Ludovico Feoli.
        pages cm. — (Routledge studies in Latin American politics)
    1. Representative government and representation—Latin America—Case
studies.   2. Legislative bodies—Latin America—Case studies.   3. Courts—
Latin America—Case studies.   4. Civil society—Latin America—Case
studies.   I. Mackinnon, Moira (Moira B.)
    JL963.R46 2013
    328.8'0734—dc23
    2012046111

ISBN 13: 978-1-138-92640-0 (pbk)
ISBN 13: 978-0-415-82433-0 (hbk)

Typeset in Sabon
by Apex CoVantage, LLC

Contents

PART III
Judiciary

PART IV
Civil Society

PART V

Figures and Tables

Acknowledgments

This volume emerged from a symposium held at the Center for Inter-American Policy and Research (CIPR), Tulane University, on March 24, 2011, organized by Moira B. MacKinnon. Our scholarly interests are very much invested in the process of democratization in Latin America and the symposium was an invitation to examine how the variables of representativeness and effectiveness—two central dimensions of democracy and democratization—interact within and between specific spheres of democratic regimes.

We would like to thank the Center for Inter-American Policy and Research (CIPR) at Tulane University for providing funding for the meeting, and the Stone Center for Latin American Studies at Tulane University for providing a venue and general support, particularly through its director, Thomas F. Reese, and his staff. We would also like to thank CIPR staff members Angela Reed, for logistical support during the conference, and Kelly Jones, for her help with preparing the manuscript for publication.

We are also grateful to the two anonymous reviewers for their comments. Finally, we thank our authors, political scientists, legal scholars and sociologists, who agreed to address the questions we proposed on representativeness and effectiveness and apply them to their countries of study.

Contributors

Eduardo Alemán specializes in the comparative analysis of political institutions and Latin American politics. He holds a Ph.D. in Political Science from the University of California, Los Angeles. He teaches courses in comparative politics, comparative legislatures, and Latin American politics at the University of Houston. His current work focuses on executive-legislative relations, parliamentary procedures, government coalitions and agenda-setting across Latin American legislatures. Professor Alemán has published articles in such journals as *World Politics*, *Comparative Politics*, *Comparative Political Studies*, *Legislative Studies Quarterly*, *Electoral Studies*, *Journal of Theoretical Politics* and *Latin American Research Review*.

María Amparo Casar is a professor and researcher at the Department of Public Administration of the Centro de Investigación y Docencia Económicas (CIDE) in Mexico City. She has a Ph.D. in Political and Social Science from Cambridge University. She specializes in the study of the Mexican Congress and executive-legislative relations, as well as on comparative electoral and presidential systems. She has published books and academic essays on topics ranging from the state intervention in the economy to Mexican presidentialism and coalition-building within Congress and between the executive and legislative branches of government. Her latest publication is *The Mexican Political System* (Mexico City: Oxford University Press). She is also a contributing editor of *Reforma* newspaper and her opinions appear regularly in major newspapers and journals as well as in radio and television political analysis programs.

Javier Couso is a constitutionalist and socio-legal scholar who specializes in the law and politics of Latin America. He holds a Ph.D. in Jurisprudence and Social Policy from the University of California, Berkeley. He is a Professor of Law and Sociology at Universidad Diego Portales (in Santiago, Chile) and also a member of the Executive Committee of the International Association of Constitutional Law (IACL). Professor Couso has been a Visiting Professor at the University of Leiden (The Netherlands), the University of Melbourne (Australia), Bocconi University in Milan (Italy), and the University of Wisconsin, Madison (United States). Recent publications include "Models of Democracy and Models of Constitutionalism: The Case of Chile's Constitutional Court, 1970-2010", in *Texas Law Review* (2011); *Constitutional Law in Chile* (Wolters Kluwer, 2011); and *Cultures of Legality: Judicialization and Political Activism in Latin America* (Cambridge University Press, 2010), with Alexandra Huneeus and Rachel Sieder, eds.

Evelina Dagnino is Full Professor of Political Science at the University of Campinas, São Paulo, Brazil. She has a Ph.D. in Political Science from Stanford University and has published extensively in several countries on democracy and citizenship, the relations between culture and politics, social movements, civil society and participation. She has been a Visiting Professor at Yale University, Goteborg University, FLACSO–Buenos Aires and Universidad de Costa Rica.

Gonzalo Delamaza has a Ph.D. in Sociology from Leiden University (The Netherlands). He is a specialist in civil society and its role in public affairs. He is a researcher of the University of Los Lagos, Chile, and director of the Center for Research in Society and Public Policies. In 2003 he was Visiting Scholar at the David Rockefeller Center for Latin American Studies at Harvard University. He has published *Tan Lejos Tan Cerca. Sociedad Civil y Políticas Públicas en Chile* (LOM, 2005), *Local Government and Human Rights* (IGPA, 2008) and *Enhancing Democracy: Public Policies and Citizen Participation in Chile* (Bergnhahn Books, forthcoming). He has publshed articles in journals such as as *Latin American Research Review*, *Reforma y Democracia*, *POLIS Latin American Review* and *Gestión y Política Pública*

Ludovico Feoli is the director of the Center for Inter-American Policy and Research (CIPR) and a Research Associate Professor in the Stone Center for Latin American Studies and the Department of Political Science at Tulane University. His research interests include the political economy of market reforms in Latin America, institutions and institutional change, and the quality of governance. He is currently the executive director of the Centro de Investigación y Adiestramiento Político Administrativo, CIAPA, in San José, Costa Rica. He has served as country expert for the Bertelsmann Transformation Index and a researcher for the Proyecto Estado de la Nación in Costa Rica. His most recent publications include "Desempeño legislativo en la primera legislatura de la administración Chinchilla," in *Programa Estado de la Nación*, and "Gobernabilidad y la medición de la efectividad legislativa desde la prensa: el caso de Costa Rica" in *Algo más que presidentes. El papel del Poder Legislativo en América Latina*, edited by M. Alcántara and M. García-Montero,

Fundación Manuel Giménez Abad de Estudios Parlamentarios y del Estado Autonómico, both in 2011. He received his Ph.D. in Political Science from Tulane University in 2007.

Matthew C. Ingram is currently a Visiting Fellow at the Kellogg Institute for International Studies at the University of Notre Dame. In the fall he will be joining the Department of Political Science at SUNY–Albany as Assistant Professor. He has a J.D. and a Ph.D. from the University of New Mexico. His research examines legal and justice sector reforms in Latin America, and the political origins of institutional change and judicial behavior, emphasizing a subnational level of analysis in Brazil and Mexico. His work has been accepted for publication in *Comparative Politics* and *The Journal of Law, Economics, and Organization*. He has also authored several chapters in forthcoming edited volumes, as well as policy and research reports on a high profile and ongoing criminal procedure reform in Mexico. His research has led to consulting, including a project with the Mexican government funded by the U.S. Agency for International Development (USAID).

Mark P. Jones is the Joseph D. Jamail Chair in Latin American Studies, the James A. Baker III Institute for Public Policy's Fellow in Political Science, and the Chairman of the Department of Political Science at Rice University. He is the author of more than 50 articles and chapters on Argentine politics and government and has given over three dozen lectures throughout Argentina for universities, think tanks, provincial governments, municipal governments, national government bodies and others. Dr. Jones received his doctorate from the University of Michigan and his bachelor's degree from Tulane University.

Moira B. MacKinnon is a Post-Doctoral Fellow at the Center for Inter-American Policy and Research (CIPR) at Tulane University. She has a Ph.D. in Sociology from the University of California–San Diego. She is a political and historical sociologist whose area of special interest is political institutions in Latin America, in particular Congress and political parties in the South Cone. She has published *Los Años Formativos del Partido Peronista (1946–1950)* (Buenos Aires: Instituto Di Tella–Siglo Veintiuno de Argentina Editores, 2002), and various articles on this topic. She is currently working on a book manuscript on her dissertation topic, a comparative study of the passage of social legislation through the Chilean and Argentine Congresses in the first half of 20th century.

Juan Pablo Micozzi is an Assistant Professor in the Department of Political Science at the University of New Mexico. His research focuses on Argentine political institutions, with particular focus on Argentine legislative politics and party politics at the national, provincial and municipal levels. His work has appeared in several edited volumes and journals such as *The Journal of Politics* and *The Journal of Politics of Latin America*. Dr. Micozzi received his Ph.D. from Rice University and his licenciatura from the Universidad de Buenos Aires.

Carlos Pereira is Professor of Political Economy and Public Policy at the Brazilian School of Public and Business Administration—EBAPE at the Getulio Vargas Foundation (FGV). He has a Ph.D. in Political Science from the New School University in New York and was recently a visiting fellow in the Latin America Initiative, Foreign Policy and Global Economy and Development programs at the Brookings Institution. He has published in *Journal of Politics, Comparative Political Studies, Legislative Studies Quarterly, Political Research Quarterly, Governance, Electoral Studies, Quarterly Review of Economics and Finance, Journal of Legislative Studies, Journal of Latin American Studies, Latin American Politics and Society* and *Journal of Politics in Latin America*. He has also coedited *Regulatory Governance in Infrastructure Industries* (Trends and Public Policy Options, No. 3, The World Bank). He has also been involved in many consultancy and research projects with interdisciplinary research teams at the World Bank, Inter-American Development Bank, Department for International Development DFID/UK, Coperación Andina de Fomento–CAF, among others.

Enrique Peruzzotti is Professor in the Political Science Department of Di Tella University and a researcher of CONICET, Argentina. His work on accountability politics, democratic innovation and civil society has appeared in *Global Governance, Human Rights Quarterly, Citizenship Studies, Journal of Democracy, Journal of Third World Studies, Journal of Latin American Studies* and *Constellations: An International Journal of Critical and Democratic Theory*. His edited volume *Critical Theory and Democracy: Civil Society, Dictatorship, and Constitutionalism in Andrew Arato's Democratic Theory* is forthcoming from Routledge.

Lucio Renno is Director and Associate Professor in the Research Center and Graduate Program on the Americas at the University of Brasilia. His research focuses on politics and governance in Latin America, particularly Brazil. Most recently his studies have focused on political crises in Latin America and the effects these have on citizens' views of democracy and democratic institutions. Professor Renno received his Ph.D. from the University of Pittsburgh. His most recent publications include *Split Ticket Voting as the Rule: Voters and Permanent Divided Government in Brazil* (with Barry Ames and Andy Baker), *Rewarding the Corrupt? Reelection and Scandal Involvement in the Brazilian 2006 Legislative Election* and *Agenda Power, Executive Decree Authority, and the Mixed Results of Reform in the Brazilian Congress* (with Carlos Pereira and Timothy Power).

Julio Rios-Figueroa is Assistant Professor at the Division of Political Studies at CIDE, in Mexico City. He received his Ph.D. in political science from New York University, and was a Hauser Research Scholar at New York University School of Law. Professor Rios-Figueroa's research focuses on comparative political institutions, constitutionalism, law and courts, and Latin American politics. His articles on these topics have appeared in journals such as *Comparative Politics*, *Comparative Political Studies*, *Journal of Latin American Politics* and *Latin American Politics and Society*. He is coeditor of the volume *Courts in Latin America* (with Gretchen Hemke), and is currently working on a book-length study of constitutional justice and democracy in Latin America.

Daniel Alberto Sabsay is Professor of Constitutional Law and Director of the LLM on Constitutional Law at the University of Buenos Aires. He has a law degree from the University of Buenos Aires and pursued postgraduate studies at the Université de Droit de Sciences Sociales et Sciences Économiques Paris II, France. He has been Visiting Professor at the Robert Schuman University (Strasbourg, France); the University of Texas–Austin; and at the International University of Andalucía (Spain). He is the President of Fundación Ambiente y Recursos Naturales, an Argentine NGO.

Part I
Introduction

Introduction
The Representativeness–Effectiveness Dilemma

Moira B. MacKinnon and Ludovico Feoli

When studying the intricacies of Latin American democracies from the 1980s until today, scholars focus on different aspects of institutions and the broader regime context in which they are immersed: elections, political parties, legislatures, executive-legislative relations, courts, judges, oversight bodies, informal institutions, alternative models of democracy, civil society, civic participation, participatory democracy, and so on. Representativeness and effectiveness, the two concepts this book addresses, are central dimensions in the analysis of these topics because they capture important aspects of democracy and democratization. As a result, there is a considerable body of literature on both. However, in spite of the development of these two individual concepts, there is surprisingly little work on institutions or regimes considering both variables simultaneously, and on their interaction and reciprocal influences. Moreover, there is little work in this direction on the judiciary, and work on civil society is not usually included in edited volumes on the topic of political representation.

This book addresses these gaps in the literature. It examines whether it is possible to apply representativeness and effectiveness to the analysis of the judiciary, congress and civil society, and what these dimensions mean in each sphere. Does one have priority over the other in the development of a strong Congress, judiciary, civil society? What are the implications for democracy? Is curtailing representativeness the only way to improve effectiveness? Conversely, is it necessary to reduce effectiveness in order to ensure representativeness? Or is a balance between both dimensions possible? How do historical trajectory and institutional design affect these outcomes?

The chapters grapple with these questions as they build on analyses of Congress, the judiciary and civil society in Argentina, Brazil, Chile and Mexico. They examine the relationship between representativeness and effectiveness in these three key spheres of democratic representative regimes, including the relationship between votes and seats, the presence of different citizen perspectives in legislatures and the dynamics of Congress; judicial oversight of institutional checks and balances and citizens' rights, accessibility of the justice system, the role of judges and civic organizations; the effect of different kinds of civic initiatives on representation, the different meanings of the term representation and the role of civil society in a representative democracy. Some chapters focus more on representativeness, others on effectiveness, but most engage both concepts.

In addition to examining the different ways the concepts of representativeness and effectiveness apply to Congress, the judiciary and civil society in the four countries included in the volume, the chapters are engaged in a larger set of theoretical debates. One of these contrasts procedural electoral arrangements to correspondence or resemblance as different approaches to representativeness in legislatures. Another refers to the conventional means of access to power and policymakers, understood in terms of elections, versus means based on social organization and the actions of civil society, and the various meanings of representation in this context. A third debate refers to representativeness in the judicial sphere and sets forth different forms by which citizens could or should influence or gain access to the judicial system: elections, progressive judges and activist courts, or civil society organizations. The chapters are also involved in debates about the ways the three spheres carry out their roles within their countries; that is, their effectiveness: whether a Congress is institutionalized and to what degree, its level of accountability and its performance as a lawmaker; whether a judicial system is independent, carries out oversight and protects citizens rights; and the role of civil society in public affairs and a representative democracy.

Below, we first look at the concept of representativeness in the three spheres: Congress, the judiciary and civil society. Then we do the same for effectiveness and, finally, we examine the relations between the dimensions both within the spheres and at the systemic level.

REPRESENTATIVENESS

Representativeness has mostly been applied to the study of Congress. In broad terms, two perspectives or emphases underlie many contemporary analyses of legislatures: one centers on the procedural arrangements that connect votes, parties and seats in the legislature, while the other focuses on resemblance, or the "presence" of citizens' views and interests in Congress. In turn, these two emphases are interpreted and applied in different ways. In this volume, Alemán, Jones and Micozzi, and Renno and Pereira can be included in the first group, MacKinnon in the second, while Casar uses criteria from both.

In the first group, some authors study the conditions and effects of election rules, the relationship between votes and seats, and coalitions in Congress (Lijphart 1990; Moreno et al. 2003; Snyder and Samuels 2001; Taagepera and Shugart 1989). Others focus on mandate responsiveness of representatives or the accountability of representatives to their constituents, through elections (Manin, Przeworski and Stokes 1999, 29, 40; Stokes 1999; Cheibub and Pzreworski 1999). Carey (2009, 7) further distinguishes between collective (party leadership is the principal to which legislators are directly accountable) and individual representation (accountability to voters, but also, potentially, to party leaders, presidents, governors, activists, interest groups and others).

The second group looks at representation in terms of resemblance or correspondence between voters and representatives. One way of understanding this conception is "descriptive representation," where representatives mirror the composition of society in terms of race, gender, class, religion, occupation, tribe, and so on (Pitkin 1967, Chapter 4), or as a selective form of representation to contingently "compensate for the effects of some other process that interferes with an expected proportionality" (as in the case of minorities) (Mansbridge 1999, 632–3, 638; Phillips 1995). Another interpretation is through "aligned objectives" between voters and representatives as in "gyroscopic representation." In this case, likeness can refer to points of view, objectives regarding policy issues, values, personal attitudes and also physical similarity, as in descriptive representation (Mansbridge 2009, 380–81). Voters select such representatives because they are self-reliant, and can be counted on to pursue the interests and objectives they stand for without external incentives or sanctions. Another line of research is the case of "substantive representation," where authors study the correspondence between political party representatives and citizens on issue representation (e.g., social welfare, economic policies, immigration) to examine citizen influence (Powell 2004).

Representation can also be considered from a different perspective to include various kinds of actions and relationships besides the electoral ones of legislatures. For example, the view that distinguishes between proxies and deputies: the former *stand for* the represented while the latter *act for* or *speak for* them, in a principal-agent relationship (Pettit 2009). Citizen juries stand for a cross-section of the community, thus representing (standing for) the whole. Similarly, new participatory institutions such as participatory budgeting and municipal health councils are formed by representative samples of the population. Judges, prosecutors, public auditors and ombudsmen, as well as other appointed officials, can be seen as representatives standing for the society as a whole. The second relationship, in which representatives act as deputies, is essential for the aggregation of multiple views into coherent positions required in large and plural representative democracies (Disch 2012, 603). Representatives in this role must act for the represented, based on what they consider their best interest (Pitkin 1967). Legislatures may act as deputies, but this role is not exclusive to them. Courts, for example, assume it when they strike down policies to protect public interests such as the environment or the constitutional rights of minorities (De Sousa 2010).

The authors of this volume writing about the judiciary and civil society examine the relevance of representation outside the legislative sphere. In judicial institutions representativeness can be a controversial concept. Therefore, a first consideration is whether judicial institutions should be representative at all, and if so, how that representation should be conceptualized. In ways akin to the conventional meaning stemming from elections, that is, through elected judges? The authors discuss the implications of elections for the impartiality of judges and their role as adjudicators of preestablished rules and legislation (Rios, Couso, Sabsay) and also whether judges do not represent interests or ideologies in a de facto manner, even when they are not elected (Ingram). A second approach is to propose "accessibility" to the justice system as an alternative to representation, since it provides greater proximity to the people's concerns (Rios). How easily can all members of society and, in particular, minorities, the poor and the marginalized, enlist the judiciary to guarantee their civil and constitutional rights (Ingram)? A third way the authors take on representativeness in the judicial sphere is by examining the embrace of socially inclusive agendas, either by judges (Ingram) or groups in civil society that advocate for social rights and by ratifying certain international and regional treaties (Sabsay). In this view, ". . . the judiciary capitalizes on its capabilities and leads the protection of minorities' rights, [and] courts become an alternative societal representative in the process of policy and social transformation" (De Sousa 2010, 89). These actions, which produce some kind of representativeness, have consequences for the effectiveness of the judiciary, as we will see below.

The separation of powers also plays an important role in generating representation by inducing the government, through checks and balances, to "reveal information about the true conditions under which it operates," thus "enabling accountability through retrospective voting" (Manin, Przeworski and Stokes 1999, 19). If elections are an imperfect mechanism of accountability, other mediated forms of accountability are also necessary. For example, bureaucrats enact policies, but politicians have to respond to voters for those policies; government is accountable to legislators, who are accountable to voters; the judiciary also holds the government accountable and protects voters from abuses. Thus, the structure of government could be "such that its various branches control each other to make the government as a whole act in the best interest of the public" (Manin et al. 1999, 25). According to these authors, unlike in the case of voting, there is a need for more research uncovering these types of effects of government structure upon representation. We believe this volume contributes to our understanding of this issue.

Representativeness is a familiar concern in scholarly work on civil society and can refer to both civil society organizations and/or the democratic regime. Although representativeness in democracy is typically understood as based on elections, the study of civil society challenges this conceptualization and expands the notion of representation to incorporate the organization of social groups that influence politics beyond electoral means (as Peruzzotti's chapter argues). The importance of this kind of representation has grown with the withdrawal of the state from the provision of public goods and the collapse of the party system in various Latin American countries. Taking up the critiques of those who question the legitimacy of civil society organizations by raising doubts about their representative status, Peruzzotti classifies the various new forms of citizen participation and specifies their varying effects and implications for the traditional electoral understanding of democratic representation. If electoral representation has certain limits or rigidities, such as a difficulty to represent marginalized or emerging constituencies, the sacrifice of deliberation to the needs of expedient decision-making, or the obstruction of direct citizen impact on politics (Urbinatti and Warren 2008, 403), civil society actors can open the way for new forms of representation and participation. Dagnino's chapter looks into the different meanings of representation and representativeness, arguing that they are connected to both historical contexts and contrasting conceptions of democracy, and that they express struggles to legitimize forms of representation that do not usually rely on formal authorization and accountability. She finds two main meanings (among various others) of the relation of representation: a more classic meaning, traditionally associated with social movements, that implies an organic link between represented and representatives and another meaning, mediation, closer to a "coincidence of interests" in which NGOs are erected as representatives of civil society *par excellence* and in which technical competence plays the key legitimating role.

How important are the activities of civil society organizations for the representative dimension of a democratic regime? This is the subject of Delamaza's chapter, which examines a society exhibiting political disaffiliation and an attendant decrease in electoral participation, a rising loss of trust in parliamentary institutions, a general decline in the support for democracy, and perhaps most importantly, the explosion of social protest on a massive scale with a manifest rejection of institutionalized political parties and representative institutions (Delamaza).

While an unprecedented number of countries are now democracies, and this regime type is becoming entrenched as the only legitimate standard for governance internationally, discontent with democracy, or at least some aspects of it, has also emerged as a problem. In some countries, popular confidence in democratic institutions is fading, voters are disaffected, trust in government is at a nadir, and there is a broadening gulf between citizens, governments and political elites (Pateman 2012). At the risk of oversimplifying, it might be said that this discontent emerges from a sense that the mechanisms of representative democracy fail to promote the interests of the majority and the *res publica*, that the social contract at the core of the democratic process has become dysfunctional. In a word, it is driven by a lack of effectiveness.

EFFECTIVENESS

Effectiveness, the second concept this book addresses, pertains to how Congress, the judiciary and civil society exercise their functions—that the legislature passes laws, acts as a public forum and exercises political control; that the judiciary validates the constitutionality of those laws and enforces them, while also processing jurisdictional disputes and protecting individual rights; and that civil society enables citizens to exercise accountability outside of elections and presses for the advancement of citizen perspectives and interests not contemplated or embraced by the legislature. Thus, the term's meaning varies according to the sphere in which it is applied, but always refers to performance.

Different approaches use different methods to evaluate the effectiveness of Congress: some are based on perception (public opinion polls and elite and expert surveys), others on capabilities (career paths, committee assignments and time demands) and a third group looks at outcomes (the number of bills passed, the proportion initiated by Congress) (see the overview in Alemán's chapter). Some authors argue that an effective Congress would have institutionalized procedures and parties that can build or impose agreements (MacKinnon), and competent, career legislators who pass good laws and are trusted (Renno and Pereira). Casar distinguishes between effectiveness of process and effectiveness of outcome, evaluating the Mexican Congress in terms of the approval rates of bills, the capacity of the three largest parties to come together actively and effectively to pass key pieces of legislation, and the level of legislative activism in bill initiation. Alemán measures effectiveness by assessing elite and public opinion polls, the levels of competency in the legislature, and the outputs generated by it, particularly in the production of laws.

In the judicial section, the authors examine different judicial bodies in their case countries—the ordinary first- and second-instance courts, the Constitutional Court, the Supreme Court, and the Public Prosecutor's Office—or the judicial system as a whole, analyzing their history and evolution and evaluating their performance. They consider a judicial system effective when judiciary institutions fulfill their oversight role in the system of institutional checks and balances, controlling the executive and legislative powers through judicial review, while also protecting the rights of all citizens equally and fairly, and adjudicating disputes impartially (Rios, Ingram), as well as reaching timely decisions that are in accordance with the Constitution and the laws (Couso). Some of the authors focus on the need for judicial independence and separation of powers, or "the perverse set of incentives" that lies at the root of the lack of independence from the executive (Rios) and the effects of a lack of institutional continuity (Sabsay), while others consider the lack of access for broad sectors of the population (Ingram).

From the perspective of civil society, effectiveness can be interpreted from either a positive or a negative perspective. From the negative theoretical perspective, an effective civil society limits (or controls) the power of the state, preventing it from establishing a despotic regime over society (Tocqueville 1969; Gellner 1994). From the positive perspective, civil society generates a strong party system and civic organizations that pressure the government for greater accountability, and deepen democracy by enhancing equality, rights, health, welfare, education, clean elections, and so forth, through their actions (Putnam 1993, Chapter 4; Edwards 2011; Waisman 2006, 19–21). Both views are present in the types of action civil society associations carry out (see Peruzzotti's chapter). An effective citizen is an associated one, as this author affirms, citing Schmitter. Effectiveness, then, is related to the capacity of citizens and civic organizations to pressure the state, make it more accountable, create new understandings and frameworks, and participate in institutionalized structures mediating between society and the state. But effectiveness also implies "the capacity to affect the political game and the production of decisions in directions favorable to their [social organizations] interests." Thus, the visibility of the represented in the places where decisions are being discussed is important. But also, for representation to be effective, technical competence is an increasingly important condition. Sometimes effectiveness may be seen as requiring a certain pragmatism which, within a context of power relations, can lead to new forms of inequality and the loss of political autonomy (Dagnino).

Sometimes effectiveness refers to the capacity of the organizations of civil society themselves, other times to the democratic regime. In this latter case, the relationship between the citizens and civic organizations and the state is examined to see whether this complex relationship results mostly from a framework of policies and programs imposed by the state or as "a response to conflicting political claims made by different groups in civil society." When the former is the case, the effectiveness of civil society in building a democracy is compromised (Delamaza).

A different way of thinking of effectiveness at the level of a democratic regime is through the concept of "governance." Tendler (1997) defines it as the pursuit of the "public good" (as opposed to private interests) understood as sound fiscal management, hiring and firing on the basis of merit (not kin), good public services, the control of corruption and low levels of poverty. While the concept, in its broadest sense, refers to the regime, it also applies to the elements that constitute the regime, its multiple institutions and arenas. Ultimately, in this case, effectiveness reflects the degree to which the society is successful in fostering cooperation and collective action. Are the different actors represented in Congress capable of advancing legislation and giving voice to majorities and minorities? Are civil society actors capable of the coordination necessary to keep the state accountable, or to nudge the state into action in areas that it neglects? Is the judiciary capable of adjudicating disputes between state powers and protecting the rights of all citizens?

REPRESENTATIVENESS AND EFFECTIVENESS

Let us now turn to the relations between the two concepts. How does the relationship between representativeness and effectiveness work in democratic regimes? In principle we want our institutions and democracies to be both representative and effective.[1] That is, we want them to be accountable and responsive to citizens' preferences and demands, accessible and open to the claims of civil society. At the same time, we want them to provide the policies, adjudications, protections and rights that they are called on to provide. Is this possible? How do these relationships work? Let us look within the spheres first and at the system level second.

One way of thinking about the interplay between representativeness and effectiveness in Congress is to compare two kinds of electoral systems: plurality versus proportional representation. But instead of following the accountability versus representativeness counterpoint that organizes the comparison of majoritarian versus proportional electoral systems (as in Powell 2000) or the centripetal versus centrifugal forces that encourage candidates who advocate centrist or median voter positions versus those who advocate extreme or dispersed positions (as in Cox 1990), we draw attention to the effectiveness versus representativeness counterpoint. It could be argued that the "majoritarian vision," as Powell (2000) calls it, is more effective because there is one clear winner, policy-making power is concentrated and responsibility thus easier to attribute; while the proportional vision, with lower exclusion thresholds, incorporates representatives from different points of view, making deliberation an important part of the process but also, according to some, thereby reducing effectiveness. There is a dilemma here: one electoral system favors effectiveness while the other favors representativeness, but neither furnishes both.

The decisiveness/resoluteness studies make a similar point. Increasing the number of veto players (Tsebelis 2002) can increase representation, but it may hinder regime effectiveness in the process by heightening the tendency towards gridlock and indecisiveness. Again, the dimensions are inversely related. The more voices that form part of the congressional scene, it is argued, the more cumbersome the process of reaching agreements and passing laws becomes. On the other hand, however, the exclusion of minorities and the concentration of power can create dangers of a different kind, weakening democracy and creating potential backlashes. The absence of broad representation may turn plural societies violence prone as the excluded struggle for recognition. Moreover, while decisiveness facilitates policymaking, it diminishes its resoluteness—what is easily passed is easily changed (Haggard and McCubbins 2001; MacIntyre 2003).

In the chapters on Congress, MacKinnon finds a similar dilemma in the comparison between the Chilean and Argentine Congresses: the former commands the effectiveness pole but at the cost of low representativeness, while the latter is representative but suffers a relative lack of effectiveness (although not necessarily as a result of its greater representativeness). Casar argues these two dimensions are not in opposition and that an increase of representativeness is not at the root of the alleged lack of effectiveness of the Mexican Congress. The author suggests de facto powers (such as interest group organizations), the lack of executive powers and the low capacities of the Mexican Congress as better alternative explanations. Alemán notes that, while the Chilean Congress seems to be highly effective—with high levels of professionalization, high enactment rates and high perceptions of effectiveness among elites and the public—it is more middling in terms of its representativeness. He also underlines that the autonomy of legislators militates against the collective accountability of parties to the national electorate. Jones and Micozzi, advancing on the representativeness dimension, find a weakening link between legislative elections and postelection actions of deputies in Congress that affects the representativeness of Argentina's democracy as a whole. Reno and Pereira argue that a legislature that is reactive, but which needs to be heard in order for policy to be approved, may be sufficiently effective and representative to assure democratic governance.

In the judicial domain, effectiveness can also be negatively correlated with representativeness, according to different theories and positions. As in the congressional sphere, there is a tension in the relationship between these two public goods. If judges, prosecutors and other judicial officials are elected (the conventional source of representation) and, therefore, possibly no longer "independent from the elected branches and the passions of the electorate," according to the Hamiltonian theory cited by Rios-Figueroa, there is a danger that the courts may "abandon their crucial role as an impartial adjudicator of previously settled legislation to the case at hand" (Rios-Figueroa, Couso). If this distances the citizenry from judicial officials, the remedy is to propose greater access to the judicial system (Rios-Figueroa) or simply to bear with it in the name of effectiveness (Rios-Figueroa, Couso, Sabsay). Another way representativeness and effectiveness can be negatively correlated in the judicial sphere is the following: some courts (such as the Chilean and Costa Rican Constitutional Courts) have, through reforms carried out in recent years, improved access to constitutional adjudication for many more citizens, increasing representativeness and contributing to the consolidation of democracy. But, at the same time, this has created "jurisprudential confusion and contradictions" (Couso) as well as practical problems such as case overload and administrative meddling by the courts, thus impacting effectiveness. That this interplay occurs along a continuum is illustrated by the Mexican case, where court access was broadened less extensively, restricting it to the other branches of government and not to the citizens, thereby limiting its impact (Rios-Figueroa).

The tension between representativeness and effectiveness can be replicated in the relationship between democracy and constitutionalism, as argued by Couso. Due to certain historical trajectories, constitutionalism—the notion that government and people should be subordinate to the law and the Constitution—is not deeply rooted in Latin America. Since the executive is popularly elected, it enjoys the mantle of popular sovereignty, while the judiciary does not. As a result, the effectiveness of the judiciary is called into question, and the executive can intervene in controversial judicial decisions.

However, according to other perspectives, representativeness and effectiveness can also be positively correlated in the judiciary. The further the judiciary is from the needs of the people (in part, precisely because it is not elected), the more difficult it is for the judiciary to become institutionalized and perform the crucial role it needs to play in the consolidation of democracy (Sabsay). To be really effective, Ingram argues, the judicial system needs to be both representative and effective. Strong and better-protected individual rights and liberties that improve the quality of democratic citizenship for broad sectors of society have to exist. This is achieved, at least in part, through progressive judges connected to social legal movements (Ingram) and/or the action of associations in civil society and international treaties that push through decisions in courts regarding environmental matters, indigenous rights and other issues, thus improving the effectiveness of judges in the eyes of the community and making justice more representative (Sabsay), in a sort of virtuous circle between representativeness and effectiveness.

Within the sphere of civil society, representativeness and effectiveness can also be positively correlated in a virtuous cycle. For example, when civil society groups organize to petition or pressure the state, often due precisely to a lack of effectiveness in a certain area (violations of rights or breaches of law and due process by public officials, corruption of politicians) and succeed in their claims, correcting the rights violation or bringing a corrupt official to trial, they are effective (in the negative sense cited above). Civic associations can also organize against the exclusion of certain constituencies (such as indigenous groups, or gays), or to engage in new forms of participatory democracy (such as participatory budgeting, or participatory health councils). Because of the limitations in electoral representation, these forms of civic action are theorized to complement and/or create—not substitute for—new mechanisms of representation where the conventional one is lacking (Peruzzotti). In other words, if the citizens and organizations of civil society succeed in creating these new mechanisms, and opening new channels, policies or laws for the citizenry, then they are effective (in the positive sense). It could also be argued that they generate more representativeness in the regime as a whole since the interests, voices and concerns of more citizens are included in the polity. Whether the organizations themselves are representative (or democratic) is a different matter (see Urbinatti and Warren 2008, and Peruzzotti, and Dagnino in this volume, on this point).

On the other hand, autonomy has often been considered "a crucial basis for the representativeness" of social movements (Dagnino). However, in order to be effective and get results, social movements sometimes must act in expedient ways, as when they prioritize results. In this case effectiveness is in tension with representativeness, a source of their radical democratic potential (Dagnino). At the regime level, better organization and mobilization can lead, for example, to a coordinated social movement that changes the direction of policy (such as the Civil Rights movement in the United States, Madres de la Plaza de Mayo in Argentina, AIDS groups in Brazil). Arguably, the same increase in mobilization may also lead to either particularistic policies or greater contention and conflict among different groups with opposing agendas, with detrimental effects for the democratic regime. Thus, there may also be tradeoffs involved between the two variables in this sphere. As effectiveness increases, representativeness may or may not increase. From a broader perspective, however, when civil society cannot carry out its role because it has become increasingly weaker, fragmented and less capable of collective action, and when this situation is combined with alienation from the channels of democratic representation like voting and political parties, then the effectiveness of a democratic regime, and its legitimacy, are affected (Delamaza).

Let us now move from the interplay of the relationships between representativeness and effectiveness within each sphere to a systemic perspective; that is, to examine how these dynamics can relate to each other when different spheres come into contact and act on each other in a democratic regime. As developed above, representativeness and effectiveness are more often inversely than directly related when examined in the context of each individual sphere, a fact that turns this relationship into a dilemma. In the legislative sphere, some authors argue that the more inclusive Congress or electoral rules are, the more likely the existence of gridlock and distributional conflicts. In the judiciary, others maintain that an increase in access for citizens to justice, or in judicial activism, can lead to a greater likelihood of institutional conflicts, power struggles, reputational damage, case logjams and administrative meddling. In the case of civil society, some argue that more organizations in pursuit of more claims may increase the probability of social conflicts, instability due to protests and erosion in the credibility of representative institutions.

However, in each of the spheres various authors in this volume find evidence of a positive correlation too. Thus, in the legislative sphere in Argentina and Mexico there is evidence that the lack of effectiveness is not due to the costs of an excess of representativeness but to other issues such as a dispersion of congressional power, insufficiently institutionalized procedures or the presence of strong pressures from powerful groups in society. A more representative judiciary that responds to social demands tends to be considered a more effective one (and vice versa), which contributes to its institutionalization, an important event in the process of democratization. In the sphere of civil society, if civic organizations are effective in their efforts to monitor the state or generate new rights or policies, they create more system-wide representativeness and effectiveness. This view of the relationship between the dimensions grows when seen from a systemic perspective. Other effects come into view, highlighting ways in which the two variables are able to reinforce each other, contributing at least partly to furthering accountability and state compliance, and improving the quality of democracy.

There is an experience taking place in the Matanza-Riachuelo river basin in Argentina that can perhaps serve to illustrate the relational perspective we are proposing here: that is, how the dynamic between representativeness and effectiveness works at the systemic level, as it moves from civil society to the judiciary, to the legislature and back to civil society, creating different effects.

The Matanza-Riachuelo river[2] is 64 km long and runs through the industrial belt of the metropolitan area of Buenos Aires. It crosses 14 municipalities of the province and part of the City of Buenos Aires and has long been the most contaminated river basin and also one of the most socially and environmentally deprived urban areas in the country.[3] In the 1990s, various grass roots and community associations organized initiatives regarding local problems in the area, but the first breakthrough only came when a local community group and an individual citizen filed complaints with the *Defensoría del Pueblo de la Nación* (National Ombudsman) in 2002. As a result, this office summoned a group of organizations to coordinate and develop a unified political strategy to address the problems in the river basin, finally overcoming the inertia and setting in motion a process of change in the river basin. The superposition of national, local, provincial and municipal jurisdictions was one of the main obstacles to agreeing on and implementing solutions. The working group that was created included some of the local associations that had made the original complaint, four national NGOs, a university and the *Defensor* of the City of Buenos Aires.[4]

Up to here we have civil society organizations and individuals working with the *Defensoría*, seeking to raise awareness and produce action from different levels of government. But in 2004, a new actor entered the scene. A group of 140 residents of the Matanza-Riachuelo river basin and 20 medical professionals from the local hospital filed a lawsuit before the Supreme Court[5] against the federal government, the province of Buenos Aires, the City of Buenos Aires, and 44 firms for damages to their health derived from environmental pollution of the Matanza-Riachuelo basin. The Supreme Court dismissed the case for individual damages but admitted an action for collective damage to the environment,[6] and in June 2006, in the second breakthrough, ordered the national and local governments to develop a plan to clean up the river basin.

In December of the same year, another important actor entered the scene. As a result of the continuing pressure from the Supreme Court, the *Defensoría* and civil society organizations, and in the midst of a strong consensus, the Argentine Congress passed a bill proposed by the executive that created the Matanza–Riachuelo Basin Authority (MRBA), a new body that united the various authorities with jurisdiction over the river basin, centralizing the governmental initiatives in the area and coordinating the work of accountability agencies so that sanctions against polluters could be enforced more effectively. It also included a commission that coordinated the implementation of the plan, and any civil society organization with a stake in the basin could join. The MRBA also set up a forum of universities to facilitate the interaction between universities with expertise in the problems of the basin and the group of experts in charge of the plan. In 2007 it approved and implemented an environmental clean-up plan.

In July of 2008, the Supreme Court ruled the MRBA had to meet certain environmental objectives within a specific timeline or face fines, designated a federal judge as the only judicial authority with jurisdiction over the case, and established a system for civil society to monitor the implementation process. It also ordered the *Defensoría del Pueblo de la Nación* to attend to citizens' suggestions and coordinate a body (*Cuerpo Colegiado*) to monitor compliance with the obligations set out in the sentence and make recommendations to the MRBA. The *Defensoría* thus played a crucial role in articulating the collegial body and transmitting the body's decisions to the Supreme Court (Peruzzotti, 24).

In March 2009 the *Cuerpo Colegiado* presented a report in which it denounced MRBA inaction regarding inspections to determine which industries were contaminating the river, the installation of a comprehensive sewage program in the basin and the eradication of illegal garbage dumping in the area. It requested the judiciary make effective the sanctions contemplated in the Court's ruling. The Supreme Court and the federal judge called public hearings (in which members of the community, NGO representatives and government officials participated) to pressure the MRBA. The federal judge took steps when the MRBA, local mayors and environmental authorities did not carry out the mandated actions. Although not all the points of the Court's sentence have been carried out to date, some ships have been removed from the river waters, the margins have been partially cleaned up, almost a third of the open-air garbage sites have been eradicated, a coastal road has been built, the population's health has been studied in a census, 256 families have been relocated, garbage collection via the river has been started for some slums and there is better control of contaminating industries.[7]

In this case, then, when politicians (generally municipal, provincial or national executives) did not respond to the demands of the citizenry and civil society associations, thus prolonging a lack of effectiveness (regarding sewage, drinkable water, health, river pollution in the area), the latter appealed to the *Defensoría del Pueblo*, an office that produced an innovative interaction between actors in civil society and the state. Then various groups appealed to the judiciary. The Supreme Court ruled in favor of the claimants, protecting collective rights to healthy air, earth and water, "adding the power of formal sanctions" (Peruzzotti, 29). In the eyes of society, these actions improved the representativeness of the judiciary, the *Defensoría* and Congress. Furthermore, the Court appointed the *Defensoría* and various civil society organizations to oversee enactment of the ruling. As a result, oversight became more effective, and national, provincial and municipal executives were forced to carry out provisions of the ruling, improving the effectiveness of civil society and the judiciary. At the same time, when grass roots organizations, NGOs, the Ombudsman and the judiciary, in a domino reaction, pressured the executive and Congress, the latter passed a law creating a body (the MRBA) that articulated the overlapping jurisdictions in the basin enabling the coordination of the complex clean-up process. The actions of civil society and the *Defensoría* jump-started a process that, through its effects on the judiciary and the legislature, enhanced representativeness and effectiveness inter- and intrasphere.

This example illustrates that a complex, virtuous circle of relations between representativeness and effectiveness (different to the relations within each sphere), can occur in a chain of actions and reactions between civil society organizations, the judiciary (in particular in this case), and the legislature. The status quo is resistant to change. A lack of accountability and/or representation, and/or effectiveness may be the detonator for civil society to pressure judicial or legislative actors to take action. The judiciary may respond to popular backing with stronger action in certain areas, judges may take initiatives to enact change, or reassert individual rights and constitutional guarantees. The legislature may respond by enacting new rights or policies that more closely reflect the needs of excluded social actors. Taken together, the actions of both may lead to the institutionalization of new forms of participation, decision-making and access (according to the case) that produce new results (attending to health, pollution, etc., in the river basin area), incorporating the formerly excluded and reflecting a deepening of democracy.

By focusing on two central dimensions of democracy, representativeness and effectiveness, in three key spheres of democratic regimes—Congress, the judiciary and civil society—this volume opens new views into the complex dynamics that underlie the democratic process. It shows that the concepts are applicable to realms where their role is not self-evident, and that they capture ways in which key spheres of the regime develop their roles in democratization processes. The judiciary, traditionally considered a nonrepresentative sphere, is found to exert a representative role in the protection of rights, citizen access to justice, and the sanction of sentences related to civic demands. Civic mobilization, often seen as an alternative to representative mechanisms, is seen to complement them, thereby strengthening representation. The governed can influence the government through multiple channels, directly and indirectly. Where representativeness and/or effectiveness fall short, this can be remedied by direct civic action, legislative action and/or judicial intervention.

Finally, and mainly, although the literature tends to present the relationship between representativeness and effectiveness as inversely correlated, the volume presents evidence that this is not always so. To the contrary, relationships in which civil society, the legislature and the judiciary are positively correlated also occur. Despite the apparent contradictions or inverse correlations within the spheres, the interrelations between the spheres can contribute to producing more effective and more representative regimes.

NOTES

1. Hagopian (2003, 124) situates what she calls "high-quality democracy" at the convergence of high levels of political representation and high levels of effectiveness.
2. The information for these paragraphs was taken mostly from Enrique Peruzzotti, "The Societalization of Horizontal Accountability: Rights Advocacy and the Defensoría del Pueblo de la Nación in Argentina" (Mimeo), and also from FARN's website at www.farn.org.ar.
3. The pollution stems from toxic waste from factories, liquid waste from clandestine sewage pipes and garbage from the more than 100 open-air landfill sites on its banks. About half of the 5 million inhabitants along its banks lack

sewage facilities, a third lack drinkable water, a large number live in "villas miseria" (shantytowns) or precarious settlements and many are afflicted with environment-related diseases (such as typhoid fever, salmonella, hepatitis A and E, cancer, etc.) (Peruzzotti, 16–17).

4. The diversity of this group brought together a crucial range of knowledge and expertise: grass roots organizations with on-the-ground knowledge of the area, groups with experience organizing neighbors' forums, and universities and specialized NGOs with skills in evaluating and generating technical reports (21).

5. ". . . which was considered the court of first instance because the defendants were the national and the provincial government" (Peruzzotti, 22).

6. The purpose of the action was to repair and prevent collective environmental damage, an Argentine creation according to law 25.675, the General Environmental Law. We thank D. Sabsay for pointing this out.

7. FARN website, accessed August 27, 2012.

Part II
Congress

1 Reflections on the Effectiveness and Representativeness of the Chilean Congress

Eduardo Alemán

In Latin America's presidential democracies, national Congresses have often been singled out for underperforming along some important dimension and deemed due for reform. The view of Latin American Congresses as weak appendices to strong presidents, for example, was prevalent among scholars until not so long ago (Wynia 1995; Wiarda and Kline 1990). In the seminal book *Presidents and Assemblies*, Shugart and Carey (1992) made the case for increasing the power of Congress vis-à-vis the president to strengthen democratic stability.

The transition from autocratic military regimes to democratic regimes brought to the forefront the study of legislatures. Congressional politics inform us about the workings of representative democracy. More than 30 years after the beginning of the "third wave" of democratization, the study of Latin American political institutions has grown considerably. The conventional view regarding Latin American legislatures has certainly changed, and most scholars no longer consider them minor institutional players. Yet the available evidence suggests a wide variation across the region in terms of the performance of national Congresses.

There is no consensus among political scientists over what constitutes an appropriate cross-national measure of congressional performance. A starting point for building such categorization involves identifying some central institutional goals and deriving some observable implications about legislative politics that reflect the degree to which these goals have been or are likely to be met. Two such fundamental aims are effectiveness and representativeness. Here I take congressional effectiveness to mean competence regarding the fulfillment of its constitutional role, usually regarding lawmaking and oversight, and representativeness to mean responsiveness to the electorate. Both concepts capture institutional goals with valence characteristics; that is, citizens would tend to uniformly prefer a more effective Congress and a strong linkage between constituents' interests and legislative behavior than an ineffective Congress and a membership co-opted by special interests.

This chapter discusses the performance of the Chilean Congress with respect to its effectiveness as a legislative body and the capacity of its membership to represent constituents' interests. It presents several measures of effectiveness, and compares the Chilean Congress with those of other Latin American countries. It also discusses the complications involved in assessing representativeness in legislatures, and presents some data on the Chilean case.

THE EFFECTIVENESS OF CONGRESS

This section examines whether the Chilean Congress is performing effectively vis-à-vis other Latin American legislatures. Whether the Chilean Congress post-1990 has underperformed or not, in terms of its institutional effectiveness, is an empirical question. While many politically informed people can answer with confidence whether the national Congress in their country is performing its constitutional role well, it is not an easy task to come up with an appropriate measure that can be applied cross-nationally. Approaches used for evaluating national congresses can be broadly grouped into three categories: (1) perception-based, (2) capability-based and (3) output-based. All three convey some important information about the effectiveness of national congresses and allow us to compare the Chilean Congress with others in the region.

Perception-Based Measures

Perception-based measures include public opinion polls as well as elite and expert surveys. They are constructed from individuals' evaluations of their national legislatures. The usefulness of surveys for examining congressional effectiveness often has to do with the appropriateness of the questions posed, in addition to typical concerns such as whether they are representative of the desired population and comparable cross-nationally or over time. Also important is the level of information deemed optimal for evaluating institutional performance. While the average citizen can provide an evaluation of Congress, this opinion is less likely to be based on information about the inner workings of Congress and more likely to be based on the political context and on complex policy outcomes than the evaluations provided by better-informed elites. Elites, while more in tune with congressional developments, can also present some challenges. For example, legislators committed to a congressional career may not be inclined to provide a negative assessment of the institution where they work. Similarly, the assessment of Congress given by business elites may be influenced by the pro or antibusiness stances of congressional majorities.

One survey that specifically asks about the effectiveness of Congress is the Executive Opinion Survey conducted by the World Economic Forum and presented in its Global Competitiveness Report. This is a survey of a representative sample of business leaders in each country.[1] This indicator is constructed from the survey question, "How effective is your national Congress as a lawmaking and oversight institution?" and scored from 1 = "very ineffective" to 7 = "very effective, the best in the world." Figure 1.1 presents the results for the period 2002–2008 for 18 Latin American countries.

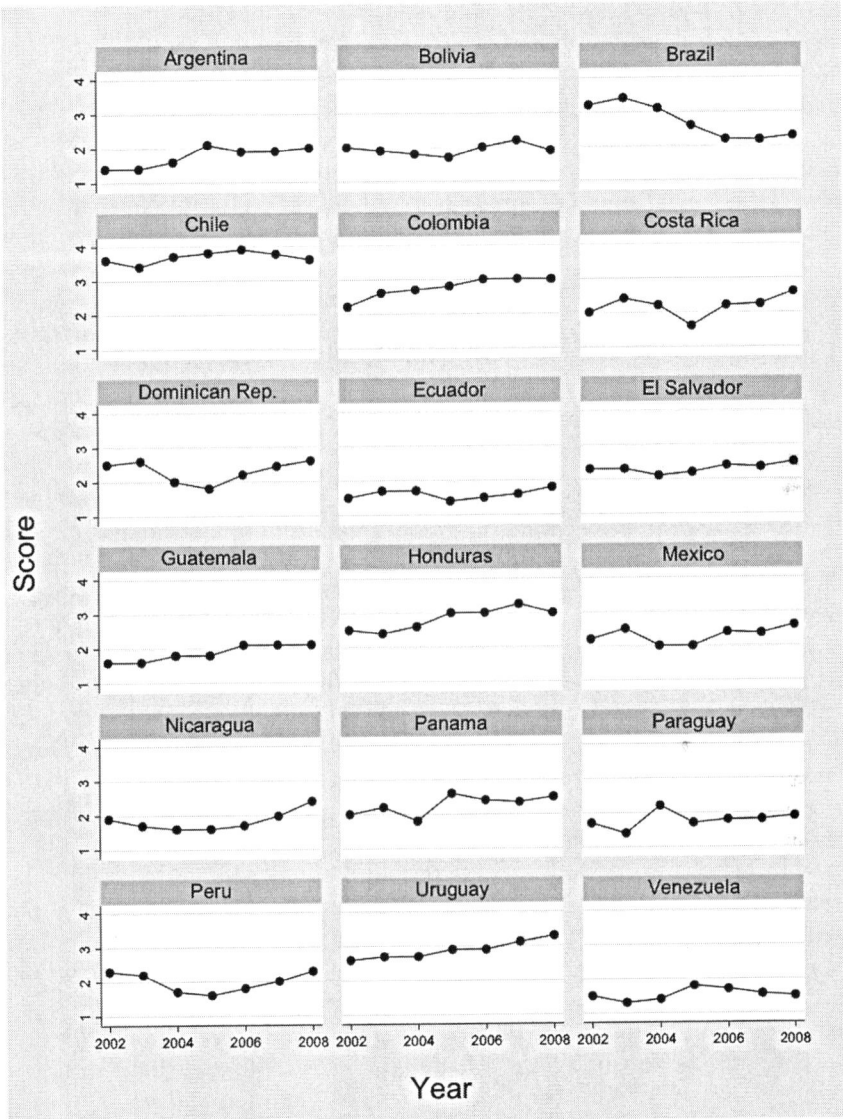

Figure 1.1 The effectiveness of congress as a lawmaking institution, 2002–2008
Source: World Economic Forum, 2002–2008

The results of the effectiveness indicators provided by the World Economic Forum show that, in general, Latin American legislatures are not well ranked. Most are positioned on the lower third of the scale, and several lurk around the bottom. Yet there are some exceptions. Over the seven-year period, the Chilean Congress is consistently ranked at the top of this group of countries. The average score for the Chilean Congress is 3.7, which is substantially higher than the average regional score of 2.3. The Chilean Congress is followed most closely by the Uruguayan Congress (average 2.9), and then by the Colombian and Honduran Congresses (both average 2.8). At the bottom of the rank, we find the Venezuelan (average 1.5) and Ecuadorean Congresses (average 1.6).

There is some empirical evidence that effectiveness, as captured by this indicator, has a relevant impact on politics, particularly on governmental coalitions. For example, Alemán and Tsebelis (2011) argue that in presidential countries, congressional effectiveness increases the likelihood that a nonpresidential party will join the cabinet and present cross-national evidence to substantiate this claim. Furthermore, Martinez-Gallardo (2011) shows that in Latin American presidential democracies, higher congressional effectiveness increases the durability of presidential coalitions. Both of these findings suggest that presidents are more likely to seek out congressional partners and maintain such coalitional arrangements when Congress is perceived to be a more effective institutional player.

Other perception-based measures include public opinion polls. The Americas Barometer survey, undertaken by the Latin American Public Opinion Project (LAPOP), asks a question pertinent to the effectiveness of Congress. The question is as follows: "Now speaking of Congress, and thinking of members/ senators and representatives as a whole, without considering the political parties to which they belong, do you believe that the members/senators and representatives of Congress are performing their jobs: very well, well, neither well nor poorly, poorly, or very poorly?" Overall, the perception of Chileans regarding their members of Congress is more positive than the average perception of citizens in other Latin American countries. The proportion of respondents rating congressional performance "poorly" or "very poorly" is shown on the top part of Figure 1.2.

Citizens gave very poor marks to members of Congress in Peru and Paraguay both in 2010 and in 2008. Members of Congress in Guatemala and Nicaragua are also perceived to be doing a rather poor job by a very large portion of the respondents. Ecuadorian legislators were very badly ranked in 2008, when close to two-thirds of respondents gave them poor marks, but improved markedly in 2010, when less than one-fourth of respondents gave such a poor assessment. At the other end of the spectrum we have Uruguay, where only a small percentage of respondents rate their legislators' performance badly (around 2% in 2010 and 14% in 2008). In Chile, Honduras, Bolivia and Colombia we also find relatively few citizens giving members of Congress bad marks (less than 20% in 2010 and less than 30% in 2008).

Alternatively, we can look at the percentage evaluating congressional performance positively (two highest categories) minus the percentage of those ranking it badly (lowest two categories). This is illustrated on the lower part of Figure 1.2. The Uruguayan and Colombian Congresses are the only ones rated positively by citizens in both surveys. Chile is ranked sixth in 2010, when it received an overall positive evaluation, and ninth in 2008, when the overall assessment was negative, as it was for most Congresses in the region.

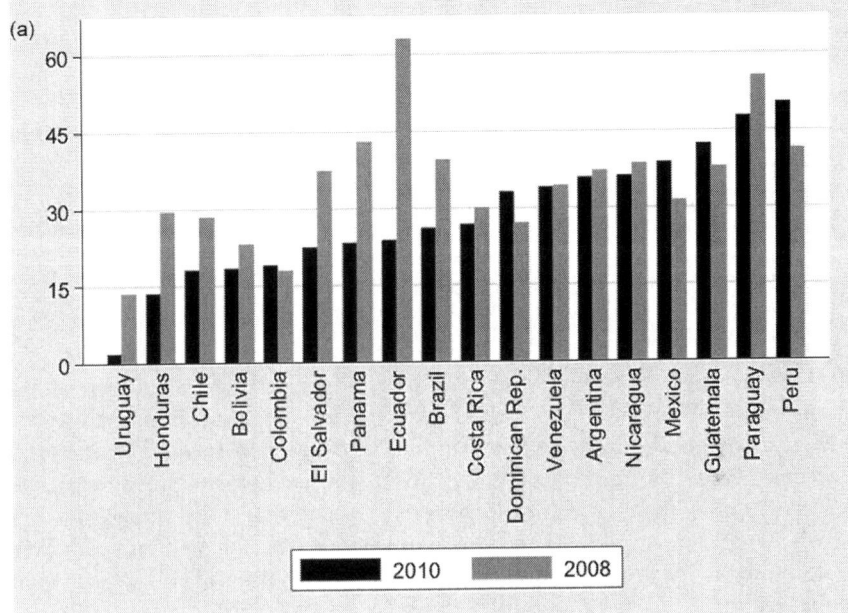

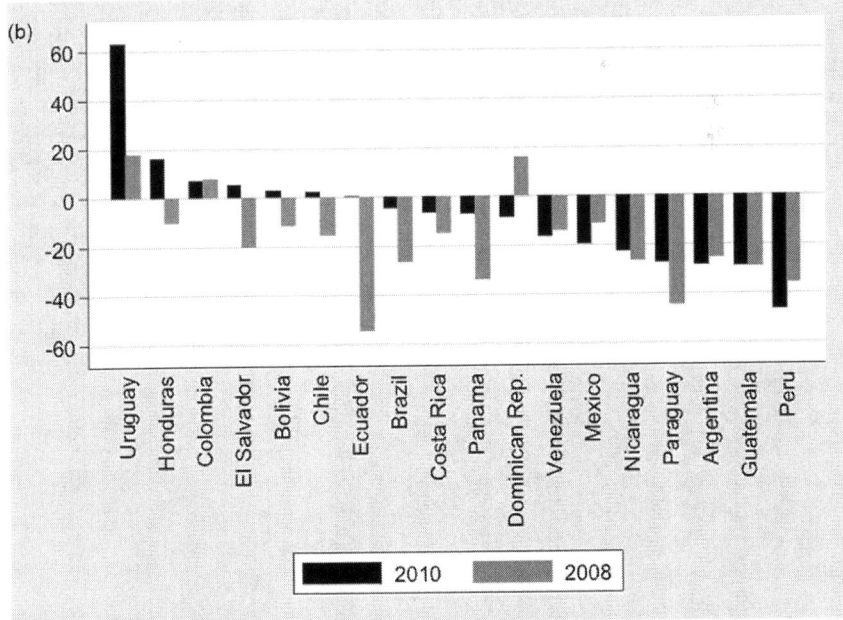

Figure 1.2   The performance of members of congress: (a) Percentage responding "poorly" or "very poorly." (b) Percentage responding "well" and "very well" minus "poorly" and "very poorly"
Source: AmericasBarometer 2008 and 2010 by LAPOP

When comparing the elite survey with the public opinion poll, we can observe differences in the consistency of rankings over time. There is a very high correlation across surveys in the congressional effectiveness evaluations provided by business elites (the year-to-year correlation is around .9), while there is a more modest correlation between country scores in the two public opinion surveys evaluating the performance on members of Congress (around .5). This is likely a reflection of differences in the weight given to the particular political context by business elites and the typical citizen when asked to evaluate the performance of Congress.

Capability-Based Measures

The effectiveness of Congress may also be inferred from the competence of its members. This is because congressional effectiveness can be argued to depend greatly on having a capable membership. While professionalization and careerism may not be sufficient conditions, it is hard to imagine an effective legislative body composed for the most part by amateur politicians—even if a small clique of professional members is able to capture the positions of power within the institution. Professionalization is typically associated with frequent congressional sessions and sufficient resources (independent staff and salaries) to allow elected members to pursue a career as legislators (Polsby 1975; Squire 2007). A legislature that spends a relatively short period of time in session is typically seen as more amateurish and less likely to act as an effective policymaking actor vis-à-vis the executive. Frequent sessions enhance legislators' understandings of the complexities behind lawmaking (Bell and Price 1975), and facilitate deliberation and policy development (Rosenthal 1996, 171). Increases in professionalization are supposed to bring about a more skillful and experienced congressional membership, better able to prioritize activities, discern between policy options, and check the power of other branches of government.

When measuring time commitments, the constitutionally established period for regular sessions can be misleading because it does not necessarily reflect how often meetings actually take place. The length of sessions established in the constitution (or internal rule of procedures) is sometimes extended by extraordinary sessions, and the frequency of meetings can also be altered by a lack of quorum. A more accurate measure to compare time demands is to count the actual number of days that members of Congress met in session. Table 1.1 shows the number of months with at least one meeting and the number of days in session for seven Latin American lower chambers in 2010.

In terms of actual days in session, Chilean and Costa Rican legislators met much more often than legislators in the other five chambers. In both countries legislators met several times a months for eleven months that year. At the other end of the spectrum we have the Argentine lower chamber, which despite having had at least one meeting a month for 10 months met in session

Table 1.1   Time in Session in Seven Latin American Countries

Lower Chamber	Months with at Least One Meeting in 2010	Actual Days in Session
Argentina	10	28
Chile	11	113
Costa Rica	11	163
Ecuador	12	63
Mexico	7	68
Paraguay	12	65
Uruguay	12	68

Source: Author's calculation based on information from congressional websites

only twenty eight times.[2] Legislators in the other four chambers met between 63 and 68 days, including Mexican deputies, which had sessions for just seven months in 2010.[3]

Turnover in congressional membership tends to decline with increases in professionalization (Moncrief et al. 2004). Tenure and reelection rates inform us about the degree to which Congress has become a place to build a political career. Political scientists have often remarked on the importance of career goals for explaining legislative behavior. In contrast to the U.S. Congress and most Western European parliaments, Latin American Congresses are largely populated by legislators serving their first term in office. Lack of experience is typically associated with less expertise. While a lack of legislative turnover can certainly bring about some other complications, the problem inside Latin American legislatures is one of membership instability. The impact of imposing term limits on legislators across U.S. states is illuminating on this matter. The evidence suggests that term limits have led to less informed legislators, inexperienced leaders, weaker committees, a greater emphasis on short-term policymaking and a shift in the balance of power in favor of the executive in terms of budgetary policy and oversight (Kurtz et al. 2007).

Latin American Congresses exhibit varying degrees of careerism. At one end of the scale we have the Chilean and Uruguayan Congresses, where average tenure is rather high and legislators get reelected at a rate that is comparable to those of established democracies in Western Europe. At the other end of the scale we have Costa Rica and Mexico, where reelection is not allowed. In countries like Peru, Argentina and Guatemala, where reelection rates are very low, the vast majority of members of Congress do not return to their legislative jobs after their term in office ends.

In Chile, the average tenure of members of Congress has increased since the transition to democracy. Figure 1.3 presents data on the tenure

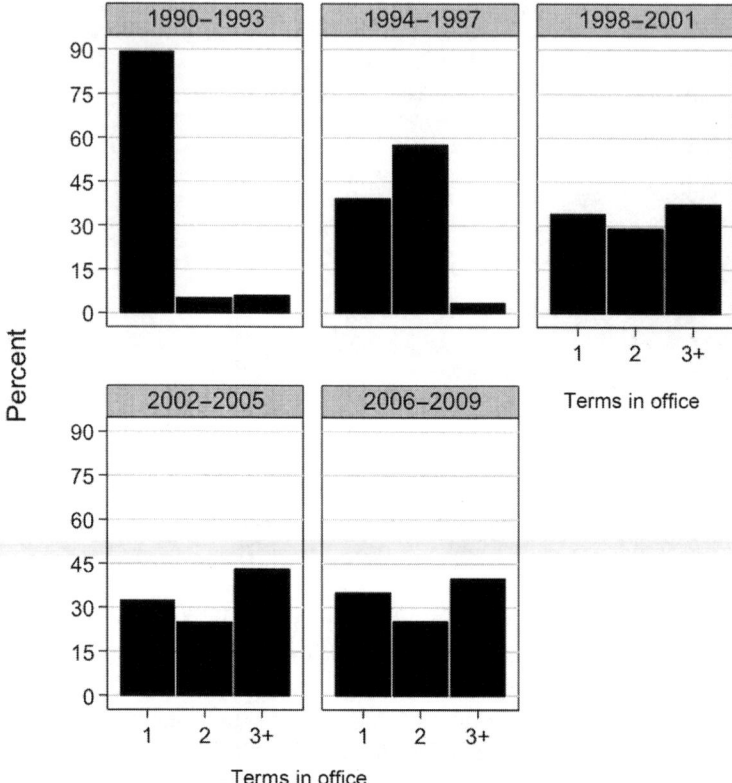

Figure 1.3   Tenure in the Chilean Chamber of Deputies
Source: Author's calculation based on information provided by Chile's Library of Congress

of members of the Chamber of Deputies from 1990 to 2009. It shows the percentage of first-time members in comparison to the percentage of members having two, and three or more terms in office. The figure illustrates how the proportion of first-timers dropped from 89% in 1990 to 39% in 1994. Since 1998, first-time members represent around one-third of the membership of the Chamber of Deputies. As expected, the share of deputies with extensive experience (three or more terms in office) was very small until 1997 (less than 6% of the membership), but since 1998 it has hovered around the 40% mark. These deputies enter office with at least eight years of prior experience and three successful electoral campaigns under their belts.

Other traits, such as the number of committee assignments and time demands, have also been used to gauge professionalization. An excessive number of committee assignments, for instance, is likely to work against policy specialization. Across Latin American legislatures, the average number of committee assignments is two, as it is in Chile, and in five countries the average number of committee assignments is just one. Only in Argentina and the Dominican Republic do we find legislators being assigned to an average of more than three committees (IADB 2006, 55).

Output-Based Measures

A third approach to evaluating the effectiveness of Congress emphasizes outcomes, particularly law production. The underlying rationale is that the work of an effective Congress should be reflected in its participation in law-making, such as in the number of bills passed, the share of laws that originates in Congress and amending activities.

Yet there are some problems with using these measures to evaluate effectiveness cross-nationally. To begin with, it is not clear that a greater number of initiated bills is indicative of more effective participation in lawmaking. In fact, the opposite has been argued (Francis 1989). While it can make sense from an electoral standpoint, initiating a very large number of bills that are unlikely to pass can hardly be considered a sign of greater institutional effectiveness. The total number of laws passed originated by members of Congress seems a priori a better measure, but again there are usually constitutional rules that are country specific which influence the initiation of bills by legislators and may distort the contribution of Congress. One measure commonly used by the legislative literature to measure efficiency is the success rate (i.e., batting average) of bills introduced (Hibbing 1991; Squire 1998). Success rates are supposed to tap into the ability of legislators to accomplish policy outputs. They intend to capture accomplishments given a specific program or set of policy proposals introduced.

There are very few cross-national studies that provide comparable data on law production. Saiegh's (2011) comparative study includes data on law production from four South American countries: Argentina, Chile, Ecuador and Uruguay. The data show that Chilean deputies introduced fewer bills than their counterparts in the other three countries, while Argentine deputies introduced by far the largest quantity. When looking at the number of bills introduced per year per deputy, the number for Argentina is 4.5 times that of Chile. The difference is less significant when looking at the number of bills passed per year, but Chile still exhibits the lowest number of the four countries.

Interestingly, when we look at the share of total bills passed that originate in Congress, the two Congresses usually considered rather ineffective by most other measures—the Argentine and Ecuadorean ones—exhibit a much higher share than the two Congresses usually considered rather effective—the Chilean and Uruguayan ones. Saiegh's (2011) results also show that approval rates for all congressional bills introduced (i.e., success rates) are higher in Chile and Uruguay than in Argentina and Ecuador. These measures of law production present some complications for cross-national evaluations, but are rather informative of changes that occur over time within countries and within legislative cohorts (i.e., between legislators).

In Chile, the participation of Congress in law production has increased since the transition to democracy. Legislators always introduced more bills than the executive, but the relative share of congressional bills out of all introduced grew markedly since 1994. The number of bills passed initiated by legislators has varied since 1990, but not too much. While 19% of laws originally introduced between 1990 and 1993 were initiated by members of Congress, the proportion for the period 2002–2005 was around 35%. Data on laws published during the year 2011 show a similar proportion originating in members of Congress. While the executive branch continues to have a preponderant role in law production, Congress appears to have become a more assertive institutional player over time. This improvement in lawmaking participation can be seen as progress in terms of legislative effectiveness.

Summary

This section has discussed three alternative approaches to evaluating the effectiveness of Congresses. The first approach relied on perceptions of effectiveness. Business elites consistently rank the Chilean Congress as the most effective in the region. Results from public opinion polls are less favorable but still better than in most other Latin American countries. The second approach centered on capabilities, particularly professionalization. The evidence suggests that within Latin America, the Chilean Congress has one of the most capable memberships. The third approach highlighted law production. In Chile, bills initiated by members of Congress make up a smaller share of all laws than in many other presidential countries. The rate of approval for Congressionally initiated bills, however, is actually higher than in many other presidential countries.

The measures examined in this section convey the idea that the Chilean Congress is a rather effective institution in comparison to other Latin American legislatures. There is room for improvement, of course, particularly in terms of the public evaluation of the performance of Congress. But one has to wonder whether we are observing in Chile the well-known phenomenon where voters hate Congress but love their own representatives. High reelection rates and discouraging opinion polls seem to suggest that this trend may be at work.

THE REPRESENTATIVENESS OF CONGRESS

The representativeness of national Congresses has been of great concern to politicians, political activists and academics. Members of Congress are elected to represent the interests of voters, yet there is no agreement over how representativeness should be measured. The concept has been used in different manners, which has implications for empirical evaluations. Approaches to studying the representativeness of legislatures can be broadly grouped into two: the behavioralist and institutional perspectives.

The Behavioralist Perspective

The representational aspect of legislative politics was of great concern to scholars influenced by the behavioral revolution of the 1950s. Many classic works on legislative politics from the behavioral era implicitly or explicitly conceptualized representativeness as responsiveness to constituents. Representativeness was supposed to be achieved by acting in the interest of and being responsive to the represented (Pitkin 1967). In the 1960s, one strand of research concentrated on examining the style and focus of legislators' representational efforts, while another concentrated on measuring congruence between the preferences of citizens and the behavior of legislators. Both offer some lessons for examining representativeness in Latin American legislatures.

In seminal works, Eulau et al. (1959) and Whalke et al. (1962) used surveys to investigate legislators' representational roles, initiating a research project that would be rather prominent in legislative studies for at least two decades. One aspect of what became known as role theory referred to legislators' views regarding which interests they ought to represent, while another referred to their individual styles of representation. Studies examined whether legislators considered themselves (1) free agents following their own judgment ("trustees"), (2) mandate-driven actors following the instructions of constituents ("delegates") or (3) more pragmatic adopters of a mixed strategy ("politicos"). While several studies sought to explain the development of role orientations, a few others attempted to link these categorizations with legislative behavior.[4] For instance, early on Souraf (1963) found some evidence that trustees were slightly more likely to vote the party line than delegates, and Kuklinski and Elling (1977) found some evidence that delegates were more likely to vote according to district preferences. More recently, Searing (1991), Studlar and McAllister (1996) and Cooper and Richardson (2006) found evidence that legislators' roles are associated with differences in the way they relate to their constituents. The usefulness of role theory to explain legislative behavior began to be challenged by the late 1970s (Friesema and Hedlund 1974; Gross 1978). As Strom (1997) notes, part of this decline can be attributed to some of the theoretical weaknesses of this approach, while part is the result of the consolidation of rational choice institutionalism in legislative studies.[5]

A second strand of research was stimulated by Miller and Stokes's (1963) seminal examination of the congruence between the preferences of voters and legislators' preferences and behavior. This approach combined constituency and elite surveys with roll-call analysis.[6] Converse and Pierce (1979), for example, examined the behavior of legislators in a country with disciplined parties—France—and concluded that defections from party unity increased congruence with constituency preferences. Since Miller and Stokes' article, several studies have reexamined the connection between constituency preferences and roll call behavior in the U.S. Congress and elsewhere. Unlike legislative role analysis, which lost prominence in the 1980s, the study of constituency influence on legislative behavior continues to be prominent in legislative studies.

Both strands of research from the behavioralist perspective provide important lessons for the contemporary study of legislative responsiveness in Latin American countries. First, they show that legislators have different views about the extent to which the preferences of electors—the often changing and ethereal will of constituents—should influence their behavior. Legislators do not always conceive the process of representation as responsiveness to the whims of constituency opinion. Second, they highlight the various behaviors that manifest responsiveness, which include not only policy responsiveness, but also constituency service (e.g., casework), securing the allocation of resources to the district and symbolic gestures (Eulau and Karps 1977). There are other behaviors aside from roll-call votes and bill initiation where responsiveness to district actors is typically manifested and can be studied. Third, examining responsiveness along the lines of the behavioralist perspective requires not only information about the attitudes and behaviors of legislative elites, but also good district-level data about constituency preferences. For most Latin American countries, the latter data are still unavailable.

There are very few works focused on Latin America that examine legislators' roles and attitudes towards representation. Marenghi and Garcia Montero (2006) and Valverde (2009) used a survey of parliamentary elites to map Latin American legislatures according to the style and focus of their members. While most countries in these studies are clustered in the middle with respect to legislators' propensity to follow party instructions versus their own free will, Chile is ranked among those furthest from following directives. In terms of focus, Chilean legislators tend to locate themselves on the particularistic end of the spectrum, expressing greater interest in promoting local/partisan interest than in promoting more general national issues. In surveys, Chilean legislators tend to respond that they primarily represent their respective district voters. For example, Nolte (2002) notes that in case of a conflict of interests, the vast majority of senators express that they would choose region over party (about 79% versus 4%), while close to 18% say they would decide based on the issue at hand. Most senators consider important bringing resources to the region, and almost half consider it very important.

But the apparent predilection for regional interests above partisan interests expressed by Chilean legislators in surveys is not readily obvious in their behavior. Marenghi's (2009) work is informative in this aspect. She notes that despite the fact that Chilean legislators overwhelmingly say they represent district voters rather than all voters or the party, give considerable importance to bringing resources into the district, and express a commitment to district voters in conflictive cases, they do not seem to translate these attitudes into district-oriented behavior; at least not in terms of the topics of the bills they initiate. Locally oriented legislation does not predominate. Siavelis (2009), for instance, is skeptic about the attitudes conveyed by legislators. He notes how their apparent predilection for district over party does not fit well with most behavioral accounts. Nonetheless, he argues that ultimately there is a rather high congruence between the overall preferences conveyed by Chilean voters in public opinion surveys and those expressed by legislators in surveys of parliamentary elites. The lack of good data regarding district preferences, as well as the lack of surveys of legislators where respondents can be identified and linked to a district, hinder the proper application of this approach to the study of representativeness in the Chilean Congress.

The Institutionalist Perspective

The interpretations of representativeness have varied within the institutionalist camp. While some authors have looked at the composition of legislatures, for example stressing the representation of the various interests and perspectives found in the electorate, others have concentrated on the incentives and constraints faced by goal-seeking legislators, for example stressing accountability mechanisms that affect legislative behavior. Unlike many works on representation, which tend to embrace a normatively favorable view of responsiveness, some works within this tradition have stressed negative aspects of responsiveness.

Institutional rules can make a legislature highly unrepresentative of the population that is constitutionally expected to embody. One obvious way is through limitations on the right to vote. Restrictions to the voting rights of women, racial minorities or illiterates—all common in Latin America during parts of the 20th century—are examples of rules that weaken the likelihood that the interests of all district inhabitants will be represented in the legislature. *De facto* restrictions on the voting rights of individuals constitutionally entitled to participate and manipulation of elections are also ways in which the representativeness of legislatures can be affected. Tainted elections tend to give disproportionate weight to the representation of some particular interests, but institutions can help to overcome this problem. The establishment of independent electoral institutes with authority to oversee elections can have a tremendous impact in restoring fair competition and lessening the unrepresentative tendencies associate with electoral manipulation, as the cases of Costa Rica in the mid 20th century and Mexico in the late 20th century illustrate.

The institutions regulating how legislators are chosen have for long been viewed as affecting the representativeness of legislative bodies. The disproportionality in the translation of votes into congressional seats is a common indicator of the degree of representativeness of the electoral rules in place. A proportional translation of a share of electoral votes into a share of legislative seats is supposed to enhance representativeness. This is a central idea behind the advocacy of proportional representation rules for electing legislators.

The size of electoral constituencies can also give rise to a disproportionate share of congressional seats allocated to voters of certain districts to the detriment of voters in other districts. Malapportionment is an affront to the principle of "one person, one vote" and distorts the representativeness of legislatures, particularly in the case of lower chambers that are supposed to be staffed according to such principle. For Snyder and Samuels (2001), malapportionment in Latin America not only has biased representation in favor of rural and conservative interests, but it has also promoted interbranch conflict and subnational authoritarian enclaves.

Others have emphasized the way in which institutions affect legislators' incentives. For instance, institutions can foster accountability to the local electorate. This should enhance responsiveness to district voters and minimize shirking. Where electoral competition encourages candidates to emphasize their own personal characteristics over the common traits of their party and voters have the opportunity to learn about legislators' actions and to punish misbehavior, responsiveness to district voters should be high. Accordingly, electoral rules that emphasized the so-called personal vote as well as frequent elections, no term limits and transparency mechanisms (e.g., recorded roll-call vote usage, information dissemination) all work to enhance the responsiveness of legislators to their electorate.

In Chile, there are no discriminatory restrictions regarding the right to vote, and clean elections are the norm. Chile's low district magnitude ($dm = 2$) and the ability of voters to select an individual candidate, encourage personalized campaigns. The relative ranking of Chile vis-à-vis other Latin American countries regarding the institutional measures just discussed appears in Table 1.2. The first column shows the average disproportionality index calculated using results for the last two elections (as of early 2011), the second column shows the malapportionment index of Samuels and Snyder (2001), the third the personal vote index from Johnson and Wallack (2007), and the fourth the length of service for lower-chamber legislators (as of 2011).

In terms of the malapportionment measure, Chile appears different than most others, with a higher tendency to regional misallocation of seats than in the typical Latin American lower chamber. The term in office for Chilean senators is also high for regional standards. But according to the other measures, the position of Chile is rather average for the region.[7]

So far, the discussion has followed the idea that representativeness is enhanced through rules that promote individual responsiveness to the electorate. But this view may be challenged on at least two grounds.

One is that the actual working of many of these rules may not have the expected effect in terms of linkages between voters and legislators. For instance, Blais and Bodet (2006) argue that PR facilitates the presence of noncentrist parties in the legislature, which increases the overall distance between voters and parties. At the same time, however, it also encourages coalition governments, which pulls the government toward the center of the policy spectrum and reduces the distance between the government and voters. So, for them, the

Table 1.2 Electoral Rules and Representativeness

	Lower Chamber Malapportionment	Electoral Disproportionality	Lower Chamber Term Length	Upper House Term Length	Personal Vote Rank
Argentina	0.14	18.2	4	6	1
Bolivia	0.17	4.9	5	5	9.2
Brazil	0.09	2.7	4	8	7
Chile	0.15	6.8	4	8	5
Colombia	0.13	4.6	4	4	12
Costa Rica	0.02	6	4		1
Dominican Republic	0.08	12.4	4	4	2.6
Ecuador	0.2	5.3	4		2.6
El Salvador	0.07	2.5	3		1
Guatemala	0.06	8.8	4		1
Honduras	0.04	3	4		1
Mexico	0.06	7.1	3	6	6
Nicaragua	0.06	4.5	5		1
Panama	0.06	9.6	5		6
Paraguay	0.04	4.3	5	5	1
Peru	0	11.5	5		5
Uruguay	0.03	2.4	5	5	3
Venezuela	0.07	8.3	5		10
Average	0.08	6.8	4.3	5.7	4.2

Source: Samuels and Snyder (2001), Johnson and Wallack (2007) and author's calculations

net effect in terms of the congruence between the electorate and legislators is likely to be nil. Or perhaps all electoral rules are fundamentally flawed regarding the aggregation of voter preferences, and do not make much of a difference in regards to representativeness (Riker 1984). So, constraints on the discretion of the rulers, such as checks on governmental power and separation of powers, may be one of the most effective ways of preventing unrepresentative governments from doing harm.

The second challenge to the perspective that emphasizes responsiveness to district voters is more fundamental. The main point here is that strengthening the representational link going from legislators to their district voters does not work so well for the interest of all voters. The emphasis on the personal vote, the attentiveness to local concerns and the recurrent pursuit of resources to the district is seen as conducive to ineffective governments, fragmented legislatures, weak legislative parties and party labels void of substantive content. These conditions undermine political parties, and ultimately make voters more uncertain about the preferences of party candidates, thereby increasing the likelihood of selecting flawed and unrepresentative candidates. Moreover, where parties are weak, electoral volatility and short-lived parties are common, which tend to make electoral sanctioning mechanisms ineffective to enhance accountability.

Collective responsibility, which puts parties at the center of the accountability link, entails a very different understanding of responsiveness (Carey 2009). Voters pick and punish political parties, and legislators are primarily responsible to party principals rather than constituents. This perspective favors a different recipe of institutional traits: rules that enhance the value of party labels, promote party institutionalization, provide parties with agenda setting power and make legislators value unity on votes. For Gerring et al. (2005), for example, centripetal institutions (including strong parties) foster decisiveness, facilitate governmental accountability, and are ultimately more effective in terms of delivering favorable policy outcomes than the decentralized institutions that characterize the world of diffuse power, where electoral laws seek to maximize local level accountability.

Chile is characterized by a well-institutionalized party system, with individual parties having coherent positions along the left-right ideological dimension and coalitions being remarkably stable. The constitution distributes significant legislative power to the executive and parties have many institutional means of promoting discipline. The behavior of legislators on roll-call votes reflects very high levels of party unity. Thus, the institutional context in Chile facilitates the assignment of responsibility for governmental decisions, and party and coalition labels matter to voters and legislators—voters can discern among candidates in terms of policy and can expect candidates for the legislature to act in a rather coherent fashion.

However, in at least one aspect, the electoral rules in place in Chile have not worked well to facilitate collective responsibility. Because the only way in which one of the two main coalitions can be defeated is if the other coalition doubles its vote-share, and both coalitions do not differ much in their share of the vote across electoral districts, elections are not such a credible mechanism to punish them. Voters may be able to clearly distinguish between competing partisan coalitions in terms of policy stances and governmental effectiveness, but they are limited in their capacity to use electoral mechanisms to sanction coalitions. They can, however, switch their support between parties to punish individual legislators.

The disenchantment of voters with the partisan offer became an important topic of discussion among Chileans during the student protests of 2011. Disagreements over educational policy led to the largest demonstrations against a sitting government since the restoration of democracy. The government of Sebastián Piñera, the first conservative government after four consecutive governments of the center-left, bore the brunt of the dissatisfaction for educational policies established long before he was elected. This contributed to the deterioration of public support, leading to the lowest presidential approval rates since 1990. Yet it is unclear whether this public disenchantment with educational policies is a symptom of an across-the-board weakening of the representational linkages between partisan coalitions and voters. As Figure 1.4 shows, the self-identification of Chilean voters with the existing coalitions has remained stable in the cases of the center-right (Alianza) and communist-dominated (Juntos Podemos) coalitions. The only significant change has been the steady deterioration of voter self-identification with the center-left Concertación.

Summary

The preceding discussion reviewed different approaches to evaluating representativeness in legislatures. The approach pioneered by the behavioralist camp, which centered on surveys of both district constituents and legislators and how attitudes relate to legislative behavior, has not been applied to the study of Latin American legislatures. While good public opinion surveys have been undertaken over the last two decades, comprehensive district level data are still unavailable for Chile. There is much to be gained from developing datasets that capture voter preferences by district. Until then, researchers will have to find other ways of examining the linkage between positions in the district and positions in Congress.

There are some fundamental differences within the institutionalist camp regarding which institutional framework is ultimately more appropriate to enhance representativeness. When conceptualizing representativeness, it is important to distinguish between the responsiveness of individual legislators to their district voters and the collective accountability of parties to their national electorate. Electoral and legislative institutions associated with locally oriented autonomous legislators are unlikely to promote unified nationally oriented ideological parties. In terms of the four specific outcomes that are supposed to have a significant impact on the representativeness of legislatures—malapportionment, disproportionality, opportunities for

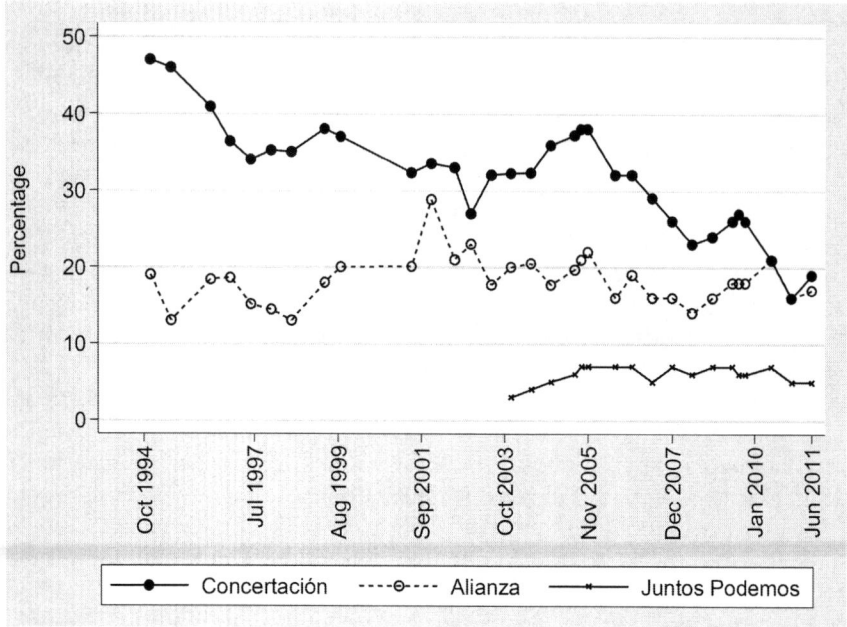

Figure 1.4   Self-identification among Chilean voters
Source: Centro de Estudios Públicos, Chile

electoral reward/punishment and incentives to attend district needs—Chile is ranked somewhere in the middle of the distribution of Latin American countries.

CONCLUSION

Paucity of cross-national information makes evaluations about congressional effectiveness and representativeness tentative at best. Overall, the Chilean Congress appears to perform effectively in comparison to other Latin American legislatures, while the representativeness embedded in the country's institutions appears typical for the region.

Many institutional reforms imply a trade-off with regards to representativeness and effectiveness, but there are some areas where reforms can advance both objectives. One is transparency. Reforms that encourage the dissemination of information regarding congressional activities, including the regular recording of votes in the plenary and in committee, would fit this category. Increasing opportunities to reward/punish legislators and their parties electorally should also work to benefit both representativeness and effectiveness. Lastly, reforms that encourage the professionalization of members of Congress should also help with the attainment of these goals. In this area, the Chilean Congress has so far performed well, even if there is plenty of room for improvement to become a more assertive check on the executive branch.

To conclude, there is a worthwhile research agenda ahead for those interested in effectiveness and representativeness in legislatures. The field is wide open, and the questions are of relevance not only to legislative scholars but also to those interested in the workings of democratic institutions.

NOTES

1. It includes domestic firms that trade in foreign markets, units of foreign firms operating in the domestic market and enterprises with significant government ownership.
2. And this number includes several "minority" sessions where quorum was not met.
3. The educational level of members of Congress has also been suggested as indicative of the membership's aptitude. Formal education has been considered an asset to tackle the complex tasks commonly confronted by members of Congress as they go about their business. Some available evidence indicates that in about two-thirds of Latin American countries, including Chile, at least three-fourths of the congressional membership has a university education (IADB 2006). Only in El Salvador, Brazil and the Dominican Republic does the proportion of university-educated legislators appear to be less than two-thirds (IADB 2006).
4. Jewell (1982), for instance, found that legislators elected under multimember districts were more likely to be trustees, while those elected under single-member districts were slightly more likely to be delegates. Cooper and Richardson (2006) also found an association between trustee self-identification and multimember districts.
5. The emphasis on norms, attitudes and socialization rather than individual preferences, incentives and strategies, and the central place given to politicians' view of their own legislative roles, eventually contributed to make role analysis a less attractive approach to the study of legislative politics. According to Strom (1997), the concept of legislative role tended to subsume legislators' beliefs, expectations, institutional functions and actual behavior without clear distinctions or causal explanations.
6. The authors presented evidence that constituency influence was more relevant in civil-rights issues, while partisan influence was more relevant on issues related to social welfare.
7. In addition, the lack of term limits and the general transparency behind legislative activity (from frequent roll-call votes to information dissemination) have worked to enhance the conditions that facilitate legislative accountability to district principals.

2 Argentina's Unrepresentative and Unaccountable Congress under the Kirchners

Mark P. Jones and Juan Pablo Micozzi

Scholars have repeatedly affirmed that over the past two decades the Argentine political party system has experienced a process of progressive denationalization. In this study we extend this line of scholarly inquiry by examining not only the pattern of partisan competition in Argentine congressional elections over the past decade, but also, and most importantly, the linkage between this progressive electoral denationalization and partisan alignments within the Argentine Congress. Through our focus on how parties interact in the electoral and legislative arenas, we highlight the profound implications of this process of denationalization of party politics for democratic representation in Argentina as well as underscore the manner in which the increasing levels of territorial fragmentation have distorted representational linkage mechanisms in the country more broadly.

If we understand by democratic representation the notion that "the actions of policy makers are supposed to be responsive to the wishes of the people" (Powell 2004, 205), the level of aggregation of the electoral supply can affect not only the nature of representation, but also the tradeoffs legislators face once in office, a reality closely tied to the effectiveness of the political system overall. Far from thinking solely in terms of patterns of imperative mandates (Pitkin 1967), the degrees of consistency between citizens' wishes and representatives' behavior are also a function of what kinds of interests ought to be represented. If voters prioritize ideology, broad policy principles or primordial partisan attachments, nationalized patterns of competition would provide a relatively clear-cut way of fostering accountability.[1] On the contrary, when the processes of partisan competition tend to be more disaggregated, the judgment of success or failure of genuine representation may be more complicated for citizens. The argument is straightforward: representatives of a given territorial unit are no more than a small share of a whole collective body governed by majority rule, and their ability to affect the policy process is noticeably limited.

Skeptical observers might counter that delegates tend to adapt their behavior to the preferences of their constituents; therefore, if competition is denationalized, it is likely to reflect similar tendencies in the voting public. However, the same hurdles for moving the status quo would hold for delegates acting on behalf of citizens interested in mere local representation.

Unless representatives engage in a giant logroll (Shepsle and Weingast 1987) where everyone wins, every subject will be frustrated by the lack of policy change. The sincere pursuit of local interests in such circumstances is likely to end up offering poor substantive representation for all citizens, contributing to unsatisfactory levels of effectiveness. Should candidates and parties, then, restrict the goals of their mandates to the pursuit of resources for their domestic audiences, irrespective of the costs, and expect to be retrospectively evaluated? Would they, as an implication, create district-based congressional delegations? Or would they prefer to forge long-lasting alliances with other actors, precisely to improve their prospective performance? These questions lie at the heart of the representational contract in a system where electoral politics have shifted from the national to the state (and lower) level. Whether the degree and quality of representation is still as robust after this change is a matter of empirical verification, a task we engage in here.

We center our analysis in the representational consequences of the long territorial chain linking voters, representatives and policy outcomes in this piece. Even though, as previously mentioned, an effective political system would largely reflect the successful implementation of (multiple) issues of salience to voters in regular elections, we can analytically separate the process of transmission of demands from their effective materialization. In sum, here we focus on how representative the contemporary Argentine political system has been, and leave the analysis of the outcomes and overall effectiveness for future research.[2]

Reviewing the Argentine experience, the progressive process of denationalization of party competition has resulted in a tremendous degree of variation in patterns of party creation and disappearance, coalition building, electoral competition, party predominance, policy priorities of delegates to federal offices and performance in the national Congress across the country's 24 electoral districts. Salient differences among provinces in these areas tend to reinforce the notion that representation is likely to be, by default, substantively different in each territorial unit. As an implication, we should observe changing patterns of competition and organization, but also clearly differentiated legislative behavior at the national level.

The results of this study represent something of a paradox, since within this context of party system denationalization, legislative parties, in particular the currently governing Frente para la Victoria (FPV) of former president Néstor Kirchner (2003–2007) and current president Cristina Fernández de Kirchner (2007–), are quite robust and dominate the legislative process, with province-based behavior restricted to a handful of local parties. Generally, scholars point to the role of congressional rules and the cartelized behavior of the majority party to explain this reality (Jones and Hwang 2005; Jones, Hwang and Micozzi 2009; Danesi 2010). However, no study has reconstructed the complete chain linking the patterns of coalitions in lists, delegation formation and legislative performance to illustrate how this logic operates. Tracking this path is necessary to fully comprehend the extent to which local politics are really detached from national alignments, and to assess the extent to which individuals and parties that have established alliances at the local level to compete in congressional elections tend to work together in the context of the national Congress. In this chapter, we systematically examine the changing patterns of alignments across parties in time and space at the electoral and legislative levels. In addition, we explore how dissimilar and even contradictory patterns of electoral coalition formation took place across and within districts in Argentina. In other terms, we try to disentangle the changing nature of province-based coalitions in national elections, and also their influence on legislative performance, empirically highlighting how politics became more denationalized over time.

As is well documented in the literature, the Argentine political party system started down the path of increasing denationalization in the early 1990s (Gibson and Suarez-Cao 2010; Leiras 2010). Multiple explanations have been presented to explain this trend, such as state reform and decentralization, the desire of local leaders to shield subnational leaderships from national shocks, and the decay of Argentine political parties as institutions. Qualitative evidence reveals how patterns of alignment have changed vis-à-vis the past, when national parties held sway regarding decisions over candidacies and alliances throughout the nation. In recent years, explicit coalitions, informal alignments and even alliances between the national government and subnational branches (or leaders) of opposition parties have become the norm. One of the most poignant examples of this dynamic was the creation in 2007 of the "Concertación" by then-president Néstor Kirchner and his spouse (and FPV presidential candidate) Cristina Fernández de Kirchner, under which provincial-level alliances were formed with governors, mayors and provincial legislators whose party represented the principal partisan opposition (the Unión Cívica Radical [UCR]) to the Kirchners at the national level.[3]

However, far from being a uniform pattern, party alignments have changed, and still change, across time and provinces. In spite of the abundance of high profile anecdotes and isolated bits of empirical data, to date there does not exist a comprehensive understanding of congressional electoral alliances in national elections in Argentina. Is variation restricted to specific districts ("fixed effects"), to national waves ("dynamic effects"), or simply to pragmatic alignments based on political convenience? Are these patterns of coalition for national offices led by subnational dynamics, or are they more affected by bargaining among local leaders and the federal government? How does this variation affect patterns of legislative behavior? These questions will be addressed via an analysis of the different patterns of electoral, bloc and voting alignments between 2001 and 2009.

THE ARGENTINE POLITICAL SYSTEM

Argentina is not a new case in the literature on federal presidential systems, which has amply demonstrated that federalism in Argentina is quite robust, and affects almost every single dimension of political competition in the country (Spiller and Tommasi 2007). With the exception of the president and vice president, every other elected official (ranging from national legislators to municipal council members) is chosen within the boundaries of its 23 provinces and the City of Buenos Aires (referred to hereafter as the 24th province). National deputies are elected from closed lists using proportional representation (PR), with the entire province serving as the constituency. The number of legislators elected from a constituency in any given election ranges from two to 35, with a median and mode of three and a mean of five. Each province renews one-half of its delegation every two years, with deputies elected for four-year terms. Senators (three per province) are elected for six-year terms using an incomplete list format, where the winning list gets two seats, and the runner up the remaining one in every province. One-third of the provinces (i.e., eight) renew their entire senate delegation every two years. This Senate electoral system made its debut in 2001, after more than a century of indirect election by the country's provincial legislatures.

The provincial nature of Argentine politics has profound implications for politics and policy. Given the strong powers possessed by governors and subnational party leaders, provincial actors tend to rule over candidate selection mechanisms for most offices (De Luca, Jones and Tula 2002), which endows them with considerable control over the behavior of these elected officials. The use of a closed list at the national legislative level reinforces these tendencies and has engendered loyalty and discipline in the Congress (Jones et al. 2002; Jones and Hwang 2005), a process bolstered by the low levels of personalization[4] on the part of deputies and the multilevel structure of political careers (Jones et al. 2002; Micozzi 2009).[5] Given the country's low reelection rate, six out of every seven legislators serve only a single term in office, the levels of expertise in Congress are low and the incentives for members of Congress to invest in Congress as an institution extremely weak (Jones et al. 2002).[6] These multistage patterns of careerism make governorships and mayoralties powerful posts from which politicians are able to exert considerable influence over the political process. In fact, governors and mayors rank highest among the half dozen categories of political posts in Argentina in terms of their rate of reelection (Micozzi 2009).

As mentioned earlier, provincial executives in Argentina have amassed substantial powers over the past two decades, transforming themselves into pivotal actors for national politics. On the one hand, the process of decentralization during the 1990s transferred multiple responsibilities to their administrations, but also allocated considerable funds to the provinces that do not require any accountability on the part of the provincial authorities (Spiller and Tommasi 2007). In parallel, provincial executives enacted institutional and constitutional reforms that removed obstacles to their reelection, changed electoral rules that let them manage dynamics of competition (e.g., the adoption of the double simultaneous vote), and increased the provincial legislative electoral system's majoritarian and partisan biases, and therein the size of the governing party's legislative delegations (Calvo and Abal Medina 2001; Calvo and Micozzi 2005). Furthermore, the governors' ability to manipulate the electoral calendars became a powerful tool. While in 1983 and 1989 every single province ran provincial elections simultaneously with the presidential contest, over time governors tended to strategically detach or attach provincial and federal elections.[7] This strategic use of the election calendar has contributed to the territorialization of party alignments in different elections over time.

A single person or small group of politicians generally dominates political parties at the provincial level (Jones and Hwang 2005). This dominance by party leaders is based principally on patronage, pork barrel politics and clientelism. In provinces where the party controls the governorship, with rare exceptions the governor is the undisputed (or at least dominant) boss of the provincial-level party. In many other provinces where the governorship is not held by the party, the party is nonetheless dominated in a comparable manner (with a greater amount of space for intraparty opponents) by a single individual.

As the previous discussion suggests, in most instances the reelection decision for members of the Argentine Chamber of Deputies (as well as the decision regarding their political future) lies primarily with the provincial-level party boss(es), and not with the individual deputy. In Argentina the electoral goals of the provincial party bosses are best served by distributive policy (since their hold on power is based primarily on patronage, pork and clientelism). They are thus primarily interested in the passage of distributive policy. Argentine provincial party bosses also tend to actively parlay their legislative support (i.e., the votes of their legislators) in exchange for financial benefits from the national executive branch in the form of transfers, subsidies, government posts and pork.

PARTIES AND ALLIANCES

Considerable scholarship (e.g., Calvo and Escolar 2005; Alemán and Kellam 2008; Leiras 2010) has underscored the progressive denationalization of the Argentine party system over the past twenty years. Utilizing distinct theoretical arguments and empirical measures, this body of work highlights two divergent processes. One, parties' performance tends to vary considerably across districts. Two, the provincial branches of parties, and even political actors who have defected from the country's two traditional parties, tend to concentrate their activities in their territorial bailiwicks, and therefore create electoral coalitions and fronts that often do not mirror national partisan alignments. Even though this literature has widely acknowledged these denationalizing tendencies, there is still uncertainty about how coherent different alliances at the provincial level have been, and also about the extent to which they broadly reflect the political and programmatic positions adopted by the national party leadership. As mentioned above, changing coalitional patterns are not restricted to parties that strategically switch as power shifts; instead, factions, leaders and well-known individuals may choose to build new local parties, rent an existing party organization, or maneuver provincial party branches into (sometimes contradictory) alliances over the years and across the provinces.

In order to shed light on these diffuse dynamics, we collected information on every single province-level coalition between 2001 and 2009 for the only office elected every two years: federal deputies. Instead of showing the district-by-district information (which would be extremely informative, but which would also require substantially more space than is available here), we organize the data at the aggregate level, and explore the coalition partners of the two major national parties, the Partido Justicialista (PJ, Peronist) and Unión Cívica Radical (UCR, Radical), during this period. For reasons of space, we restrict the presentation of our election specific data to the two "book-end" elections of the Kirchner era to date (2003 and 2009). Tables 2.1 (2003) and 2.2 (2009) provide information on the parties allied with either the PJ or UCR in one of the 24 provinces in the congressional elections. Table 2.3 summarizes the information for the 2001–2009 period by providing the alliance patterns (vis-à-vis the PJ and UCR) of the six most common PJ/FPV and UCR alliance partners. It also details the number of instances per year when the PJ/FPV and UCR allied together in one of the country's 24 districts.

Many of the aforementioned patterns of denationalization are readily apparent in Tables 2.1, 2.2, and 2.3. First, patterns of coalition are changing and, at times, chaotic. Both the PJ and UCR have joined alliances with a specific party in different districts in the same year. Local branches of small national parties (e.g., Frente Grande [FG], Movimiento de Integración y Desarrollo [MID], Partido Demócrata Cristiano [PDC], Partido Demócrata Progresista [PDP], Partido Intransigente [PI], Unión del Centro Democrático [UCEDE]) have tactically chosen their alliance partners based on provincial level factors, regardless of any (if existing) federal party direction. This crazy-quilt pattern of conflicting alliances with minor national parties has been approved by the respective PJ and UCR national party organizations, thereby resulting in provincial-level electoral alliances which differ both across districts but also from broader national trends. Moreover, over the past decade instances have emerged where the two principal pillars of the Argentine party system (the PJ and UCR) have actually allied in several provinces (e.g., Corrientes, Neuquén), all while at the same time remaining bitter rivals at the national level and in the other provinces.

Second, the aforementioned changing coalitional patterns have in a plethora of elections ruptured the boundaries of ideological coherence. Both the UCR and PJ have in different years and provinces allied with center-left and left parties such as the Partido Socialista (PS), FG, Patria Libre (PL) and Libres del Sur (LDS), as well as with center-right actors like the UCEDE, Acción por la República (AR) and Movimiento de Independencia Nacional (MODIN).

Table 2.1 Partido Justicialista and Unión Cívica Radical Alliance Partners, 2003

2003		2003	
PARTIDO JUSTICIALISTA	23	UNION CIVICA RADICAL	24
UNION CIVICA RADICAL	1	JUSTICIALISTA	1
FRENTE GRANDE	5	FRENTE GRANDE	2
MOVIMIENTO DE INTEGRACION Y DESARROLLO	4	MOVIMIENTO DE INTEGRACION Y DESARROLLO	4
DE LA VICTORIA	4	DE LA VICTORIA	1
POLITICA ABIERTA PARA LA INTEGRACION SOCIAL	3	POLITICA ABIERTA PARA LA INTEGRACION SOCIAL	1
DEMOCRATA CRISTIANO	2	DEMOCRATA CRISTIANO	4
ACCION POR LA REPUBLICA	2	ACCION POR LA REPUBLICA	1
UNION DEL CENTRO DEMOCRATICO	2	UNION DEL CENTRO DEMOCRATICO	1
INTRANSIGENTE	1	INTRANSIGENTE	5
PARTIDO SOCIALISTA	1	PARTIDO SOCIALISTA	2
UNION Y LIBERTAD	1	UNION Y LIBERTAD	1
CONSERVADOR POPULAR	4	RECREAR PARA EL CRECIMIENTO	3
MODIN	3	DEL FRENTE	2
AFIRMACION PARA UNA REPUBLICA IGUALITARIA	2	SOCIALISTA POPULAR	2
DEMOCRATA LIBERAL	2	AUTONOMISTA	1
NACIONALISTA CONSTITUCIONAL	2	BASES Y PRINCIPIOS DE CHACO	1
ACCION DESARROLLISTA	1	BLOQUISTA	1
ACCION NATIVA	1	CONCERTACION POPULAR	1

ACCION PARA EL CAMBIO	1
ACCION POPULAR	1
AUTENTICO FORMOSENO	1
AUTONOMISTA	1
CAMBIO DEMOCRATICO DE TUCUMAN	1
DEL PUEBLO	1
DEMOCRATA PROGRESISTA	1
EL BLANCO FRENTE INDEPENDIENTE DEL NORTE	1
FEDERAL	1
FORTALEZA	1
FRENTE DE LOS JUBILADOS	1
FRENTE FEDERAL DE CORDOBA	1
GESTION ESTADO Y SOCIEDAD TODOS AHORA	1
MEMORIA Y MOVILIZACION	1
MOV. DE REIVINDICACION NAM QOM	1
MOVIMIENTO CIVICO DE SALTA	1
MOVIMIENTO DE ACCION POPULAR	1
MOVIMIENTO DE BASES	1
MOVIMIENTO DE PARTICIPACION POPULAR	1
MOVIMIENTO DE RECUPERACION POPULAR	1
MOVIMIENTO GRANDE DE LA ESPERANZA	1
CORDOBA EN ACCION	1
DEMOCRACIA POPULAR PARA EL FRENTE SOCIAL	1
FEDERAL	1
FRENTE CON TODOS	1
MOVILIZACION	1
MOVIMIENTO AMPLIO DE UNIDAD	1
MOVIMIENTO DEMOCRATICO FEDERAL	1
MOVIMIENTO FEDERAL SANTACRUCENO	1
MOVIMIENTO FEDERALISTA PAMPEANO	1
MOVIMIENTO POPULAR CORDOBES	1
MOVIMIENTO POPULAR JUJENO	1
NUEVO PAIS	1
POR UN NUEVO JUJUY	1
RED DE PARTICIPACION POPULAR	1
SOCIALISTA DEMOCRATICO	1
UNIDAD CATAMARQUENA	1

(Continued)

Table 2.1 (Continued)

2003	2003
MOVIMIENTO INDEPENDIENTE DE PARTICIPACION	1
MOVIMIENTO POPULAR PROVINCIAL	1
MOVIMIENTO POPULAR TUCUMANO	1
MOVIMIENTO REGIONAL DEL PUEBLO	1
MOVIMIENTO TIERRA COLORADA	1
NUEVA GENTE	1
NUEVO FRENTE	1
PROVINCIAL RIONEGRINO	1
RENOVADOR DEL OESTE	1
SOCIAL DEMOCRATA	1
SOLIDARIDAD Y ORGANIZACION PARA LA LIBE	1
UNIDAD POPULAR	1
UNIDAD Y PROGRESO	1
UNION SOCIAL	1
UNION VECINAL DE CORDOBA	1
VANGUARDIA PROVINCIAL	1
VECINOS UNIDOS	1

Source: Author's calculations

Table 2.2 Partido Justicialista and Unión Cívica Radical Alliance Partners, 2009

2009		2009	
PARTIDO JUSTICIALISTA	24	UNION CIVICA RADICAL	24
UNION CIVICA RADICAL	1		
DE LA VICTORIA	13	DE LA VICTORIA	1
INTRANSIGENTE	11	INTRANSIGENTE	3
DEMOCRATA CRISTIANO	4	DEMOCRATA CRISTIANO	2
CONSERVADOR POPULAR	4	CONSERVADOR POPULAR	1
POLITICA ABIERTA PARA LA INTEGRACION SOCIAL	2	POLITICA ABIERTA PARA LA INTEGRACION SOCIAL	1
NUEVA DIRIGENCIA	2	NUEVA DIRIGENCIA	1
MODIN	2	MODIN	1
MOVIMIENTO DE INTEGRACION Y DESARROLLO	1	MOVIMIENTO DE INTEGRACION Y DESARROLLO	4
FEDERAL	1	FEDERAL	3
UNIR	1	UNIR	1
DEMOCRATA PROGRESISTA	1	DEMOCRATA PROGRESISTA	4
MOVIMIENTO CIUDADANO	1	MOVIMIENTO CIUDADANO	1
MOVIMIENTO DE LEALTAD RADICAL	1	MOVIMIENTO DE LEALTAD RADICAL	1
POR LA GENTE	1	POR LA GENTE	1
POR LA JUSTICIA SOCIAL	1	POR LA JUSTICIA SOCIAL	1
FRENTE GRANDE	10	PARTIDO SOCIALISTA	11
HUMANISTA	6	AFIRMACION PARA UNA REPUBLICA IGUALITARIA	6

(Continued)

Table 2.2 (Continued)

2009		2009	
COMUNISTA	4	COALICION CIVICA	2
PROYECTO POPULAR	4	CONSENSO FEDERAL	2
POLO SOCIAL	3	GEN	2
MEMORIA Y MOVILIZACION SOCIAL	2	ACCION CHAQUENA	1
MOVIMIENTO DE ACCION VECINAL	2	ACCION DEPARTAMENTAL DE VALLE VIEJO	1
NACIONALISTA CONSTITUCIONAL	2	ACCION NATIVA	1
NUEVA GENERACION	2	ALTERNATIVA PARA UNA REPUBLICA DE IGUALES	1
PROGRESO SOCIAL	2	BASES Y PRINCIPIOS DE CHACO	1
RECREAR PARA EL CRECIMIENTO	2	CAMBIO 2000	1
ACCION PARA EL CAMBIO	1	CRECER CON TODOS	1
ACCION POPULAR	1	DE LA PARTICIPACION POPULAR	1
ACCION POR LA REPUBLICA	1	DE UNIDAD CATAMARQUENA	1
AUTENTICO FORMOSENO	1	DEMOCRACIA POPULAR PARA EL FRENTE SOCIAL	1
BLOQUISTA	1	ENCUENTRO FEDERAL ENTRERRIANO	1
CAMBIO CORDOBA	1	ENCUENTRO POPULAR	1
CAUSA REPARADORA	1	FRENTE DE INTEGRACION SOCIAL PARA UN CAMBIO	1
CHACO DE PIE	1	INTEGRACION CATAMARQUENA	1
COMPROMISO POPULAR	1	INTEGRACION Y MOVILIDAD SOCIAL	1
DE LA CONCERTACION	1	MILITANCIA CATAMARQUENA	1
DE LA PARTICIPACION POPULAR	1	MOVILIZACION	1

DE TODOS POR LOS DERECHOS SOCIALES	1
DEL FRENTE	1
DEMOCRATA DE CATAMARCA	1
DESARROLLO Y JUSTICIA	1
EL BLANCO FRENTE INDEPENDIENTE DEL NORTE	1
EL FRENTE Y LA PARTICIPACION NEUQUINA	1
ENCUENTRO DE LA VICTORIA	1
ES POSIBLE	1
ESPACIO ABIERTO	1
FORJA	1
FORTALEZA	1
FRENTE DE LOS JUBILADOS	1
FRENTE DEL PUEBLO	1
FRENTE FEDERAL DE CORDOBA	1
FRENTE PARA EL CAMBIO	1
FRENTE PARA LA ESPERANZA	1
FRENTE PARA TODOS	1
FUERZA TRANSFORMADORA	1
LIBRE EN MOVIMIENTO	1
LOS DESOCUPADOS	1
MOVIMIENTO DE IDENTIDAD POPULAR	1
MOVIMIENTO DE PARTICIPACION CIUDADANA	1
MOVIMIENTO JUSTICIA Y LIBERTAD	1
MOVIMIENTO PATAGONICO POPULAR	1
MOVIMIENTO POPULAR CATAMARQUENO	1
MOVIMIENTO POPULAR JUJENO	1
MOVIMIENTO TINOGASTENO	1
MOVIMIENTO VECINALISTA PROVINCIAL	1
NACIONALISTA CONSTITUCIONAL	1
NORTE FEDERAL	1
NUESTRO COMPROMISO	1
NUEVA GENERACION	1
NUEVA GENTE	1
NUEVO ESPACIO DE OPINION	1
NUEVO FRENTE	1
NUEVO MOVIMIENTO	1
PAMPA SUR	1
POPULAR SANTARROSENO	1
RECREAR PARA EL CRECIMIENTO	1
SOLIDARIDAD Y ALTRUISMO	1

(Continued)

Table 2.2 (*Continued*)

2009		2009	
MOCOMER	1	TODOS POR CATAMARCA	1
MOVIMIENTO BRENENSE	1	UNIDAD POPULAR MENDOZA	1
MOVIMIENTO DE ACCION POPULAR	1	UNIFICACION POPULISTA	1
UNION DEL CENTRO DEMOCRATICO	1	UNION POR LA RIOJA	1
37 OTHER PARTIES	1		

Source: Author's calculations

Table 2.3   Alliance Patterns of the Six Most Common PJ and UCR Alliance Partners by Year 2001–2009

POLITICAL PARTY	2001		2003		2005		2007		2009	
	PJ	UCR	PJ	UCR	PJ	UCR	PJ	UCR	PJ	UCR
MID	2	9	4	4	5	2	1	8	1	4
PDC	1	2	2	4	3	1	4	0	4	2
FG	0	11	5	2	8	3	9	0	10	0
PI	0	6	1	5	3	6	9	4	11	3
DLV	0	0	4	1	13	2	12	1	13	1
PS	0	10	1	2	1	5	2	3	0	11
PJ/UCR Behavior										
PJ	24	0	24	1	24	2	23	2	24	1
UCR	0	24	1	23	2	24	1	24	0	24

Source: Author's calculations

A third trend is related to the intertemporal flexibility of parties in coalitional terms. Actors that mostly allied with one of the national parties (i.e., the UCR and PJ) at time *t* massively switched to the other only a few years later. For instance there are the cases of the FG and PI, which at the start of the past decade primarily allied with the UCR, but by the end of the decade primarily allied with the PJ/FPV (see Table 2.3). Of course, this process is not independent from the changes in national level party alignments (with the PJ moving from the center to the center-left as time passed during the 2000s), which also resulted in several other progressive parties (e.g., the Partido Comunista [PC] and PL) moving to ally with the PJ/FPV. However, other actors also shifted their alliances brusquely during this period, such as the cases of the Partido Bloquista (PB) and the Partido Renovador de Salta (PRS), two conservative provincial parties in the provinces of San Juan and Salta respectively with strong ties to the military dictatorship that governed Argentina between 1976 and 1983. Both were allied with the UCR at the start of the decade and with the FPV/PJ by the end of the decade.

A fourth issue relates to specific unusual alliances. Even though we are not analyzing every alliance across time in detail, particular coalitions do illustrate that province-based dynamics not only differ from national behavior, but also from any logical intuition based on ideological coherence. For example, the 2009 congressional election in the province of Corrientes illustrates how three parties with dissimilar backgrounds joined together in the same electoral front. The Correntinos por el Cambio alliance consisted of three parties: the PJ (traditionally mass based, populist and flexible, and whose ballot featured a photo of Eva Perón), the PC (as its name suggests, the Argentine communist party, whose ballot featured a photo of Che Guevara), and the UCEDE (a conservative party founded by one of the country's most visible advocates of neoliberal economic policies, Álvaro Alsogaray). It is hard to imagine a national politician of any of these parties successfully defending a federal coalition with each of these partners. However, as previously noted, subnational dynamics have an autonomous life in the Argentine political system.

FROM VOTES TO SEATS: PARTY ALLIANCES AND LEGISLATIVE BLOCS

Another dimension of the decomposition of the traditional party system can be seen in congressional activity. We have already discussed how electoral alliances can reflect multiple political motivations. It is also clear however that political dynamics play a role during legislative tenure, and legislators can leave their parties and blocs, create new ones, join others, form a unipersonal bloc, or leave office for multiple reasons.[8] In fact, even in the case of the well-structured U.S. Congress, as well as in other countries, there exist many examples of party switching (Nokken and Poole 2006; Desposato 2006), "internal" party creation (Samuels 2003), and varying degrees of party cohesion

(Poole and Rosenthal 2001; Carey 2009). Returning to the Argentine case, it is clear that within the political context described above, legislators can engage in a variety of strategic behavior during their mandates. These instrumental shifts can be manifold, and can also occur at multiple stages of a legislative mandate.

The first decision subject to manipulation takes place immediately after taking possession of the seat, and involves the decision of which legislative delegation to join. This choice is not a minor one for several reasons. On the one hand, the internal rules which allocate power in the Argentine Chamber of Deputies are majoritarian,[9] a reality that affects salient factors such as committee assignments, committee chair posts, delegation leadership positions and budget and contracts to hire personnel. On the other hand, delegation membership affects the probabilities of bill passage; namely, members of the majority bloc have higher chances of legislative success (Alemán and Calvo 2010). However, individuals are not operating in a vacuum, having been elected from closed party lists and often as part of a national or subnational coalition or alliance. In parallel, local leaders have powers to affect individuals' political fates. Therefore, strategic decisions are, in fact, constrained *ex ante*.

Let us assume that, in a *normal* world, a legislator should belong to the list from which she was elected. Therefore, electoral and legislative brands (labels) should not differ. However, as described above, not only can individual legislators (or more commonly, the legislator's principal, the party boss) make unilateral decisions about the blocs they join, but also, given that party alliance strategies tend to vary across time and province, legislators elected from the same list in the same province may in fact belong to parties which are rivals at the national level. In parallel, several party branches or factions can have a particular position vis-à-vis the national government that may also be different from that of the federal party leadership. Therefore, nothing insures that there will be consistency between the electoral supply and the destination of those representatives elected by voters. Thus, the relationship between electoral and legislative alignments can be heavily influenced by the degree of party system nationalization.

The transition election of 1983 represented the peak of party system nationalization in Argentina. That year, electoral alignments were principally determined by the national parties, which coordinated candidacies throughout the 24 electoral districts, and tended to reproduce federal patterns of competition almost everywhere. Ten parties and alliances won seats in the Chamber in 1983, with these deputies subsequently forming eleven Chamber delegations. Eighteen years later, in 2001, 40 parties and alliances won seats in the Chamber, and subsequently joined 36 distinct delegations. Even though partisan fragmentation has increased in Argentina, especially since 2001, very few relevant parties have been created at the national level. Instead, local parties and leaders have opted to develop specific patterns of alliances, coalitions, and province-based frames to insulate their districts from national shocks.

Table 2.4 Labels Employed by the PJ and UCR in Chamber Elections, 2001–2009

Year	PJ (and allies) Label	N	UCR (and allies) Label	
2001	JUSTICIALISTA	14	ALIANZA PARA EL TRABAJO, LA JUSTICIA Y LA EDUCACION	7
	ALIANZA FRENTE DE LA UNIDAD	1	UNION CIVICA RADICAL	6
	ALIANZA FRENTE FUNDACIONAL JUSTICIALISTA	1	ALIANZA 2001 PARA EL TRABAJO, LA JUSTICIA Y LA EDUCACION	1
	ALIANZA FRENTE JUSTICIALISTA	1	ALIANZA FRENTE CIVICO JUJEÑO	1
	ALIANZA FRENTE JUSTICIALISTA POPULAR	1	ALIANZA FRENTE CIVICO Y SOCIAL	1
	ALIANZA FRENTE JUSTICIALISTA POR SANTA FE	1	ALIANZA FRENTE DE TODOS	1
	ALIANZA FRENTE JUSTICIALISTA TODOS PARA EL CAMBIO	1	ALIANZA FUERZA DE UNIDAD POPULAR	1
	ALIANZA FRENTE PARA EL CAMBIO	1	ALIANZA GRANDE	1
	ALIANZA FRENTE UNION POR BUENOS AIRES	1	ALIANZA POR MENDOZA	1
	ALIANZA UNIDOS POR SAN JUAN	1	ALIANZA POR SAN JUAN	1
	FRENTE PARA LA UNIDAD	1	ALIANZA SANTACRUCEÑA	1
			ALIANZA SANTAFESINA	1
			FRENTE DE TODOS	1
2003	JUSTICIALISTA	12	UNION CIVICA RADICAL	8
	ALIANZA FRENTE DE TODOS	2	ALIANZA FRENTE DE TODOS	2
	ALIANZA FRENTE PARA LA VICTORIA	2	ALIANZA CONCERTACION PARA EL DESARROLLO	1
	ALIANZA FRENTE DE LA UNIDAD	1	ALIANZA CONVERGENCIA POR SANTA CRUZ	1
	ALIANZA FRENTE JUSTICIALISTA COMPROMISO POR MENDOZA	1	ALIANZA FRENTE ALTERNATIVA PAMPEANA	1

Year	Party	Seats
	ALIANZA FRENTE JUSTICIALISTA PARA EL CAMBIO	1
	ALIANZA FRENTE JUSTICIALISTA PARA LA VICTORIA	1
	ALIANZA FRENTE MOVIMIENTO POPULAR	1
	ALIANZA UNION POR CORDOBA	1
	FRENTE FUNDACIONAL POR EL CAMBIO	1
	ALIANZA FRENTE CIVICO Y SOCIAL	1
	ALIANZA FRENTE DE UNIDAD PROVINCIAL	1
	ALIANZA FRENTE JUJEÑO	1
	ALIANZA FRENTE JUNTOS POR SAN LUIS	1
	ALIANZA FRENTE PROVINCIA UNIDA	1
	ALIANZA FRENTE SOCIAL ENTRE RIOS TIENE FUTURO	1
	ALIANZA FRENTE SOCIAL Y PRODUCTIVO	1
	ALIANZA FRENTE UNION POR TUCUMAN	1
	ALIANZA UNIDOS POR SALTA	1
	LEMA RIOJANO POR EL TRABAJO Y LA PRODUCCION SOCIALISTA	1
2005	ALIANZA FRENTE PARA LA VICTORIA	14
	ALIANZA FRENTE JUSTICIALISTA PARA LA VICTORIA JUSTICIALISTA	3
	ALIANZA FRENTE DE TODOS	2
	ALIANZA FRENTE JUSTICIALISTA	2
	UNION CIVICA RADICAL	11
	ALIANZA FRENTE DE TODOS	2
	ALIANZA CONCERTACIÓN PARA EL DESARROLLO	3
	ALIANZA ENCUENTRO PARA EL CAMBIO UNION CIVICA RADICAL	1
	ALIANZA FRENTE CIVICO PARA LA VICTORIA	1

(Continued)

Table 2.4 (Continued)

Year	PJ (and allies) Label	N	UCR (and allies) Label
	ALIANZA FRENTE CIVICO PARA LA VICTORIA	1	ALIANZA FRENTE CIVICO POR SANTIAGO
	ALIANZA UNION POR CORDOBA	1	ALIANZA FRENTE CIVICO Y SOCIAL
	DE LA VICTORIA	1	ALIANZA FRENTE CIVICO RADICAL INTRANSIGENTE
			ALIANZA FRENTE JUJEÑO
			ALIANZA FRENTE PROGRESISTA, CÍVICO Y SOCIAL
			ALIANZA FRENTE RADICAL, DEMOCRÁTICO, CÍVICO Y SOCIAL
			MOVIMIENTO POPULAR FUEGUINO
2007	ALIANZA FRENTE PARA LA VICTORIA	14	UNION CIVICA RADICAL
	JUSTICIALISTA	4	ALIANZA CONCERTACIÓN UNA NACIÓN AVANZADA
	ALIANZA FRENTE DE TODOS	2	ALIANZA FRENTE CIVICO Y SOCIAL
	ALIANZA FRENTE JUSTICIALISTA PARA LA VICTORIA	2	ALIANZA CONCERTACIÓN PARA UNA NACIÓN AVANZADA
	ALIANZA FRENTE JUSTICIALISTA CHACO MERECE MÁS	1	ALIANZA FRENTE CIVICO POR SANTIAGO
	ALIANZA FRENTE PARTIDO JUSTICIALISTA	1	ALIANZA FRENTE DE TODOS
	FRENTE PARA LA VICTORIA SANTACRUCENA	1	ALIANZA FRENTE JUJEÑO
			ALIANZA FRENTE JUNTOS POR SAN LUIS

Year	Party	Seats
	ALIANZA FRENTE PAMPEANO CÍVICO Y SOCIAL	1
	ALIANZA FRENTE PARA LA VICTORIA	1
	ALIANZA FRENTE POR UNA NACIÓN AVANZADA	1
	ALIANZA UNA NACION AVANZADA	1
	ALIANZA UNA SAN JUAN	1
	FRENTE CAMBIEMOS PARA CRECER	1
	ALIANZA ACUERDO CIVICO Y SOCIAL	6
	UNION CIVICA RADICAL	5
	ALIANZA FRENTE ACUERDO CIVICO Y SOCIAL	2
	ALIANZA FRENTE CIVICO Y SOCIAL	2
	ALIANZA CONCERTACIÓN FRENTE PARA LA VICTORIA	1
	ALIANZA CONCERTACIÓN PARA EL DESARROLLO	1
	ALIANZA ENCUENTRO POR CORRIENTES	1
	ALIANZA FRENTE CAMBIEMOS PARA CRECER	1
	ALIANZA FRENTE CÍVICO FEDERAL UCR	1
	ALIANZA FRENTE DE TODOS	1
	ALIANZA FRENTE FEDERAL, CÍVICO Y SOCIAL	1
	ALIANZA FRENTE PAMPEANO CIVICO Y SOCIAL	1
	ALIANZA FRENTE PROGRESISTA CÍVICO Y SOCIAL	1
2009	ALIANZA FRENTE PARA LA VICTORIA	8
	JUSTICIALISTA	6
	ALIANZA FRENTE CHACO MERECE MAS	1
	ALIANZA FRENTE CORRENTINOS POR EL CAMBIO	1
	ALIANZA FRENTE JUSTICIALISTA DE LA DIGNIDAD Y EL PROGRESO	1
	ALIANZA FRENTE JUSTICIALISTA DEL PUEBLO RIOJANO	1
	ALIANZA FRENTE JUSTICIALISTA ENTRERRIANO	1
	ALIANZA FRENTE JUSTICIALISTA ES POSIBLE	1
	ALIANZA FRENTE JUSTICIALISTA PARA LA VICTORIA	1
	ALIANZA FRENTE POR LA INTEGRACION	1
	ALIANZA FRENTE RENOVADOR DE LA CONCORDIA	1
	FRENTE PARA LA VICTORIA	1

Source: Author's calculations

Here we provide several indicators of the aforementioned processes. First, we show the different labels adopted by the lists joined by the two most prominent national parties, the PJ and UCR. As can be observed in Table 2.4, differences across districts abound. While party leaders in several provinces have opted to highlight the traditional party name or its contemporary equivalent,[10] others frequently have linked their labels to the province. Table 2.4 shows how dissimilar the brand names of the two principal parties have been over time and across provinces during the past 10 years, and also clarifies how parties followed different degrees of utilization of the national label.

Within Peronism, references to the party name have been maintained in most cases, even though they have varied substantially. Changes after 2003 (the starting point of the Kirchner era) reflect the emergence of the Frente para la Victoria label. This linkage of the provincial lists to the national label was principally the consequence of two major goals of the provincial level Peronist leaders. First, they wished to identify themselves with the successful brand name of the national government and its popular policies. Second, they desired to signal that they, and not another list, represented the "true" party faction supported by the Kirchners. It is noteworthy that, for several years, the number of Peronist lists in the sample is greater than 24. This situation, the product of severe factionalism, occurred where the Peronists in a province chose to resolve their internal dispute in the general elections, rather than via primaries or other internal party selection mechanisms. Paradoxically, in an environment that the literature recognized as teeming with territorially based power structures, territorial references do not abound on the Peronist side of the spectrum. This suggests that these provincial cues are not needed, as Peronist governors (during this period three-fourths of the provinces were governed by Peronists) have a well-developed presence with near-universal name recognition in their provinces.

Within Radicalism, the variance in the labels utilized is much greater than among Peronists, while the explicit use of the party name is much less common across the board. In the UCR one witnesses Radical governors in office utilizing distinct names to detach provincial level electoral competition as much as possible from national trends with UCR provincial leaders (in provinces where the party did not control the governorship) also making a concerted effort in many instances to distance themselves from their discredited national organization. In the case of the successful Radical governors, there existed a tendency to utilize a name for their list that was completely devoid of any reference to political parties (Frente Cívico y Social in Catamarca, Concertación para el Desarrollo in Rio Negro, Frente de Todos in Corrientes, and Frente Cívico por Santiago in Santiago del Estero). In several cases, as noted in the previous section, Peronists and Radicals allied at the provincial level. Unsurprisingly, these alliances occurred in districts where other parties have traditionally held the governorship like Neuquén (i.e., the Movimiento Popular Neuquino [MPN]) and Corrientes (i.e., the original members of the Pacto Autonomista Liberal [PAL] and its descendents). In these cases, the alliance labels were generic and inclusive ("Frente de Todos") or used the (popular) leitmotiv created by the Kirchners, Frente para la Victoria.

For any frequent observer of Argentine politics, these above-mentioned tendencies are far from new. With more or less salience, these changing party labels are one of the dimensions of the stated process of denationalization. In contrast to the Argentine case, in one of the arguably most decentralized political systems in the world, Brazil, parties have broad labels that do not restrict their *raison d'être* to their states, even though their action in office may have had clear territorial orientations (Ames 2002).[11] Moreover, not even the Southern Democrats in the United States used the adjective to differentiate from their liberal colleagues, nor did they create local labels to send signals to their electorates. In the Argentine case, the process of the territorialization of politics had a correlate in multiple dimensions. Party strategies, alliances and even labels have been notably influenced by this phenomenon.

FROM THE OATH TO THE SEAT: PARTY DELEGATION FORMATION

After provincial-level political parties have made the decision to either run alone or with allies, selected their alliance partners, negotiated the positions of the candidates on the closed party lists, campaigned and won seats, they have one last decision to make: which legislative delegation to have their deputies join. We already discussed how volatile the patterns of coalition and list building are across districts in Argentina. A natural question that emerges from this prior analysis is how this inchoate set of alliances affects legislative behavior. If we extended the argument developed above and followed a purely rational approach, we might be tempted to conclude that every party delegation from each district should have a separate legislative bloc, and then negotiate votes for local goods, following dynamics similar to the "giant logroll" depicted by Shepsle and Weingast (1987). However, the internal rules of the Argentine Chamber are majoritarian, and local powerful actors tend to delegate power to the leadership of the majority party, which functions as a legislative cartel (Jones and Hwang 2005; Calvo 2007; Danesi 2010). Thus, repeating the rationalist exercise, almost every single actor would have interests in joining the majority coalition. Far from discussing what kind of winning coalition tends to prevail in this body, it is clear that individuals also have party backgrounds, identities and ambition, and leaders with varying goals. Depending on these and many other factors, representatives will decide what legislative delegation they will join. Recall however from the prior discussion, that in most instances the individual legislator responds to a governor or other party leader, and thus the delegation they join is most commonly determined by their "boss," not by the individual deputy.

For this study, we analyzed the size of party delegations by electoral list in four different Congresses (2004–2005, 2006–2007, 2008–2009, 2010–2011), and compared them with delegation composition at the beginning of their mandates. Due to space limitations, only the tables for the 2004–2005 (Table 2.5) and 2010–2011 (Table 2.6) legislative periods are provided here, reflecting the first and last full sessions of the presidential mandates of Néstor Kirchner and Cristina Fernández de Kirchner. Clearly, compression does exist, and deputies tend to join already existing blocs. Looking at the first period (2004–2005), if we restricted our observation to the electoral lists, we would conclude that no party held more than a third of the seats. However, the right column confirms that the Peronist bloc comprised an absolute majority of the seats during the 2004–2005 period. Comparing both columns in detail, it is noteworthy that few of the names on the left are actually kept on the right side. Specifically, only the PJ, UCR, Afirmación para una República Igualitaria (ARI) and PS maintained the seats won under their own labels. Most other deputies joined these established groups, created new ones (e.g., the Frente del Movimiento Popular [FMP] or Encuentro [ENC]), or opted to form single-member blocs. In a similar vein, several deputies needed to be relocated regardless of their preferences. Fourteen deputies had been elected in 2001 by the Alianza para la Producción, el Trabajo, y la Educación (UCR and the Center-Left Frente País Solidario [FREPASO]) witnessed their coalition disintegrate following the election, and thus were forced to seek a new legislative home.

The pattern in subsequent legislative sessions in terms of the levels of compression and predominance of the two major national parties does not differ exceptionally from the 2004–2005 period. However, over the past few sessions we have witnessed a marked increase in the number of medium-sized (i.e., approximately 10 deputies) congressional delegations. Some of them have reflected fragmentation of the party system at the electorate level (e.g., Propuesta Republicana [PRO], Coalición Cívica [CC], PS), while others reflect splits in the governing party (e.g., Peronismo Federal [PF]), or splits in the opposition in favor of the governing party (e.g., Concertación).

Finally, we present systematic information on the electoral origins and legislative destination for the 2010–2011 Chamber, examining the correspondence between the list upon which the deputies were elected (in 2007 and 2009) and the delegation to which they belonged as of March 1 in 2010 when the first ordinary session of the 2010–2011 session began. Table 2.7 illustrates the extreme variance both in terms of the name of the list on which the deputies were elected and the delegations which they ended up joining. We highlight in bold the most salient cases. For instance, the non-Peronist opposition Acuerdo Cívico y Social alliance saw its deputies dispersed primarily among its three principal constitutive parties, the UCR, the Partido Generación para un Encuentro Nacional (GEN) and the CC (and in a few districts the PS).[12] The governing FPV experienced the largest number of defections, a reality partially explained by the obvious fact that it had the

Table 2.5 Party List and Delegation Joined, 2004–2005 Chamber Session

LIST FROM WHICH ELECTED	N	LEGISLATIVE DELEGATION JOINED	N
JUSTICIALISTA	84	JUSTICIALISTA	128
UNION CIVICA RADICAL	15	UNION CIVICA RADICAL	44
ALIANZA PARA EL TRABAJO, LA JUSTICIA Y LA EDUCACION	14	A.R.I	11
ALIANZA FRENTE DE TODOS	6	FRENTE DEL MOVIMIENTO POPULAR	7
ALIANZA FRENTE COMPROMISO PARA EL CAMBIO	5	PARTIDO SOCIALISTA	6
ALIANZA FRENTE POPULAR BONAERENSE	5	CONVERGENCIA	4
A.R.I	4	ENCUENTRO	4
ALIANZA FRENTE CIVICO Y SOCIAL	4	FRENTE POPULAR BONAERENSE	4
ALIANZA FRENTE DE LA UNIDAD	4	MOVIMIENTO POPULAR NEUQUINO	4
ALIANZA FRENTE JUSTICIALISTA POR SANTA FE	4	AUTODETERMINACION Y LIBERTAD	3
ALIANZA FRENTE POLO SOCIAL	4	FREPASO	3
ALIANZA UNION POR CORDOBA	4	FUERZA REPUBLICANA	3
ALTERNATIVA PARA UNA REPUBLICA DE IGUALES	4	PARTIDO NUEVO CONTRA LA CORRUPCION	3
AUTODETERMINACION Y LIBERTAD	4	UNIDAD FEDERALISTA	3
MOVIMIENTO POPULAR NEUQUINO	4	BUENOS AIRES	2
ALIANZA ACCION FEDERALISTA POR BUENOS AIRES	3	COMPROMISO PARA EL CAMBIO	2
ALIANZA FRENTE JUSTICIALISTA TODOS PARA EL CAMBIO	3	FRENTE CIVICO SOCIAL	2
ALIANZA FRENTE NUEVO	3	RENOVADOR DE SALTA	2
ALIANZA FRENTE PARA LA VICTORIA	3	SINGLE-MEMBER DELEGATIONS	22
ALIANZA SANTAFESINA	3		
FUERZA REPUBLICANA	3		
SOCIALISTA	3		
AFIRMACION PARA UNA REPUBLICA IGUALITARIA	2		

(*Continued*)

Table 2.5 (Continued)

LIST FROM WHICH ELECTED	N	LEGISLATIVE DELEGATION JOINED	N
ALIANZA ALTERNATIVA PARA UNA REPUBLICA DE IGUALES	2		
ALIANZA CONCERTACION PARA EL DESARROLLO	2		
ALIANZA FRENTE CIVICO JUJEÑO	2		
ALIANZA FRENTE FUNDACIONAL JUSTICIALISTA	2		
ALIANZA FRENTE JUSTICIALISTA	2		
ALIANZA FRENTE JUSTICIALISTA COMPROMISO POR MENDOZA	2		
ALIANZA FRENTE JUSTICIALISTA PARA EL CAMBIO	2		
ALIANZA FRENTE JUSTICIALISTA PARA LA VICTORIA	2		
ALIANZA FRENTE MOVIMIENTO POPULAR	2		
ALIANZA FRENTE PARA EL CAMBIO	2		
ALIANZA FRENTE POR UN NUEVO PAIS	2		
ALIANZA FRENTE RENOVADOR	2		
ALIANZA FRENTE UNION POR BUENOS AIRES	2		
ALIANZA FUERZA PORTENA	2		
ALIANZA GRANDE	2		
ALIANZA UNIDOS POR SAN JUAN	2		
FRENTE FUNDACIONAL POR EL CAMBIO	2		
FRENTE PARA LA UNIDAD	2		
RENOVADOR DE SALTA	2		
UNIDAD FEDERALISTA	2		
SINGLE-MEMBER LISTS (only one person elected from the list)	29		

Source: Author's calculations

Table 2.6 Party List and Delegation Joined, 2010–2011 Chamber Session

LIST FROM WHICH ELECTED	N	LEGISLATIVE DELEGATION JOINED	N
Elected by list	N	Joining bloc	N
ALIANZA FRENTE PARA LA VICTORIA	60	FRENTE PARA LA VICTORIA - PJ	85
JUSTICIALISTA	17	UNION CIVICA RADICAL	43
ALIANZA FRENTE JUSTICIALISTA PARA LA VICTORIA	16	PERONISMO FEDERAL	29
ALIANZA ACUERDO CIVICO Y SOCIAL	15	COALICION CIVICA	19
ALIANZA UNION PRO	13	PROPUESTA REPUBLICANA	11
UNION CIVICA RADICAL	11	FRENTE CIVICO POR SANTIAGO	7
ALIANZA FRENTE COALICION CIVICA	9	PARTIDO SOCIALISTA	6
SOCIALISTA	8	PERONISTA	6
ALIANZA FRENTE CIVICO POR SANTIAGO	7	GEN	5
ALIANZA PROPUESTA REPUBLICANA	7	MOVIMIENTO PROYECTO SUR	5
ALIANZA FRENTE DE TODOS	6	NUEVO ENCUENTRO POPULAR Y SOLIDARIO	5
ALIANZA PROYECTO SUR	5	FRENTE CIVICO - CORDOBA	3
ALIANZA FRENTE CIVICO Y SOCIAL	4	MOVIMIENTO POPULAR NEUQUINO	3
ALIANZA FRENTE PROGRESISTA CIVICO Y SOCIAL	4	SI POR LA UNIDAD POPULAR	3
ALIANZA FRENTE RENOVADOR DE LA CONCORDIA	4	CORRIENTE DE PENSAMIENTO FEDERAL	2
ALIANZA SANTA FE FEDERAL	4	CORDOBA FEDERAL	2
ALIANZA UNION	4	DE LA CONCERTACION	2
AFIRMACION PARA UNA REPUBLICA IGUALITARIA	3	LIBRES DEL SUR	2

(*Continued*)

Table 2.6 (Continued)

LIST FROM WHICH ELECTED	N	LEGISLATIVE DELEGATION JOINED	N
Elected by list	N	Joining bloc	N
ALIANZA COALICION CIVICA	3	PARTIDO JUSTICIALISTA LA PAMPA	2
ALIANZA FRENTE CIVICO	3	SINGLE MEMBER BLOCS	16
ALIANZA FRENTE CIVICO FEDERAL UCR	3		
ALIANZA FRENTE DEL PUEBLO RIOJANO	3		
ALIANZA FRENTE JUSTICIALISTA ES POSIBLE	3		
MOVIMIENTO POPULAR NEUQUINO	3		
ALIANZA CONCERTACION PARA EL DESARROLLO	2		
ALIANZA FRENTE ACUERDO CIVICO Y SOCIAL	2		
ALIANZA FRENTE CAMBIEMOS PARA CRECER	2		
ALIANZA FRENTE CHACO MERECE MAS	2		
ALIANZA FRENTE JUSTICIALISTA CHACO MERECE MAS	2		
ALIANZA FRENTE JUSTICIALISTA ENTRERRIANO	2		
ALIANZA FRENTE PAMPEANO CIVICO Y SOCIAL	2		
ALIANZA FRENTE PARTIDO JUSTICIALISTA	2		
ALIANZA FRENTE POR LA INTEGRACION	2		
ALIANZA NUEVO ENCUENTRO	2		
FRENTE PARA LA VICTORIA SANTACRUCENA	2		
PARA LA CONCERTACION CIUDADANA	2		
SINGLE MEMBER LISTS	19		

Source: Author's calculations

Table 2.7 Electoral List Label and Legislative Delegation Correspondence, March 2011

Label of the Electoral List from Which Deputies Were Elected	Legislative Delegation to Which Deputies Belonged	N
ALIANZA ACUERDO CIVICO Y SOCIAL	**Coalicion Civica**	5
ALIANZA FRENTE DE TODOS	Coalicion Civica	1
ALIANZA FRENTE PROGRESISTA CIVICO SOCIAL	**Coalicion Civica**	1
ARI	Coalicion Civica	2
COALICION CIVICA	**Coalicion Civica**	8
COALICION CIVICA-PARTIDO SOCIALISTA	Coalicion Civica	1
SOCIALISTA	Coalicion Civica	1
ALIANZA CONCERTACION PARA EL DESARROLLO	Consenso Federal	1
PARTIDO JUSTICIALISTA	**Cordoba Federal**	2
ALIANZA UNION PRO	**Corriente de Pensamiento Federal**	1
UNION-PRO	Corriente de Pensamiento Federal	1
CONCERTACION	De la Concertacion	1
FRENTE PARA LA VICTORIA	**De la Concertacion**	1
ALIANZA FRENTE PARTIDO DEMOCRATA - PRO	Democrata de Mendoza	1
ALIANZA FRENTE PROGRESISTA CIVICO SOCIAL	**Democrata Progresista**	1
DIALOGO POR BUENOS AIRES	Dialogo por Buenos Aires	1
ALIANZA FRENTE CIVICO	Frente Civico - Cordoba	3
ALIANZA FRENTE CIVICO POR SANTIAGO	Frente Civico por Santiago	3

(Continued)

Table 2.7 (*Continued*)

Label of the Electoral List from Which Deputies Were Elected	Legislative Delegation to Which Deputies Belonged	N
FRENTE CIVICO POR SANTIAGO	Frente Cívico por Santiago	4
ALIANZA FRENTE CIVICO Y SOCIAL	Frente Cívico y Social de Catamarca	1
ALIANZA FRENTE DE TODOS	Frente de Todos	1
FRENTE PARA LA VICTORIA	**Frente para la Victoria - Partido Bloquista**	**1**
ALIANZA FRENTE CHACO MERECE MAS	Frente para la Victoria - PJ	2
ALIANZA FRENTE JUSTICIALISTA ENTRERRIANO	**Frente para la Victoria - PJ**	**1**
ALIANZA FRENTE JUSTICIALISTA PARA LA VICTORIA	Frente para la Victoria - PJ	12
ALIANZA FRENTE PARA LA VICTORIA	Frente para la Victoria - PJ	10
ALIANZA FRENTE POR LA INTEGRACION	Frente para la Victoria - PJ	1
FRENTE CORRENTINO PARA EL CAMBIO	Frente para la Victoria - PJ	1
FRENTE DEL PUEBLO RIOJANO	Frente para la Victoria - PJ	2
FRENTE JUSTICIALISTA CHACO MERECE MAS	Frente para la Victoria - PJ	2
FRENTE JUSTICIALISTA PARA LA VICTORIA	Frente para la Victoria - PJ	2
FRENTE PARA LA VICTORIA	**Frente para la Victoria - PJ**	**38**
FRENTE PARA LA VICTORIA - PARTIDO JUSTICIALISTA	Frente para la Victoria - PJ	1
FRENTE PARA LA VICTORIA-PJ	Frente para la Victoria - PJ	2
FRENTE PARA LA VICTORIA-PRS	**Frente para la Victoria - PJ**	**1**
FRENTE RENOVADOR DE LA CONCORDIA	Frente para la Victoria - PJ	4
PARTIDO JUSTICIALISTA	**Frente para la Victoria - PJ**	**5**
PARTIDO UNIDAD FEDERALISTA	Frente para la Victoria - PJ	1
ALIANZA FRENTE FEDERAL	Frente Peronista Federal	1
ALIANZA ACUERDO CIVICO Y SOCIAL	GEN	2

COALICION CIVICA	GEN	2
SOCIALISTA	GEN	1
ALIANZA FRENTE DE TODOS	Liberal de Corrientes	1
FRENTE GRANDE	Libres del Sur	1
FRENTE PARA LA VICTORIA	**Libres del Sur**	1
MOVIMIENTO POPULAR NEUQUINO	Movimiento Popular Neuquino	3
ALIANZA PROYECTO SUR	Movimiento Proyecto Sur	5
ALIANZA ENCUENTRO POPULAR PARA LA VICTORIA	Nuevo Encuentro Popular y Solidario	1
ALIANZA NUEVO ENCUENTRO	**Nuevo Encuentro Popular y Solidario**	1
FRENTE PARA LA VICTORIA	Nuevo Encuentro Popular y Solidario	2
FRENTE PARA LA VICTORIA	**Partido de la Concertacion - FORJA**	1
PARTIDO FEDERAL FUEGINO	Partido Federal Fueguino	1
PARTIDO JUSTICIALISTA	**Partido Justicialista La Pampa**	2
ALIANZA FRENTE PROGRESISTA CIVICO SOCIAL	Partido Socialista	1
COALICION CIVICA	**Partido Socialista**	1
COALICION CIVICA-PARTIDO SOCIALISTA	Partido Socialista	1
PARTIDO SOCIALISTA	Partido Socialista	1
SOCIALISTA	Partido Socialista	2
ACCION POR LA REPUBLICA	Peronismo Federal	1
ALIANZA FRENTE CIVICO FEDERAL - UNION CIVICA RADICAL	**Peronismo Federal**	1
ALIANZA FRENTE JUSTICIALISTA ENTRERRIANO	Peronismo Federal	1

(Continued)

Table 2.7 (Continued)

Label of the Electoral List from Which Deputies Were Elected	Legislative Delegation to Which Deputies Belonged	N
ALIANZA FRENTE JUSTICIALISTA ES POSIBLE	Peronismo Federal	3
ALIANZA FRENTE UNION POR SAN JUAN	Peronismo Federal	1
ALIANZA SANTA FE FEDERAL	Peronismo Federal	4
ALIANZA UNION PRO	**Peronismo Federal**	**9**
FRENTE JUSTICIALISTA PARA LA VICTORIA	Peronismo Federal	1
FRENTE PARA LA VICTORIA	Peronismo Federal	3
FRENTE PARTIDO JUSTICIALISTA	Peronismo Federal	2
FRENTE UNION PRO DIGNIDAD	Peronismo Federal	1
PARTIDO JUSTICIALISTA	**Peronismo Federal**	**2**
FRENTE PRIMERO JUJUY	Peronismo Jujeño	1
ALIANZA FRENTE POR LA INTEGRACION	Peronista	1
FRENTE PARA LA VICTORIA	**Peronista**	**2**
FRENTE PARA LA VICTORIA-PJ	Peronista	1
PARTIDO JUSTICIALISTA	**Peronista**	**1**
UNION-PRO	Peronista	1
ALIANZA PRO - PROPUESTA REPUBLICANA	Propuesta Republicana	5
ALIANZA PROPUESTA REPUBLICANA	Propuesta Republicana	1
FRENTE PARA LA VICTORIA-PRS	**Renovador de Salta**	**1**
ALIANZA UNION PRO	**Propuesta Republicana**	**3**
UNION-PRO	Propuesta Republicana	2
ARI	Proyecto Progresista	1

FRENTE PARA LA VICTORIA-PRS	Renovador de Salta	1
ALIANZA SALTA SOMOS TODOS	Salta Somos Todos	1
ALIANZA NUEVO ENCUENTRO	**SI por la Unidad Popular**	1
COALICION CIVICA	**SI por la Unidad Popular**	1
SOCIALISTA	SI por la Unidad Popular	1
ALIANZA ACUERDO CIVICO Y SOCIAL	**Union Civica Radical**	9
ALIANZA CONCERTACION PARA EL DESARROLLO	Union Civica Radical	1
ALIANZA CONCERTACION PARA UNA SOCIEDAD JUSTA	Union Civica Radical	1
ALIANZA ENCUENTRO POR CORRIENTES - ACUERDO CIVICO Y SOCIAL	Union Civica Radical	1
ALIANZA FRENTE CIVICO FEDERAL - UNION CIVICA RADICAL	**Union Civica Radical**	2
ALIANZA FRENTE CIVICO Y SOCIAL	Union Civica Radical	3
ALIANZA FRENTE DE TODOS	Union Civica Radical	3
ALIANZA FRENTE PAMPEANO CIVICO Y SOCIAL	Union Civica Radical	2
ALIANZA FRENTE PROGRESISTA CIVICO SOCIAL	**Union Civica Radical**	1
CONCERTACION PARA UNA NACION AVANZADA	Union Civica Radical	1
FRENTE ACUERDO CIVICO Y SOCIAL	Union Civica Radical	1
FRENTE CAMBIEMOS PARA CRECER	Union Civica Radical	2
FRENTE JUJENO	Union Civica Radical	1
FRENTE PARA LA VICTORIA	**Union Civica Radical**	3
FRENTE PARA LOS CORRENTINOS-PA	Union Civica Radical	1
UNION CIVICA RADICAL	Union Civica Radical	10
ALIANZA PROPUESTA REPUBLICANA	Valores para mi Pais	1

Source: Author's calculations

most deputies to begin with.[13] While a large majority of the delegations members remained in the FPV bloc, more than a dozen (14 total) sought other destinations and contributed to the FPV delegation's movement from majority to plurality status in the Chamber. Finally, deputies elected under the ostensibly anti-Kirchner Justicialista label made some interesting decisions. Many of them joined the governing FPV bloc, others joined the PF, and two pairs decided to create province-based delegations (Córdoba Federal, Partido Justicialista La Pampa), highlighting their territorial origin. This description does not exhaust the plethora of cases where individuals of a list joined distinct legislative delegations. However, it helps to demonstrate that denationalization, province-level dynamics and party system change are now ingrained facets of the Argentine political party system.

CONCLUSION

In this chapter we have provided ample evidence of the extreme level of party system denationalization that has taken place in Argentina over the past 20 years. In doing so we underscore the tenuous linkage between congressional elections and the postelection actions of deputies in the Chamber and the resulting impact of this reality on the quality and nature of democratic representation in Argentina. In particular, we highlighted the virtual inability of Argentine voters to hold transient electoral alliances with widely varying names and partisan composition accountable as both reinvent themselves annually while their deputies join delegations in Congress that often bear little resemblance in name or programmatic goals to the electoral alliances supported by voters at the ballot box in congressional elections.

During the tenure of Presidents Néstor Kirchner and Cristina Fernández de Kirchner, Argentina's democratic system has become increasingly unrepresentative. Voters select candidates from closed lists, which vary in name and alliance composition across provinces during a given election year and over time within the same province. Furthermore, the linkage between the labels under which deputies are elected and the delegations which they join upon their arrival in Congress are tenuous at best, and, lastly, often subject to frequent change during a deputy's brief tenure (one four-year term on average) in the Chamber. These factors combined severely compromise the ability of Argentine citizens to hold the individual deputies in particular, and the legislative branch more generally, accountable for their actions, and weaken the ability of the legislature to effectively check the powerful Argentine executive branch.

NOTES

1. Authors have identified this process as the "attribution of bias" (Duch and Stevenson 2008).

2. For recent work on factors related to bill passage, roll-call vote behavior, and the use of vetoes and decrees by the president in Argentina, see Calvo (2013), Jones, Hwang and Micozzi (2009), and Palanza and Sin (2014) respectively.

3. A prime example is that of Vice President Julio Cobos (2007–2011) who, as the UCR governor (2003–2007) of the province of Mendoza (the most populous province governed by a member of the UCR), was chosen by the Kirchners to be Cristina Fernández de Kirchner's running mate in 2007. While Cobos (along along with the other four UCR governors; from Catamarca [Eduardo Brizuela de Moral], Corrientes [Arturo Colombi], Río Negro [Miguel Saiz] and Santiago del Estero [Gerardo Zamora] respectively) backed the Kirchners in 2007, the national-level UCR supported its own presidential–vice presidential ticket, comprised of Roberto Lavagna (who served as President Néstor Kirchner's Minister of Economy for the first two and a half years of his presidency) and Gerardo Morales (at the time of his nomination, the national president of the UCR), as well as competed against the FPV in congressional, provincial and municipal electoral contests.

4. In this context low personalization limits the degree of autonomy enjoyed by each legislator when making legislative and political decisions. This is a product of party-based electoral rules and the powerful impact of provincial leaders on the political careers of most legislators.

5. Political careers are considered multilevel when politicians tend to look for multiple positions across different levels of government (i.e., the municipal, state and federal tiers).

6. The Argentine Chamber has historically had the lowest rate of immediate reelection of any national legislative body in Latin America with the exception of those that expressly prohibit immediate legislator reelection. While the staggered move from the indirect to direct election of senators in Argentina impedes an overtime comparison of reelection rates for the Senate, such a comparison is possible for the Chamber. Under the Kirchners (2003–2009) the average rate of immediate reelection in the Chamber was 17%, very similar to that under former presidents Carlos Menem (1989–1999) (18%) and Raúl Alfonsín (1983–1989) (20%). For the years in which senators who were elected for full six year terms were up for reelection (2007 and 2009), the average reelection rate was an identical 17%.

7. In 2007 and 2011, only eight and seven of the 24 districts held their gubernatorial elections concurrently with the presidential contest.

8. Clearly, variation in rules (electoral and legislative) affects expected behavior. Systems that make parties the owners of the legislative seats are likely to have lower levels of party switching than those where the seat belongs to the individual legislator, while rules that inhibit the creation of new parties will reduce the probability of legislative delegations splintering.

9. By majoritiarian, we mean that a simple majority vote determines the appointment of the president of the Chamber (i.e., the speaker) and the chairs of the congressional committees. Furthermore, it is customary in Argentina that the plurality party chairs, as well, receives the most members on the Chamber's most powerful committees.

10. References to Peronism and the Partido Justicialista are traditional, while references to the Frente para la Victoria (FPV) reflect the more "modern" label adopted during the Kirchner era.

11. It can be reasonably argued that the rate of legislative party switching, new party creation and existence of "parties for rent" make party references sterile in Brazil. Far from denying this, we argue that the explicit territorial concentration of political actors is a powerful signal by itself, and it reflects a direction in patterns of organization and competition. In concrete terms, the

reference, albeit vague and ambiguous, to an ideological or social principle (workers, liberalism, democracy or even the environment) provides different cues compared to hypothetical parties like "Paulistas United" or "Mineiro Heart." While the Brazilian case is representative of the former tendency, Argentina (in theory less decentralized) functions much more like the latter. A valid counterargument could lie in the fact that Brazilian politics have always been decentralized, and therefore there is no need to reflect these state-based bailiwicks in labels, while the process of territorialization of politics in Argentina is more recent, with the provincial-national party ties still retaining some residual relevance for provincial parties.

12. An extreme example of postelection dispersion of alliance partners can be seen in the anti-Peronist Frente Progresista Cívico y Social (FPCS) in the Province of Santa Fe in 2009. The FPCS was an alliance consisting of the PS, the UCR, the PDP, the CC, the PC and Pampa Sur (PSUR) (the latter a dissident Peronist splinter group). The FPCS elected four deputies in 2009, each of whom joined a distinct congressional delegation upon assuming office on December 10, 2009. One joined the UCR delegation, one the PS delegation, one the CC delegation and one formed the PDP delegation (consisting solely of himself).

13. During the Alfonsín and Menem presidencies, party-switching was relatively uncommon. Under the Kirchners, however, the Chamber witnessed a very high level of party-switching. For instance, among the 127 deputies who initially formed the class of 2005–2009, 39 (31%) switched delegations during their four-year term, with 11 defecting from the FPV to an opposition delegation, 8 from an opposition delegation to the FPV, 19 between opposition delegations, and 1 between FPV-aligned delegations.

3   Effectiveness and Representation

Effects on Federal Deputies' Career Choice and Reelection

Lucio Renno and Carlos Pereira

The discussion about career choices and legislative institutionalization is central in the debate about legislative politics. The argument is straightforward: legislators will run for reelection when they profit from being a member of Congress. In other words, if legislators are enticed by reelection, they will work to strengthen and professionalize the legislative branch and increase their own power in the policy-making power. Hence, career paths and Congress institutionalization are intertwined. In addition, this line of argument posits that more competent legislators will be rewarded with votes in elections, increasing the quality of representation in the legislative branch; that is, being responsive to voters' demands pays off.

Therefore, legislators' effectiveness, or ability to produce outcomes (independent of their cost, which refers to efficiency), should induce higher reelection rates, if voters reward effective legislators with votes in their reelection attempts. The representativeness of the legislative branch, and of legislators themselves, is in place when voters, in general, hold incumbents accountable based on criteria of effectiveness. Therefore, a political system that functions optimally would see a virtuous cycle in which the most effective policy-makers in the legislative branch are conducted back to office election after election based on voters' evaluations of their performance. Hence, legislators' effectiveness reinforces representation in a continuous feedback loop between these two important dimensions of the functioning of political systems. Effectiveness and representativeness go hand in hand.

In empirical terms, we should expect that representative legislatures tend to be composed by competent, effective legislators, who influence policy results, contribute to improve voters' living conditions and play a role in controlling the government. Voters are the most apt to judge performance: if such performance is evaluated based on objective criteria such as incumbents' performance, and by rewarding effective politicians, then we can say a legislature, and congressperson, is representative. On the other hand, we can also claim that a more effective and representative legislature is also one that invests in becoming always more professionalized and institutionalized.

It must be clear here that voters are the ultimate judges of effectiveness and how representative and responsive a representative and an institution are. Therefore, contrary to Manin et al. (1999), we claim that it is impossible for there to be a representative and responsive politician, institution or government that is not accountable. We concur with the above-cited authors in that a representative politician or institution is one that assures that policy outcomes reflect interests expressed through clear signals, in the form of demands from the different constituencies (Manin et al. 1999, 8). We depart from their interpretation in arguing that in democratic regimes only voters can assess representativeness. If so, then the imposition of sanctions based on outcomes, which is how Manin et al. (1999) define accountability, is the ultimate form of assessing representation.

Moreover, if the evaluation of outcomes is based on criteria of effectiveness (Manin et al. 1999, 8), then representativeness and effectiveness are linked through mechanisms of accountability engendered by elections. Effectiveness, representativeness and accountability are inherently intertwined. If voters employ effectiveness criteria to judge federal deputies, then we can say that incumbents are representative and responsive.[1] When the general patterns of incumbent evaluation are based on such criteria, then we can say that the entire institution that incumbents belong to also moves in the direction of the virtuous cycle we referenced above.

The question, then, is how to measure representativeness. Our claim is that representativeness is assured if voters employ criteria based on effectiveness to judge politicians. Hence, the issue is how to measure effectiveness criteria. There are many different ways of measuring effectiveness of Congress (e.g., surveys, law production, etc.). We have decided to do so using the legislators' choices of career and their performance in office. In order to verify these claims, we investigate the determinants of Brazilian federal deputies' career choices—if they decide to run for reelection or not—and their electoral success in their bids for different offices—if elected or not. Different from previous studies that focus either on federal deputies' reelection determinants (Ames 1995; Samuels 2000, 2001; Pereira and Renno 2002) or on their career paths exclusively (Samuels 2003; Leoni, Pereira and Renno 2004), we argue that these phenomena cannot be analyzed separately. They are inexorably linked because career paths depend on electoral expectations, as well as on performance in office.

If we find that federal deputies simply run for reelection because it is the safest bet, instead of a consequence of their performance in office answering voters' demands, then we argue that reelection is not a sign of effectiveness in office and of strengthened representation. If federal deputies chose office and win reelection in spite of their performance, then we face a situation in which there is a rupture between effectiveness and representation. In our view, basically, this would mean that voters are not able to hold incompetent politicians accountable and that other factors such as vote buying or expensive campaigns may overshadow wrongdoing or incompetence in office. The links of representation would be fractured in this situation.

Hence, exploring the determinants of career choice and reelection is an interesting way of evaluating if criteria for holding incumbents accountable

are based on evaluations of the effectiveness of federal deputies in performing their tasks as representatives. We argue, therefore, that representative
legislators are effective in producing outcomes that are in the interest of their
constituencies. Therefore, it is voters who decide on the effectiveness (and
representativeness) of incumbents. If voters rely on criteria related to legislators' effective behavior while in office, then we provide clear evidence that
effectiveness is rewarded. If voters' choices, on the other hand, are not related
to legislators' performance in office, but to other factors such as the amount
of campaign finance or how the vote is distributed across the electoral district, then we might raise doubts if legislative effectiveness leads to reelection.

In the next section, we examine the determinants of career choice and
reelection success in Brazil. We point out factors that include federal deputies' participation in the lawmaking process, such as presenting legislative
proposals, being the rapporteur of legislative proposals and occupying important positions in the hierarchical structure of the Chamber of Deputies.
We also examine federal deputies' strategies for allocating budgetary amendments oriented to the local level, which is another form of performance in
Congress seen as central to federal deputies' engagement in policy-making.
All of these factors are associated with federal deputies' performance in office and would serve as an indicator that the most competent ones are being
reelected. Finally, we also examine if federal deputies are reelected because
they spend a lot of money during the campaign or because of their votes in
prior elections, which would indicate determinants of electoral success that
are somewhat independent of their performance in office during their current
tenure.

WHY ARE REELECTION ATTEMPTS IN BRAZIL SO PREVALENT?

Where legislative seats are valuable career goods, reelection attempts should
be high and Congress will be designed in a way that facilitates reelection
(Mayhew 1974). Career choices and reelection rates are related to the effectiveness and representativeness of the legislative branch. There should
be a reciprocal relationship between professional resources available for
legislators and reelection rates. We do not argue, however, for a one-way
causal arrow. That is, we acknowledge that experimenters or some random
processes exogenously manipulate professional resources. Levels of such resources are instead established by the legislature itself. In particular, legislators that are planning to seek reelection should support the development of
such professional resources. Enhancing legislative resources increases their
political opportunity. If competent legislators populate Congress, it will be
more influential in the policy process, increasing its effectiveness and representativeness. We argue here, therefore, that there is a strong association
between several factors, but the direction of causality is not specified. Again,
there is a clear reinforcement mechanism in place, which closely associates

reelection, career choice, institutionalized legislative branch, effectiveness and representativeness. The factors are closely related and co-vary positively.

In general, incumbents run for the office with the best combination of low electoral risk and high payoff in terms of perks of office: "The decision to run results primarily from a matching of individual ambition and the context of the opportunities available to the potential candidate" (Kazee 1994). Consistent with this literature, we also assume that if no risks were present, all politicians would pursue higher office.

In Brazil, this clearly means running for executive level offices at the federal and state levels, as well as in larger municipalities, those with greater political resources, powers and budgets, and the Senate, where politicians have longer tenure, as well as power, prestige and greater perks. All choices, however, come with a price: different levels of risk to bear. Our claim, following the literature on career choice (Rohde 1979; Squire 1988; Swift 1987; Kiewiet and Zeng 1993; Hall and Van Houweling 1995; Brady et al. 1999; Hibbings 1999; Santos 1999; Patzelt 1999; Kernell 2003; Samuels 2003; Leoni et al. 2004; Carson 2005), is that the expected probability of victory is a central determinant of political ambition. Samuels translates this debate to Brazil and argues that turnover rates in Brazil are high because the best legislators decide to run for offices outside the legislative branch, more specifically executive level offices at the state and municipal levels (2000, 2003). His claim, however, is that this occurs because the legislative branch is not effective in influencing public policy (Samuels 2000, 2003). In the United States, just the opposite occurs: reelection rates are high and legislative careers stable because the House of Representatives is a good place to work.

But the literature above places less emphasis on an alternative explanation, which must also be considered. Federal deputies run for reelection because the stakes of seeking higher office are too high. Hence, legislators may choose to run for reelection not because of any special interest in the legislative branch, but because the risk of losing the election is lower when attempting reelection. In this way, if few other factors influence career choice and reelection, such as performance in office, this may indicate a case in which reelection itself does not indicate a reward to effectiveness.

Empirically, we argue that the best form of understanding career choice is to compare the expected probabilities of victory for different offices. Modeling electoral success therefore becomes an integral part of the study of career calculi. In order to understand why candidates choose a certain office, it is necessary to know which factors increase incumbents' predictability of the outcome of elections for different offices. To estimate the predictability of the outcome, it is mandatory to model electoral success and estimate the probabilities of victory for the different offices, controlling for federal deputies' individual traits. That is, we need to estimate what would be the difference in the likelihood of victory for a federal deputy when running for different offices.

With this purpose in mind, we interweave two strands of literature that do not intersect as often as they should: the research on career choice and the research on reelection success (Mayhew 1974; Fenno 1978; Jacobsen 1983; Cain et al. 1987; Stein and Bikers 1994; Ames 1995; Bikers and Stein 1996; Katz and Sala 1996; Samuels 2001, 2002; Pereira and Renno 2003; Carson and Roberts 2005). We apply a theoretical model to explain the case of Brazil, and investigate what factors increase the likelihood of incumbents running for reelection and getting reelected.

If such factors are decided based on the federal deputy's performance in office, we face potential indicators of legislators' effectiveness playing a role in increasing representativeness, through voters rewarding competent legislators based on their performance within Congress as well as on the basis of the direct benefits they provide to their constituencies. If the decision to run for and win reelection is based mostly on expectations that winning such office is likelier, then winning reelection may represent exclusively a residual category, based much more on opportunity than on predisposition and will to hold the office in order to contribute effectively to the policy-making process. Reelection may be a sign of opportunism only, and not of competence. The implications of this to the overall functioning of the legislative branch may be deleterious, in that it may create distortions in its impact on national level policies.

ELEMENTS OF CAREER CALCULI

All discussions about incumbents' career choice are based on a very simple model that can be summarized by the following equation:

$$U_{(O)} = P_{(O)} \, B_{(O)} - C$$

The expected utility $U_{(O)}$ of running for a specific office is a function of the probability of winning office $P_{(O)}$ weighted by the benefits of the office $B_{(O)}$, discounting the costs (C) of running.[2] Our claim is that of these three groups of factors, the hardest to estimate is the probability of victory. The probability of winning office therefore becomes a key factor in career choice. Hence, to explain career choices, one must model what the determinants of reelection success are. Even in the basic explanatory model of career decisions, estimating probabilities of electoral victory is a central component.

On the other hand, we argue that the benefits and costs of running for the different offices are fixed in Brazil and quite predictable. The benefits of office refer to the perquisites attached to holding a specific electoral post. In Brazil, executive level offices offer the highest benefits. Senatorial offices have high perks, in the form of higher staff funding and longer terms. The Senate also has a decisive say in lawmaking and is composed by a smaller number of elected representatives, which may facilitate the influence of individual senators in the decision-making process.[3] Therefore, the benefits associated with these posts will always be a stimulus to run for higher offices.[4]

The costs of running are also more predictable than the probability of victory. Races for governor and senator are, on average, more expensive than races for federal deputy. Our own data indicate that campaign expenditures for higher offices are about five times greater than running for reelection. Holding all else constant, when it comes to campaign costs, incumbents would be more inclined to attempt reelection. But, for the purposes of our argument, what really matters is that incumbents have a very good idea of what each different race will cost.[5]

On the other hand, the probability of victory in the different races is much harder to forecast than the benefits and costs of running, therefore it requires modeling. It could be argued that the probability of victory in running for higher offices should be smaller than when seeking lower office. A simple reason for this is that senatorial, mayoral and gubernatorial elections are ruled by plurality and majority systems. The number of offices available is lower when running for higher office. In races for federal and state deputy, ruled by open-list proportional representation and at-large districts with high magnitude, the number of slots available is much higher. However, the relationship between number of seats available and probability of electoral success is far from perfect. Even if the correlation is strong, the difference in the probabilities of victory for the different offices is not predefined and is subject to the interference of several variables. The comparison between the probabilities of victory for the different offices can vary more widely from election to election and from district to district than any of the other components in the classic career calculi equation.

Therefore, the estimation of the probability of victory for each distinct office is fundamental to making viable career choices. Because the probability of victory is itself a function of several distinct variables, it requires modeling. *That is the main reason why the study of electoral success can contribute to analyses of career choice.* After all, studies of electoral success focus exactly on identifying the factors that influence the probability of victory for a specific office.

Furthermore, it is through the examination of the factors that influence electoral success that we can make inferences about the criteria voters employ to evaluate their representatives.

A MODEL OF ELECTORAL SUCCESS

Incumbents who decide to run for office, independent of which office, know that their performance in office will affect their future electoral success. As Mayhew has claimed, however, they do not know exactly what factors will assure their victory in the upcoming elections (1974). For this reason, they diversify their portfolio of electoral strategies, and a model of electoral success should include variables related to the various dimensions of legislators' attempts to survive politically. To test these assumptions, our model has three classes of variables: (1) electoral factors, (2) aspects related to the incumbent's power within political parties and the Chamber of Deputies, and (3) legislators' performance within the Chamber of Deputies in the lawmaking process. The last two factors are indicators of legislative effectiveness at the individual level. If they influence election results, then we move in the direction of identifying a link between effectiveness and representation. The electoral dimension, defined as the amount of campaign expenditures and votes in prior elections, are seen as determinants external to the legislator's performance within the Chamber of Deputies. Hence, the determinants of electoral success will allow us to evaluate if indicators of federal deputies' effectiveness in the performance of their tenure pay off electorally.

The electoral dimension is modeled using several variables. First, the total amount of votes in the previous election is included as an indicator of the incumbent's political capital. We hypothesize that this variable should have a positive impact on electoral success since it is expected that the larger the amount of votes obtained in the previous election the safer the incumbent will be in the next election. This variable is also a proxy for name recognition, and indicates a reason to vote in the current election that is not necessarily based on the incumbents' performance in office, but prior reputation. The incumbents' pattern of vote spatial distribution should also affect electoral success (Ames 1995). Concentration is measured by the percentage of the total votes a candidate receives on the single municipality where that candidate received most of his/her votes. This is also, to a great extent, a legacy of prior political career. We expect that concentration of votes would make legislators electorally vulnerable, especially in very competitive municipalities and electoral districts. We also included in the model a measure of electoral competition at the district level, indicated by the number of candidates per seat in the district. The more competitive the district, the harder it should be to get elected, which is a key reason for incumbent turnover, according to Samuels (2000). Campaign expenditures also affect electoral success in Brazil (Samuels 2001, 2002). Hence, this variable is a component of both the cost of running for office as well as a determinant of how successful the election bid is. Therefore it molds the probability of electoral victory. We test this hypothesis using each candidate's declared campaign expenditures. This variable also indicates the relationship with donors and candidate self-financing, which is quite common on elections for federal deputy. Hence, it is not clearly an indicator or consequence of performance in office.

A second set of variables is related to the performance of incumbents within parties and the legislative branch. First, we measure the incumbent's position inside the hierarchy of the party. This variable is a dummy with the value of 1 indicating whether the incumbent is a party leader and 0 otherwise. Party leaders are more visible actors within and outside Congress. We expect that being a party leader should pay off in elections. We also include a variable indicating if the incumbent was a member of the directing table of the Chamber of Deputies, the leadership body responsible to set the agenda of the Chamber. As these federal deputies control many resources inside the Chamber, they should also be more likely to win elections.

Finally, we control for the performance of the incumbent inside the Chamber. We include a measure of seniority, indicated by the number of terms the incumbent has prior to the current one; number of projects in which the incumbent was a rapporteur; and the number of legislative projects (*projetos de lei*) initiated by the incumbent that were approved by the floor. If these variables significantly affect career choice and reelection success, then they indicate that competent performance within the Chamber, on the policy-making process that affects issues of broad interest, are criteria in holding representatives accountable. Therefore, we could claim that effectiveness affects representation.

We also test for the impact of individual budgetary amendments in electoral success, which we consider a central element of federal deputies' performance in office. Most incumbents distribute amendments throughout their home states, which are disbursed to specific publics and localities. However, presenting the amendment does not assure appropriation. Because of the contingent nature of the Brazilian budget, which just authorizes expenditures but does not obligate the executive to comply with congressional decisions, the executive branch has the final word for the appropriation of amendments. Hence, we include in the model the mean percentage of the total value of amendments presented by the federal deputy that were appropriated by the executive branch benefiting the entire district for the four-year term. Our expectation is that having a higher percentage of the statewide amendments executed will have a positive impact on electoral success.[6] This effect will indicate a form of accountability focusing on local level issues (Pereira and Renno 2003) and oriented towards effectiveness in disbursing funds with diffuse costs and concentrated benefits, typical of distributive policies (Lowi 1964).

We emphasize here that all forms of participation in Congress are seen as legitimate forms of exercising the mandate. The use of budgetary amendments is usually relegated to a secondary position, as being a simple form of clientelism (Ames 2001). We argue here that it is, instead, a form of action oriented to solving immediate and pressing needs of local electorates. Such amendments allocate important resources to fund infrastructure, public health and education projects in localities that would not have access to these funds from other sources. Hence, the ability of congresspersons to affect the allocation of budgetary funds is an indication of the power of the Brazilian National Congress, especially in comparison to Latin American counterparts such as in the case of Argentina.

Therefore, we follow Eulau and Karps (1977), who associate the concepts of representation and responsiveness and argue that there are many forms for legislators to represent the interests of their constituencies. We focus here on policy responsiveness and allocation responsiveness as two central forms of assuring representativeness through effectiveness. Federal deputies who deliver policy proposals through legislative bills and goods through budgetary amendments are conducting their job in accordance to prescriptions of the 1988 Brazilian Constitution and neither forms of performance can be superior to each other. It is a matter now of evaluating which ones voters more highly prize.

DATA AND RESULTS

To test these hypotheses, we rely on a unique dataset of incumbents' electoral and legislative performances in the last three consecutive legislative elections in Brazil: 1998, 2002 and 2006. Our data is composed of all federal deputies, main office holders (*titulares*) and substitutes (*suplentes*) that held office in the 50th, 51st and 52nd Legislatures.[7] So, in addition to the model specified above, we add three controls to the model. First, we include a dummy variable identifying main office holders. Second, we include dummies for the years of 2002 and 2006.[8] Third, we control for incumbent's age. Age should have a negative effect in electoral success, given the extenuating demands of an election for federal deputy in Brazil, and increase the likelihood of retiring.

Incumbents choose to run for reelection because this choice of career has the highest victory rate of all career choices. Table 3.1 shows the rate of victory for each different type of career ambition in 1998, 2002 and 2006 elections and the percentage of incumbents who attempted each office in parenthesis. Regressive ambition indicates running for state deputy, static ambition indicates running for reelection to the Chamber of Deputies and progressive ambition indicates running for the Senate, state governor, vice-governor, president or vice-president. This is the simplest form of showing that incumbents who run for reelection have a much higher success rate than those who run for any other office.

Table 3.1 Federal Deputies' Career Choice and Electoral Success: 1998 and 2002

	1998 Election		2002 Election		2006 Election	
Form of Ambition	Run (%)	Success (%)	Run (%)	Success (%)	Run (%)	Success (%)
Regressive Ambition	4	55	4	43	4	32
Static Ambition	75	65	71	68	73	61
Progressive Ambition	6	25	9	27	4	31

Source: Author's calculations

It is clear that running for reelection is the preferred option for the majority of incumbents and is the safest bet, the one with the highest rate of electoral success. About two-thirds of those who attempt reelection are successful in their bid and usually 70% of all incumbents run for reelection. This is true even in the 2006 elections, in which many federal deputies were involved in mega-scandals of corruption that rocked the Brazilian political system. Reelection rates in 2006 were slightly lower than in previous years. However, as Renno (2008) and Pereira et al. (2011) have shown, this is due to the fact that the reelection rates of the federal deputies involved in scandals that attempted reelection were much lower than they were for those who did not have their names associated in scandal, therefore bringing the overall rate down.

The second safest bet is to run for state deputy, a form of regressive ambition. It is interesting to note that running for state deputy should have a higher probability of victory, given that there are always more offices available in such races and that the electoral district is identical to that of races for federal deputy. Empirically, however, this is not the case, which indicates that the relationship between number of offices and probability of victory is not linear. The other options—running for vice-president, president, vice-governor, governor and senator—are considered forms of progressive ambition. All had much lower success rates.

Looking only at the percentage of victory is identical to analyzing a naïve model, one where the personal characteristics of each individual incumbent and the effects of such variables on the probability of victory are ignored. This leads us to the second form of evaluating the likelihood of victory, by modeling electoral success.

Apparently, there is a high incidence of success in winning reelection. It is fundamental now to evaluate what factors influence winning reelection. To what extent is this electoral outcome a consequence of the effectiveness of the incumbent in office?

Table 3.2 reports the change in the probability in electoral victory for all the offices for which federal deputies ran. Therefore, we examine here what determines the electoral success of incumbents, independent of which office they are running for. The dependent variable in both models is a dummy; therefore we use maximum likelihood estimation. Since some federal deputies appear more than once in the dataset, we correct for clustering at the individual level and we estimate robust standard errors. The model includes all the factors that explain electoral success, mentioned in the previous section of this article plus a very important variable, "Ambition," indicating for which office the incumbent ran. This is the variable described in Table 3.1, indicating regressive, static and progressive ambition. We use this variable later, to simulate the differences in probabilities of victory when moving from regressive to static and to progressive ambition. The model controls for the legislature, through dummy variables, and state and individual level random variation by using distinct estimation procedures; that is why we

Table 3.2   Regression Coefficients for Federal Deputies Who Win Election for All Offices: Brazil, 50th, 51st and 52nd Legislatures

Variables	-1 Mixed Effects Logistic Regression with Random Errors for States and Federal Deputies	-2 Probit Regression with Clustering by Federal Deputy and Robust SE
Ambition/Career Choice	-1.64***	-0.93***
	(-0.28)	(-0.17)
Main Officeholder	0.53***	0.35***
	(-0.19)	(-0.11)
Campaign Expenditures	0	0
	(0)	(0)
Lagged Vote	0.00***	0.00***
	(0)	(0)
Electoral Concentration	-1.20***	-0.83***
	(-0.35)	(-0.19)
Candidates per Seat	0.02	0.01
	(-0.06)	(-0.03)
Senior	0.04	0.03
	(-0.05)	(-0.03)
Party Leader	0.27*	0.16*
	(-0.15)	(-0.09)
Member of Directing Table	0.12	0.07**
	(-0.08)	(-0.04)
Project Rapporteur	0	0
	(0)	(0)
Projects Approved	0.22	0.11
	(-0.22)	(-0.11)
Budgetary Amendments	0.95***	0.62***
	(-0.35)	(-0.2)
Age	-0.03***	-0.02***
	(-0.01)	(0)
2002	-0.39	-0.2
	(-0.25)	(-0.14)
2006	-0.72**	-0.35**
	(-0.28)	(-0.15)
Constant	4.29***	2.46***
	(-0.8)	(-0.46)
Observations	1374	1374
Number of Groups	27	852 Clusters on Federal Deputy

Standard errors in parentheses
***p < 0.01, **p < 0.05, *p < 0.1
Source: Author's calculations

include two models in Table 3.2. The results are identical in both models, which increases our confidence in the findings.

We find that some variables have the expected effect in electoral success. The variable that indicates career ambition has the expected negative effect. Since it has an ordinal scale, moving from regressive to static and to progressive ambition, our theory expects that the likelihood of victory will decrease as one attempts higher offices. In other words, running for reelection does provide a higher probability of electoral survival. Lagged vote, indicating political capital, electoral concentration, party leadership, budgetary amendments and age all have the expected effects.

Therefore, we find that two forms of performance in office, holding a position inside the party and affecting the appropriation of budgetary amendments, affect reelection success to different offices. In addition, two electoral variables have the expected effect: vote in the prior election and electoral concentration, which indicate some form of inertia in the electoral luck of incumbents, independent of their performance in office. Approving legislation or being a rapporteur are not of the criteria that define election results: There seems to be a limited form of accountability in place, one that focuses more on local-level politics and in holding positions of high visibility inside political parties.

Next we simulate the likelihood of the incumbent with identical traits in all independent variables, held at their mean, winning elections for the different offices. To do so, we use the Clarify commands in Stata 10 to estimate the first differences in the variable Ambition, indicating how a change from static to progressive ambition results in changes in the probability of winning (King et al. 2000; Tomz et al. 2003).[9]

We find that an incumbent is 36% more likely to win the election if she decides to run for reelection instead of running for higher office and 24% more likely to win reelection than winning the election for state deputy. Therefore, we claim that running for reelection has a more predictable outcome for federal deputies: they know they are more likely to win reelection than other offices. In other words, the uncertainty of victory is higher when running for offices outside the Chamber of Deputies than when running for reelection.

Finally, we must verify what are the factors that affect exclusively the change of winning reelection to the Chamber of Deputies. In Table 3.3, we include only the federal deputies who ran for reelection to the Chamber. We find that all of the variables related to the electoral traits of the incumbent, including prior vote, electoral concentration, campaign finance and competition in the electoral district, have the expected results. Holding important positions in the hierarchy of the Chamber, like being a party leader and a member of the House leadership, also increase the likelihood of being reelected. Finally, budgetary amendments also have the expected positive effect. On the other hand, performance in the legislative process has no effect.

Table 3.3   Regression Coefficients for Federal Deputies Who Win Reelection for All Offices: Brazil, 50th, 51st and 52nd Legislatures

Variables	Logit Regression with Clustering by Federal Deputy and Robust SE
Main Officeholder	0.36*
	(−0.18)
Lagged Vote	0.00***
	(0)
Electoral Concentration	−1.21***
	(−0.32)
Campaign Expenditures	0.00***
	(0)
Candidates per Seat	−0.00***
	(0)
Member of Directing Table	0.13*
	(−0.07)
Party Leader	0.31*
	(−0.17)
Senior	0.05
	(−0.06)
Project Rapporteur	0
	(0)
Budgetary Amendments	0.81**
	(−0.38)
Projects Approved	0.27
	(−0.22)
Age	−0.03***
	(−0.01)
2002	−0.17
	(−0.24)
2006	−0.54**
	(−0.23)
Constant	1.08**
	(−0.47)
Observations	1273
	798 Clusters on Federal Deputy

Standard errors in parentheses
***p < 0.01, **p < 0.05, *p < 0.1
Source: Author's calculations

CONCLUSION: IMPLICATIONS FOR LEGISLATIVE POLITICS AND PROFESSIONALIZATION

While some pundits criticize high reelection rates as evidence of a "political mafia," the maintenance of a core of specialized and experienced legislators is widely seen as essential to an effective and efficient legislature. Where legislators have experience and specialization, they can effectively oversee bureaucracy, provide a counterweight to the powerful executive branch (in presidential systems), and generally produce higher quality policy and legislation. Many systems, however, lack experienced legislatures; turnover is frequent, and a legislative term is merely a brief stop on the path to other political opportunities.

In some systems immediate reelection is prohibited by constitutional or other legal restrictions. But in most Latin American countries, reelection rates are a function of legislators' career ambitions. Where legislative seats are valuable career goods, reelection rates should be high. Consequently, if the legislature does not foster long-lasting careers where politicians can gain necessary experience and knowledge to become professionals, reelection rates should be low and the chances of the legislative branch becoming a central actor in policy formulation are bleak.

Despite the fact that deputies have improved their direct and indirect salaries,[10] the Brazilian Congress seemingly does not provide enough professional or institutional incentives for incumbents to seek reelection. In reality, it is quite the opposite. The decision-making process in the Chamber is centralized on the hands of few legislators; the executive interferes constantly in legislative business by issuing decrees (*Medidas Provisorias*) and unilaterally calling urgency time procedures on specific bills; an individual legislator can be substituted by party leaders at any time from standing and special committees, which decreases incentives for specialization and experience; legislators are not allowed to initiate legislation on specific issue areas such as budgetary and administrative policies, and so on.

Immersed in such an unwelcoming institutional environment, it is puzzling that the great majority of legislators keep running for reelection. This paper argued the reason that incumbents tend to run for reelection is that the career decision federal deputies make is mostly determined by the predictability of electoral success. In other words, federal deputies' choice of career is guided not only by the incentives of the position pursued but also by the electoral viability of that choice. The higher utility of being elected to these offices is weighed against the risks and costs one must incur.

In addition, we find that the determinants of reelection are not based, to a great extent, on the federal deputies' performance in the lawmaking process. Instead, effectiveness in getting budgetary amendments approved and in holding positions in the decision-making hierarchy of the Chamber (being a party leader and a member of the directing table) is more decisive for incumbents' electoral luck. Performance evaluation is based on certain aspects of how deputies conduct their work, mostly oriented to local forms of accountability (Pereira and Renno 2003). As we argued before, this is not a sign of limited representation, but an indication that in an unequal and poor country like Brazil, voters expect federal deputies to work on improving local living conditions through transfers of federal funds.

On the downside, performance in the electoral arena, such as prior vote and campaign finance, plays a very significant role in electoral success. In addition, the decision to run for reelection is conditioned on the risk of avoiding more likely losses in races for other offices. To a certain extent, it appears that running for reelection is a residual category, and not the most preferred option to start out with. Hence, these results indicate there are some limits to voters' ability to hold their representatives accountable.

On the other hand, the great majority of legislatures, particularly in Latin America, exert a reactive role in the policymaking process (Cox and Morgenstern 2001). In fact, despite the widespread belief in the importance of legislative influence for democratic governance, the great majority of legislatures play a minor role among contemporary liberal democracies. A clear outlier is the U.S. Congress. According to an index of legislative budget institutions proposed by Wehner (2010, 55), the U.S. Congress is the only legislature with the institutional capacity to exercise very strong influence over public finance. This index of legislative scores for the United States is about three times greater than legislatures in countries such as France, Australia, Canada and the United Kingdom, among other consolidated European democracies. This finding contradicts the received wisdom that a strong legislature is a necessary condition for effective democratic representation. A legislature that is more reactive, but which needs to be heard in order for policy to be approved, may be sufficiently effective and representative to assure democratic governance.

NOTES

1. The difference between representativeness and responsiveness is also blurred by our understanding that voters are the ultimate judges of both in democracies.
2. We replicate this equation from Samuels (2003). It is a reduced form of the equation in Leoni et al. (2004) and Kiewiet and Zeng (1993).
3. All of these offices provide higher payoffs than running for reelection in the Lower House. For a ranking of offices in Brazil, see Samuels (2003).
4. Incumbents may also run for a particular office because of partisan pressures or to increase name visibility. This would be an indirect benefit of running for office, and it is hardly measurable. In Brazil, this used to be particularly true in the case of left-wing political parties when they were in the opposition. These parties tended to appoint their better-known incumbents to executive posts even if they had minimal chances of victory.
5. Costs of running for office also refer to reputation costs of losing the election and the cost of being excluded from access to the perks of office. Only campaign finance is measurable. The other costs are subjective in nature, which renders them hard to operationalize.

6. There is a debate in Brazil about what is the electoral role of amendments in races for reelection with three main positions. Individual budgetary amendments, a surrogate for pork barrel politics, positively affects reelection bids (Ames 1995; Pereira and Renno 2003). Budgetary amendments have no effect on reelection success (Figueiredo and Limongi 2007; Mesquita 2009). Budgetary amendments have an indirect effect in elections, by only affecting campaign finance donors' propensity to support candidates (Samuels 2002). We do not test these arguments here because we are not evaluating electoral success only in races for reelection. However, our results do show that budgetary amendments are very important to assure electoral success for federal deputies who decide to run for some office.

7. We believe it is important to include all politicians who held office in the Chamber because if we included only *titulares*, we would arbitrarily exclude from the population *suplentes* who held office for long periods of time. In 1998, our sample includes 488 *titulares* and 120 *suplentes*. In 2002 there are 496 main office holders and 124 substitutes. In 2006, there were 511 deputies that became *titulares*, because some were *efetivados*, and 116 *suplentes*. We also dropped the cases of incumbents who were forced to either step down from office because of scandals or who were expelled from the Chamber, as well as incumbents who passed away.

8. In 1998, all federal deputies had the right to nomination to run for reelection, if they so wished. In the 2002 and 2006 elections, this rule no longer was in place. We control for this change by including the dummy variables for the different elections.

9. Our simulations are based on the results of model 2 on Table 3.2.

10. There has been a continuous increase in legislators' salary. In 1985, total compensation (including indirect payments for housing and travel) was approximately R$11,000. By 2003, this increased about six times to approximately R$60,000. A similar increase can be seen in staff resources—rising from R$10,000 in total salary in 1995 to $35,000 in 2003. However, the maximum number of staff per legislator has not changed, it remains 20.

4   Representation and Decision-Making in the Mexican Congress

María Amparo Casar

The appearance of a minority government for the first time in 1997, while the PRI was still ruling, and the recurrence of this phenomenon for the fifth time in a row, have caused wide concern regarding the capacity of the Mexican political system to process all sorts of policy decisions, particularly those with a potential to foster growth and make possible the delivery of public goods and services demanded by the population. This concern arises from a poor performance of the economy, from the growing perception that the political arena is more a battleground where no agreements can be reached than one that encourages democratic consensus, and from a decline in the approval of democracy and its institutions. All three suspiciously coincide with the appearance and recurrence of minority governments since 1997.

The argument runs as follows. The poor performance of the economy finds its explanation in the absence of structural reforms, including labor market, energy, telecommunications and fiscal reforms. In turn, the absence of these reforms is blamed on a minority government incapable of reaching agreements in these key areas. Much of the same happens in other policy areas that most actors—including the executive branch—find in need of legislative action like the justice or health and education systems. Performance in all these fields is undoubtedly unsatisfactory. Consequently, the population is showing mounting disaffection towards both government and the democratic regime. The conclusion is that since the advent of pluralism in Congress, the Mexican political system has fallen into a sort of stalemate that hinders progress.

These views are dominant in the political arena where most parties and the executive have unmistakably expressed that the Mexican presidential system is "worn out" or "depleted" and in need of refurbishing.

Although not dominant, on the academic side there is also an extended perception that executive-legislative relations and the political decision-making process have suffered as a result of pluralism and, in particular, as a result of the absence of a majority for the president's party. In fact, after five minority governments, the discussion about the need for political reform is being framed in terms of whether representativeness and efficiency are at odds and, if such is the case, which one of these two values should be upheld.[1]

The debate on representativeness versus effectiveness goes beyond the relation between the executive and legislative branches of government. It attempts to assess the influence of the overall constitutional arrangement adopted by nations on the performance of countries in a variety of fields and indicators such as economic growth, income distribution, labor productivity, social well-being and political and civil rights.

Political science has been unable to draw robust conclusions on how or to what degree constitutional arrangements—even within the boundaries of democratic regimes—influence the performance of countries. Nor has it been able to determine whether representativeness is at odds with effectiveness. For example, in their comparative studies, both Lijphart (1999) and Powell (2000) show that neither forms of government—parliamentarism/presidentialism—nor representation systems—plurality/proportional—can be clearly associated with a superior economic performance. The most likely conclusion is that there is no single best constitutional system and that Constitutions need to be tailored to fit the culture, traditions, needs and possibilities of each country (Dahl 2003, 96–97).

Bearing this conclusion in mind, in this chapter I present the evolution of representativeness in the Mexican Congress—in particular in its Chamber of Deputies—and review the general changes that have occurred in the policy-making process within the Mexican political system.

I then turn to the distribution of power in the Lower House and examine the evidence to support the idea that increased plurality has transformed it into an ineffective institution (when not an ungovernable body) incapable of reaching agreements and fulfilling its constitutional lawmaking. In particular, I assess whether there are grounds to endorse the thesis that the outcome of increased representativeness and of minority governments since 1997 has been that of paralysis or of "legislative failure."

Finally, I discuss the alternatives posed by different actors in the current discussion of political reform in Mexico and their probable consequences.

REPRESENTATIVENESS AND EFFICIENCY

Representativeness and efficiency are both elusive concepts, although there is more agreement as to the meaning of the former and the ways to measure it. Representativeness has to do with the free and fair access of political organizations that articulate and represent different social views and interests to the formal institutions that are popularly elected. Once this precondition is met, representativeness refers to the degree to which Congress reflects and ensures that these different views and interests in society are present and confronted in the debate by legislators with different positions and then translated into the provisions of the law.[2]

Undoubtedly the Mexican Congress has grown in terms of its degree of representativeness over the last 30 years. From 1946 until 1985 the Partido

Revolucionario Institucional (PRI) mustered over 85% of the vote in federal legislative elections and gathered 90% of seats on average in the Chamber of Deputies. The situation was even worse in the Senate, where all seats went to the president's party until 1988. In spite of the fact that elections were regularly held and at least four opposition parties were present in each electoral process, it was hardly possible to speak in any meaningful sense of a minimum degree of representativeness in the Mexican political system.

Thereafter, the representativeness of Congress began to expand until, in 1997, Mexico experienced its first minority government as a result of the opposition's gain of a legislative majority during the midterm elections.

The expansion of representativeness was the consequence of a series of reforms that gradually leveled the field for electoral competition, guaranteed fair elections and, most notably, introduced a mixed electoral system that included 60% (300) plurality and 40% (200) proportional representation

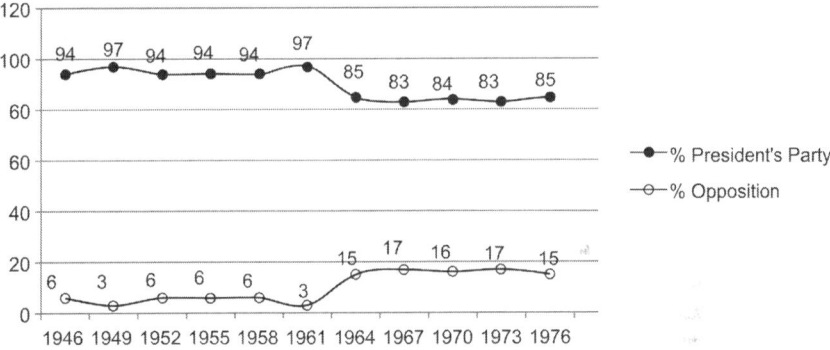

Figure 4.1 Chamber of Deputies (1946–1976) president's party versus opposition
Source: Author's calculations

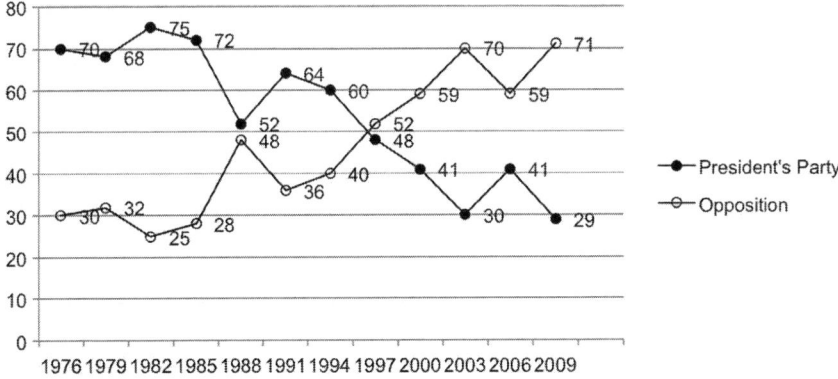

Figure 4.2 Chamber of Deputies (1976–2009) president's party versus opposition
Source: Author's calculations

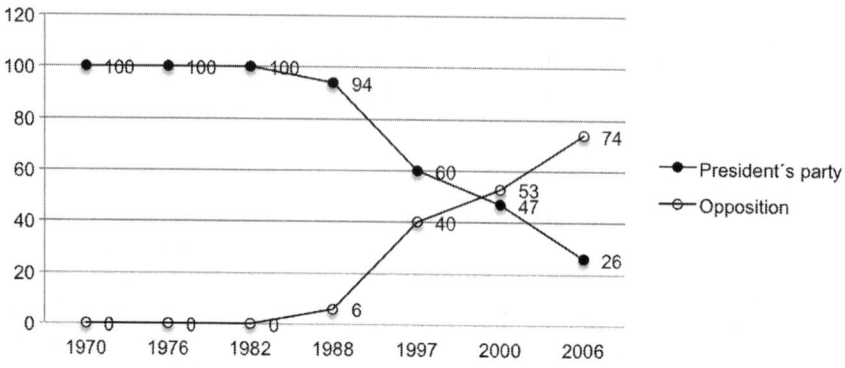

Figure 4.3   Senate 1970–2006 president's party versus opposition
Source: Author's calculations

seats. It is also important to mention that since 1992 no single party has been allowed to hold more than 60% of the seats in the Chamber of Deputies. Among other consequences, this rule precludes the possibility of amending the Constitution through the votes of a single parliamentary group because the needed majority is two-thirds (66%).

Although there is no consensus around how to measure the degree of representativeness of a system, there is ample evidence that, at least since the late 1980s, the Mexican Congress stands at a reasonable level of representativeness with an effective number of 3.2 parties and an overrepresentation limit—rate of percentage of votes against the percentage of seats—fixed at a maximum of 8 points. It is worth mentioning, however, that the representativeness of the system is flawed by the exclusion of independent or nonpartisan candidates.

In addition, and as a consequence of its plural composition, the Mexican Congress has also enhanced its internal representativeness. Parliamentary groups are represented on a proportional basis both in committees and governing bodies, and have fair rules to express themselves in debates and to participate in the decision-making process at both the committee and floor levels. In addition, there are rights established to protect the minority when calling hearings and setting up special commissions. Likewise, there is no question about the centrality and the publicity of congressional debates that are not only broadcast via the congressional television channel but are also amply reviewed in newspapers and magazines.

Finally, if we consider the origin of bills to be a measure of representativeness, it is evident that all parties are adequately represented as sponsors of the many initiatives turned to committees. The following figure shows the percentage of bills endorsed by each of the three major parties in the last four legislatures.

The concept of effectiveness is more difficult to define and pinpoint. Effectiveness may be taken to mean parliament's capacity to initiate and pass legislation coupled with the capability of congressional parties to come to agreement (see MacKinnon in this volume) or, more generally, the

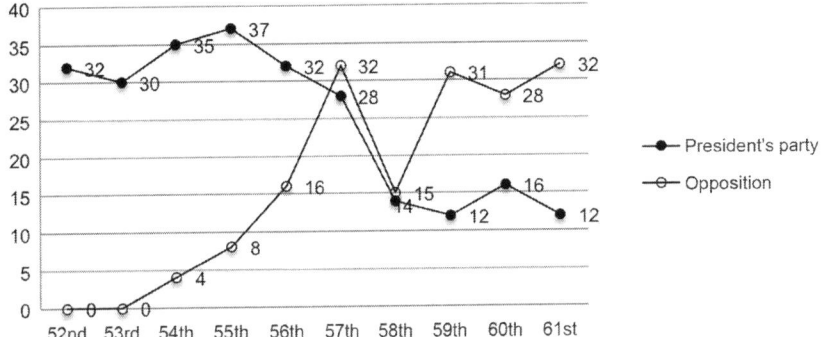

Figure 4.4 Distribution of committee chairman's Ordinary Commissions Chamber of Deputies
Source: José Abel Rivera Sánchez, "Cambio institucional y democratización: la evolución de las comisiones en la Cámara de Diputados en México," *Política y Gobierno* 11, no. 2, México: 2° semestre de 2004; and *Cámara de Diputados*

Table 4.1 Origin of Bills in the Chamber of Deputies, 1997–2009

	57th (1997–2000)	58th (2000–2003)	59th (2003–2006)	60th (2006–2009)
PRI	80	264	941	634
	–17%	–28%	–36%	–26%
PAN	168	253	540	590
	–35%	–27%	–20%	–24%
PRD	163	290	474	632
	–34%	–30%	–18%	–26%
OTHERS	66	142	679	585
	–14%	–15%	–26%	–24%
TOTAL	477	949	2634	2441

Source: Author's calculations

competence of Congress to fulfill its constitutional role regarding lawmaking and oversight (see Alemán in this volume).

Diverse measures have been suggested to assess the efficacy of Congress, from the number of bills that are processed by committees and reach the floor, to the number of bills passed together with the time required to pass them. In the end, as Saiegh (2010a, 2010b) suggests, most measures reveal something meaningful about executive-legislative relations but they are of limited value in assessing a legislature's full influence on policy making, let alone its effectiveness.

In what follows, and bearing in mind the difficulties of determining the effectiveness of congressional work, I argue, on the basis of data, that (1) the expansion of representativeness in the Mexican Congress is not at the root of the supposed lack of reforms, (2) that compromise and agreements are more the rule than the exception and (3) that paralysis and stalemate are not the inevitable fate of minority government.

This certainly does not mean that all reforms have been coming through or that effectiveness, understood as the robustness of Congress as an active policy-making body, cannot be improved. It puts the recent performance of Congress in perspective and attempts to contribute to the representativeness/effectiveness debate.

The initial claim is that the debate most often mistakes effectiveness in outcome—adequate policy decisions given certain ends—with effectiveness in process, that is, the procedure whereby decisions are reached. It is to the latter that I will refer.

In terms of the policy decision-making process, things have certainly changed since the demise of the PRI as the hegemonic (1940–1979) and then dominant party (1982–1997) in Congress.

It is clear that that the long-standing dominant position of the PRI enabled the executive and its party to centralize and concentrate policy-making power and that this was made possible by a combination of a noncompetitive structure of access to power, and the mechanism that enabled party unity and its compliance to presidential will and initiatives.

Whether a system that concentrated formal power in the hands of the president was more effective in terms of policy outcome is debatable. What is not, however, is that the decision-making process flowed swiftly within Congress and that legislators behaved mostly as rubber stamps.[3]

When as a result of a number of electoral reforms, Mexico moved from a single-party regime into a dominant party and then to a stable three-party system,[4] the decision-making process became far more complex. Parties and their parliamentary groups became real players and, as in any other democratic polity, the system began to require negotiation and compromise within Congress and between the executive and legislative powers.

As stated above, since that time there is a growing sense that necessary decisions have not been coming through, that parties are unwilling to reach a compromise, that opposition in Congress sees itself as a force that systematically blocks the presidency, that conflict reigns and, ultimately, that the Mexican institutional framework is ill equipped to deal with plurality. I will examine each of these claims.

There is little argument regarding the profound changes brought about by the end of the hegemonic and then dominant party system, and the fact that these changes were not limited to the enhancement of representativeness in Congress. Within the formal political realm, that is, disregarding the *de facto* powers,[5] the policy-making process became less centralized and concentrated and a number of political actors that had had practically no say in the heyday of the PRI became crucial. These include not only legislators but also party leaders, governors, justices and members of the autonomous organisms that were created during the last decade of the 20th century and the first years of this century (*Banco de México, Comisión Nacional de los Derechos Humanos, Instituto Federal de Acceso a la Información, Auditoría Superior de la Federación*) (Casar 2010). Given these changes, it did not come as a surprise that the lawmaking process became not only more cumbersome but also more prone to open conflict.

Setting aside the question that by design any presidential system is intended to make a change in the *status quo* difficult, undoubtedly veto players have grown in numbers and assertiveness while the institutional arrangement of the Mexican political system has not adopted rules conducive to either the creation of legislative coalitions or the solution of intractable disagreements.

To begin with, Mexico has a bicameral structure that, in addition, is symmetrical. Consequently almost any initiative—the budget being the most important exception—has to go through an identical process in two chambers that usually present a different distribution of power. This forces a two-round negotiation because party votes are disciplined and consistent within each chamber but not across both chambers. That is, members of the same party may vote as blocks but in different directions in the lower and upper chambers.

Second, the growth in the number of parties has made negotiations more difficult, and shifting coalitions rather than permanent ones are now the rule. Seldom has the president's party been able to maintain a permanent coalition with "small" parties, let alone with any one major opposition political force.

Third, by design, any constitutional reform requires two-thirds of legislators in both chambers and, at the same time, electoral provisions establish that no party may hold more than 60% of seats. Thus, the concurrence of members of more than one party is needed. It must be added that by law, half (16 in all) of the local legislatures—which are also organized around a mixed electoral system—have to confirm the passage of a constitutional reform. This introduces another veto point in the legislative process.

To all these veto players it is necessary to add the judiciary and the array of unelected bodies that, while not strictly speaking veto players, do restrain legislative powers and complicate the legislative work.

Finally, it must not be overlooked that in the new democratic context, public opinion and interest groups can play a more active role in trying to openly influence policy decisions in contrast to what used to be a closed and secretive process. The former, by making use of their voice through access to information and the free press, and the latter by moving freely to lobby different parties.

The question is whether all these changes have turned Congress into a veto machine with the overarching purpose of blocking most legislation proposed by the president, preventing the executive from advancing its agenda of policy reform or, at least, creating an inefficient institution incapable of building consensus and reaching policy decisions. In what follows, I offer some data that run counter to this general perception.

Parties have become very active bill initiators. Although the executive has never been the major bill sponsor, the number of bills presented by actors different from the executive has certainly soared since plurality came about. There has been a marked change in the number and proportion of bills initiated by parties[6] in Congress, rising from 55% in 1982–1985 to a striking 99% in the last legislature. In absolute numbers, the executive went from sponsoring 139 (45%) bills in 1982–1985 to just 37 (1%) in 2006–2009.

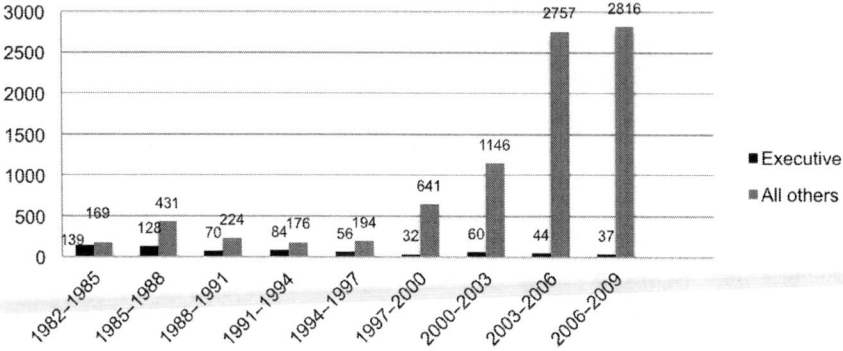

Figure 4.5   Bill initiators Chamber of Deputies (1982–2009)
Source: Casar (2008) and *Cámara de Diputados*

Table 4.2   Approval Rate Chamber of Deputies, 1988–2009

Legislature	Presented	Approved	%
54th 1988–1991	294	131	44.56%
55th 1991–1994	260	158	60.77%
56th 1994–1997	250	108	43.20%
57th 1997–2000	673	195	28.97%
58th 2000–2003	1206	281	23.30%
59th 2003–2006	2800	478	17.07%
60th 2006–2009	3059	538	17.50%

Source: Memorias de la LII Legislatura (1982–1985), Cámara de Diputados; Nacif (1995), *Cuadernos de apoyo* (1994 and 1997), *Diarios de Debates* (1997–1998), *Sumario de Actividades Legislativas* (1997, 1998 and 1999), Gaceta Parlamentaria (2000–2010)

The approval rate for all bills has equally diminished. While the approval rate was almost 45% in the 54th legislature when opposition parties secured for the first time almost half of the lower house seats, it plummeted to 17.5% in the 60th (2006–2009). Nonetheless, these numbers must be taken with caution, for the diminished rate may be explained by the inordinate growth of bills that was, over the same period, of around 800%. Taken in absolute terms, the number of initiatives that reached the floor and were approved rose from 131 to 538.

The approval of executive bills has also diminished, but it remains high. From 1940 to 1970, no executive bill was defeated on the floor.[7] In the period 1982–1988, when the PRI was still the dominant party and firmly in control of the legislative agenda, the success rate of executive bills was of 97%. Thereafter it started to decrease. During the last four legislatures—all of them with no party majority—the success rate of executive initiatives averaged 73.5%.

Thus, although the approval rate of executive initiated bills has undoubtedly gone down, the idea of a systematic opposition to executive bills does not find sound empirical basis. In fact, compared to other Latin American countries, Mexico is well above the sample average, which is 65% (Saiegh 2010). Moreover, contrary to this view, floor-voting analysis shows that most of them are passed with broad coalitions that include the three largest parties.

On average, 58.5% of all bills were approved through coalitions that included members of all parties represented in Congress. The figure for executive-sponsored bills is lower but still high. All-party coalitions for executive initiated bills was at 44%.

Table 4.3 Approval Rates of Executive Bills

PRI Hegemony	PRI Dominance	Minority Governments
Single party system	Dominant party system	Three party system
100%	97%	73.50%

Source: Author's calculations

Table 4.4 Number of Executive-Initiated Bills Chamber of Deputies, 1997–2009

Status	57th Legislature (1997–2000)	58th Legislature (2000–2003)	59th Legislature (2003–2006)	60th Legislature (2006–2009)
Introduced	32	60	44	37
Approved	25	47	23	32
Pending	6	12	19	5
Rejected	1	1	2	0
Approval Rate	78%	78%	52%	86%

Source: Casar (2008) and *Cámara de Diputados*

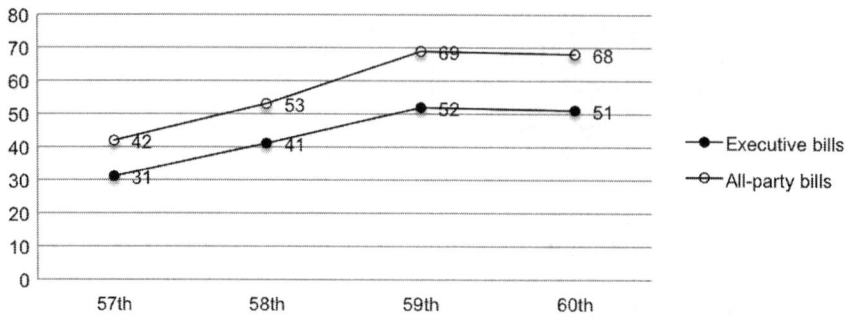

Figure 4.6   All-party coalitions (floor voting) Chamber of Deputies (1997–2009)
Source: Casar (2008) and *Cámara de Diputados*

If we exclude the emergent or small parties from floor voting coalitions (parties that account for only 10% of seats in the Chamber of Deputies), the numbers rise. Floor coalitions of the three major parties were formed, on average, 71.5% of the time for all initiatives and 55% of the time for executive bills.

In fact, the most frequent coalition in Congress for bills that reach the floor—regardless of origin—is that formed by the three largest parties.[8] Figures do not warrant the claim of a paralysis in quantitative terms neither for constitutional reforms that require two-thirds of legislators, nor for ordinary laws that require a simple majority of members present in any one session.

During the last period of PRI dominance (1982–1997) Congress passed 39 constitutional reforms involving the transformation of 175 articles. During the last five periods of minority governments (1997–2012), Congress passed 67 reforms involving the amendment of 167 constitutional articles.

These figures constitute but a rough indicator of legislative activity. Among other things, they do not account for the subject and content of bills, the amendments made to executive-sponsored initiatives in committees or for the executive postponing or withholding altogether controversial legislation out of fear of failure.[9] Nonetheless, they also serve to question the idea of a paralyzed Congress. Over the now 14-year period of minority governments in Mexico, important pieces of constitutional reform and legislation have been passed, among them the energy, pensions, electoral, banking, human rights, public access information and security and justice reforms. Others, it is true, have not been able to gather the needed majority to be passed and are still waiting for approval, most notably the fiscal, labor, education, telecommunications, anti-trust and political reforms.

In spite of the fact that the available evidence does not seem to side with the thesis of paralysis or deadlock, there is still a sense that pluralism has performed far worse than it could have and that there has been a lack of action or at least a poor performance in many of the fields that all parties agree are in need of reform, and that since the advent of minority government there is more political conflict than political action.

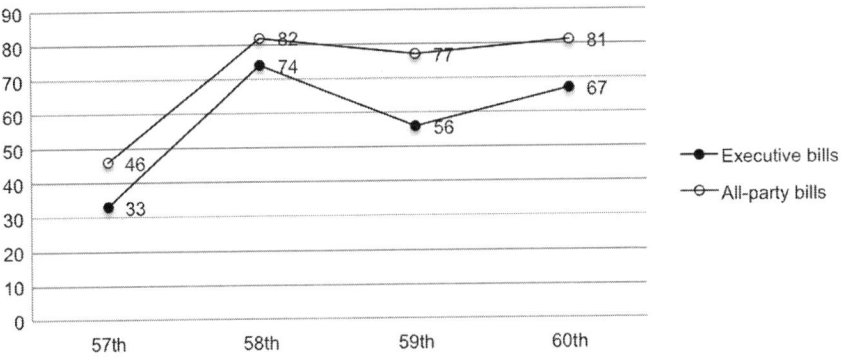

Figure 4.7 Three major parties' coalitions (floor voting) executive versus all others Chamber of Deputies (1997–2009)
Source: Casar (2008) and Cámara de Diputados

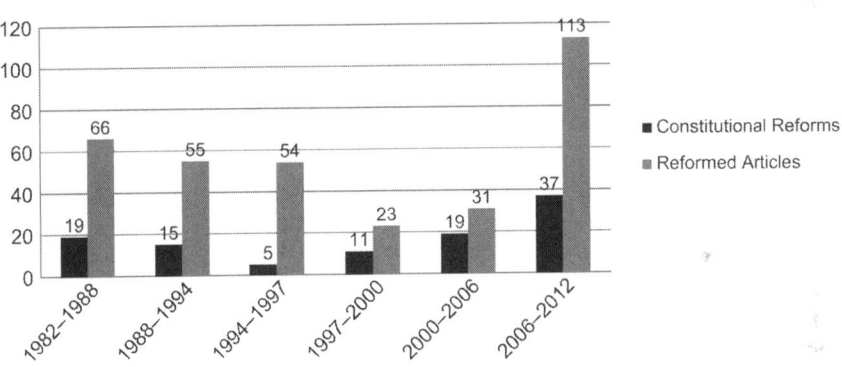

Figure 4.8 Constitutional bills 1982–1997 versus minority governments.
Source: Casar and Marván, forthcoming

These perceptions can be explained by the poor performance of the economy and the deterioration of public safety. Opposition parties in Congress and the president blame each other for these problems. Congress alleges a lack of executive efficiency, while the president accuses Congress of electorally motivated obstruction. In fact, the constant public clash between powers—usually magnified by the media—enhances the idea of a fruitless confrontation between the president and opposition parties. Finally, it is also true that unparliamentary behavior, such as the closing of congressional sessions when a minority is defeated on the floor, or the "time wasted on rowdiness and disorder and theatrics replacing debate," have contributed greatly to the image of Congress as a dysfunctional institution.[10]

At any rate, the question remains as to what extent the pending reforms have not been approved as a consequence of minority government, or whether the particular arrangement of the Mexican presidential system is responsible for what is termed an inefficient decision-making process.

THE INSTITUTIONAL ARRANGEMENT ARGUMENT

Albeit with different fine points, the dominant view within political and academic elite is that Mexico has a faulty institutional arrangement and that the way out of the supposed paralysis or deficient and/or unsatisfactory decision-making process is political reform.

The widely held diagnosis is that the Mexican presidential system is poorly designed because it promotes party fragmentation at the ballot box, does not promote the formation of legislative coalitions and does not foster cooperation between the executive and legislative branches of power. In addition, it provides no mechanisms to surmount crisis situations or deadlock. Elements of these arguments can and should be questioned.

To begin with, there is no mention of the fact that the presidential system, regardless of the particular form it assumes, was designed to inhibit or at least to slow the pace of change of the *status quo*, that one of the basic tenets of presidentialism is the freedom of voters to decide in the ballot box whether or not to give a majority to one party (to form a unified or minority government) and that in presidential systems majorities cannot be decreed because they are not necessary to form a government but, instead, that most of the time they have to be negotiated on a case-by-case basis.

Surprisingly enough, it has not even been argued that if policy decisions to change the *status quo* have not been taken, it is not because of some system failure but rather because it has not been in the interest of political forces to do so as they think the current situation benefits them, and its transformation might hurt them politically or electorally.

Against those who contend that enhancement of representativeness and the lack of a majority for the president's party are to be blamed for the absence of the so-called structural reforms, it can be argued that, during the last two decades in which the PRI was still dominant and not in need of any type of coalition, neither pension, education, energy nor fiscal reforms were passed. All of them were already in the public and academic debates and were deemed essential for the performance of the economy by most parties, and yet no action was taken.

It can also be argued that when political parties agree on any one issue they will negotiate at once, creating the necessary majorities to reshape the Constitution and laws, forgetting that the system hinders the decision-making process. A good example of this is the 2007 electoral reform, which received the unanimous support of the three main political forces against the two media conglomerates.

If further evidence was needed, one could point to the fact that in the current legislature (2009–2012) the PRI holds a near majority (47.4%) by itself and a majority formed by its alliance with the Partido Verde Ecologista (PVEM). These two parties account for 51% of the seats in the Lower House. Nonetheless, they have been reluctant to pass important reforms like the fiscal, labor, education and national security laws, all of which figure in their electoral platforms or political programs.

These facts acknowledge one of two things: either political discourse is little more than demagogic and parties and presidents were never serious about those reforms for their electoral consequences or, most likely, apart from parties who are the formal players on the congressional arena, there are other players in the game that are weighty and effective enough to hamper reforms.

The Mexican political system may not be flawless, but it would be a mistake to disregard the challenge posed by de facto powers to the decision-making process. De facto powers are those interest-group organizations that are able to overpower elected authorities and impose policies—or obstruct the passage of reforms—even if their power is informal and comes from grants and privileges[11] bestowed by these same elected authorities in successive governments in their search for support or personal benefit.

THE PROPOSED ALTERNATIVES AND THEIR POLITICAL CONSEQUENCES

As argued above, in addition to the consensus regarding the system's flaws, parties in Congress agree that there is no other way out but political reform. However, they are divided as to what type of reform should be prompted.

The debate—mirrored in the academic community—is whether to alter the "access to power" side of the equation or that of the "structure of powers," that is, the equilibrium of the power system. In particular, there is a clash on whether it is wiser to reform the electoral rules in order to promote the creation of majorities at the ballot box or whether to explore the alternatives for reducing overlapping areas of competence and establishing mechanisms that may punish legislative inaction and help overcome stalemates.

Regarding representativeness, most parties and party fractions argue that the whole point of the Mexican democratic transition was precisely to end the majority rule exercised by the PRI for over 70 years through fair elections and a mixed system that included 40% of the seats elected through proportional representation in the Lower Chamber and a mixed system of majority, minority and proportional representation seats in the Senate. They thus advise either maintaining the present electoral formulas or even moving forward into a pure proportional system. There are, however, exceptions. The Lower House PRI parliamentary group, for example, has argued in favor of reducing the proportion of plurality versus proportional representation seats, of eliminating the 8% over-representation rule presently in force and/or of introducing a governability clause that would automatically grant 51% of seats to the party that gathers a 35% or 40% of electoral votes.

If we move to the balance of powers dimension, opposition parties counter any serious attempt at strengthening the powers of the executive or even reducing the overlap of powers so as to avoid or diminish potential conflict between the two branches. Moreover, both the PRI and the PRD argue for further limiting the presidency and rebalancing the equilibrium of powers in favor of Congress and of the sharing of powers now reserved to the executive. Such is the case with proposals like cabinet ratification, congressional approval of the development plan (*Plan Nacional de Desarrollo*), establishment of more autonomous organs, referenda power, congressional censure and the dismissal of ministers (Casar 2010).

In sharp contrast, the current governing party (Partido Acción Nacional) calls for formulae with the potential to reduce party fragmentation, create a single-party majority in Congress, and strengthen the executive. In the first category, they propose a reduction of the size of both chambers and altering the ratio of plurality versus proportional representation, establishing a majority run off for presidential elections, separation of executive and congressional elections in time, and raising the barrier entries for parties. In the second category they propose to strengthen the executive's legislative powers through the introduction of a relatively light urgency procedure for executive bills, the introduction of a line-item veto, and making the presidential budget the reversionary outcome if Congress does not reach a decision.

In the end, political forces in Mexico have not been able to agree on the nature of the political reform. On the one hand, there is fear and resistance to altering the electoral system because of the negative consequences it may have for both stability and legitimacy. On the other, after over seven decades of a very strong and unchecked presidency, most political actors refuse to accept the constitutional strengthening of its powers.

Mexico is not the first country to face the representativeness/effectiveness dilemma. Many countries in Latin America—especially those that after prolonged periods of authoritarian rule drafted new Constitutions—engaged in the discussion of how far and in what direction to alter each side of the equation. Following the literature on constitutional change, it must be noted that in terms of electoral rules, most constitutional changes in the last two decades in Latin America have involved a shift from plurality rule for presidential election to a majority run-off (or qualified plurality in some cases) system. This change has been coupled with the restoration or adoption of proportional rules for congressional elections. The combined effect of the electoral rules for electing legislators and presidents has supported and reinforced multipartism in the region.[12] To "overcome" this situation, presidents have been forced to form government coalitions, or to rely on legislative coalitions, in order to further their agendas.

However, these electoral system trends have been often accompanied by the strengthening of legislative powers for the executive: exclusive introduction of legislation or reserved policy areas, power to issue provisional decrees, capacity to propose binding referenda and right to demand urgency procedures.[13]

Brazil is probably the best example of a multiparty system—even of a highly fragmented system—in which decisions have come through in the last two decades and where presidents have been able to push their agendas through in spite of their minority position in successive legislatures.

As Cheibub and Limongi (2000) argue, this has been possible by a virtuous combination of strong legislative powers of the president with a legislative organization that is highly centralized, with "a tight control over the agenda by speaker and party leaders" and where institutional arrangements promote party discipline and "conspire against the capacity of members of Congress to pursue their own particularistic interests." Thus, it is possible to conclude that political reformers have avoided the representativeness versus efficiency trap and have resisted the temptation of a reversal of representativeness.[14]

So where then does Mexico fall compared to other Latin American countries in terms of its constitutional trends? Like most nations, Mexico has moved toward greater proportionality in its electoral system, and it is characterized by a reasonable degree of representativeness, with an average of seven parties participating in Congress, and three of them accounting for 90% of seats. With 3.2 effective parties it does not qualify as a system with excessive party fragmentation.[15] It must be added that parties are highly cohesive and disciplined with a Rice Index for the three major parties ranging between 92 and 99 (Casar, 2008). However, the president's party contingent in Congress since 1997 (last five legislatures) has been rather low, with an average of 38% of seats in the Lower House and 45 % in the Senate making legislative coalitions necessary.[16]

If Mexico is aligned with Latin American trends regarding representativeness, the same cannot be said about the strengthening of executive powers, which may be the missing link in executive-legislative relations in Mexico. The Mexican transition left the structure of powers of the legislative and executive powers practically untouched. If anything, the balance of power has been tipped in favor of Congress. In terms of reactive powers, the Mexican executive has package veto power but no exclusive powers to initiate legislation in any policy area except for the budget. In terms of proactive powers it is at a disadvantage vis-à-vis many of its Latin American peers, for its budgetary powers are limited, it cannot enact new legislation by decree and it cannot even declare a legislative proposal as urgent. Moreover, not even the budget bill is subject to a reversionary point.[17]

The other missing link may be the structure of Congress itself. In spite of the fact that recent organizational changes have gradually made Congress a more democratic body,[18] the legislative organization and processes are highly centralized and party-centered, with "a tight control over the agenda by speaker and party leaders," and the internal institutional arrangements (and the electoral system itself) promote party discipline.

Nonetheless, the Mexican Congress remains a body with poor capacities that lacks professionalization, a seniority system in committees, independent professional bodies, and internal mechanisms to curb antiparliamentary conduct or purposeful delaying of legislation. It is also in need of internal mechanisms that could ease the decision-making process and overcome stalemates either within each chamber or between the Lower House and the Senate.

Lack of capacities derives, at least in part, from the absence of consecutive reelection. Every three years the Lower House is integrated with 500 hundred individuals, most of whom have never had prior parliamentary experience. The same is true for the Senate.

Mexico stands as the country with the lowest parliamentary experience rate in Latin America. In the last decade only 12.7% of legislators in the Lower House had had previous experience, and only 5% in the Upper Chamber.[19]

FINAL REMARKS

In this paper I have argued that Mexico has reached a democratic stage where electoral rules guarantee free and fair competitive elections and a reasonable degree of representativeness, inasmuch as Congress reflects the different views and interests in society and ensures that they are presented and confronted in legislative debates to be translated into the provisions of laws.

I have shown that—in spite of perceptions to the contrary—legislative failure has not been the rule in the now 15 years of minority government that have prevailed in Mexico, and that interparty coalitions have been successfully formed to pass several important pieces of legislation. Finally, alternative explanations for the lack of action regarding many of the structural reforms that many deem necessary were put forward. These include the presence of

Table 4.5 Number of Legislators with Prior Legislative Experience

	58th		59th		60th		61st	
	Dep	Sen.	Dep	Sen.	Dep	Sen.	Dep	Sen.
PRI	51	3	3	2	26	7	61	2
PAN	12	0	9	0	11	5	12	0
PRD	7	1	16	1	12	2	3	0
PT	3	0	2	0	4	0	7	0
CONV	–	–	2	0	3	0	1	0
PANAL	–	–	–	–	2	1	2	0
PVEM	–	–	1	0	5	0	–	–
PSD	–	–	–	–	1	0		
IND	1	0	2	0	–	–		
TOTAL	74	4	35	3	64	15	86	2

Source: *Cámara de Diputados*

de facto powers, the lack of executive powers and the low capacities of the Mexican Congress. These arguments and findings do not mean that rules for democratic governance need not be improved in order to both enhance representativeness and achieve a more efficient decision-making process. In both these respects, Mexican democracy faces important challenges.

The degree of representativeness may not be questioned if we make reference to the number of parties and views represented in Congress, but it is certainly questionable in relation to the linkage between the membership of Congress and the citizenry. Public opinion shows an extended dissatisfaction with the workings of democracy, and particularly with the performance of parties and legislators. According to *Latinobarómetro 2010*, only 27% of Mexican citizens are satisfied with the workings of democracy, and barely half (49%) of them support the democratic regime. Furthermore, among all institutions or actors, legislators and parties are the least trusted and appreciated.

Finally, when asked whether they feel represented by their legislators, a large majority responds that they are little or not at all represented by them.

Along with the challenge of representativeness, there is also that of improving the effectiveness of the system. Although collaboration within Congress and between executive and legislative powers cannot be guaranteed, the Mexican political system could certainly benefit from some reforms in its institutional make-up.

Table 4.6   Trust in Institutions

Institution	Grade (1-10 Scale)	Confidence %
Universities	8	37.4
Church	7.8	42.1
Army	7.5	32.3
Media	7.4	22.4
Entrepreneur	7	17.2
Federal Electoral Institute	6.7	15.5
Supreme Court	6.7	14.9
President	6.5	13.7
Senators	5	5.8
Unions	5.9	6.7
Policemen	5.8	6.5
Deputies	5.8	5.3
Political Parties	5.8	5.2

Source: Consulta Mitofsky, June 2011

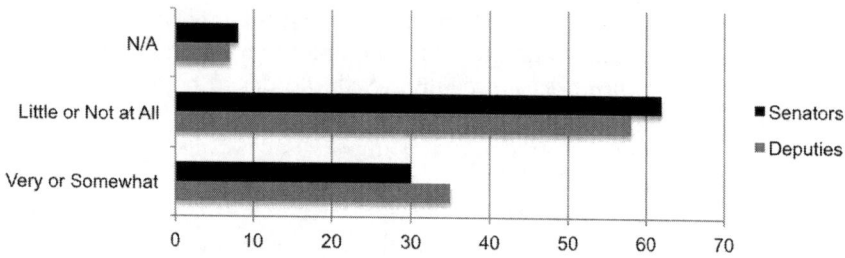

Figure 4.9   Perceptions regarding the representativeness of legislators
Source: Buendía and Laredo, "Percepciones sobre el Desempeño Legislativo," August 2010,
www.buendíaylaredo.com

Assuming that minority governments will continue to be a structural feature of Mexican politics and that most probably any president will have to
deal with rather small legislative contingents in the coming years, it would
seem reasonable to introduce reforms that have proved useful in other
countries.

In my view, what needs to be avoided is the widely held idea that a political reform should have as its main premise either the restriction of representativeness or the weakening of the presidency. Experience has shown
that, deprived of the majorities and associated partisan powers imposed by
the previous undemocratic electoral system, the Mexican president is not as
powerful as he or she was thought to be. On the other hand, it is clear that
a presidential system demands cooperation in order to push through the
presidential or any alternative political agenda, to start addressing some of
the most pressing social and economic problems of the country.

If what is needed is the creation of legislative majorities, putting incentives in place for cooperation and making the decision-making process more
efficient, a number of alternatives seem at hand.

First, the electoral system can be reformed, not to diminish representativeness, but rather to avoid the fragmentation of the party system, to promote the transformation of electoral alliances into parliamentary coalitions
and to allow for a stronger link between legislators and their constituencies.
These goals could be approached through reelection, increasing the entry
barriers of small unrepresentative parties to the political arena and by the
introduction of rules that promote electoral coalitions.

Second, it seems advisable to review those constitutional articles that far
from averting conflict between the two branches tend to encourage it, and
that could place the system in situations of crisis (e.g., ambiguity in veto powers, budget proceedings and rules for the replacement of the president should
the need arise).

Third, it would be worth exploring putting in place incentives to foster
collaborative relations between the executive and the legislature, as well as
granting proactive powers to the executive.

Fourth, the legislative process could be made less protracted by introducing scheduling rules for committee and floor discussion and voting. At the same time it would be worthwhile to increase the Congress' professional capacities through the introduction of nonpartisan advisory boards.

NOTES

1. For an academic discussion of this debate in reference to the different bills of political reform recently (2009–2010) put forward by the executive and political parties in the Mexican Congress, see Negretto 2010.
2. See MacKinnon and Feoli in the Introduction to this volume.
3. The fact that Congress was not the political arena where lawmaking was decided does not mean that the president could do as he pleased. Protracted negotiations were held outside Congress with both interest groups and political factions within what was once called the "revolutionary family."
4. "Several smaller parties survive thanks to generous public financing and open coalition rules. From 1990 to 2005, between six and eleven parties held official registration . . . ." Nonetheless, the three major parties—PRI, PAN and PRD—have systematically won 90% of the vote in federal elections and 95% of the legislative seats (Langston 2009).
5. I draw on Acemoglu and Robinson's (2006) distinction between de jure and de facto political power. The former is that which comes from political institutions. In contrast, de facto political power comes from the ability of one group or groups to overwhelm elected authorities through means and resources—force, wealth, corruption, mobilization—which allows them to choose or impose whatever policy is in their best interest at any given point.
6. The Mexican Constitution allows legislators, the executive and local legislatures to present bills in Congress.
7. De la Garza (1972). This does not mean that all executive bills were passed or went unamended. Congress did not act on several and it filed others.
8. For a detailed analysis of voting behavior and coalitions formed in the Chamber of Deputies, see María Amparo Casar, "Los Gobiernos sin Mayoría en México: 1997–2006."
9. There are several examples of the executive's strategy of not presenting controversial legislation in face of the certainty that it will be defeated. Such was the case of Salinas postponing or withholding the introduction of reforms that were to alter longstanding traditions such as state-church relations, agrarian property rights or labor legislation; of Zedillo's pension reform; of Fox's political reform and of Calderón's telecommunications reform.
10. In this respect, see the argument developed for the Indian Parliament by Kapur and Mehta (2006).
11. These include fiscal privileges that drain public finances, monopolies that hinder competition in strategic economic sectors, trade union leaders that check efforts at modernization, competitiveness, efficiency and transparency in state-owned enterprises and private industries that capture regulating bodies and administrative units.
12. As of 2003, for instance, only 6 out of 18 countries in Latin America had an effective number of parties in the single or Lower Chamber of Congress of less than 2.5. In most cases, the president's party has had a minority status in Congress (Jones 2010).
13. However, it is also true that a tendency to introduce higher limits on the president's power to appoint political offices was observed. Many Constitutions

have restricted the power of presidents not only to appoint cabinet ministers but also local or regional executive authorities and judges of the Supreme or Constitutional Court (Negretto, 2009).

14. These authors have convincingly argued that "explanations of parliamentary behavior and of policy outcomes overemphasize the importance of the separation of powers and the characteristics of electoral and party legislation" and that "they overlook the role of other institutional characteristics, especially the president's legislative powers and the internal organization of the legislative work."

15. In contrast, Brazil has a 7.8. In fact, out of the 11 countries included in Jones's study, Mexico stands as the third country with a lower NEP (see Mark Jones [2005]).

16. According to Jones (2010), the presidential party's Lower (or single) Chamber and Senate contingents in Latin America are 39% and 41% respectively.

17. For a discussion of reactive and proactive powers, see Mainwaring and Shugart (1997).

18. For example, in the past, the PRI's majority in Congress allowed that party to control the committee assignment process, resulting in the absolute control of all and each of the committees. It was not until 1988 that the PRI was forced to give up the presidency of 4 out of 39 committees, with another 8 following in 1991 and 16 more in 1994. These occurrences were followed by a resolution to divide the presidencies of committees and their composition in proportion to the seats held by each party (Casar 2002 in Morgenstern y Nacif) and later to place the two most important governing bodies of Congress—the presidency of the Directive Board and of the Junta de Coordinación Política—successively in the hands of different parties.

19. According to Saiegh (2010), Mexican legislators have the least parliamentary years of experience in Latin America: 1.9 years. The average for his sample of countries is 4.3 years.

5 Congress in Action
Representativeness and Effectiveness in Chile and Argentina (1900–1930)

Moira B. MacKinnon

This chapter presents a study of how the Argentine and Chilean Congresses operated at the turn of the 20th century. For both countries involved, the four decades of social and political modernization from about 1890 to 1930 were tumultuous and significant. They were tumultuous because the governing elites had to deal with protest from the working classes, a new social actor generated by industrialization and urbanization who aspired to political participation and social equality through the institutionalization of rights. At the same time, new political parties emerged and suffrage expanded, changing the ways in which politics had been carried out until then. This period was significant in itself, but also because in Argentina, these years led up to a coup that inaugurated a period of over 40 years of pendular movement from dictatorship to democracy, while in Chile, on the other hand, after various coup attempts and a military regime, there began a period of democratic continuity that lasted until 1973.

The study examines the passage through both Congresses of 11 pieces of social legislation from their inception in different bills to their final approval as laws, through the indicators of two variables: representativeness and effectiveness (developed below). After an analysis of the bills and laws, and the dynamics of Congress in terms of the indicators of these variables, I find that the Argentine and the Chilean Congresses were very different institutions. The former was more representative: it held within it a greater diversity of views and interests, the voices of both employers and workers were present in different perspectives, the provisions of bills and laws tended to benefit larger portions of the population, debate played a crucial role in the passage of a bill, provisions were changed and many legislators participated. Consequently, the Argentine Congress acted more like a public forum, a place of public deliberation. The Chamber of Deputies was the engine of social legislation. It was characterized by a horizontal, open logic, driven by debate and voting. At the same time, the assembly did not follow strict procedural rules, it lacked specific conflict-solving mechanisms and power was dispersed; sometimes, important matters were not resolved. It was thus also less effective. The Chilean Congress, on the other hand, was effective: laws progressed more rapidly and efficiently down the legislative path, congressional rules on procedures were more complex and adhered to more strictly, the agenda and other important matters were never decided in the plenary, and there existed a clearly defined mechanism, often resorted to, for dealing with intractable conflicts. Congress fulfilled the role of a lawmaker. The main chamber for dealing with social legislation was the Senate, which displayed a top-down, power-concentrated logic. At the same time, the process and content of the bills was mostly locked in at meetings held previously to their arrival on the chamber floors and subsequently hardly changed by debate, which, consequently, was less important. There were fewer voices, less difference between positions and fewer bills on the different issues, and the provisions of the bills favored a smaller group of people. Thus, it was also less representative.

Congress is understood as the political synthesis of a country's capacity to respond to and process conflict—in this case, complex social conflict originated in worker protest and unrest. The study follows the activity in the assemblies of deputies and senators from the various political parties as they carried out daily congressional business, debating and resolving the issues that came before them, and the different ways in which they processed the worker issue both from the point of view of the content of the debates and the procedures they followed. Thus, the study provides a window into how these two Congresses actually worked—a matter that has not received enough study, and will hopefully contribute to a better understanding of them. Also, contrary to the popularly held opinion that Congresses in Latin America have been historically weak and subservient to the executive,[1] it shows two quite strong Congresses that played an important, although different, political role.

The chapter proceeds thus: The next section develops the concepts of representativeness and effectiveness and their indicators in a congressional context. The passage through Congress of various social legislation bills in terms of the indicators of the variables follows. The last section contains the conclusions.

The first years of the 20th century, from about 1890, were a moment of inflection in many countries of South America. With the turn of the century came the "social question," a period of "social tension, worker protest and intellectual ferment which commences with industrialization itself" (Morris 1966, 78–9), a central component of which was the worker issue (Suriano 2000, 2–3). Waves of strikes and union organization swept both countries with peaks between 1902 and 1908/10 and 1917–1921, in particular in 1919 (de Shazo 1983, 103–4, 308–9; Panettieri 1967, 201, 137; Collier and Collier 1991, 92–3). While governments first reacted to strikes and unionization with repression, as the social question became a public issue instead of a police matter and was discussed in other countries of the world, part of the elites in both countries came to understand the need to respond through social legislation besides repression.

The second important process that was occurring was an expansion of democratic institutions. In Chile, during the years of the so-called Parliamentary Republic (1891–1925) two coalitions, the Liberal Alliance (centered round the Radical party) and the Conservative Coalition (grouped round the Conservative party) competed for power in Congress. The Socialist Worker party emerged in 1912 and became the Communist party in 1922. The Argentine party system started developing in the 1890s, but it was only in the second decade of the 20th century that a competitive regime comparable to the Chilean one introduced after the civil war in the 1890s, finally developed (Remmer 1984, 32). Besides the Conservatives, the Radical, Demócrata Progresista and Socialist parties emerged and began competing for and winning votes (Cantón 1966; Molinelli 1999, 256–8, 239). Suffrage expanded, in particular in Argentina, under the 1912 Roque Saenz Pena suffrage law, and led to the Radical party winning the elections for the first time in 1916. This law established the incomplete list system under which majority and minority parties in each province were represented in the Lower Chamber (the winner received two-thirds of the seats and the minority one-third), senators were elected by the provincial legislatures. In Chile, legislators were elected under a system of proportional representation. The electoral law of 1890 replaced the complete list or winner-take-all system with the cumulative vote in all elections.[2]

REPRESENTATIVENESS AND EFFECTIVENESS

In order to examine the ways in which legislators went about deliberating on the worker issues and shaping a new set of citizenship rights, the passage of the laws will be examined in terms of two variables: representativeness and effectiveness. Work on representation in assemblies tends to fall into one of the two following perspectives: while some authors examine the relationship between voters and legislators by studying the rules and procedures that make representation possible, others focus on correspondence or resemblance, the "presence" of citizens' views and interests in institutions. In turn, each perspective is interpreted and applied in different ways. Within the first group, some authors study the conditions and effects of election rules, the relationship between votes and seats, and coalitions in Congress (Lijphart 1990; Taagpera and Shugart 1989; Snyder and Samuels 2001; Jones and Micozzi, this volume) or, emphasize "sanctions" through either mandate representation (or responsiveness) or accountability representation (Pitkin 1967; Miller and Stokes 1963; Manin et al. 1999, 8, 16, 29; Stokes 1999). The second approach to representation emphasizes "correspondence" or "resemblance," also understood in different ways: for example, parliaments' capacity to reflect society, such as for J. S. Mill[3] and the Anti-Federalists.[4] Another way of understanding this kind of representational link is selective representation sometimes approved for underrepresented constituencies (such as women, or French speakers, or African Americans) (Mansbridge 1999; Phillips 1995). More recently, Mansbridge shifts attention from a "sanctions model" to a "selection model"; a crucial element of her "gyroscopic representation" is "aligned objectives" (that is, similar policy preferences or interests, and/or personal attitudes), between representative and constituent (Mansbridge 2003, 522; 2011, 623). Another group of authors study what Powell (2004) calls "substantive" representation: they examine the correspondence between citizens' support for a party and their representatives' policy positions and behavior once in the legislature. The idea of resemblance in representation also underlies the support for proportional representation (Powell 2000).

In this chapter, following the second emphasis, representativeness refers to the degree to which a country's Congress ensures that the different views and interests in society are present in the debates, confronted by the legislators who belong to political parties with different positions, and then translated into the provisions of the laws. Congress is considered representative when different legislators that express a plurality of views and interests have been elected and participate in the debate—not necessarily when members from the different social classes or groups in a country can be found in the national assembly.[5] Since the policy issue at stake here is social legislation concerning workers and employers (their rights, their organizations, working conditions, etc.), the more different legislators, from any political persuasion, social class or other cleavage, who in public debate defend a bill or clauses thereof that either protect employers or empower workers, from the different perspectives their constituents may hold, and include at least part of these different positions in the bills, the more representative the legislature.

Political representation existed long before elections became the dominant mechanism for choosing authorities, which means that other forms of informal representation had also developed (Knights 2009) and played a part together with elections. Thus, although part of the population in Chile and Argentina had been voting for many years by the first three decades of the 20th century, other forms for pressuring elected authorities existed concurrently with elections such as the petition, public rallies and street protests. Petitions from different worker associations requesting that legislators pass certain social legislation bills appear frequently in both countries' congressional records, in particular when a bill is on the agenda to be considered.[6] Street rallies were an old and very frequent way that various sectors of society participated and tried to influence political events in both countries, in particular in Argentina, from early on in the previous century (Sábato 1998; Rocchi 2000). Thus, through petitions and rallies "both the franchised and the unfranchised could find a voice" (Knights 2009, 53–4), an important fact in Argentina where, in the first years of the century most of the workers were foreigners and could not vote.

The indicators that capture representativeness are the following: (1) Diversity of views and interests expressed in the different origins of bills (presented by different political parties, different members of one political party, or by different political parties within a coalition) and in the debates. The diverse positions express the lines of fracture or disagreement regarding social legislation, individual rights and the place of the workers and the state; (2) The role of debate: the number of participants, the time spent on debate, engagement (i.e., importance given to debate regardless of results, discussion versus presentation, importance of persuasion and oratory), the existence of debate on core ideas and meanings of the bills; (3) The possibility of producing changes in the provisions of a bill through debate in the assembly; (4) The content of the bill-then-law in terms of clauses that enable or constrain workers, in principle balancing claims from workers and employers.

The second variable used here to examine congressional performance is effectiveness. Different approaches have used different measures. Following Alemán's classification (see this volume), some are based on perception (public opinion polls and elite and expert surveys), others on capabilities (career paths, committee assignments and time demands) and a third group on outcomes (the number of bills passed, the proportion initiated by Congress). In a historical study only some of these measures are available. In this chapter, effectiveness refers to Parliament's capacity to initiate and pass legislation based on two features: the degree to which it has developed differentiated offices and procedures that facilitate the operation of a complex institution (Cox 2008, 27, 4–7) and the capabilities of the congressional parties of articulating or imposing positions and interests on both individual members of parties and on parties that may not agree. The indicators that measure this dimension are: (1) how time and activities are structured; (2) the degree to which rules are adhered to; (3) locus: where the bills are initiated (by the executive or by a chamber) and especially where decisions are taken about content and process (in the assembly, in the committees, in external or private meetings), where opposing opinions are expressed; (4) how intractable disagreements are dealt with; (5) how long it takes for a bill to be approved; and (6) length of time a law is in force. Thus, effectiveness is based on how Congress functions.

These indicators inform two crucial roles that Congress plays—those of public forum and lawmaker—in its mediating capacity between society and the state. There of course other functions Congress must carry out such as oversight of the executive, and socialization and training of future political leaders (Smith 1974, 21) but they will not be examined here. In principle, Congress should be both representative and effective, since the lack of either dimension creates problems, as will be seen below.

THE PASSAGE OF THE LAWS

The analysis that follows is based on data collected through archival research of congressional records from 1900 to 1930 (and 1946 in the case of Argentina) and, of course, secondary literature.[7] For both countries it includes: the trajectory of each bill from the moment it was submitted to when it was finally passed (or not), including the other bills on the issue (i.e., not only the committee-reported bills); the daily unfolding of congressional business, discussions regarding the procedure of the bills; debates in general and in particular of the bills held on the floor of both chambers and in joint committees when applicable; the text of the approved laws; and controversies and daily debates on social issues and events (such as strikes, stoppages, political rallies, etc.) and references to the bills that do not form part of the actual debates on bills. The passage of each bill is examined in terms of the indicators of representativeness and effectiveness as it moved through each chamber.

The bills on which the information is based are the following: (1) the bills and law regulating trade unions—the most important and difficult of the social laws because it implied a redistribution of power between employers, workers and the state; (2) various bills containing workplace rights: the law of Sunday Rest in both countries, the Eight-hour Workday bill in Argentina, the blue collar labor bill in Chile, the Putting Out law in Argentina (which regulated work and salaries in the "sweating shops," as they were called); (3) the white collar labor law (which regulated working conditions for this group of workers in Chile; in Argentina the same laws applied to all workers); (4) the Deputies' bill on conciliation and arbitration in Chile; and (5) some aspects of the Laws of Residence in both.[8]

Representativeness

As regards representativeness, Argentina's Parliament reveals the presence of a more varied range of interests and perspectives on topics related to working conditions, individual rights and the role of the state (often debated in the chambers in relation to social legislation), and deeper differences generally related to party origin. It also grants a greater role to public debate and, finally, shows more inclusiveness in the positions and legal provisions that benefit workers to a higher degree. The Chilean Congress presents a narrower set of voices and a more hierarchical and exclusionary mode of functioning, the important points of the laws are discussed and decided outside the chamber in smaller groups, and the laws constrain the workers to a higher degree. Let us look at each indicator in more detail.

Diversity of Interests and Views—One way of assessing the existence of diversity of views and interests is examining the bills presented. The bills presented by members of different political parties in the Argentine Congress reveal greater differences than Chile's: there were bills from each of the major parties (and often various bills from each one) containing very different proposals regarding the issues at stake, starting from 1900. In Chile there were generally two bills, one from the Liberals and one from the Conservatives, most concentrated between 1919 and 1921–1922, and the differences tend to be less stark. Thus, in Argentina, there was multiplicity in terms of party origin and time; in Chile, concentration (see Table 5.A1 in the chapter appendix).

A second way diversity of views and interests can be assessed is by looking at whether legislators defending different political positions participate in the debate.[9] Surprisingly, the congressional debates (and bills) show that there was less difference between party positions in Chile than in Argentina (before and after 1912). In both countries, positions in the debates varied by showing more or less respect for individual rights and the legal order, and regarding views on public or social order. These topics typically came up when legislators discuss strikes and police action during demonstrations, strikes and worker protest and also (in particular in Argentina) during the debates on the state of siege and the Law of Residence bills when respect for the Constitution and the laws, and the separation of powers also came up. A second hub on which opinions differed was social legislation: how much/little trade unions and workers and their actions should be controlled or not, how much state intervention in the workplace, how much control or independence in internal union governance, and of course, more or less beneficial work conditions (more or fewer hours of work, etc.). Finally, a third difference rose only in Argentina (since Chile was centralized) between those who defended provincial (often but not always against the bill proposed) or more national (generally in favor of the new law, see Sunday Rest and Eight-hour Workday bills) positions in respect of the scope of the provisions in the bills.

The Argentine Conservatives were more concerned with issues of social order produced by the strikes and demonstrations and the situation of employers, and tended to be less supportive of workers although their opposition to social legislation is often much weaker than expected. There were no Conservatives who defended recalcitrant antisocial legislation positions[10] (even in 1904–1905); if any believed in them in private, they did not express them in public. And although there were Catholics, their influence was much less dominant and not translated into these bills as in Chile.[11] The Argentine Socialists were the eternal champions of workers' rights: social legislation was the core of their electoral program and from the first day they reached Parliament, they struggled and campaigned to get that legislation on the congressional agenda and, once it was there, to get the best possible law for the workers, submitting bills and requesting information and reports from the executive regarding the fulfillment of the existing social laws. They were always against repressive measures and their positions regarding the autonomy of the worker organizations were laissez faire. The Argentine Radicals, in power from 1916 to 1930, had to battle on many fronts. There was more ideological heterogeneity in their ranks: some were more socially conservative and less supportive of strikes and social legislation in particular at the beginning of the first administration; others, more pro labor, coincided with the Socialists. However, Radicals were much more tolerant and supportive of workers than most Conservatives. The bills and positions in debates were almost always identifiable by political party. Party origin was an important variable in the Argentine Congress (see also Smith 1974, ch. 4).

In the Chilean Parliament, there was less difference regarding the "social or public order" issue. Except Malaquías Concha and a few other members of the Democrat party, legislators tended to view worker protest as a public order issue and favor a more repressive attitude to union activity and strikes—in particular in the first half of the period (as in the Sunday Rest debate and frequent statements in the chambers on strikes and worker protest). Although the provisions of Liberal Alliance bills tended to be more favorable to workers than the Conservative ones, on many occasions in the debate both in the chambers and the joint committee, these differences disappeared surprisingly quickly. The Democrats consistently upheld the need for social legislation to protect workers, supported a new, more interventionist role for the state in social issues and defended positions of more freedom and autonomy for the workers' organizations, and the right to associate and to strike. They were also the only ones who voted against the Law of Residence in 1918. The Catholic reformist Conservatives posited a more authoritarian, controlling legal order for workers and their organizations, and fewer benefits regarding their working conditions (as in the debate of blue collar labor bill and the joint committee debate of the trade union bill). In fact, it is surprising that although Chile already had various long-standing political parties, except for the Democrats, positions regarding the social question did not constitute the lines that divide them. Even more, it is sometimes difficult to see what the distinguishing differences were.[12]

Role of Debate—Was the debate in the chambers an important step in the process of passing a law? Did legislators dedicate time and energy to debating? Were they invested in persuading their colleagues and countrymen? Were important aspects of the bills questioned, and was it possible to effect changes in the bills through debate? Was Congress a public forum with a national audience? These were the questions considered for this indicator. Debate in the chambers is important simply because it shows the existence of public deliberation: Congress is considered more representative if more voices and more public deliberation takes place.[13] In a nutshell, debate was important in Argentina; many legislators engaged in it (in particular in Deputies) (Table 5.A2 in the chapter appendix), core principles of the bills were always questioned and sometimes debated intensely, and different perspectives were expressed. In Chile, on one hand, there was less interest in social legislation and fewer legislators participated, bills were more predefined, and there was less political difference between groups.

Engagement in Debate—While the Chamber of Deputies was the engine as regards initiating social legislation in Argentina, the Senate was in Chile; moreover, until the Senate started drawing up social bills, various initiated in the Lower Chamber did not get very far.[14] Since debate tended to be longer and more intense in Deputies in both countries, there is a lot more discussion and exchange between different positions on social issues among the legislators in the Argentine Deputy Chamber than in the Chilean Senate (and Deputy Chamber). In the Chilean Senate, rather than a debate between different views, there were long, opposed presentations by the leading legislators arguing in favor or against certain provisions (see debate on the labor contract in the Senate, a very important bill) and short interventions by others on specific subjects (for example, on the sale of alcohol and on reporting information to the government), but they did not really engage with each other in debate—or engage little. Most Chilean senators did not participate in the discussion of the important articles of the bill on trade unions. Either they knew the law was going to pass whatever they thought of it—this attitude of opposition but resignation to the fact that it would pass anyway is visible in some opinions—or they did not have an opinion on these issues. The legislators who did not agree with the position of a leading senator were allowed to speak but their words had little or no effect, as the more powerful senators did not engage with them; those who opposed spoke alone.[15] Either the former legislators were marginal or the bill was already so defined once it reached the floors—this seems to be the case always—that those who opposed it sounded out of place; they did not matter. Neither did the more powerful legislators—in particular, in the Senate—try to persuade the others of their position. Even the authors of a bill did not make an effort to bring their fellow legislators over to their side; their style was more one of presentation (e.g., see Juan Concha on the blue collar labor bill). There was more debate and exchange of opinions and reasons in the joint committee, which of course was much smaller (11 members who are generally not all present). The Chamber of Deputies was always more dynamic than the Senate, all through the years. However, as indicated, this chamber in Chile did not play an important role in the principal laws (trade union, blue collar), which were initiated and approved by the Senate and then sent to the Joint Committee. Even the white collar labor law, which was initiated by Deputies, was combined with another bill previously defined by the joint committee and when they debated it, many legislators were absent, a signal that the bill had been mostly defined already.

In Argentina, debate took up much more time and energy; in particular, as indicated, in the Lower Chamber. In the Senate there was more debate outside the chamber, like in Chile (Sunday Rest, also in the Putting Out bill, the Eight-hour Workday bill). Legislators ranked the abilities of the speakers[16] while stenographic recordings of the debates evoke a cinematic quality: they intersperse comments such as "Laughter," "Hilarity" (political sparring and jokes are frequent), "Applause," "Prolonged Applause," "The members leave their seats to congratulate the Speaker," and so on. The debate where the different positions are clearly expressed tends to clarify the often complex legal points and also contemporary events (such as strikes, rallies, arrests and murky situations surrounding them). These features are valid both before and after 1916; that is, during both the Conservative and the Radical eras. In the Chamber of Deputies, the Socialists, for example, from 1904 to 1930 frequently lost the votes on clauses of different bills because they were always a minority but dominated the debates on social legislation by the strength of their innovative ideas and the force of their arguments. Because they studied and prepared for the debates they made their counterparts improve and specify their arguments. And in contrast to the Chilean legislators, the Radicals and the Conservatives took them on, thus allowing them to be the protagonists and, more importantly, making a good debate possible. Furthermore, not only did legislators engage, they also tried to persuade the other legislators—as an important function of political debate is to be able to arrive at the consent of the majority (Manin 1997, 198)—and acted as if addressing not only the audience in the chamber, but the nation also.

Probably related to this desire to persuade, the art of oratory was prized and admired. Legislators often expressed their ideas in eloquent, beautifully worded sentences, using rhetorical flourishes, metaphors, suspense, emotion and irony. Debate was long and could be passionate, even spectacular (in particular at the beginning of the century during the era of Parliamentarism, as Manin [1997] calls the first period). It could also be philosophical, mercurial and complex—possibly because of the existence of very different informed opinions; also conflictive, abrasive and rowdy. During the Radical years, the pages taken up by debates grow exponentially[17] and a higher number of legislators participate. The debates in Chile were more low key, staid and formal in the Senate; more dynamic in Deputies, and in both chambers more procedurally ordered, often more controlled, more resigned, concise and to the point. Chilean legislators are focused on expressing their ideas and getting a law passed or changed if possible; they fought with each other, of course, but appear in their interventions not to care as much about the wording on one hand, or the galleries, the public and posterity, on the other. The Argentine deputies give the feeling the country is listening to them, even more, hanging on their words (and up to a point they were—the newspapers published congressional speeches until the 1950s at least). Thus, in Argentina debate in itself was an important part of passing a bill; in Chile, less so.

Debate on Core Ideas, Meanings and Implications of the Bills—While the core principles of the bills were always questioned in Argentina, even in the earlier Conservative Parliament where less ideological variation could be presumed, in Chile they were not, possibly due to opposition to and disinterest in social legislation (for example, the blue collar labor and the union bill in the Senate in 1919), and to more agreement, and also to the fact that bills were not very susceptible to change: they arrived in the chambers after decisions regarding their content had already been taken in smaller, more authoritative spaces.

Changes in Bill Provisions—How much were bills changed by debate? This indicator measures the effect, the importance of deliberation in the chambers and the ability a chamber had to modify legislation; it is also tied to the rules and practices of how a bill was shaped and how debate was carried out in each Congress. If a bill is hardly or never questioned or changed, it moves through the chambers much faster and effectively but it also means that parties and members who did not participate in the previous, smaller decision-making spaces (either party, intraparty or committee meetings) had less say in the drawing up of a new law and so can also be related to effectiveness.[18] Debate in Argentina generally changed the bills, often in important ways. The chambers were the space in which different positions met, argued, and determined the contents of a bill on the basis of a committee-reported bill. In Chile, as indicated above, debate was less important and did not have much effect. The passage through the chambers emerges as just one more step in a process that must be completed rather than an important stage in shaping a future law (Table 5.A3 in the chapter appendix). Thus, this finding supports both the greater representativeness of the Argentine Congress and the greater effectiveness of the Chilean one (and the lack of representativeness of the Chilean Congress where all bills were predefined and most congress members could not participate in their determination).

Contents of Debates and Provisions of Bills and Laws—The contents of the bills and laws are considered more representative if the positions of both employers and workers regarding the different provisions of the bills are expressed in the debates and found in the clauses of the law. There is evidence of the positions of both groups in the Argentine Congress's debates and controversies and in the bills passed. The provisions in all of Argentina's trade union bills (except the 1919 committee-reported bill never debated on the floor) and final law are more permissive and enabling for workers than the Chilean ones (see Table 5.A4 in the chapter appendix for examples). The rules of unionization tended to promote an articulated, strong labor movement on the basis of craft or industrial activity with the possibility of federating. The 1945 trade union law, much resisted by the employers, followed various pre-existing tendencies. In Chile, the law established compulsory unionization on the basis of the individual firm for plant unions, with no federation, atomizing and weakening the labor movement. Besides, the rules tend to not intervene in the internal governance of unions in Argentina, while in Chile, the industrial unions were meticulously regulated by the provisions in the law.

Thus, the Argentine Congress is considerably more representative than the Chilean one since the four indicators reveal a greater diversity of interests and perspectives present in the origin of the different bills and the positions in debates, a greater role granted to public debate, bills and laws that show the presence of both voices, employers and workers, and they tend to benefit workers more than the Chilean laws do.

Effectiveness

The indicators of effectiveness reveal a more structured and differentiated Congress in Chile, and one probably nearer to Cox's "legislative state of nature" (2008, 141) in Argentina. Let us turn to the indicators.

Time Organization—In Argentina the topic and legislators' interest are more important than the organization of time; sessions are less structured, exchanges are not measured out by the minute, frequent mini-debates develop, there are fewer limits on topic and time, proposals are discussed and defined in the chamber, and sometimes the agenda is discussed in the plenary. There is a freewheeling order in the debate; there are fewer rules and these are more flexible. In the Chilean Congress, on the other hand, time reigns supreme: sessions are structured in slots, all topics are predefined and clearly demarcated,[19] there are allotted times and spaces for each matter, there is no debate in the chamber outside of debates on actual bills, a spontaneous debate on the floor is extremely rare, issues are mentioned and the assembly moves on. Proposals about the agenda are discussed and defined outside the chambers, never in the plenary; debate is more orderly and disciplined, and the rules are more complex and strict. The sentence-long statements and absence of debate imply they are discussed and coordinated elsewhere and that a disciplined practice of rules of procedure exists. As indicated, the exchanges during the first hour are also much more controlled in Chile from the point of view of time.[20] In Argentina, legislators often just say "*Pido la palabra*" and speak—although the president complains when he is not previously informed by those who wish to speak. In Chile, legislators debate different positions only during the debate of a bill in the "second hour" (which generally seems to last two hours). After the second hour is over, the session is closed. I have only found one bill in which the session had to be suspended because of the absence of legislators (see next point). This occurs more frequently in the Argentine Congress, where debate continues until a certain agreed upon time is reached or, frequently, until legislators start leaving the chamber (in the Radical period), while Chile's sessions end because it is time to do so. Deputies are told to shorten their speeches, other deputies complain and request everyone shorten their comments, some apologize—but their time is never de facto cut off, measured and controlled as it is in Chile.

Chile's procedural rules are stricter, and the behavior of legislators in the chambers is more solemn and formal, and also much more hierarchical, as is reflected in the debates and even in the way stenographers record the names,[21] in particular in the Senate. In Argentina, there is a more egalitarian and informal way of functioning; more people participate in this daily discussion of matters with fewer limits on topic and time. This way of working in the Argentine assembly is present from the beginning (i.e. the Conservative era), although sometimes the functioning is more formal.

Adherence to Rules—More instances of "adapting" or "changing" the rules can be found in Argentina; adherence to rules and respect for procedure is superior in the Chilean Congress. Some examples of "rule flexibility" in the Argentine Congress are the following: the 1904 Sunday Rest bill was not strictly committee reported because the committee could not agree on one version; however, those who did not agree with the text reported allowed it to be debated because there was widespread interest in passing the law before the session period ended.[22] In the course of the debate, the bill was substituted for another one written up by a legislator as he listened and this version was the one finally passed by the Chamber of Deputies. Another example: although an interparliamentary committee had already reported the Putting Out bill that the Conservative-dominated Senate started treating in March 1918, the bill was exchanged for another one agreed upon by two senators from the committee and another Conservative senator in meetings held outside the chamber (similar to the Chilean senators) (del Valle Iberlucea and Olaechea y Alcorta, CS, June, July, August 1, 1918; de Tomasso, DS, CD, September 1918). There were periods in which legislators were absent, causing the chamber of Deputies to suspend the sessions (in both, a quorum was needed to maintain the chamber working). On the other hand, the debates on the trade unions in the Senate in 1926 and the eight-hour workday in 1921 and 1928 kept to the rules.

In Chile, the absence of legislators was rare and the problem soon solved by calling the deputies back to the chamber (BS, CD, 6 September 1923) or, as in the case of the white collar labor bill, closing down the discussion in particular. The Chilean deputies were not totally above changing the rules.[23] However, I only found one example of stepping outside the usual procedure in the records. To conclude, the Chileans were much stricter with procedure: they had more complex rules and they followed them to a greater degree. Rules were more institutionalized, although at the same time there were more informal meetings outside Congress to decide provisions.

Locus—That is, where do things happen? Where were bills initiated? Where was the content decided? *Initiation* refers to where the process of the passage of a bill through Congress actually started, in a committee belonging to one of the chambers (see Table 5.A5 in the chapter appendix). Where bills are initiated is important because the different origin and composition of Deputies and Senate influences the contents and the passage of the bill and eventually contributes to shape the role of Congress. The importance of the executive has to be analyzed for each individual bill. In both countries the Chamber of Deputies held more dynamic debates and tended to be less conservative. While in Argentina the Chamber of Deputies propelled social bills and the Argentine Senate tended to follow Deputies' leadership on these issues, "correcting" some "overidealistic" provisions passed by the deputies as one legislator put it (in particular before 1916), in Chile social bills proposed in Deputies were postponed, sent to bodies under the control of the Senate or the joint committee, or simply dropped (see endnote 14). In Chile, the Senate is the important chamber in social legislation. Showing relatively strong Congresses in both cases, the main pieces of social legislation studied here were initiated by the legislative, except the Argentine 1945–1946 trade union law and understandably, since it was regarded as a matter of national security, both countries' Laws of Residence.

Where is the content of the bills defined? Which space (committee, the Chamber of Deputies', the Senate, the Joint Committee, or other external meetings) is most influential in defining the provisions of a bill? In both assemblies committees reported the bills first. As indicated, in Argentina debates were an important part of the procedure to get a bill passed and bills could undergo important changes in plenary debates while in Chile, debates mattered much less and the important decisions regarding contents and the process a bill would follow (e.g., whether it will be discussed in Deputies or in a special committee) were always defined in committee meetings, informal meetings between members outside the plenary and, presumably, meetings between party leaders and government officials. Bills were passed with few changes or none at all, which speaks of the importance of these prior instances. In Argentina, the content of the Sunday Rest law in 1905 was defined partly in the Committee, partly in Deputies and also in the Senate; the main provisions of the Putting Out law were partly agreed on outside the Senate chamber, and then debated and defined on the floor. In both cases the content of the provisions of the bill underwent important changes in their passage through the chambers. The eight-hour workday was debated and defined in committees first and then Deputies' with few changes in 1928 (since it had been debated in detail in 1921 and afterwards); the 1926 trade union bill in the Committee and was discussed only in the Senate and defined there (changed on the floor); and the 1946 final trade union law passed by both houses in December 1946 was defined by the executive with input from union leaders (Torre 1990). In Argentina, bills tend to be defined on the floor.

In Chile, the content of the bills was always defined before reaching the floor, even at the very beginning of the 20th century, during parliamentarianism when, according to Manin (1997, 205), opinions are formed on an individual basis *within* the debate in the chambers, not in party spaces or in committees. This feature of a bill that does not change could reveal a greater development of parliamentary offices, but above all I think that at this early date, it shows a great concentration of power. The bills left the chambers almost the same, word for word, as they had entered (Sunday Rest, Plant Unions, Craft Unions, blue and white collar labor contract and the Law of Residence). The Eight-hour Workday (part of the blue collar law) law was defined in the Senate and so was the trade union law for plant unions; the craft union bill was defined in the joint committee. The Senate labor contract bill (1920–1921) was the one that suffered most changes comparatively—under the influence of the Washington Convention—and it is interesting that these are not agreed upon in the debate; they appear with no warning at the next session, already included. Mostly, we do not know how or why this happened (unless it is mentioned in the debate), making Congress more opaque on one hand and, on the other hand, more effective. The same happened in the Sunday Rest debate (1907), when suddenly the debating and the dissenting voices were silent; some fundamental negotiating has taken place outside the chamber, presumably between party leaders, but we do not find out what it centered on.

Mechanisms for Intractable Disagreements—The typical mechanism in Chile to solve a disagreement is what I call "the ascending spiral" mechanism: when debate stalls, decisions are kicked up a step to a smaller set of actors who make the decisions—a constant, fundamental feature of the Chilean Congress. At system level, when both the Senate and the executive had a rival bill and code they wanted to get passed during a very tense political period—and both were stalled in the Lower Chamber's social legislation committee—the way out of the impasse was proposing a joint committee to study the matter, and after some time, it did so and prepared the bills. This mechanism is used in many other circumstances: in the Senate, when Democrat M. Concha objected strenuously to the articles on minimum salary in the Conservative labor contract bill, a few senators met separately, outside the chamber, to agree on a version of those articles which then appeared in the bill. Various other times during the debate of this bill, it is obvious that meetings have been held and new material added to the bill, but we never learn exactly how they came to decide on the provision. On another occasion, when the legislators cannot agree on a point in the joint committee, a meeting of only two is proposed (although finally not carried out). This ascending spiral, in which fewer and fewer people acquire more and more power to define an issue, bears a curious resemblance to the voting system included in the law on trade unions.[24] It also is a useful coordinating mechanism that keeps disagreements firmly under control in small spaces.

In Argentina, there are clearly fewer of these mechanisms. The usual one is to debate, and sometimes agreement is reached; other times, only deadlines and voting put an end to debate, or nothing is done leading to impasses or inaction. I have only found one example of a smaller committee being proposed or formed (in Deputies, a committee of five is proposed in order to harmonize the different preferences regarding some articles of the Sunday Rest bill). Many more bills died in Argentina (there is a law that establishes that after two years a bill that has not been considered expires), also many more were submitted to Congress than in Chile; but they also prescribed due to a different kind of problem. The 1921 Eight-hour Workday bill was debated and passed in Deputies but expired in the Senate which simply did not debate it (the Senate, "that mass grave of social legislation," as Socialist deputy Adolfo Dickmann calls it [DS, CD, September 18, 1928]). The eight-year delay seems mostly due to the standoff between the Radical party in power and their adversaries, the Conservatives who controlled the Senate. In the case of the trade union bills—that remarkably cannot get approved for at least 20 years—there was debate in 1904, but the fact that it was a chapter within a complex and precocious labor code, among other reasons, makes its passage very difficult. In 1919 a committee-reported bill was agreed upon between Conservatives and conservative Radicals, but it did not reach the floor probably due to executive (President Yrigoyen) and worker opposition. There followed the debate and approval of a Socialist-based committee-reported bill in the Senate in 1926, but it did not reach the Chamber of Deputies (perhaps due to Alvear's and employer opposition). The Argentine Congress cannot find a way of passing this difficult bill; it did not have a vertical political logic or enough independent power from social forces to push the trade union bill through, as the Chilean Congress did, although only up to a point—for it was the military also that finally sanctioned the law.

Time for a Bill to Pass—The starting date chosen is the month when a bill that is to be debated is first mentioned, which is generally about one month before the actual debate in the first chamber it is considered in. At that moment, in both countries there is jostling for space on the agenda and specific comments and information about the bill coming up. The ending date is the month the bill is passed by the last chamber to approve it,[25] or when Congress approves it under the military coup, as in Chile in 1924. It takes Chile between two and four years to pass a bill; it takes Argentina between 3 months and 20 years (Table 5.A6 in the chapter appendix). So, it takes Chile less time and the time is less variable too, which speaks to more regularity.

Time in Force—In strong contrast to Argentina, Chile's law on trade unions together with the other main labor laws passed in 1924/1931, except for some changes such as in the rural sector and the copper miners special statute (Angell 1972, 57), remained the same in their fundamentals until 1979–1981 when, under Augusto Pinochet, another military man, a new one was drawn up (Drake 2003). In Argentina, the trade union law tended to be altered with each change of regime after 1955.

The Chilean Congress was more effective than the Argentine Congress. It was more differentiated and tightly structured, rules were adhered to more strictly, times were shorter, there were mechanisms for solving disagreements, and decisions regarding process and contents were taken in small spaces among few participants, expressing the power-concentrated logic in this Congress.

CONCLUSIONS

The comparison of the Argentine and Chilean legislative processes shows two very different institutions at work. The Argentine Congress is more representative: the trajectories of the laws passed in the Argentine Congress reveal a multiplicity of bills coming from different political parties (Conservatives, Socialists, Radicals, Peronists) between 1904 and 1946 and an array of different positions on the different issues in the debates, generally closely correlated to the political parties and groups within them. Bills in Chile show concentration of origin and time and little difference between them: the bills were proposed by Liberals and Conservatives, mostly between 1919 and 1924 (see also Morris 1966, 160). It is surprising that Chile, with an older, more institutionalized party system, should have so little diversity of opinion expressed in bills and debates. This does not mean there were no ideological differences in the Chilean Congress but that political parties do not represent systematic differences regarding the social question; besides, as mentioned above, Socialists and Communists were not present in the debate.[26]

Second, debate clearly played a more important role in the Argentine Congress. It was a crucial part of the passage of a bill, particularly in the Chamber of Deputies: it took up more time, more legislators participated, the main ideas of the bills were examined and often debated long and passionately; the debate had concrete effects on the provisions of the bill often producing changes in them; and everybody engaged more regardless of the real possibilities of winning passage of their own preferences.[27] Finally, the contents of the bills favored a wider proportion of the population and to a greater extent. Arguments were often presented with care and meticulous study behind them, and efforts to persuade, metaphors, irony, rhetorical flourishes all played their part. Oratory was a valued talent. The debates were also a public spectacle: spectators often filled the galleries and debates were published in the newspapers. The conjunction of these features show that Congress in Argentina acted as an important public forum, a place where a wide array of views and perspectives were expressed: "… local and particularistic interests and discontents, the executive represents the majority but in the assembly different constituencies exist and dissenting voices and local viewpoints are heard ... the latent and otherwise unrepresented interests of the public take place there" (Fennel 1971, 163). Although Fennel was speaking of Argentina at the end of the 1950s and during the 1960s, his characterization can be applied to the years studied here.[28]

In Chile, debates in the chambers were less important: they tended to be shorter, more to the point and fewer legislators took part in them; positions against certain provisions or bill could be expressed but everyone knew the debate would soon end without changing the bill in any important way. There tended not to be an engaged debate about opposing ideas and contrasting arguments from different political positions. A reason for this could be that the important points of all the bills were always resolved before or after the floor debate but not *in* it, and that the Senate was the main forum for social legislation. Moreover, there was less ideological distance between positions, and also perhaps resignation or acceptance—as indicated, controversial parts of the bills and the process the bills followed were defined by party and government leaders. Legislators who disagreed with provisions of the bills evoked little response, no one took them on—in particular in the Senate. The passage through the chamber was nearer to being a formality for passing the bill than an important stage in shaping it. Finally, the two Congresses produced different laws. The voice of both workers and employers was present in the bills and debates of the Argentine Congress reinforcing its representativeness, while the workers' voice in Chile was much weaker than the employers', and this is reflected in the bills and laws both on trade unions and working conditions.

Regarding the second variable, effectiveness, the Chilean Congress regulated the available actions and the plenary time to a greater degree; rules were more institutionalized and enforced more strictly. There was a preordained place for each issue, and daily congressional activity moved forward with more organization and much less debate than in Argentina. Legislators obeyed stricter rules regarding speaking and the length of their utterances. Bills were hardly changed once defined in committees; they took less time to move down the legislative path and remained in force longer once approved. Decisions about key controversial provisions and process were invariably taken outside the chambers in small spaces. In the Senate, it is possible to glance into how things worked behind the scenes when the senators refer to their meetings outside the chamber to decide issues. In this sense, Congress was more hierarchical and opaque in Chile, and this seems to have contributed to its effectiveness in passing social legislation.[29] Ministers were often in both chambers, answering questions, keeping the wheels oiled with information and responses from the executive. The fluid, frequent—almost daily—presence of ministers in both chambers is not found in Argentina. Although this happens during the Conservative period, at the beginning of Yrigoyen's term, relations between the executive and the legislative are fraught, which is visible in the frequent attempts at interpellations and how they unfolded when they were held. Relations improved during Alvear's term.

The Argentine Congress's activities and time were less structured than Chile's. Legislators participated in mini-debates on more topics on a daily basis, there was not such a marked difference between the plenary and administrative meetings outside the plenary and between different parts of the congressional day, time was seldom parceled out in pre-allotted slots and strict segments as it always was in the Chilean assembly and sometimes assembly sessions even revolved round the agenda. The strict, brief, focused exchanges in the "first hour" of the Chilean assembly on a daily basis did not occur in the Argentine Congress. Rules were less dominant. There were more absences in the Argentine Chamber during the Radical period and legislators sometimes took the liberty of innovating procedures. Sometimes important bills could not be passed; they remained "suspended" in the process. All these characteristics, together with a quicker legislative process for each bill and a longer time of the laws in force, reveal the workings of a more effective lawmaker in Chile. The power of the Senate, dominated by the Conservatives, and the taking of decisions in small spaces before the passage of the bill through the chambers, are two factors that explain the Chilean Congress's capacity to articulate or impose positions and push a bill through in spite of widespread opposition.

Another factor expressive of the differences between both Congresses is that while in Argentina the Chamber of Deputies was the engine of social legislation, in Chile it was the Senate. The Argentine Chamber of Deputies stamped a more dynamic, inclusive and challenging character on the debate and the content of social legislation. Its more heterogeneous composition, due to a larger electorate and the federal character of the country's political organization, produced more public deliberation. On the other hand, it was the Chilean Senate that played the crucial role in the Chilean polity, initiating and passing the most important social bills and dominating their passage in the joint committee, deciding over the other chamber.[30] The origin of a bill is important here in as far as the dynamics and composition of each chamber tends to imprint a different character on the content and process of the bills and thus characterize the role of Congress contributing to make it either a more important participant in the public sphere (Argentina) or a more powerful (and conservative at this point in history) lawmaker (Chile). At the same time, the fact that bills supported by the executive do not necessarily get passed (in both cases, Yrigoyen and Alessandri's), that Congress can define the contents and delay or block the passage of bills, and initiate most of the important laws, indicate that these were two relatively strong Congresses that the executive could not control or ignore, but instead had to negotiate with.

Finally, an important principle in the functioning of the Chilean Congress is "the ascending spiral" principle. As mentioned, almost all the issues related to the passage of the bills were proposed, treated and decided in small arenas with few actors (parallel informal meetings, committees, the joint committee), reducing the assemblies to just one more stage of the process. And when there were disagreements at important junctures in the chambers or in the joint committee, the mechanism to solve them was the ascending spiral, part of a vertical, power-concentrated logic. Pushing the decision space up and away from the wider, more crowded arenas of the chambers towards increasingly exclusive ones was an effective way of resolving disagreements, and also very different from the disorderly but more horizontal logic of the Argentine Congress. In the latter case, the system was more centered around debating and voting—this last was the mechanism par excellence that defined the content of the bills; there was more and more debate until everyone was exhausted and started leaving the assembly, or until the deadlines imposed the need of a definition and the vote decided (Law of Residence 1902, Sunday Rest 1904/5, Eight-hour Workday in 1928). There were fewer mechanisms to deal with intractable disagreements in this Congress. When these situations appeared and could not be overcome—as in the difficulties of passing a law regulating trade unions—there was an impasse, the passage of a law could be postponed for years. These points show the dispersion of power in the Argentine Congress: there were not any mechanisms for overcoming these situations and also, perhaps, the politicians did not have enough power independently of the social forces—in particular, employers who preferred to negotiate in the market without any state intervention.

Why was Argentina more representative and Chile more effective? I will only outline three possible reasons that will have to be developed elsewhere. I will argue that the first reason that Argentina was more representative was the extension of suffrage: a higher proportion of the population voted in Argentina (Canton, 1966) and they voted in freer conditions than in Chile, which meant that the legislators had more incentives to compete for the vote. Furthermore, because more people voted, legislators had to answer to more social demands. Many fewer people voted in Chile until the 1950s (Remmer 1984) and elections were more subject to manipulation that held the vote captive. These two conditions reduced the impact of the workers' vote and parties (Drake 1991). Second, Argentina had (and has) a federal political organization, an institutional design that captured a greater variety of interests, allowing a more diverse representation of interests and perspectives, which affected the composition and therefore the dynamics of Congress. Chile had (and has) a unitary, centralized political organization that subsumed the provincial level: the *intendents* were appointed by the president. At the same time, both factors contributed to producing more social and political homogeneity, and control, in the Chilean Congress, which, in turn, increased legislators' coordination abilities, and thus their effectiveness.

I will suggest that a third factor that explains the Chilean elite's better coordination abilities is the result of a historical legacy. In Chile after independence, there was institutional continuity (the colonial state continued through the independence revolution), while in Argentina soon after independence the colonial state broke down and 50 years elapsed before a central state was reconstituted in the 1850s and 1860s. The fact that many provinces lived a fully independent life for so long shaped very distinctive local or provincial communities and elites. Elite homogeneity would seem to help consensus, and passing bills while elite division and heterogeneity leads to a more varied presence of ideas and interests and a richer debate but also to more difficulties for creating agreement.

To conclude, the comparison of the two cases presented here seems to provide evidence of the representativeness-effectiveness dilemma: in order to be effective, Congress has to sacrifice representativeness, and conversely, in order to be representative, Congress has to bleed effectiveness. However, although in Chile effectiveness was closely related to a lack of representativeness, it was also related to a more vertical power-concentrated logic and a more differentiated Congress. Likewise, Argentina's lack of effectiveness was not related to a greater capacity of representation or an excess of deliberation, but rather to a dispersion of power and a lower level of institutionalization. However, this study shows some kind of balance between these two dimensions is necessary for a workable Congress. In other words, a degree of representativeness or a degree of effectiveness by themselves are necessary but not sufficient conditions for a Congress to work well.

NOTES

I would like to thank Matt Shugart, Eduardo Silva, Ludovico Feoli, and Carlos Waisman for their helpful comments on earlier drafts of this paper. I am also very grateful to CIPR for being such a supportive and welcoming place of work during my postdoctoral fellowship.

1. See, for example, the authors cited in Fennel (1971, 152) and Molinelli (1991, 106); but also Shugart and Carey (1992), Morgenstern and Nacif (2002, 1, 5).
2. In this system each voter had as many ballots as his province had electors, and it was not obligatory to mark all the possible preferences so he could accumulate his votes for the candidates he chose and not distribute them; minorities had a better chance of obtaining a representative this way (S. Valenzuela 1985, 104; Monteón 1982, 25).
3. J. S. Mill's *Considerations on Representative Government* ([1861]1991) cited in Manin, Pzeworski and Stokes (1999, 32). Following Pitkin, these authors and others question the assumption that "electing politicians who somehow mirror or reproduce the composition of the electorate achieves representation," recognizing Pitkin's pioneering comments in this direction (32, 37–8).
4. "When the Constitution was being debated in 1787–88, the Federalists advanced their principle of distinction and the Anti-Federalists opposed that principle, arguing that representation required "likeness" and "resemblance" to constituents so that representatives could "possess their sentiments and feelings" (Brutus, cited in Manin 1997, 110); Mansbridge (2009, 387).
5. In the Argentine "Conservative" parliament of the beginning of the 20th century, various legislators, who were not legislators from the Socialist party, nor workers, clearly defended the workers' rights to rest on Sundays for different reasons (e.g., O'Farrell, Roca, Pinedo in the debate on Sunday Rest, DS, CD, 1904–1905). In the Chilean Parliament, for example, during the debate

on retirement for railway employees, some legislators defend the right of the wage laborers to retirement as well as that of the machinists and the white-collar employees' (Malaquías Concha, Quezada; BS, CD, November 18, 1909 to March 4, 1910).

6. The constitutional right of petition existed in both countries.

7. The Diario de Sesiones (DS) in Argentina and Boletín de Sesiones (BS) in Chile, Senate and Chamber of Deputies in both cases. Debate and everyday legislative affairs in both countries were recorded verbatim. The Chilean joint committee debates on social legislation were recorded by the secretary (i.e., not verbatim). In Argentina: (A) Chamber of Deputies: 1901–1908, 1910, 1917–1930, 1946. (B) Senate: 1901–1905, 1917–1930/32, 1946. In Chile: (A) Chamber of Deputies: 1902–1907; 1910–1911, 1915–1924. (B) Senate: 1904–1907, 1910–1911, 1917–1924 (Library of Congress in Santiago, Chile; Biblioteca del Maestro Collection, Di Tella University Library, in Buenos Aires, Argentina.)

8. These were antiimmigration laws that authorized the executive power to expel any foreigner whose behavior "compromised national security or disturbed the public order." Years are specified in the Appendix.

9. The information in this indicator is based on the review of all the bills, but see the most important ones in Chile: debates in the joint committee on the trade union bills, and in the Senate on the blue collar bill.

10. As, for example, the Chilean Radical MacIver in the debate on the blue collar bill (BS, CS, November 12, 1920), or such traditional views as legislator Mujica in the debate on Sunday Rest (BS, CD, September, 1904). The characterization of workers as lazy and vicious and the need to apply more force to them are not even tangentially touched in the Argentine debates on bills.

11. The Conservatives included the "liberal reformist" Conservatives (as Zimmerman 1995, aptly calls them) who together with some Socialist and other intellectuals drew up the 1904 code; the more authoritarian ones (represented by the committee-approved trade-union bill of 1919), and the modern Conservatives of the Demócrata Progresista party (after 1914), very active in the Eight-hour Workday bill debates.

12. This characterization coincides with previous work. "An individual's loyalty or contribution to coalition programs, labor bills included, cannot necessarily be assumed from his party affiliations" (Morris 1966, 155; also Monteón 1982, 56). Two examples illustrate the degree to which party labels were not very important for expressing different positions. When the members of the Joint Committee had to vote on which bill of the three possible (the Conservative bill, Ramírez Frías's, or the government's) would serve as the basis for the discussion of the trade union law, seven members out of eleven voted for the Conservative or Senate bill: 4 Conservatives and 3 Liberal Alliancists. The second remarkable vote was on whether plant unions were to be compulsory or voluntary; the proportion was seven to two in favor of mandatory unions within the firms. Only two Alliancist legislators voted for voluntary unions (ACM, December 15, 1922; 61–2). Although there seemed to be a close majority of Alliancists, in fact the positions of the members of this Committee are all much nearer the Conservative Senate bill than the government's "Liberal" one.

13. See Manin (1997) and Mansbridge (2003), who explain and emphasize the "deliberative function of democracy" and its implications in different ways.

14. For example, the Senate stopped deputy-initiated bills: a bill on workers' savings fund (1909 and 1910), it rejected a bill regulating women's and minors' work (1908) (BS, CD, August 19, 1909), and discarded a proposal to create an Office of Labor Information (BS, CD, August 22, 1910) as well as the Conciliation and Arbitration bill (BS, CD, July 28 and October 12, 1921).

15. For example, Torrealba in the Senate during the debate of the bill on working conditions; Senator Zanartu who expressed his objections in the Hour of Incidental Matters, outside the debate on the labor bill, and Lamieres, Torreblanca, Lisoni in Deputies on December 3, 1918 during the debate of the Residence Bill.

16. Columba (1949, 1951, 1952), the congressional stenographer and caricaturist for almost 50 years, tells of various conversations with deputies in which they would discuss and rank the eloquence of the orators (e.g., 58, 177–8).

17. From 1900 to 1912, the Lower Chamber produces generally two volumes, exceptionally three a year; after 1912 they increase sharply to between five and seven a year until the end of the 1920s.

18. Although in party democracy, debate is supposed to take place in party spaces before debate in the chambers (Manin 1997, 205), the fact that there is little or no public debate in the chambers means less participation anyway because not all parties are represented in the committees and joint committees on social legislation. Besides, it is arguable if Chile's Congress during these years can be classified as party democracy instead of parliamentarianism in Manin's terms.

19. For example, in the first part of the day, different issues are just expressed or briefly arranged, there is a slot for "Incidents" (the Hour for Incidental Matters), generally used by legislators to express personal views on events or a matter considered of public interest and one for "*Indicaciones*" (brief motions and preferences regarding the issues and their order on the agenda and possible ways of execution).

20. For example, during an exchange on an immigration bill, one legislator (M. Concha) cannot answer another (Subercauseaux) directly; he has to wait until the chamber gives him permission to. The president decides to postpone the end of the session 15 minutes and then, as no one opposes the motion, he grants Deputy Concha five minutes to speak. Another example: Deputy Undurraga, is talking about reforms to the Senate bill on working conditions. He has not finished his speech and requests that he be able to finish; he is asked how many minutes; he requests 15 but goes over, and he is stopped again. He requests another 3 minutes, and is granted 3 more (BS, CD, July 12, 1923).

21. For example, some are simply "Sr. Rioseco" or "Sr. Díaz," while others—considered, apparently, socially or politically senior—are "Sr. Huneeus (Don Alejandro)" or "Sr. Concha (Don Malaquias)." Besides, the presidents of the chambers tend to be stricter, at least in word, with exclamations from the galleries, which are much less frequent (or less recorded).

22. Roca proposes exactly this procedure 13 years later in the Senate (it is not clear if they follow the suggestion) (DS, CS, September 13, 1917).

23. As deputies struggled to debate the white collar labor bill in the face of repeated absences of fellow legislators, a deputy motioned that due to these absences, the debate in particular should be closed and they should proceed to voting on the bill (BS, CD, Yrarrázaval, Joaquin, June 14, 1923). A month later we learn that this resolution was defined outside the assembly to the chagrin of various legislators, who critique the decision in later sessions, justified as the only way to pass a bill since the complaining legislators did not attend the sessions slotted for discussion of the bill. Ismael Edwards Matte, an influential Conservative deputy, comments, "it is a procedure not contemplated in the prescribed practices to accelerate and contribute to [the bill's] dispatch" (BS, CD July 13, 1923).

24. The regulations of internal trade union matters determined that some votes were worth more than others: the 1924 law established that the workers or employees who had completed three years of consecutive service in the company had the right to two votes and one more vote for every two additional

years of consecutive service in the election of the plant union authorities. Those with less than three years at the company apparently could not vote. Furthermore, only the members of the board could choose the president and secretary, not all the workers.

25. In other words, not the moment the committee starts meeting to discuss it because it is more difficult to pinpoint correctly and it is not clear whether all the information necessary to determine the dates could be gleaned from the records; besides, the time from when a bill is reported to when it is debated on the floor can vary immensely. The end point could also have been the regulatory executive decree—that second instance that is necessary in Roman law. However, for the purpose of studying congressional effectiveness, approval by the last chamber to pass the bill was more appropiate.

26. Two Socialist Worker party candidates won seats in 1921, but a combination of reasons kept their influence at bay: they arrived in Congress late since the main labor laws would soon be defined. That same year the debate was whisked up into the more rarefied airs of the joint committee, where the Socialists had no place at the discussion table, and the Democrats at this later date, like the other parties, fell into line with the Conservatives. Besides, the Socialist legislators were not as convinced of the importance of Congress and legislation (Grez Toso 2001; Morris 1966, 205–8) as the Argentine Socialists. It fell to the Democrats to emphasize the importance of the social issue in the first years of the century.

27. An example of how debate matters and how the legislators take part is the fact that in 1928 the assembly argued about rural workers being included or not in the Eight-hour Workday bill in spite of the fact that those who promoted the idea, the Socialists, lost the vote 71 to 16. It was known from the beginning that the great majority of the assembly was against the idea and yet they debated it, led by the Socialists, for a time equaling over 100 pages of text.

28. Both Fennel (1971) and Smith (1974, 11), writing in the 1970s, underscore the Argentine Congress's role as a national forum ("a microcosmic representation of effectively competing forces in the national community").

29. Although the literature shows this period as one of frequent parliamentary immobility and infighting, this is not the case of the passage of social legislation.

30. Studying the Chilean Congress in the 1960s, Agor (1971) also finds a very strong Senate.

Appendix

Table 5.A1   Bills by Political Origin

Bills and Laws	Argentina	Chile
Sunday Rest	Chapter from JVG 1904 code, drawn up by "liberal reformist" Conservatives and Socialists, prepared by Legislation Committee	Bills by a Democrat, one from Conservatives, main one from Radicals. This bill is atypical in both countries.
Eight-hour Workday[1]	Bills from all political parties (1895 to 1928): Conservatives, Socialists, Radicals, more than one from Socialists and Radicals	Claim also upheld since previous century by Democrats; in 1919, bill from the Liberal Alliance and from Conservatives (included in Blue and White Collar Labor bills).
Blue Collar Labor		Includes various issues, Conservative Senators 1919.
White Collar Labor		First version from Deputies Legislation (author unknown, supported by Radicals, National Union Liberals and Democrats).
Trade Unions	Various bills: Conservatives (1904, 1919, 1933), Socialists (1913–1926), Radicals (1919, 1921), Peronists 1945/6	One from Conservative senators (1919), two from Liberal Alliance (1919 and 1921).
Putting Out	Interparliamentary bill of Radicals and Socialists, then negotiated with Conservative bill	
Law of Residence	Presented by executive but based on bills presented by Conservative legislators (1902)	Presented by executive but based on bills presented by Conservative legislators (1918).

1. While Chile included all the working conditions into the labor bills of blue or white collar workers, Argentina passed a separate law on each major aspect (trade unions, duration of the work day, putting out, minimum salary, work of women and minors, etc.)

Source: Author's creation

Table 5.A2   Legislators Who Participate in the Debates

Law	Argentina		Chile	
	Deputies	Senators	Deputies	Senators
Sunday Rest	21	3	12	3
Eight-hour Workday	25	5		7:3 (11 JC)
Trade Unions		6		3 (11 JC)
White Collar Labor			8/10	
Putting Out	2	7/8		
Total	69/70		31 + Joint Com: 41[1]	

1. I have included 11 for the joint committee although they are seldom all present
Source: Author's creation

Table 5.A3   How Content Changes through Debate

Law	Argentina	Chile
Sunday Rest	Deputies changed all the content of the bill (e.g., new clause: employers had to pay workers for Sunday), Senate changed scope to the capital; provinces passed their own laws	Bill entered and exited without a single clause being changed
Eight-hour Workday	Two not fundamental changes in 1928 debates (long-debated bill)	Approved blue collar labor bill very similar to original in essentials but is bill with most changes, comparatively (minimum wage and scope)[1]
Trade Unions	1926 Senate debate: relatively important changes, more state control (changes in statutes, unions could take part in conciliation and arbitration, etc.)[3]	Plant unions and craft unions bills change very little in Joint Committee, features reaffirmed, some benefits shorn off[2]

(*Continued*)

Table 5.A3 (*Continued*)

Law	Argentina	Chile
Putting Out	Important changes, e.g., less state control of factories	
White collar labor conditions		Remains the same all the way through; non-fundamental changes (e.g., explicit mention that domestic service was excluded)
Law of Residence	No change	No change

1. The biggest change was M. Concha's definition of the minimum wage. The groups of workers included and excluded became more clearly defined: industry and not commerce nor agriculture. The articles on the length of the workday left the Senate approved almost exactly the same as the original articles, only clearer and lengthened. The bill becomes tidier and more precise but the eight-hour workday can still be transformed into a twelve-hour one; new mothers are not given more than 40 days' rest after giving birth; there is no direct state control over articles sold in company stores, etc. The most remarkable lack of change was in the workday article, which remained the same

2. For example, workers are granted an extra vote after each two additional years at work instead of one year (taken to 3 in 1924 when approved under military duress); the 10% value of the salaries employers had to pay their workers was reduced to 6%; union powers of control over their firms accounting was curtailed (BS, Senate, November 1920–January 1921; Actas de la Comisión Mixta [joint committee], 87)

3. For example, the government had to approve any alteration of an association's statutes; the bill had to clearly express that incorporated associations could take part in the conciliation and arbitration proceedings thus enabling associations to fulfill the primary objective of the worker corporations (DS, Senate, September 27, 1926, Sp. 913); and a provision saying that worker associations could take part in the election of worker representatives for the Labor Council and that they represented the trade in the designation of delegates for whatever object the special laws might establish

Source: Author's creation

Table 5.A4 Content of the Laws

Law	Argentina	Chile
Sunday Rest	Forbade work in factories, workshops, stores and other establishments and places of work. Only exceptions expressed in the law and its regulations. Work on Sunday forbidden.	Employers would grant a day of rest on Sunday "to those individuals who had worked all the working days of the week," more employer discretion, work not forbidden.

(*Continued*)

Table 5.A4   (*Continued*)

Law	Argentina	Chile
Eight-hour Workday	One law for all workers and employees, 8 hours a day, 48 hours a week (3 regulated exceptions) Rural and domestic workers not included	Two different laws, 8 hours a day or 48 hours per week, but permits up to 10 hours for blue collar, 12 for white and 56 a week if paid extra. Rural and Domestic workers not included
Trade Unions	Unionization on basis of craft/then industrial activity, can federate; 3 levels of organization allowed (factory, region, national)	Different laws for plant and craft unions, mandatory on basis of individual firm (for plant unions), cannot federate for economic reasons craft unions can-white collar workers have privileges, were less important.
Putting out law	". . . It eliminates the conventional salary and replaces it with the minimum mandatory wage determined by joint committees" (Unsain, 1952:19).	
Law of Residence	Similar in both countries	Similar in both countries

Source: Author's Creation

Table 5.A5   Where Bills Were Initiated

Argentina	Chile
1904–1905 Sunday Rest (Dep)	1905–1907 Sunday Rest (Dep)
1918 Putting Out law (Sen)	1919 Blue collar labor bill (Sen)
1919 Committee-reported trade union (Dep). 1926 Senate approved one (Sen)	1919 Trade union bill (plant) (Sen)

(*Continued*)

Table 5.A5   (Continued)

Argentina	Chile
1921 Eight-hour Workday bill and 1928–1929 one that was passed (Dep), plus various other bills (Dep)	1919–1921 Trade union bill (craft) Dep and Exec
	1922 White collar labor bill (Dep/Sen)
Executive: Trade union bills (1904, 1921, 1933) and the 1945–1946 (passed)	Executive: 1917 decree regulating hours in state railways (Minister Ind.)
Law of Residence	Law of Residence

Source: Author's creation

LOCUS—INITIATION

In Argentina, the following bills were initiated by the *first chamber*, some with executive support: the law of Sunday Rest—the process was started by a motion of the Socialist deputy to adapt the pertinent chapter from the executive's Code into an independent bill in 1904; the motion was supported by all the Congressional parties. The 1919 committee-reported trade union bill was based on a Conservative's bill and an agreement between conservative Radicals and Conservatives, was probably opposed by the executive who was more well disposed to the worker issue and got no further. Ten other bills (1919) and a code (1921) were also submitted to the Chamber of Deputies at this time. The Eight-hour Workday bill of 1921, based on two bills by a Radical and a Socialist deputy, was passed by Deputies in 1921 and then stalled in the Senate. In 1928–1929, the bill was passed by both chambers. These bills were supported by the executive. The 1918 bill on the Putting Out system was initiated in the *Senate*. The bill began as an inter-parliamentary (i.e. joint committee) bill in 1913. It probably ended up being put forward in the Senate because the original three deputies had completed their mandates but the original senators remained in office. Moreover, Senator del Valle Iberlucea, a Socialist and a foreigner, had participated in the social surveys carried out for the 1904 code, and was a firm supporter of social legislation and of this bill. The 1926 trade union Senate-approved bill was initiated in the Senate. The committee-reported bill was based mostly on a Socialist bill and had been presented previously in Deputies. The Law of Residence was initiated by the *executive* in both countries, in both cases using legislators' bills that had been submitted previously. It also presented various trade union bills but they did not even reach the committee stage (e.g. the "liberal reformist" Gonzalez 1904 code, the Radical 1919–1921 bills and

Table 5.A6　Time to Pass a Law

Law	Argentina	Time	Chile	Time
Sunday rest	Sept 1904–Sept 1905	1 year	Nov 1904–Aug 1907	almost 3 years
Putting out	June 1918–Sept 1918	3 months		
Eight-hour workday	June 1921–August 1929	8 years 2 months	Nov 1920–Sept 1924	3 years 10 months
Trade union law	1904– chapter of labor code; 1919– committee-reported bill; 1926– Senate debates and passes a bill; 1945/6– passed by Congress	20 years[1]	Nov 1920–Sept 1924	3 years 10 months
White collar labor			July 1922–Sept 1924	2 years 2 months

1. The number of years varies depending on the date one starts counting: 27 years starting at 1919, when a bill was first debated in a committee of the Chamber of Deputies; 20 years from 1926, when a bill was first debated on the floor of the Senate; or even 42, going back further to the first Labor Code in 1904, which included a chapter on worker associations but was never debated. Using the same criterion used to count in the other cases, it took 20 years

Source: Author's creation

code, the Saavedra Lamas code in 1933). However, the 1945–1946 Peronist decree/law on trade unions bill finally became law.

In Chile the law on blue collar labor contract (which contained various important issues within it such as women's and minors' work and the eight-hour workday, treated in separate laws in Argentina) and the one on plant unions—the most important social bills—were initiated and passed by the *Senate* on the basis of a bill from the Conservative party in 1919. The bills proceeded through the joint committee and were passed under the military pressure in 1924. The craft union law was based on a bill originally drawn up by two deputies from the Liberal Alliance and a chapter from Alessandri's code (drawn up by Moises Poblete Troncoso). It was treated only in the joint committee, not in the chambers. The white collar labor law was initiated by the *Lower Chamber* in 1922 as was the Sunday Rest bill in 1905. The *executive* (Alessandri) presented a labor code (in 1921) that also went to the joint committee, and President Sanfuentes before him, proposed a bill on the length of the workday. In the case of initiation, besides the numbers, the bills themselves are important: the Chilean Senate was the powerful chamber in the process of passing social legislation: besides passing the most important laws, its members were the most powerful members of the joint committee.

Part III
Judiciary

6 Effectiveness and Accessibility of Justice System Institutions in Mexico's Transition to Democracy

Julio Rios-Figueroa

The hegemonic party regime that characterized Mexico for most of the 20th century led to a protracted transition to democracy driven by a series of political reforms that combined with a series of socioeconomic changes. The gradual melting down of an authoritarian regime has shaped the institutional architecture of the justice system, which after more than a decade of democratic governance still exhibits traits from the authoritarian past. In particular, the Mexican justice system has a pyramidal architecture in which the president of the Republic and the Supreme Court exert considerable influence over the functioning of the whole justice system: the former through its control of the Public Prosecutor's Office (*Ministerio Público*) and the latter through its control of the administration of the judiciary and its concentrated power of constitutional review.

The argument of this chapter is that the institutional architecture of the Mexican justice system is related to low levels of access to justice for Mexican citizens and to mixed results in terms of effectiveness. In particular, the Public Prosecutor's Office has not been effective in prosecuting crimes and promoting respect for the law. And while the Supreme Court has been an effective arbiter of political disputes, its role in the protection of individual rights has been much less successful. A new set of recent and ongoing reforms to the justice system, however, may impact accessibility to justice and effectiveness in the protection of rights in unprecedented ways.

The chapter is divided into three parts. In the first, I briefly discuss the concepts of representativeness and effectiveness as applied to justice system institutions. In the second, I show how the series of successive reforms (or lack thereof) to two key justice system institutions in Mexico (the Supreme Court and the Public Prosecutor's Office) has produced a system that works relatively well for politicians but definitely not as well for ordinary citizens. In the last part, as a form of conclusion, I discuss a set of recent and ongoing reforms that may drastically alter the shape of the Mexican justice system by considerably expanding access to justice.

REPRESENTATIVENESS AND EFFECTIVENESS IN
JUSTICE SYSTEM INSTITUTIONS

Accessibility as a Surrogate of Representativeness in Justice System Institutions

The concept of representation can be understood in different ways, making the debate on whether a government is more or less "representative" ultimately dependent upon the underlying concept (Pitkin 1972). Nonetheless, when applied to governments the term representative necessarily implies election, the "central institution of representative government" (Manin 1997, 7). Of course, variation in electoral systems can make governments more or less representative (Powell 2000) but in every case elections are central. It follows that using the concept of representation to analyze justice system institutions implies gauging the pros and cons of electing judges, prosecutors and other officials that populate these institutions.

The long-standing view of the judiciary as a coequal participant, with the executive and legislative branches of government, in the system of checks and balances emphasizes that judges should be relatively independent—from both the elected branches and the passions of the electorate—to effectively prevent the arbitrary exercise of power. The judiciary, in the famous Hamiltonian formulation, has "neither force nor will, but merely judgment," and this judgment is better exercised in accordance with the Constitution (that contains the will of the people) when institutional features such as a long tenure, salary protections, and appointment procedures assure that courts are "an intermediate body" between the people and its elected representatives (cfr. Hamilton et al. 2001, 496). Hamilton warned that if the function of protecting rights and enforcing the Constitution was left "to the people, or to persons chosen by them for the special purpose, there would be too great a disposition to consult popularity" (Hamilton et al. 2001, 498).

In general, therefore, based on the influential Hamiltonian perspective, justice system institutions in most countries are designed to be not representative—that is, not directly elected by the people. As previously mentioned, whether direct popular election of high court judges would make them "representatives of the people" is a matter of a debate that ultimately hinges upon the underlying concept of representation, and upon the peculiarities of the electoral system chosen to elect the judges. For the purposes of this chapter, suffice it to say that most countries fill the offices of their justice system institutions through different appointment methods that very rarely involve direct elections, and in this sense, in general, these institutions are designed to be not representative (see, for example, Malleson and Russell 2006).

There are relevant exceptions where high court judges (and other officials such as prosecutors) are directly elected, such as some states of the United States and Bolivia.[1] Critics of judicial elections point to, among other things, the potential undermining of judges' neutrality produced by political campaigning, a process in which judges either receive support in hopes of certain type of future decisions or where judges actually render certain types of decisions in search of future support. The second of these fears correspond to the old Hamiltonian warning and there is some evidence that it is well founded: elected judges in Pennsylvania tend to give longer sentences for similar crimes as the Election Day approaches (Huber and Gordon 2004).

Defenders of judicial elections, in turn, claim that if judges are to nullify laws enacted by directly elected representatives then they also should be directly elected. Some scholars echo this argument and, while not explicitly defending direct elections of judges, do consider that decisions made by directly elected representatives are under certain circumstances superior than those made by indirectly elected judges (see Waldron 2006). In addition, other arguments point out that direct elections provide an easier means to get ride of bad judges. In the U.S. case, a recent defense of judicial elections systematically challenged the empirical accuracy of some of the critics' warnings, in particular regarding the effects of judicial partisanship on turnout and the effect of campaign contributions on judicial election outcomes (Bonneau and Hall 2009). In general, one of the main arguments in favor of electing judges is that this mechanism would bring them, and the justice system, closer to the interests, feelings and needs of the citizens, which is the ultimate guiding principle in a democracy.

In this chapter, I side with the long-standing view that justice system institutions should not be representative, in the sense of not directly elected, mainly because of the advantages for judicial decision-making derived from distancing judges both from the government and from the people. However, it is clear from the arguments in favor of judicial elections that judges and justice system officials should not be too removed from the concerns of the ordinary citizens. This is particularly true in civil-law countries where young would-be judges join the judicial system right after law school and start climbing up the hierarchical-bureaucratic apparatus for a number of years,

oftentimes producing a corps of civil servants more concerned with their corporation than with providing just relief to ordinary citizens (Damaska 1986).

In particular, I argue that accessibility to the justice system can accomplish the function of bringing the justice system institutions closer to the citizens' concerns.[2] The more accessible the justice system, the more permeable such system would be to societal values and to the concerns of ordinary citizens. Accessibility of the justice system is determined by several factors including the legal possibilities for channeling disputes to the courts, the availability of lawyers or of technical assistance at a low or no cost for people with scarce resources, and the rights and opportunities for victims to participate in the prosecution of crimes (see Guarnieri and Pederzoli 1999, 91). The remainder of the chapter provides a broad assessment of the degree of accessibility of Mexican justice system institutions considering these factors.

Effectiveness in Justice System Institutions

This chapter argues that effectiveness in justice system institutions should be assessed by looking at the roles, or function, these institutions play in the political system. Notice that this empirical focus on judicial effectiveness is different from the more common focus on judicial efficiency, i.e. the processing of backlog cases, the time-to-resolution of cases, the automatization of judicial procedures, and so on. While efficiency considerations are no doubt important, and will be mentioned in the analysis of the Mexican case, the chapter focuses on effectiveness.

In particular, to gauge effectiveness it is useful to distinguish between two roles of the justice system, and in particular of its high courts. Supreme and constitutional courts are located in the intersection of a horizontal dimension that relates them to the other branches of government and a vertical dimension that relates them to the citizens. On the horizontal dimension, high court judges are in charge of overseeing the functioning of the institutional checks and balances that is the hallmark of the moderate exercise of political power. On the vertical dimension, they are in charge of protecting the rights of the citizens, both "negative" ones such as freedom of expression and "positive" ones such as the right to health care, which are inscribed in Constitutions to realize the full potential of its citizens.[3]

Interestingly, the high court and, in particular, constitutional judges do not perform their two roles equally at all times; sometimes they display more effort on one or the other. For instance, while the Costa Rican Supreme Court's constitutional chamber has been able to act both as a check on the government and a protector of rights, the Brazilian or the Mexican Supreme Courts have distinguished themselves for being more effective arbiters of political disputes than protectors of rights (see Helmke and Rios-Figueroa 2011). It is therefore useful to assess effectiveness of judicial institutions on both dimensions. This is what the reminder of the chapter does for the case of Mexico.

It is noteworthy that the relationship between accessibility and effectiveness, as understood in this chapter, can be positive. In particular, more access to justice to ordinary citizens can be positively related with effectiveness the rights protection function of courts, because the courts will be more aware of the ordinary citizens problems and they will also have more opportunities (e.g., more cases) to guarantee rights.[4] On the other hand, the relationship between accessibility to justice and effectiveness in the check-and-balance function of courts is not clear. What matters more for judicial effectiveness in the political-arbiter role is independence and neutrality from the political actors not necessarily access to justice to ordinary citizens. For an effective performance of this role, a handful of salient cases can have a huge impact (thus more access is not necessary) whereas the rights protecting function arguably requires a stream of consistent decisions over a period of time to produce a lasting impact.

POLITICAL DYNAMICS AND THE PYRAMIDAL ARCHITECTURE OF THE MEXICAN JUSTICE SYSTEM

During the 1920s, in the aftermath of the armed phase of the Mexican Revolution (1910–1920), the multiplicity of political forces continuously threatened to derail the already precarious postrevolutionary regime. To channel this diversity of political forces, and in the shadow of the assassination of the president elect, revolutionary leader and former president General Plutarco Elías Calles pushed for the creation of an umbrella political organization under the name of National Revolutionary Party (PNR, 1929). During the administration of General Lázaro Cárdenas (1934–1940), the party successfully integrated the army, the organized workers, and the organized peasants into its structure and changed its name to *Partido de la Revolución Mexicana* (PRM, 1936). A decade later, when the party took its current name *Partido Revolucionario Institucional* (PRI, 1946), it had already been established as the single most important political machine in the country within which most decisions regarding "who gets what, when, and why" were made.[5]

One of the most interesting features of the PRI was its capacity to remain in power for more than seven decades (1929–2000). Through a series of gradual reforms the PRI adapted successfully to changing internal and external conditions while simultaneously holding on to power. These reforms touched on every issue of the political and social system. The electoral reforms since 1977 are the paradigmatic example of constant and hard bargaining between the PRI—that did not want to lose much—and opposition forces—that needed to gain enough—that made possible the PRIísta order for 71 years. The judicial system was no exception. In what follows, I provide a brief account of the transformations suffered by the Mexican Supreme Court and the Public Prosecutor's Office.

The Mexican Supreme Court

The Mexican judicial system, as established in the Constitution of 1917, has been reformed several times since the enactment of the Constitution: out of a total of 397 reforms between 1917 and 2010, 42 (16.3%) were reforms to the judicial system (López Ayllón and Fix-Fierro 2010, 355). Three sets of reforms can be distinguished: one set aimed at subordinating the Supreme Court politically (from 1928 to 1950), another set aimed at increasing the administrative efficiency of the Court and the judiciary (from 1951 to 1987), and a final set aimed at empowering the Supreme Court as a constitutional tribunal (from 1987 to 2011).

From the aftermath of the Mexican Revolution, circa 1920, until the consolidation of the hegemonic party regime, three reforms—that took place in 1928, 1934, and 1944—basically affected the appointment and tenure of Supreme Court judges, and they had as one of their main goals to politically subordinate the Supreme Court to the dynamics of the one-party system. These reforms can be understood as a political reaction to independent Supreme Court decisions during the 1920s that, according to the government, were delaying the implementation of the revolutionary program regarding, for instance, the expropriation and redistribution of land (see Marván 2010, 309–311; James 2006).

In 1928, a constitutional amendment augmented the number of Supreme Court judges from 11 to 16 and modified their method of appointment: instead of exclusive congressional appointment by a two-thirds vote, the reform gave the president the right to propose a candidate, subject to Senate ratification. In 1934, another amendment again increased the number of judges to 21 and transformed the original life tenure of Supreme Court judges into a six-year tenure coincident with the presidential administration. Ten years later, in 1944, life tenure was restored with an interesting caveat: the president of the Republic could initiate proceedings to remove a judge who exhibited "bad behavior." Moreover, despite the restored life tenure the Supreme Court had already been incorporated into the dynamics of the hegemonic party regime: from 1944 to 1994 most presidents appointed more than 50% of justices during their terms and almost 40% of the justices lasted less than five years, coming and going according to the presidential term (Magaloni 2003, 288–9; see also Caballero 2010).

Once the Supreme Court and the rest of the judiciary were successfully incorporated into the corporatist logic of the PRI, there was another series of reforms aimed at improving the administrative efficacy of the judiciary, both by concentrating administrative power in the Supreme Court and by expanding the number of lower federal courts, to deal with the ever-increasing caseload. Two reforms are noteworthy examples of this trend. First, in 1951 a constitutional amendment approved the appointment of auxiliary judges to the Supreme Court and also created a new layer of circuit courts with the aim of reducing the highest court's caseload regarding *amparo* suits,[6] namely the cases where an individual citizen challenges a state action based on the argument that a public authority had violated her constitutionally protected rights (see Caballero 2010, 149–52). In 1968, again to overcome the backlog, another reform decided to limit the Supreme Court's appellate jurisdiction and to transform the collegial circuit courts, which were doubled in number, into last courts of appeals for most cases (see Caballero 2009, 166–70).

The culmination of the series of reforms aimed at improving the administrative efficacy of the judiciary took place in 1987, when a constitutional amendment transferred to the Supreme Court the power to control the material resources of the judiciary, including not only the budget, but also decisions over the number and jurisdiction of courts. These new capacities added to the Supreme Court's control over the appointment and promotions of lower court judges, a prerogative that the Court had enjoyed since 1917. By the end of the 1980s the Mexican Supreme Court had become a powerful administrative body very much involved with the dynamics of the hegemonic party that, nonetheless, still had weak powers of judicial review.

The reform of 1987, however, by limiting even further the jurisdiction of the Supreme Court to "important cases" also signals the beginning of a new series of reforms aiming at the empowerment of the Supreme Court as a constitutional tribunal. The key reform in this transformation process took place in 1994 when the Supreme Court was delegated considerable powers of judicial review and its membership was reduced and renewed in order to increase its legitimacy and independence vis-à-vis the other branches of government (see, for example, Fix-Fierro 2003). The 1994 reform substantially increased the judicial review powers of the Mexican Supreme Court by creating instruments of both concrete and abstract control with the possibility of generating *erga omnes* effects.[7] Moreover, most of the judges proposed in 1995 by the president and confirmed by the Senate were the product of consensus between at least two political parties, the PRI and the right-leaning PAN (*Partido Acción Nacional*), and the reform granted them an effective 15-year tenure (see Sánchez, Magaloni and Magar 2011).

However, access to the two new instruments of constitutional review created or strengthened in 1994 (the action of unconstitutionality and the constitutional controversy, respectively) was allowed only to political authorities such as political parties, the representatives of the three branches of government, or a legislative minority. Ordinary citizens do not have standing to use these instruments, and this is also true for most autonomous organs such as the Federal Electoral Institute (IFE) or the Federal Institute of Transparency and Information (IFAI).[8] Moreover, the other instrument for constitutional review, the amparo suit, was not only weak mainly because of its limited, *inter partes* effects, but also because of its de facto inaccessibility for ordinary citizens because throughout the years it had became technically complex and quite expensive.

To understand why the reforms concentrated power in the Supreme Court while limiting access to citizens it is necessary to look at the motivations behind the reform of 1994: to have a neutral arbiter to solve political conflicts, a role that the executive (which had been, simultaneously, leader of the hegemonic party and president of the country) was no longer capable of carrying out successfully in a context of increasing political fragmentation. As Beatriz Magaloni has argued, multiple-party politics created incentives for President Zedillo to delegate power to the judiciary (2003, 267). As the era of hegemonic *presidencialismo* was fading, politicians of multiple partisan affiliations began to occupy elected offices; "the president's leadership was challenged, first by members of different parties, and soon by his own copartisans. The president thus delegated to the Supreme Court the power to rule on constitutional issues as a means to solve this dilemma" (Magaloni 2003, 268).

The limitations of the reform of 1994 are also evident regarding the creation of the judicial council and the (eventually successful) Supreme Court resistance to this innovation. The reform of 1994 also created a judicial council to which was delegated the enormous administrative power formerly enjoyed by the Supreme Court, both in terms of the administration of the judiciary's budget, and also in terms of the appointment of judges and the management of their careers. The political motives behind the creation of the council were, first, to make the constitutional jurisdiction the special focus of the Supreme Court, and second, to reduce the Supreme Court's corporatist management of judicial careers. According to former Justice Jorge Carpizo, Supreme Court judges used to take turns to fill a vacancy at any level of the judiciary, and the new judge's career was overseen by his "mentor" on the court, so that after some time each Supreme Court judge had his own loyal clientele within the judiciary (Carpizo 2000). Also, Supreme Court judges protected unprofessional and dishonest judges whom they had mentored, reasoning that public scandals damaged the reputation of the entire judiciary.[9]

The judicial council was originally composed by a majority of judges selected by lottery, a method that effectively took away from the Supreme Court the control over lower court judges and over the material resources of the judiciary. The Supreme Court did not like this and it started to lobby strongly in order to regain control over the administration of the judiciary and the administration of the judicial career (see Fix-Fierro 2003; Carpizo 2000). The pressure was successful: in 1999, after four years of an interesting battle between the council and the Supreme Court, a constitutional amendment changed the mechanisms used to appoint judicial council members (see Pozas Loyo and Rios-Figueroa 2010, 2011). In essence, the amendment transformed the selection by lot of judges from different levels into a direct designation by the Supreme Court of judges from the district and circuit courts. This effectively gave the Supreme Court control over the majority of seats in the council, which automatically gave back to it control over the material resources of the judiciary and the careers of lower court judges.[10]

In sum, since 1999 the justice system concentrates a lot of power on the Supreme Court, an institution that dominates the system, combining functions of constitutional tribunal, last court of appeals, court of cassation and administrator. The Mexican Supreme Court is the interpreter of the Constitution; it has the power to attract cases deemed "transcendent and important"; it oversees lower courts jurisprudence by resolving conflicts of interpretation among lower courts; and it oversees the administration of material and human resources of the whole judiciary (indirectly, via its influence over the judicial council).

The Mexican Supreme Court: A Court for Politicians not for the People

The series of reforms to the Supreme Court and the protracted transition to democracy in Mexico have created an effective court for solving political disputes but not for protecting the rights of ordinary citizens (see essays in

Vázquez 2007; see also Sánchez, Magaloni and Magar 2011). For decades, the Supreme Court and the judiciary in general were reformed to become just another piece in the dominant party system that characterized Mexico for 71 years; the PRI was able to incorporate it into its institutional structure together with the other organs of government, worker unions, peasant movements, the army and business (Casar 2002; Weldon 1997). Since the 1994 reform, the Mexican Supreme Court has notably increased its participation in the checks and balances and the resolution of conflicts among political authorities, in particular after the increase in political fragmentation in 1997 and the defeat of the PRI in the presidential race of 2000 (Rios-Figueroa 2007; Sánchez, Magaloni, and Magar 2011).

However, the Supreme Court's performance regarding the protection of individual rights has been much less effective. This is due, in an important part, to the restricted access to constitutional justice, simply because many rights violations cases do not reach the Supreme Court. But there are other factors that contribute to the poor performance of the Court regarding rights protection, for instance, the weakness of the "support structure"[11] (Epp 1998) for rights litigation in Mexico or the ideological and pro-judicial restraint attitudes of some Supreme Court judges (Magaloni 2007; Sánchez, Magar and Magaloni 2011). Moreover, as I have argued, the series of reforms that have created a multifunctional Supreme Court, and in particular its huge administrative load, also play a role. In particular, Supreme Court judges cannot concentrate on interpreting the Constitution, providing persuasive arguments for their decisions, writing clear and concise sentences and disentangling the abstract meaning of the rights clauses present in the Constitution. They have instead focused on applying the more familiar and clearer (but by no means unambiguous) political rules of the game.

The Public Prosecutor's Office

In the last 20 years, there have been numerous reforms to the constitutional clauses that regulate the criminal procedure as well as to the criminal code. Actually, in the last two decades these areas suffered more reforms than in the previous 60 years. For instance, constitutional Article 19 (which regulates procedural aspects of the prosecutors and judges when a person is detained) was reformed in 1993 for the first time since 1917. Similarly, Article 16 (which establishes the basic rights of due process) was reformed only once before 1983, but has been already reformed five times since 1990. According to experts in criminal law, the turning point regarding criminal procedure was 1993, when the whole set of articles related to the detention and trial of a suspect were changed (Garcia Ramirez 2001). Since then, reforms on these issues accelerated until the complete overhaul of the criminal procedure in the constitutional reform of 2008, which implied an abandonment of the inquisitorial process and a gradual eight-year transition to an adversarial procedure.[12]

However, the basic institutional structure of the public prosecution has remained practically untouched since 1917. This institutional structure creates perverse incentives because it subordinates the public prosecution to the president of the Republic. The Mexican president freely appoints and removes the *Procurador General de la República* (the equivalent to the attorney general in the United States) and the *Procurador*, in turn, freely appoints and removes all the *procuradores* at lower levels.[13] There are internal mechanisms of control, such as periodic visits and reviews, that allow officials at higher levels to monitor their subordinates, but ultimately all *procuradores* report to the *Procurador General*. At the same time, the office of the Mexican attorney general is legally very powerful, in the sense that it enjoys much discretion in the three steps that characterize the prosecutorial process: investigating, charging and sentencing. This combination of political subordination with strong legal power has been characterized as a "strong institution with weak officials" (Zepeda Lecuona 2000, 339).

The Mexican executive has traditionally chosen the political use of prosecutorial power to exert pressure on friends and enemies alike. The popular saying *para mis amigos todo, para mis enemigos la ley* ("for my friends, everything—for my enemies, the law") is particularly true regarding the Mexican *Ministerio Público*.[14] A famous recent case involved former president Vicente Fox's attempt to legally disqualify former Mexico City mayor, Andrés Manuel López Obrador, as presidential candidate for the 2006 election. But there are also cases related to corruption, the typical plot being a special prosecutor selected to investigate a high-level official who concludes that there is not sufficient evidence to charge him. The performance of the prosecutorial organ has been pointed out as the very "heart of the immunity problem" that characterizes the Mexican criminal justice system (Zepeda Lecuona 2000). In fact, the politicized *Ministerio Público* is one of the main factors explaining the relatively high corruption levels in Mexico (see Rios-Figueroa 2012).

While the Mexican prosecutorial organ is relatively efficient at getting things done for the political bosses in selected cases, it is extremely inefficient for prosecuting the vast majority of criminal offences that affect common citizens. One of the problems is the relation between the prosecutors and the police. While in many countries the investigatory police usually act as a filter for minor offences and other common cases that do not merit prosecutorial revision, in Mexico the prosecutors deal with every single case, even the minor offences and cases that turn out to be not criminal but, for instance, administrative offences (Zepeda Lecuona 2000, 212). The consequence, of course, is that prosecutors have an immense caseload, and this generates processing delays. Lost files and poor attention to the citizens are the norm. This inefficiency, in turn, creates opportunities for prosecutors demanding "speed money" and citizens who are willing to pay the bribe in order to expedite their cases (or frustrated citizens who simply do not bother to either report crimes or collaborate with investigations). Needless to say, both the investigatory police and the prosecutors not only do not feel dignified but some of them actually acknowledge that their job is to produce a "file of lies" instead of searching for the legal truth in the cases before them (see Azaola and Ruiz 2009).

The strange (and dysfunctional, for a young democracy) combination of perverse incentives and huge legal power for the Public Prosecutor makes sense once we take into account that it was the cornerstone of the coercive power of the authoritarian PRI regime for most of the 20th century. As Ana Laura Magaloni explains, in the context of the authoritarian regime, the task of the *Ministerio Público* was not to conduct a professional investigation of a crime but instead to hide the arbitrariness of the police to detain people and to obtain confessions (Magaloni 2010, 15). The capacity to unleash the force of a legal prosecution on a political enemy served as the proverbial stick that the Mexican executive wielded to coordinate behavior according to its interests. The successive presidents under the PRI regime did use this capacity, even against prominent members of the political and entrepreneurial elite who "step out of the bounds" informally established by their administrations.

The judge, once the *Ministerio Público* presented these cases to him, merely checked if the file contained the legal requisites, declared the defendant guilty, and then proceeded to sentencing. As mentioned in the previous section, because the Supreme Court had been successfully incorporated into the dynamics of the hegemonic party regime, it did not serve as a check to the prosecutors and very rarely overturned lower judges' decisions, validating their corrupt practices. For instance, in one infamous decision the Mexican Supreme Court decided that confessions extracted by prosecutors with the use of physical force (i.e., torture) were accepted as evidence in a trial as long as there were other pieces of evidence that corroborated the confession.[15]

Ministerio Público in Mexico: The Long Shadow of the Past

The performance of the public prosecutors has not changed with the transition to democracy. The arbitrariness and the rights violations committed by the police and the prosecutors are still common, and the judges continue to validate them. Interestingly, the judiciary has not been capable of building its authority and independence vis-à-vis the *Ministerio Público* (Magaloni 2010, 18). One figure tells it all: in Mexico only 25% of all crimes are reported to the police, and the bulk of the detainees are captured *in fraganti* not after an investigation. Now, of those crimes reported, only 4.5% are investigated and of those, only 1.6% taken before a judge (Zepeda Lecuona 2004, 398). However, if a case reaches a judge it is almost sure that the judge will declare the defendant guilty. In Mexico City, the percentage of guilty sentences between 1997 and 2008 is never less than 85%, and in 2007 it was 93% (Magaloni 2010, 19). That is to say, judges validate in almost all cases the work of the prosecutors even though they know the ways in which the prosecutors usually proceed. It was not until 2006 that the Supreme Court in a series of decisions started to consistently uphold the basic criminal due process rights, establishing sensitive limits to prosecutorial, police and military discretion.[16]

In sum, regarding the prosecution of crimes, the subordination of the *Ministerio Público* to the president, coupled with the huge legal powers and discretion that the prosecutors enjoy, produces a system that may be efficient for those in power but definitely not for the ordinary citizens. The chances to challenge or even question the actions of the prosecutors or the police are severely limited. Moreover, compared to criminal systems such as those in Chile or Guatemala, in Mexico the chances for the victim of a crime (or her relatives) to aid in the investigation by themselves or through their lawyers are very limited (Perlin 2006). This situation is supposed to change with the reform of the criminal process, which will be discussed in the next section of the chapter.

RECENT JUDICIAL REFORMS IN MEXICO: A FORTHCOMING RIGHTS REVOLUTION?

Mexico's protracted transition to democracy produced justice institutions that lack accessibility and are efficient for politicians but not for the people. Recent reforms have the potential to considerably expand access to justice for ordinary people. Whether these reforms will have a positive effect will depend, in part, on how the justice system processes the expected surge in legal activity. In the remainder of the chapter, I briefly discuss three recent or ongoing reforms that have the potential to radically transform the Mexican justice system. The first is the reform of the criminal legal process. While this reform will change the inquisitorial process for good, transforming it into an adversarial one, it is important to note that the key institution in charge of the investigation, the *Ministerio Público*, remains untouched. The second and third reforms will be analyzed together: they are the so-called "human rights" reform and the reform of the amparo suit. These two reforms will dramatically open access to justice for ordinary citizens.

Criminal Process Reform

In July 2008, an ambitious constitutional reform to the criminal process was approved. It stipulates that by 2016 all criminal trials in Mexico will be carried out in an adversarial process. The reform affects prosecutors, the police, the judges and the links among them. According to the reform, the new process encompasses four stages: investigation, pretrial stage, oral trial and sentencing. The main actors vary depending on the stage; the police and the prosecutor are the protagonists in the first two and judges will preside over the last two. However, a judge will oversee the performance of the police and the prosecutors during the investigation phase, and judges who are overseen by their superiors in the appellate system will conduct the rest of the stages. In a nutshell, at least in theory, in the new process there will be no unchecked actors who can abuse their discretion. While these oversight mechanisms are good news, especially regarding the prosecutors, the basic incentive structure of the *Ministerio Público* remains untouched: they are still subordinated to the executive.

It should also be pointed out that the reform of the criminal process expands access to the victims so that they (or their relatives) can participate at different points of the process. The reform, in the first place, allows challenging a prosecutorial decision to file a case. But perhaps more importantly, it allows that in certain cases the victims or their relatives can by themselves present their cases before a judge. This will effectively empower the victims, and will also incentivize the prosecutors to have very good reasons to convince the victim not to go to trial. This is an ongoing reform that, as mentioned, will have to be fully implemented by 2016. As of this writing (October 2012), the reform has not made much progress and is actually fully working only in a handful of states, the most important of which is Chihuahua (David Shirk 2011). The experience of Chihuahua shows the impressive amount of efforts (economic, political and social) that are needed to fully activate the new process. So far, however, at least according to some evaluations, the results are encouraging (Zepeda Lecuona 2011).

HUMAN RIGHTS AND AMPARO REFORMS

Between April and July of 2011, yet another couple of important constitutional reforms that directly affect the justice system were approved in Mexico. The first reform transforms the human rights regime in the country. First, it expands the catalogue of actionable rights: the reform introduces in the constitution the term "human rights" instead of "individual guarantees," which is not merely a linguistic change because whereas "individual guarantees" are located in the first 29 articles of the Constitution, "human rights" can be found anywhere in the Constitution or in international treaties. The human rights reform also gives new powers to the National Commission of Human Rights (CNDH). Among the most important are the power to investigate cases of grave violations of human rights[17] and to give the results of investigations to prosecutors; the power of subpoena; the power to call on public security forces; and the capacity to demand detailed explanations from actors that fail to act according to the CNDH's recommendations.

While the reform of human rights is important in itself, its potential was considerably augmented by the simultaneous reform of the amparo suit: the individual instrument of constitutional complaints that is the main legal tool for rights protection in Mexico. This reform, at least in theory, considerably expands the accessibility, scope and applicability of the amparo. Contrary to the old amparo that was accessible only for someone with a "juridical interest" in a case (someone directly affected by a public authority), the new amparo will be accessible for anyone with a "legitimate interest," and it will be useful for filing so-called *acciones colectivas*, which are similar to class actions. Contrary to the old amparo that was only useful for challenging governmental acts allegedly violating one of the "constitutional guarantees" present in the first 29 articles of the Constitution, the new amparo will be useful for challenging government acts that violate any human right recognized by the Constitution or by international treaties. Last but not least, contrary to the old amparo that produced only *inter partes* effects, decisions in at least some new amparo cases will be applicable to greater number of people.

Rights Revolution in the Horizon?

Whether these recent reforms actually produce a rights revolution in the country remains to be seen. On the one hand, some studies have documented a prudent but consistent change since about 2005 in the jurisprudence of the Mexican Supreme Court favoring the protection of, for instance, the right to privacy, some criminal due process rights, and the right to health (e.g., Madrazo and Vela 2011; Pou 2011; Magaloni and Ibarra 2008). Moreover, at least in theoretical terms, the reforms have the potential to produce a surge in rights litigation and a transformation of the judicial landscape: studies on Costa Rica and Colombia (e.g., Wilson and Rodríguez Cordero, 2006) argue that expanding access produces a rights revolution even in countries lacking a strong "support structure" (Epp 1998). Karina Ansolabehere (2009) has found that the Colombian constitutional court is much more active protecting rights than the Mexican Supreme Court, in large part because of ease of access to justice in the former country and the lack thereof in the latter.

However, there are at least three notes for caution. First, the effects of the reforms will depend on how creatively and extensively litigants use the new amparo and how expansively judges interpret the "legitimate interest" standing in these suits. Of course, both the litigants' and the judges' decisions will be shaped by the governmental reactions to the potential judicialization of previously "political" issues. Second, as this chapter has argued, the institutional structure of the judiciary is currently poorly designed to meet an important increase in judicial activity. On the one hand, the Supreme Court concentrates too many jurisdictional and administrative functions, which makes it inefficient. On the other hand, the public prosecutors still work under perverse incentives that favor their loyalty to the executive and not to the citizens and the law. It is unclear to what extent the reforms can have positive effects if this basic institutional architecture remains unchanged. A third note of caution is that the recent reforms can combine in virtuous or vicious ways. If lawyers use creatively the new amparo, the judges welcome the new flow of cases and human rights arguments, and the criminal process reform starts to generate better prosecutorial and police practices, then there will be motives to celebrate. But if, for instance, lawyers creatively use the new amparo, judges welcome the flow of cases and arguments, but the prosecutorial and police practices do not improve, then a "juridical perfect storm" may be on the horizon.[18]

To conclude, let me focus on the third of the challenges. This chapter has argued that one of the sources of the ineffectiveness of the Public Prosecutor's Office, in both its functions of check-and-balance tool and rights protector, in Mexico is the perverse set of incentives created by the institutional architecture of the procuration of justice. The "perfect storm" may well be the outcome if this institutional architecture is not modified. Regarding the Supreme Court, a virtuous combination of the recent reforms to the amparo suit and the human rights regime will have as an effect an important increment in accessibility to justice in Mexico and, as argued in the previous paragraph, an increase in effectiveness in the court's role of rights protector. However, a vicious combination may bring not only ineffectiveness in rights protection but also perhaps an increase in inefficiency regarding the processing of an increasing numbers of cases and petitions. In contrast to climate conditions, for good or for bad, whether a perfect storm or clear skies dominate the horizon in Mexican politics will depend on the decisions of political actors.

NOTES

1. The first direct elections of high court judges in Bolivia took place on October 16, 2011.
2. The so-called political appointment of high court judges (i.e., involving the participation of the executive, the legislative and sometimes other organizations such as the universities or the administrative courts) also serves this function.
3. These are arguably the two main roles for high court judges but certainly not the only ones. For instance, they are also in charge of securing to the greatest extent possible the uniformity of decisions made throughout the judiciary. They thus authoritatively solve the disagreements that occur regarding the interpretation of the laws when courts reach different outcomes in similar cases.
4. Note that to avoid the "jurisprudential confusion" created by expanding access (as Couso warns in his chapter in this volume), high courts should be given discretion to select only some cases to decide (some sort of *certiorari* power) and rules for making jurisprudence sticky should be created (some sort of *stare decisis* doctrine).
5. This is a sketch of an interesting and much more complex story. See the chapters and references in Marván (2010).
6. Especially those *amparos* filed against decisions of local judges, the so-called *amparo directo*. "Amparo" is sometimes translated as *habeas corpus*, but it encompasses more than what this term implies in English. Amparo is more broadly an instrument of individual constitutional complaints.
7. The 1994 reform added to the *amparo* suit an instrument of constitutional review that can be used by any citizen to protect against state violations of individual rights, the so-called action of unconstitutionality and the constitutional controversy. Constitutional controversies involve problems between different levels and branches of government, both vertical and horizontal. Therefore,

any dispute between a state and the federal government or the executive and the legislative, generally with regard to attributions, can be brought before the Supreme Court. State governors, municipal presidents, the three powers of the Union and the three powers of any state can refer constitutional controversies to the Supreme Court (Mexican Constitution, Article 105). Standing in constitutional controversies is thus restricted to public authorities representing the institution whose functions are allegedly encroached. Actions of unconstitutionality are instruments of abstract review that involve cases where there is a contradiction between a general rule or an executive order and the Mexican Constitution. Standing in actions of unconstitutionality in Mexico is also restricted to public authorities (Article 105, Mexican Constitution).

8. The exception is the National Commission of Human Rights, CNDH, but only since 2006.

9. The corporatist logic within the judiciary reached its summit in 1993, when a former Supreme Court judge was convicted on corruption charges in a case in which circuit judges had liberated a defendant charged with the rape and murder of a little girl after their "mentor" on the court asked them to do so in exchange for a sum of money paid by the defendant.

10. There is not much systematic information on the performance of the judicial council. Scattered data published in some analyses and by the council itself suggest that the subordination of the council to the Supreme Court in 1999 had immediate consequences. For instance, regarding the selection and appointment of lower court judges, Fix-Fierro (2003, 288) reports that between 1995 and 1998 the council decided not to ratify nine district and two circuit court judges. Interestingly, in 1999 the council appointed forty new district court judges, 90% of which were clerks of Supreme Court Judges (González Compeán and Bauer 2002, 235). In contrast, there seems to be no noticeable change regarding the sanctioning and destitution of lower court judges. On the one hand, between 1995 and 1998 only two judges were fired (Fix-Fierro 2003, 235). On the other hand, data from the council show that the number of judges sanctioned (sanctions go from a private warning to destitution) has been declining dramatically and that the number of judges fired goes from a low 8 in 2003 (there is no data prior to 2003 in the webpage of the council) to a super low 2 in 2008. It is not clear what explains the decline in sanctions of judges, but one hypothesis is that the subordination of the council to the Supreme Court produces more leniencies as it used to be the case before 1994.

11. The "support structure" refers to the existence of a network of lawyers, NGOs and individuals who either litigate or contribute to finance litigation in favor of rights (Epp 1998, 2–3).

12. This reform will be further discussed in the second section of this chapter. The institutions in charge of securing public safety (e.g. the police, the secretary of public security, the investigative police) have also undergone important transformations (Bergman 2007). Many of these reforms are still in implementation phase at the time of this writing.

13. Since 1994 the executive choice of *Procurador General* has to be approved by the Senate, but the president still freely removes her.

14. Interestingly, different Latin American countries claim the original authorship of this popular saying. In Mexico, there is debate as to whether the author was Benito Juárez or Porfirio Díaz. But Brazilians claim authorship by Getulio Vargas, Argentineans by Juan Domingo Perón and Peruvians by Oscar Benavides. And very probably this is only a partial list.

15. Tesis de Jurisprudencia. Semanario Judicial de la Federación. Amparos Directos 151/90 y 251/90. Primera Sala, Octava Época, tomos VII-Enero y X-Septiembre, pp. 193 y 248.

16. For instance, in a series of cases the Court has ruled that prosecutorial accusations based on hearsay, illegally obtained evidence and other questionable practices are simply not allowed and thus insufficient for convicting the suspects. In a 2011 decision the Court decided to limit the scope of the military jurisdiction, complying in this way with a ruling against the Mexican State by the Interamerican Court of Human Rights.
17. This "faculty of investigation" used to be part of the Supreme Court functions.
18. Mexican Supreme Court Justice José Ramón Cossío has warned about this possibility. See *El Universal*, July 13, 2011: http://www.eluniversal.com.mx/editoriales/53725.html.

7 The Role of Chile's Constitutional Court in the Consolidation of Democracy (1990–2011)

Javier Couso

THE TENSION BETWEEN "EFFECTIVENESS" AND "REPRESENTATIVENESS" IN THE JUDICIAL DOMAIN

The relationship between the ideals of representativeness and effectiveness of political institutions has long been a concern for political theorists,[1] particularly since democracy became "the only game in town" (Linz and Stepan 1996). Indeed, we typically expect democracies to have institutions that are both representative of the people they serve as well as effective in the delivery of the public goods they are supposed to provide. There are, however, instances in which there might be a trade-off between democratic representativeness and effectiveness. This is, I submit, the case with judicial institutions, where representation often translates into lack of impartiality (Peabody 2011). Therefore, while we expect most of the institutions of modern democratic regimes to be *both* representative *and* effective, in the case of judicial institutions we should accept to sacrifice a degree of representativeness in order to get effective courts—that is, ones that deliver timely decisions adopted in accordance with the Constitution and the law. Indeed, recent history suggests that, in the case of the judiciary, effectiveness is negatively correlated with representativeness (Burbank and Friedman 2002). In other words, the more "representative" a court is—that is, the more responsive to the preferences of the people—the more likely it will be to abandon its crucial role as an impartial adjudicator of previously settled legislation in the case at hand.

The negative correlation between effectiveness and representativeness in the domain of judicial institutions is particularly evident in criminal law cases, where public outcry in the face of heinous crimes often clashes with the due-process guarantees of the alleged perpetrators. Thus, an "effective" judge will on occasion set free someone who she thinks may have indeed perpetrated the crime, but whose due-process rights were violated by the police at the investigation stage (for example, in the evidence-gathering process), even if this decision makes the majority of the population feel outraged by it (here the powerful image of a sheriff in the Wild West protecting an accused man from a mob that wants to lynch him comes immediately to mind).

Of course, criminal law is the realm in which the clash between effectiveness and representativeness in the judicial domain is more pronounced. But, even in constitutional adjudication, Supreme or Constitutional Courts will on occasion have to make "effective" decisions that are nonetheless "nonrepresentative" (i.e., unpopular). The reason for this is that the very legitimacy of judicial institutions (including that of the Supreme Court or constitutional courts) lies in that they are supposed to adjudicate preexisting rules and principles that they had no part in elaborating.[2] To put it in other words, precisely because judges are not elected by the people—but instead designated in view of their expertise in the legal field—their legitimacy ultimately depends on being seen as "applying" constitutional values and rules elaborated by the representative bodies, instead of judicially "creating" new legislation through their decisions. Indeed, in a democratic regime it is extremely hard to justify the introduction of legislation by unelected officials, even when it is done under the disguise of merely adjudicating preexisting law.

The previous reflections, of course, assume that judges are not elected by the people. And although it is true that there are experiences of elected justices in some states of the United States and, more recently, in the case of Bolivia, those experiences are rare and have been generally disappointing in terms of their "effectiveness" (Case 1992–1993; Laserna 2010).

THE PARALLEL TENSION BETWEEN DEMOCRACY AND CONSTITUTIONALISM IN LATIN AMERICA

The tension between representativeness and effectiveness in the judicial domain is particularly relevant in the transitional democracies of Latin America, where many countries are still dealing with issues of state-formation and where the values associated with the rule of law and constitutionalism are still weak (Shor 2006; Loveman 1993). Indeed, the lack of a "culture of legality" in many states of the region on occasion allows populist political leaders to openly attack the courts for issuing judicial decisions they disagree with, but which are consistent with the Constitution and the laws of the country. These attacks often end with the intervention by the representative branches—in particular, the executive branch—in the judiciary, which in turn destroys any meaningful understanding of an "effective" judicial institution. This suggests that the clash between "effectiveness" and "representativeness" in the judicial domain noted above is particularly acute in Latin America.

To sum up this point, without a general consensus within society of the need to have judicial institutions that are both independent from the government and loyal to the Constitution and the laws, there is little hope of attaining what O'Donnell calls "horizontal accountability,"[3] that is, the mutual control of the different branches of government, something that is indeed a crucial factor in the sustainability of democratic rule.

A related issue is that of the irregular fate that constitutionalism—that is, the notion of limited government—has experienced in the region (Adelman and Centeno 2002). Indeed, if we take into account that constitutionalism per se has a complex relationship with democratic self-rule, it is all the more so in Latin America, where democracy *preceded* constitutionalism. Let me explain this point further.

As it is well known, in the expression "constitutional democracy" the first element constrains the second one. Indeed, Constitutions—although crucial for "constituting" democracy—are centrally about limiting government, even democratic self-government. The fact that the latter is an accepted feature of consolidated democracies has to do with the historical sequence that took place there. Indeed, in those countries the limits on government imposed by constitutionalism and the rule of law *preceded* the rise of democracy. Given this sequence, the whole "point" of constitutionalism was originally to limit a power that was, after all, imposed on the people (the monarchy), not to limit democratic rule. In such a context, constitutionalism worked for the people, not against them. When those constitutional monarchies gradually became democratic regimes, the people had grown accustomed to accepting that any form of government—even a democratic one—should be limited by the values of constitutionalism and the rule of law.

The problem in Latin America is that the sequence has generally been the reverse of that experienced by consolidated democracies. Indeed, because in most of Latin America constitutionalism and the rule of law were traditionally weak, democracy—at least electoral democracy—was achieved *before* constitutionalism had taken hold, something that makes the latter appear as an illegitimate constraint on democratic self-rule. This is particularly the case with constitutional adjudication, which by its own nature implies the nullification of democratically enacted law by nonelected judges.

If, as it is the case in Latin America, there is no strong tradition of constitutionalism (understood as the general acceptance of the virtues of limited government), it becomes difficult to justify to the people that the outcome of democracy should be sacrificed on the altar of constitutionalism by a few unelected officials. In other words, when constitutionalism first appeared in the Western world—almost 300 years ago—it could be regarded as a mechanism protecting the people from governments imposed upon it, but nowadays, when democratic self-rule is considered the only legitimate form of government, constitutionalism and the rule of law may appear to work against the people (or, at least, against the majority of them).

Of course, all of the above assumes that the democratic regime is working properly, transmitting the preferences of the majority of the people in a reasonably accurate way, but the case still remains that if a society has not internalized the relevance of constitutionalism and the rule of law, the danger of a populist leader inciting intervention of the judiciary in cases of unpopular judicial decisions would be rather high.

After this general reflection on the tensions inherent to the relationship between representativeness and effectiveness in the judicial domain, and the related issue of the historically troubling relationship between democracy and constitutionalism in Latin America, I turn my attention to the role that the Chilean constitutional court played in Chile's democratic recovery.

THE CONSTITUTIONAL COURT OF CHILE

Chile is generally considered to have experienced one of the most successful transitions to democracy in Latin America (Haggard and Kaufman 1997). In fact, in the last two decades since the end of General Pinochet's authoritarian regime (1973–1990), the country has seen the gradual consolidation of its democratic regime, accompanied by sustained economic growth, respect for the rule of law and a low degree of corruption.

As in many countries that started their democratic transitions in the 1990s, Chile has had a constitutional court during its own transition,[4] so the question arises as to what was the contribution of this institution to this country's return to democracy. But here we confront a rather peculiar situation, because, contrary to many Latin American states, which expanded constitutional adjudication to help processes of democratization (such as Brazil and Mexico), in Chile the authoritarian government itself established a system of constitutional adjudication with the goal of protecting the military regime's political and economic design from the perceived threat posed to it by the incoming democratic regime. This makes the question about the role that this institution played in Chile's democratic transition all the more interesting. Before analyzing the latter, however, I will provide a brief account of Chile's Constitutional Court.

The court is regulated by Chapter VIII of the Constitution of 1980. It has 10 members, who serve in it for nine years and who cannot be reappointed. Three are designated by the head of the executive branch; two by the Senate; and two by the Chamber of Deputies, with the agreement of the Senate. The last three are appointed by the Supreme Court. In order to be considered as a candidate, a person should be a lawyer with at least 15 years in the profession. Members of the court cannot be removed, but have to leave it when they reach 75 years of age.[5] The court works either *en banc* or divided in two panels, but the most important decisions are always decided *en banc*.

The court has strong powers of judicial review of existing laws, law-projects and administrative acts, making it a politically important body. Its powers include: (1) the mandatory review of the constitutionality of laws that interpret the Constitution and the so-called "organic constitutional laws" (which require four-sevenths of the existing members of Congress for their approval, repeal or amendment); (2) the review of the constitutionality of bills being discussed in Congress when so requested by the president of the Republic, the Senate, the Chamber of Deputies or at least a quarter of the senators or deputies; (3) the review of the constitutionality of a constitutional reform or an international treaty under discussion, when the president of the Republic, the Senate, the Chamber of Deputies or at least a quarter of the senators or deputies request it; (4) the declaration of the "nonapplicability" of an otherwise valid statute whose application to a specific case originates an unconstitutional result[6]; and (5) the declaration the unconstitutionality of laws that have been previously declared nonapplicable.

The rulings of the constitutional court cannot be appealed, and the norms that it declares unconstitutional cannot become law in the case of the control of the constitutionality of a law-bill approved by Congress. In the case of an existing law that is declared unconstitutional, it will be expelled from the legal system by the publication of the decision, without retroactive effect. Finally, in the case of an administrative act that is found to be unconstitutional, it will cease to have any legal effect by the decision of the constitutional court alone.

THE ROLE OF THE CONSTITUTIONAL COURT IN CHILE'S DEMOCRATIC RECOVERY

As we saw in the previous section, Chile's constitutional court was introduced in 1980 by the military regime with the purpose of protecting the authoritarian political and economic design from being dismantled by the democratic regime when it eventually returned. However, in what represented a complete surprise for the framers of the Constitution of 1980, the very constitutional court that was meant to protect the military regime's political and economic architecture eventually paved the way to its end, through a landmark decision that deserves to be described in some detail. The decision was issued in 1985,[7] and involved a law-project regulating the plebiscite set to take place in 1988 to confirm (or not) the person designated by the military junta to be the president of the Republic until 1997 (who was widely expected to be General Pinochet). The bill was automatically reviewed by the constitutional court because it regulated one of the matters the Constitution of 1980 declared to be of an "organic" nature, which are always subject to the control of their constitutionality.

The law-project under scrutiny included a transitory clause prescribing that the electoral court would only start to function "*at the date of the first election of deputies and senators*,"[8] that is, after the 1988 plebiscite (since the first such election was set to take place in December of 1989). The relevance of this law project was that it effectively meant that the crucial plebiscite scheduled for October of 1988 would be held without an electoral court in place. Conscious of the importance of the bill that the constitutional court had to review, and aware of the increasingly independent mind of one of the leading members of the Court, Eugenio Valenzuela,[9] the military government decided to have the law-project sent to the court when he was on a trip overseas.[10] Alerted by a fellow member of the tribunal, Julio Philippi,[11] of the bill sent by the junta, Valenzuela immediately returned to Chile, just in time to participate in the court's discussion of the constitutionality of the project. Heavily influenced by Valenzuela's leadership,[12] the constitutional court ultimately declared in a divided (4–3) vote that the electoral law-project under review was unconstitutional, thus forcing the government to have a clean plebiscite in 1988.

It is hard to overestimate the relevance of this ruling. Indeed, a leading analyst of Pinochet's regime, Carlos Huneeus, claims that the day of that judicial decision the general effectively lost his chance to continue in power until 1997 (Huneeus 2006). The reason for this blunt assessment is that there is every reason to believe that, had Pinochet been able to do so, he would have repeated the electoral fraud that took place in the previous plebiscite, which introduced the Constitution of 1980.[13]

Interviewed by the author, Eugenio Valenzuela explained that what he did was simply to follow a legal and constitutional tradition he was proud of. Recognizing that he had been a supporter of the military coup and the economic policies of the Pinochet regime, he said he thought it would be unacceptable to be part of a legal maneuver to ensure General Pinochet's election for yet another eight years. A few years later, in early 1990, Justice Valenzuela's independence and assertiveness in this decisive case led to retaliation. In one of his last acts as president of the Republic, Pinochet removed Valenzuela from the court, replacing him with a far less prestigious jurist, who was nonetheless considered by the general to be more loyal to the military. For all its ulterior political relevance, constitutional court's Decision no. 33 (and a few others, also connected with the regulation of the 1988 plebiscite)[14] was not the norm in the otherwise large jurisprudence concerning "organic" legislation issued by the constitutional court between 1981 and 1990. Indeed, the electoral decision just mentioned was rather exceptional, not merely under the authoritarian rule, but more importantly, also in the transitional period, which started in 1990. Indeed, during the first decade and a half from the beginning of the transition to democracy, the constitutional court took a rather deferential stance toward the government and Congress, as I have documented elsewhere (Couso 2005), thus playing no role in furthering democracy.

THE 2005 AMENDMENT AND THE NEW ROLE OF CHILE'S CONSTITUTIONAL COURT

After 15 years of passivity, a constitutional reform aimed at eliminating the last "authoritarian enclaves" of the 1980 charter (in 2005, when Chile's transition was widely regarded as having been completed), would dramatically change the status quo of the constitutional court, thanks to the changes it introduced in the composition and powers of the latter.

These reforms were incorporated by a small group of jurists advising the different political parties, and their significance went largely unnoticed by the political elites, particularly the very congressmen who voted in favor of them, whose gaze was set on the other important amendments introduced by the 2005 constitutional reform, such as the end of unelected senators and the introduction of a clause giving the president of the Republic the power to remove the commanders in chief of the armed forces (Fuentes 2011; Couso and Coddou 2010).

The key reforms introduced to the constitutional court were the elimination of judges from the Supreme Court from its membership (and their replacement by politicians and constitutional scholars), and the transfer from the Supreme Court to the constitutional court of the "writ of nonapplicability," a procedural change that opened the door of the constitutional court to ordinary people and lower court judges (this last reform increased in a dramatic way access to the court, and represents—as stated in the Introduction to this volume—a key element of representation).

With regard to the first reform, it should be noted that, until the 2005 amendment, almost half of the members of the constitutional court (three out of seven justices) were acting members of the Supreme Court, who split their time between the two courts. These judges were deeply embedded in the traditional culture of the "regular" judiciary, one prone to deference to the elected branches and avoidance of political conflict (Hilbink 2007; Peña 1994). Given this context, the elimination of justices from the regular judiciary and their replacement with academics and former politicians represented a major factor in the new, more activist attitudes displayed in the constitutional court's jurisprudence since 2006 (Couso and Hilbink 2011).

The second crucial reform to the constitutional court, the transfer of the writ of nonapplicability to it, meant that for the first time in the court's history it could decide actual cases and controversies brought about by regular people, not just political elites. The importance of this element of the constitutional reform cannot be underestimated. First, it produced a dramatic increase in the caseload of the constitutional court.[15] Moreover, the transfer of the writ of nonapplicability to the constitutional court encouraged a more activist stance on the part of these full-time justices because it opened the court to "popular actions,"—that is, suits brought by ordinary people—while before it had been open only to elites (the president of the Republic, Parliament, the comptroller general). This helped make the court much more visible to the population because of the drama normally associated with actual cases as opposed to the abstract review of legislative proposals. Furthermore, thanks to this writ, the constitutional court can now exercise judicial power and influence policy-making without having to constantly confront the government in a direct fashion because the cases would typically involve two private parties. That said, the post-2005 constitutional court has also been more likely to directly confront the government in its preventive (or a priori) jurisdiction.

It should be noted that the transfer of the writ of inapplicability from the Supreme Court to the constitutional court and the change in standing rules also opened up new opportunities for ordinary judges at any level to challenge the constitutionality of a law that pertains to a case before them. Whereas in the past only parties to the case (or the Supreme Court *de oficio*) could file a writ of nonapplicability, now any judge from the regular judiciary who thinks a law she must apply is unconstitutional can send such a claim directly to the constitutional court, whose membership no longer includes any of her superiors from the Supreme Court. This new ability of lower court judges to circumvent the Supreme Court and appeal to an external body (and one which is actually above the Supreme Court when it comes to constitutional interpretation) means that a lonely judge at the bottom of the regular judicial hierarchy can now (in theory) play a crucial role in getting a law declared unconstitutional without needing to persuade her superiors in the Supreme Court.

CONCLUSION

In this chapter, I first analyzed the tension that exists between representativeness and effectiveness in the judicial domain, arguing that a well-functioning judiciary would necessarily be "unrepresentative" in certain ways, due to the very role that is assigned to it in a constitutional democracy, in particular to protect the fundamental rights of individuals and minorities in an impartial fashion. Furthermore, we saw how the above-mentioned tension is reproduced in the relationship of constitutionalism and democratic rule, something that is particularly acute in Latin America, where electoral democracy preceded constitutionalism and the culture of legality, both key elements to establish the legitimacy necessary to resist attacks from populist leaders fighting judicial decisions they do not like. Finally, the chapter explored the way these issues unfolded in the case of Chile's constitutional court and its contribution to the democratic recovery of the country, concluding that after a stunning decision by a court still operating under the military regime (which actually opened the door to the transitional period), the constitutional court did little to further the democratic regime, taking instead a passive role that only ended when democracy was already consolidated (in 2005) and due to factors that have little to do with the transitional logic.

Due to the changes described in the last section of the chapter, Chile's constitutional court is now a key player in the country's policy-making process, and therefore an important political actor. In this new role, it sometimes gets the support of the population or, on the contrary, receives strong criticisms, but so far it seems to have won enough legitimacy to act independently of both the government and powerful private actors. Given this context, it seems likely that it will manage to continue making a difference in Chile's politics for many years to come. The question that remains unanswered, however, is if in the future the court will serve as an effective mechanism of governance or rather one that complicates policy-making unnecessarily, given that in recent years its activism has been accompanied by jurisprudential confusion and contradictions that have produced complex problems that have been severely criticized within the legal academia (Marshall 2011).

At any rate, the reforms introduced to the constitutional court in 2005 can be said to have increased its representativeness, giving broader sectors of the citizenry recourse to constitutional adjudication and thus to the protection of their constitutional rights. Also, to the degree that a stronger constitutional court contributes to the consolidation of democracy in Chile, one can say that it has helped this regime to be more representative. Having said this, the drawbacks of an activist (but confused) constitutional court highlighted above suggest that effectiveness may be an unintended casualty of the transformations analyzed in this chapter. This might be another way in which representativeness and effectiveness are inversely related in the judicial domain.

NOTES

1. In effect, the tension between representativeness and effectiveness can be traced all the way back to Plato's well-known defense of elitism in his *The Republic* (360 B.C.) (See Plato 2003.)
2. Habermas's distinction between *"discourses of application"* (which, he argues, are what constitutional judges should utilize when engaging in constitutional adjudication) and *"discourses of justification"* (which he says ought to be utilized by legislative assemblies when defending the fairness or convenience of bills) is on point here. See Habermas (1994).
3. See O'Donnell (1999).
4. The intellectual sources of the constitutional court were varied. It was inspired by a mixture of Spain's constitutional court of 1978, Germany's constitutional court of 1940 and France's *conseil constitutionnel* of 1958. Even though it was charged with abstract and a priori constitutional review, as opposed to the first constitutional court, it included a mandatory review of the so-called "organic laws" (*Leyes Orgánicas Constitutionales*), as well as the constitutional review of executive decrees. See Couso (2003).
5. See article 92 of Chile's Constitution.
6. The nonapplicability due to unconstitutionality, known in Spanish as *recurso de inaplicabilidad por inconstitucionalidad*, is a legal mechanism at the disposal of any individual who wants to challenge a piece of legislation whose application to a particular case has an "unconstitutional result" due to the way it was applied. While under the Constitution of 1925 and during the first 25 years of the Constitution of 1980, the writ of nonapplicability had to be filed before the Supreme Court. It was transferred to the constitutional court with the constitutional amendment of 2005.
7. Decision no. 33, September 24, 1985.
8. The clause was Article 11, a transitory article of the 1980 Constitution.
9. Valenzuela was a prestigious jurist who had been an attorney in one of Chile's most important public legal agencies, the *Consejo de Defensa del Estado*.
10. Interview with Eugenio Valenzuela, former justice of Chile's constitutional court (July 6, 1999, in Santiago, Chile).

11. Phillippi was a widely respected international law scholar who had gained enormous prestige for his contribution to Chile's negotiations and international litigation concerning its border disputes with Argentina.

12. The decision emphasized that the electoral law meant to regulate the plebiscite of 1988 was in stark contradiction with Chile's centuries-old tradition of having "clean" electoral rules, something which had been a source of national pride in a region characterized by widespread electoral fraud.

13. Robert Barros, commenting on this decision by the constitutional court, wrote:

> Undoubtedly, the Courts' 24 September 1985 ruling on the organic constitutional law regulating the Tribunal Calificador de Elecciones (TRICEL), the special electoral court, was the most consequential. The court struck as unconstitutional a transitory article that left oversight of the presidential plebiscite to an ad hoc electoral court and ruled not only that this plebiscite had to be supervised by the TRICEL but that the full electoral system specified in the main body of the text had to be in place for the plebiscite. This meant that the plebiscite would be constitutional only if it took place with electoral registries and independent oversight and counting. Like all of the court's rulings, this decision was final and not subject to appeal. (Barros 2002, 27)

14. Barros mentions Decision no. 38, of October 1, 1986, on an organic law regulating voter registration and the Electoral Service; Decision no.43, of March 23, 1987, regulating political parties law; and Decision no. 53, April 13, 1988, on the organic constitutional law on popular votes and counts. This set of laws did all involve matters with impact on the plebiscite scheduled for October 1988, and in most cases the court's rulings contributed to making that election fairer. Of all such rulings, Barros highlights the crucial importance of the one granting both sides in the plebiscite equal, free time on television and paid access to the print media and radio (see Barros 2002, 28).

15. Whereas before the reform, the court issued 30 to 35 decisions per year (all of them abstract review), during the period 2006–2011 that number increased tenfold, averaging nearly 300 decisions per year, most of these in inapplicability (concrete) cases. One important consequence of this change is that the court is now a full-time job for its members, whereas until 2005 most of the judges worked part-time.

8 Courting from the Left

Judicial Effectiveness and Representativeness in the Brazilian State of Acre

Matthew C. Ingram

Judicial strength is crucial for democracy and development. Effective judicial institutions—accessible, efficient and independent—enhance the ability of ordinary citizens to vindicate their rights and liberties, leading to the fuller enjoyment of civil rights, or what scholars have called the "civil dimension" of democratic citizenship (Marshall 1965; O'Donnell 1993; UNDP 2004). Regarding economic development, effective courts facilitate the enforcement of contract and property rights, improving economic transactions (Kaufman, Kraay and Zoido-Lobatón 1999; Cross 2002). Further, effective courts are also representative to the extent that they perform these functions well for broad sectors of society, not just for political or economic elites or dominant majorities. In short, strong courts are vital for both democracy and markets, so understanding the sources of judicial strength—understood here as effectiveness and representativeness—is a vital concern for scholars and policymakers alike.

This chapter makes two principal claims regarding the study of court strength: one conceptual and one causal. Drawing on a central theme in this volume, I frame judicial strength in terms of effectiveness and representativeness. Much of the literature discusses court strength in terms of various aspects of judicial performance, and the concept of effectiveness resonates easily with discussions of functional institutions, so I anticipate readers will readily accept a discussion of effectiveness with regard to court strength. But representativeness is more controversial, appearing at first glance to be anathema to common conceptions of judicial strength. In a common formulation, courts are not supposed to be venues of popular opinion or majoritarianism; quite the opposite, courts are supposed to act as a check or brake on majoritarian politics—to be counter-majoritarian. However, I argue that a closer look at underexplored aspects of both effectiveness and representativeness with regard to the judiciary, particularly in light of broader debates on the relationship between democracy and the rule of law, yields two insights relevant to core themes of this volume. First, *contra* Rios and Couso in this volume, effectiveness and representatives can be understood as not inherently in tension with each other—that is, this is not a zero-sum game. A balance or even synergy between the two is possible; indeed, from a normative perspective, this balance is desirable. Second, the reconstructed concept of representativeness is consonant with a broader understanding of court functions (and thus, with what "effectiveness" means beyond a formal functional analysis), and that attention to a broader, macro-level notion of effectiveness can benefit the comparative study of judicial institutions in democratic societies.

Second, I focus on the explanatory role of ideas in building strong courts. Existing research tends to emphasize the material, cost-benefit calculus of judicial reform. That is, politicians do not build stronger, more effective judicial institutions because they have strong moral or ethical commitments to do so; rather, they do so mainly if it is in their rational interest. Contrasting starkly with the normative democracy- or development-oriented reasons for wanting good, functional courts, this dominant view in current literature posits that strong courts are the result of politicians' narrowly self-interested behavior. Stated otherwise, politicians do not craft stronger courts because it is the right thing to do; they do so because it is the safe or expedient thing to do. A prominent account in this tradition is that electoral competition in democracies generates uncertainty for politicians, who in turn create effective, democratic courts in order to protect themselves once out of office (Ramseyer 1994; Magalhães 1998; Ginsburg 2003; Finkel 2008).

While this literature has greatly increased our understanding of institutional change, two shortcomings remain. First, electoral openings and rational incentives for reform frequently appear long before institutional change takes place, so these accounts do not explain differences in the *sequence* and *timing* of reform. Second, rationalist accounts based on electoral openings do not anticipate the precise *shape* or *content* of reforms. Drawing on recent scholarship that pays greater attention to the role of ideas in shaping reform (Hilbink 2007a, 2007b, 2008, 2009; Woods 2008; Rodriguez-Garavito 2011; Ingram 2012), I offer an account of key reform episodes in the Brazilian state of Acre—including timing and content—based primarily on nonmaterial, ideational motivations. I argue that crucial instances of reform cannot be understood without serious attention to ideas.

The chapter is organized as follows. First, I clarify the concepts of judicial effectiveness and representativeness. Second, I present the theoretical argument regarding the causal role of ideas, followed by a discussion of methods and case selection. The main analysis then focuses on reform dynamics in the crucial case of Acre. Looking ahead, I find that (1) representativeness is not necessarily always in tension with effectiveness, and can sit comfortably alongside effectiveness in our understanding of court strength; and (2) progressive, left-leaning ideas exert a meaningful influence on crucial episodes of institutional change, especially in enhancing representativeness.

CONCEPTUAL CLARIFICATION: EFFECTIVENESS AND REPRESENTATIVENESS IN THE JUDICIARY

Conceptual difficulties abound in the study of judicial strength. Existing research in public law highlights these difficulties, wrestling with the concepts of accessibility, efficiency, independence, power, authority, assertiveness and accountability (e.g., Kapiszewski and Taylor 2008; Helmke and Rosenbluth 2009; Rios-Figueroa and Staton 2010; Helmke and Rios-Figueroa 2010; Brinks 2012), as well as compliance, enforcement and even the substantive societal impact after a judicial process has concluded (e.g., Rosenberg 1991; Frymer 2003; Staton and Romero 2011; Kapiszewski and Taylor 2012).

Acknowledging this conceptual complexity, I reconcile the concepts of effectiveness and representativeness in four steps by (1) building on the debate on majoritarianism versus counter-majoritarianism; (2) distinguishing between majoritarianism and representativeness; (3) drawing on notions of "substantive rule of law" from debates on the relationship between democracy and rule of law, debates that ask us to consider *for whom* courts must be effective; and (4) distinguishing between micro- and macro-level effectiveness. Taken together, these steps help conceptualize judicial strength in a way that accommodates both effectiveness and representativeness.

Countermajoritarianism and Representativeness

Effectiveness has a relatively straightforward, conventional application to the study of courts. Effective courts are those that perform their societal function of dispute resolution well. To be sure, dispute resolution breaks down into the multiple moving parts noted previously, including the ability to be heard in adjudicatory fora (access), the timeliness of decisions (efficiency), and the impartiality of decisions themselves (independence). Conceptually, effectiveness is complex and has many faces, but is not controversial.

Conversely, representativeness is, at first glance, conceptually much simpler but more controversial when applied to the judiciary. Conventionally, representativeness captures the idea that a court and its decisions should be congruent with or "look like" society. In a literal sense, the composition of courts should reflect the composition of society. More figuratively, courts and their decisions should reflect popular will, which quickly translates as majority will. The controversy hinges on the fact that, while representative institutions may be more democratic, we may not want particular institutions—namely, courts—to reflect majoritarian impulses, since checks and balances may be compromised and minority rights may then be vulnerable to an unconstrained majority. A rigid form of separation of powers justifies the normative preference for a nonrepresentative judiciary. By exploring additional dimensions of the concept of representativeness—that is, by making it more complex—I argue it becomes less controversial when applied to the judiciary, and yields insights regarding the broader concept of judicial strength in comparative perspective.

The conventional account outlined briefly previously is that in a democracy, of the three branches of government, the judiciary is the only nonpolitical branch. The executive and legislative branches are populated by elected officers, translating popular will to these branches. The democratic legitimacy of these institutions rests on their ability to aggregate popular will from constituencies—on their ability to express majoritarian preferences. Thus, if democracy is government by the people, then these majoritarian institutions have the most democratic legitimacy. Courts are not only *not* supposed to be majoritarian from a normative perspective in democratic theory, but they are also generally understood not to be majoritarian in practice. Normatively, courts are the place where respected legal minds referee the proper application of laws and guard against the creation of laws and other forms of state action that, though popular and supported by the majority, offend core democratic principles. Courts protect minoritarian rights from the "tyranny of the majority" and serve as a nonpolitical check on the political branches. Practically, judges are generally appointed, not elected, and thus at least one step removed from the sovereign to which elected officials are accountable. Thus, in a classic and widely accepted formulation in studies of democratic constitutionalism, courts are deliberately designed to be *un*representative (see Vallinder 1995, citing de Tocqueville 1969; Mill 1859; Stone Sweet 2000; Murphy 2007, 1–19). Indeed, this very unrepresentativeness is the source of a criticism in the last 50 years of constitutional courts and judicial review as countermajoritarian and therefore undemocratic institutions (e.g., Bickel 1962).

Yet this conceptualization of representativeness is limited and therefore limiting. Representativeness is not anathema to concepts of judicial strength for at least two reasons related to the countermajoritarianism debate. First, in practice, judges and judicial behavior are more representative of majoritarian interests than is frequently assumed. Judges are not apolitical technocrats who appear spontaneously on the bench. Rather, judges come from elite social ranks that are frequently aligned with dominant classes and must be vetted by majoritarian stakeholders (see Rios, this volume). Further, they are selected by political leaders, and their successful appointment frequently depends on negotiations among dominant political majorities. In short, "[a]n institution that routinely promotes presidential ambitions is no more countermajoritarian than the presidency" (Graber 2008, 367; see also Greenwood 2001). Juries, constitutional juries and civic constitutional fora (Zurn 2011) further undercut claims that courts are countermajoritarian. Lastly, some judges are even elected, demonstrating little difference with their executive and legislative counterparts, though the idea of judicial elections is nearly sacrilegious in the civil law world. Still, even in some prominent civil law countries, such as Portugal and Spain, the political connections of judicial officers are patent, not latent. Indeed, transparency regarding the political affiliations of judges, even at the highest level, is understood to lend democratic legitimacy to the courts in countries with traditions of parliamentary supremacy and Kelsenian model of constitutional review (e.g., Amaral et al. 2009; Fabrinni 2008). To some extent, separation of powers and popular sovereignty are in tension with each other, and at least some constitutional designs resolve this tension strongly in favor of popular sovereignty, making the composition of their constitutional courts representative in a very literal sense. Similarly, judicial behavior in a wide variety of systems frequently follows majority opinion. As noted by Graber (364), "[w]hat courts hardly ever do is protect powerless minorities that have no champions among the power-holding majority." Thus, the composition and behavior of the judiciary is not uniformly subject to criticism of democratic deficits due to unrepresentativeness.

Second, judicial review of legislative or executive action is countermajoritarian only in an idealized form and infrequently in practice, so Bickel's criticism is formalistic, or true only in an ideal sense (Graber 2008). Where courts rule against state action conducted by the popularly elected branches, but the underlying state action was not in the interest of the majority, then courts are the de facto protectors of majoritarian concerns. Where courts are making decisions but these decisions cannot be classified as judicial review—as in most cases of ordinary litigation—then the countermajoritarian difficulty does not even come into play. Following Graber (2008), Bickel's notion of courts as countermajoritarian is difficult to reconcile with democratic theory only if we restrict our understanding of judicial functions to a very formal and ideal dimension. The "countermajoritarian difficulty" is not really difficult at all if we consider the broader range of roles that judges and courts perform in democratic societies, including the mostly nonconstitutional adjudication that occurs in state courts in large federal systems like Brazil.

Majoritarianism versus Representativeness

From a normative perspective, perhaps we should want judges and courts to be not majoritarian, but representative. That is, even if we accept arguments about countermajoritarianism, representativeness is consistent with countermajoritarianism. An analogy to electoral rules and the general principle of proportionality clarifies the difference. In designing electoral laws, majoritarianism stands for the idea that the will of *most* people—be it a plurality, simple majority, or super majority—should be followed (e.g., Lijphart 1999). The starkest example of this is the winner-take-all nature of single-member-district-plurality (SMDP) elections, where one person wins in a zero-sum contest based only on the fact that they received more votes than anyone else, even if their total is less than a majority of registered voters, and even less than a majority of the voting age population. Majoritarian electoral systems are simple, clear and efficient, but this efficiency in electoral processes comes at a cost in representativeness, a cost that can be countered with different electoral rules, for example, varieties of proportional representation, or PR (e.g., Rae 1967; Lijphart 1999; Shugart and Carey 1992). Generally, PR systems maximize representativeness by making the composition of legislative bodies proportional to the range of views expressed in the population. Thus, even if minority views are not expressed in the final policy, all views are represented, or have a voice, in the process of translating votes to seat shares in a legislative body, something that occurs less frequently in majoritarian systems.

Analogizing these trade-offs to courts, we may have normative reasons to want courts to be not majoritarian but representative. That is, in the substance of a judge's work, it is normatively clear that courts should not simply echo the preferences of popular majorities. However, perhaps the decision making of courts should reflect all views in a society, balancing as full a range of principles and values as possible, of which the majoritarian position on a particular question is but one factor to be considered, and arriving at a reasoned conclusion based on what the law says, what would be agreeable to most people, what would benefit most, and what norms of justice and equity demand, all without sacrificing any fundamental democratic values or principles. Starkly put, we may want courts to be *more representative than elected bodies.*

The general principle of proportionality supports this proposition. Notions of fairness and equity inhere in proportionality. For instance, judges frequently assess the share of responsibility among parties to a dispute, weigh the severity of a punishment against the seriousness of an offense, or engage in any number of balancing analyses. Even in evaluating the resources available to litigants (in civil disputes) or between the state and the criminally accused (in criminal cases), judges evaluate the "equality of arms"—the extent to which the power distribution among parties is equitable, intervening when necessary so that it is not might that makes one right, but rightfulness itself. Thus, no matter what the electoral rules by which political offices were filled—majoritarian or proportional—courts in democratic societies must seek to level the legal playing field; that is, they must have a "PR mindset." Stated otherwise, courts seek to abide by principles of justice and equity, not just formal legality. Courts are not majoritarian or countermajoritarian, but broadly representative. Where laws may be perfectly proper from a procedural standpoint and may also not violate any substantive constitutional principles, we may want courts to be fully representative of society's interests, not elite, plurality or majority interests. In this regard, courts should be protective of democratic values and human rights beyond those ensconced in laws and Constitutions. Reflecting a tension any law student is faced with in the first term of study, we may want courts to represent not just what is legal, but also what is just, fair and equitable.

This is what Greenwood (2001) suggests in arguing that the political branches and courts both make decisions that reflect democratic values, but that the decision-making system of each is different. Political branches make decisions according to aggregative principles—norms established during the process of deliberation itself—while courts make decisions according to normative principles—norms established prior to the process of deliberation. That is, where Bickel and other advocates of a countermajoritarian difficulty see a uninomic world—a world where all decisions are measured against an aggregative model—Greenwood sees a polynomic world with two main models, aggregative and normative (Greenwood 2001, 784, 789–790). The aggregative model is majoritarian but the normative one is not. Further, in the same manner that PR electoral rules are more representative than majoritarian rules, the normative model is more representative than the aggregative model in that courts consider not just the majoritarian preferences in their decisions, but also minoritarian preferences and fundamental principles.

In some cases, effectiveness and representativeness may overlap conceptually. For instance, a court that is effectively independent is presumably also representative. That is, by being autonomous from political influence we might conclude that a court is representative not just of dominant elites or majorities, but that it is making decisions according to the normative principles outlined by Greenwood, and therefore representative. However, a court may be overly independent and therefore insulated from oversight, so independence does not necessarily translate into representativeness. Insularity can be counteracted by accountability, so accountability would then overlap with representativeness. In any case, effectiveness and representativeness are not irreconcilable.

Rule of Law, Democracy and Representativeness

Substantive conceptualizations of the rule of law and democracy also help reconcile effectiveness and representativeness. Rule of law scholars distinguish between two main conceptualizations of the rule of law (ROL): procedural and substantive (e.g., Tamanaha 2004). The hallmark of procedural ROL is the proposition that government must be bound by law, which unpacks into various components: laws must be clear (i.e., provide definite guidance), public (open, transparent), general (apply to all), and prospective (cannot legislate against past activities) (see related discussion of constitutionalism by Couso, this volume). Kleinfeld (2006) adds the feature of procedural economy, or efficiency. Taken together, these procedural features are supposed to guarantee the nonarbitrary exercise of power. Substantive ROL accepts all these properties but adds explicit protections for concrete individual rights and liberties (e.g., property, privacy, food, healthcare, even housing). The advantage of procedural ROL is that it is universal and generalizable; lacking substantive content, it travels rather effortlessly from one context to another. This strength is indeed its weakness, falling prey to conceptual "stretching" (Sartori 1970) as the ease with which procedural ROL travels allows it to apply to systems most observers would be reticent to qualify as consistent with the spirit of "rule of law." For instance, Nazi Germany, apartheid South Africa and the slavery or Jim Crow regimes in the United States all meet the minimum requirements of procedural ROL (e.g., Tamanaha 2004, 93–96), yet I imagine few readers would want to hold these examples up as beacons of the rule of law.

For these reasons, substantive ROL can offer a more meaningful and satisfying alternative. However, its very meaningfulness—the fact that the concept includes concrete rights that we associate with democratic ideals but about which there may be disagreement—renders this variant of ROL vulnerable to criticisms of being culturally specific or even undemocratic (Kleinfeld 2006). For example, within the United States, ideological divisions prevent a single country from agreeing on a host of rights-related issues (e.g., gay marriage, abortion, death penalty, gun ownership), and any direct imposition (or removal) of these rights would be seen as autocratic by those who oppose (or support) them.

Democracy can also be conceptualized in either procedural or substantive terms. Procedural democracy can have as little as a single property: formal elections (e.g., Schumpeter 1942; Przeworski 1991). Again, this minimum definition travels well, but most observers would find it unsettling to call single-party or other forms of electoral authoritarianism (Schedler 2005) "democratic" simply because they hold elections. Even in advanced democracies with multiple parties, myriad barriers to participation exist, including access to a full spectrum of quality information, education that affords an ability to understand policy options offered by candidates, and the ability to get to the ballot box on election day. Further, some people or groups are more effective at organizing interest groups and parties, building political campaigns and running for office. The substantive form of democracy calls for all of the procedural elements plus a bundle of explicit freedoms and rights that make participation fully effective, including the freedoms of speech, association and the press, and the attendant rights to information and education.

The disjuncture between procedural and substantive definitions of democracy and rule of law highlights the gap between democracy *in theory* and democracy *in practice*. In theory, if all people had equal endowments, resources or capabilities (Sen 2000), the procedural versions of both democracy and rule of law would suffice. However, this is not the reality of most countries, especially in Latin America, which is persistently the most unequal region of the world (UNDP 2004). Thus, the pursuit of the democratic ideal requires a series of firmer supports in order to bring practice in closer alignment with theory.

Returning to the issues of judicial effectiveness and representativeness, this context of persistent inequality conditions how we understand both concepts and the relationship between them. In highly and stubbornly unequal societies, the effectiveness of courts remains dramatically uneven, working well for those who have the requisite endowments and capabilities—education, information and material resources—and working poorly for those who do not. Even without being openly partial or politically dependent, courts in highly unequal societies tend to represent the interests of dominant political and economic elites (e.g., the political class in Mexico; see Rios, this volume), and in civil law countries courts can also be intensely corporate, i.e., institutionally self-interested (Rios, this volume, citing Damaska 1986). Both phenomena are inconsistent with fuller notions of democracy. If we take ideals of democracy and rule of law seriously, especially the substantive versions outlined previously, courts in these societies ought to strive to represent interests beyond those of dominant political and economic elites, who compose a minority of the population, and seek to be more deeply representative.

This kind of representativeness asks us to consider *for whom* courts are effective and *of what* they are representative. I agree with Couso and Rios (this volume) that traditional separation of powers doctrines advise against judicial institutions that are responsive to popular political pressures. That is, judicial representativeness should not derive simply from direct elections or popularity. However, returning to the context of highly unequal societies, if courts work well for elites, should they not also strive to work well for the poor, underserved and *underrepresented*? What might the challenge of bringing judicial institutions "closer to citizens' concerns" (Rios, this volume) or "closer to society" (Sabsay, this volume) require of courts? If the position of politically dominant elites is representative in a formal sense (i.e., majoritarian in the formal political process) but there is evidence that substantial sectors of the population—perhaps even de facto majorities—require protection against this position or simply remain un- or under-served, ought not courts to check dominant minorities, even if those minorities occupy formally majoritarian institutions? In this context, which branch carries the mantle of representativeness? What kinds of changes in the ways courts do business might make the judiciary more representative of the interests of the poor and marginalized? These questions require a broader understanding of representativeness beyond formal sources of judicial office. That is, these are questions that go beyond the concern with direct elections for judges (e.g., Rios). The empirical analysis in the Brazilian state of Acre offers examples of what answers to these questions can look like, including courts bringing their services to communities instead of requiring people to come to them, and courts expanding the range of services they offer in order to address issues more representative of community needs. Thus, in both form and content, courts can change in ways that enhance representativeness, bringing them in closer alignment with substantive conceptualizations of democracy and the rule of law.

Micro- and Macro-Level Effectiveness and Representativeness

Micro-level court effectiveness refers to the aforementioned conventional qualities of dispute resolution: courts must perform this central function in a manner that is accessible, efficient and independent. At a macro-level, however, I propose courts must also be effective in a broader sense: they must contribute to the quality of democracy. Courts that deny or delay justice, or demonstrate favoritism, partiality or political capture erode public trust and confidence in institutions, thereby undermining support for democracy and generating incentives for individuals to resolve conflicts in fora outside the auspices of state-sanctioned institutions. In the extreme, this defection from the state's justice institutions can lead to the privatization of violence (e.g., vigilantism, lynchings). Conversely, courts that are open to all, efficient and fair, build public trust and enhance the quality of democracy.[1] Beyond the qualities of accessibility, efficiency and independence, however, macro-level court effectiveness implies a substantive component; that is, even if accessible, efficient and independent, the outcomes of dispute resolution must also resonate with the public's broader sense of fairness, legitimacy, or—for lack of a better word—justice. That is, they must resonate with ideas that are consistent with the ideals captured by substantive definitions of democracy and rule of law, including respect for fundamental rights and liberties, and the real, generalized effectiveness of these rights. If substantial sectors perceive courts as fora fundamentally unfriendly to the real effectiveness of these rights for broad swaths of the population, public trust will suffer no matter how accessible, efficient or independent courts may be for a select few. Thus, in terms of macro-effectiveness, *representativeness can be seen as a component of effectiveness*. As was the case with purely procedural forms of democracy and ROL, courts that only attend to their micro-effectiveness risk neglecting meaningful sources of their institutional legitimacy, a legitimacy that is closely tied to fairness, equity and representativeness.

In sum, while the conceptual boundaries are not fixed and can sometimes overlap, effectiveness speaks more directly to the capacity to perform functions well, namely, adjudication, while representativeness asks us to consider to what extent that function meets the needs and reflects the interests of democratic society as a whole. That is, "effective for whom?" In this sense, effectiveness and representativeness are sufficiently distinct with regards to the judiciary that we can speak of them separately as different concepts and jointly as two dimensions of the broader concept of judicial strength. However, a macro-level perspective of effectiveness suggests that representativeness is a dimension of broader definitions of effectiveness. In either case, effectiveness and representativeness are reconcilable—as either separate components of a narrower concept of court strength, or as causally related to each other in broader discussions of judicial effectiveness in democratic societies.

THEORY: EMPIRICAL IMPLICATIONS OF IDEATIONAL ACCOUNTS

Ideational explanations highlight the influence of nonmaterial, principled-programmatic commitments. That is, actors react less to material, cost-benefit calculations inherent in interest-based, rational-strategic accounts and respond more to deeply held commitments of a nonmaterial nature regarding the role of courts in society. Notably, clearly conceptualizing the nature of ideas can be difficult, posing methodological challenges. Nonetheless, such difficulty "cannot justify shrinking from elements that are deeply constitutive of institutions" (Smith 2008, 55).

Comparative studies of judicial reform help conceptualize the kind of principled-programmatic commitments highlighted here. These studies teach us that both left- and right-leaning actors can promote reform, but for very different reasons. That is, leftist and rightist actors are both motivated by ideas, but the content of their ideas differs. Conversely, the absence of these commitments identifies actors as nonideological.

Programmatic actors on the political left tend to emphasize the social dimension of democracy, favoring a stronger role for public institutions in the tutelage of fundamental rights, and seeking to enhance the real, effective substance of individual rights and liberties. These substantive protections contribute to the depth and quality of democratic citizenship. Conversely, programmatic actors on the political right tends to emphasize individualism and economic factors, favoring a reduced role of the state and the security and predictability of property and contracts, as well as public safety in the quest to establish the right business conditions for efficient markets. Stated starkly and provocatively, leftist actors favor social democracy and rightist actors favor market democracy.

This ideational contrast between programmatic left and right—and the effect of these programs on the judicial sector—finds support in the comparative literature on court building. This literature includes Woods's (2008) progressive "judicial communities" in Israel and Hirschl's (2004) promarket, neoliberal elites in Israel, Canada, South Africa and New Zealand. Hilbink's (2007b) study of the key roles of leftist parties and a progressive clergy in "politicizing the law in order to liberalize politics" in Spain's transition to democracy also supports the argument. More recently, Nunes (2010b) highlights the role of market-oriented judicial elites in the construction of the Colombian constitutional court. Separately, Hilbink (2012) and Rodriguez Garavito (2011) also draw attention to ideologically tinged visions of constitutionalism, contrasting a new progressive, left-leaning *neo*constitutionalism against a conservative, right-leaning neoliberal constitutionalism.

Concrete empirical implications flow from theoretical propositions based on principled-ideological commitments. First, we should see actors framing reform projects as part of broader projects of either (1) democracy promotion or (2) market promotion. However, behavior that conforms to this expectation is only weak evidence in favor of the argument since actors motivated by rational-strategic interests may also articulate principled justifications. Still, a necessary empirical implication is this kind of ideational framing. Second, an observable implication that is unique to ideational arguments—and therefore behavior that comports with this expectation offers stronger evidence in favor of principled commitments—is that principled behavior can be costly in ways that rational-strategic behavior is not. That is, where conventional "electoral market" arguments (Ramseyer 1994) anticipate an analysis of material costs and benefits that leads to risk-averse behavior, ideational logics suggest nonmaterial principles motivate actors, so we may observe costly or risky behavior, resonating with what social movement scholars have termed "high-risk activism" (McAdam 1986). To be sure, electoral accounts frequently claim to explain the seemingly costly and counterintuitive puzzle of sitting majorities delegating power to the courts. However, the key insight of those accounts is that delegating power to courts is actually *less costly* for declining or outgoing majorities in the long term than failing to delegate that power and later being a political minority in the absence of a protective court. In contrast, the ideational argument advanced here anticipates that principled actors—even electorally ascendant ones—may delegate power to courts because doing so conforms to an *idea* of the proper role of courts in society. If we observe this costly behavior—specifically, an executive self-constraining by creating a stronger judiciary when electoral uncertainty is low or absent, or judges engaging in risky or costly activism when material incentives would lead us to anticipate the opposite—this constitutes strong evidence of principled rather than prudent behavior. Behavior that is similarly risky or costly favors concluding that behavior was motivated by ideas, not interests.

Two analytic clarifications are in order. First, echoing Hilbink (2009), I do not argue that ideas are the only explanatory factors at the exclusion of rational-strategic calculations. As others have shown, it is possible for more narrowly self-interested motivations to yield strong courts (e.g., Landes and Posner 1975; Magalhaes 1998; Ginsburg 2003; Finkel 2008; Whittington 2007; Brinks 2010; Nunes 2010a). However, building on this research, I find that crucial instances of reform and reform efforts involved actors who took substantial material risks in order to pursue reform, resonating with the "high-risk activism" found by social movement scholars (McAdam 1986), and cutting against dominant accounts of reform as the rational outcome of short-term, material, self-interested calculations. This kind of costly activism cannot be understood without serious attention to ideas. Second, I do not argue that progressive ideas are the only kind of ideas that matter. Where ideas generate other-regarding or altruistic behavior, these ideas might have origins in right-leaning ideologies (e.g., Gillman 2008; Hirschl 2004; Nunes 2010b; Rodriguez-Garavito 2011). However, that is not what the evidence shows here. Building on the conceptualization of representativeness and the previous theoretical argument, this finding is consistent with the idea that we should expect the political left to engage in court strengthening projects that enhance both effectiveness and representativeness together. In sum, the results help us understand reforms that challenge dominant accounts based on the material self-interest of politicians, and the analysis highlights the understudied role of judges and other institutional insiders in effecting reform, contributing to our understanding of institution building in new democracies.

METHODS AND CASE SELECTION

The tracing of reform processes in this state draws on 15 personal interviews, archival research, and direct observation.[2] I identify key moments in the post-1985 life of courts in the state of Acre, and these moments of reform or reform effort function as landmarks in the institutional landscape of the judiciary. I then employ process tracing to build an analytic narrative that examines the sequence, timing, and content of changes in order to explain the causes of the reforms and their success or failure (Hall 2003; Bennett and George 2005; Gerring 2007). Working backwards from the outcome of interest—institutional change or reform effort—I identify the causal linkages the lead to such an outcome.

The selection of Acre follows the logic of "crucial" cases (Eckstein 1975; Gerring 2008). According to this approach, crucial or difficult tests of theories come in two varieties, "most likely" and "least likely." A "least likely" case is one that, "on all dimensions *except* the dimension of theoretical interest, the case is predicted not to achieve a certain outcome, and yet does so" (Gerring 2008, 659; emphasis in original). Acre poses this kind crucial test for the theoretical argument that progressive commitments can bring about judicial empowerment, marked as the state is by historically low levels of electoral competition, turnover with the PT but then electoral dominance by the PT itself, low levels of state wealth and resources, a weak business/commercial environment and distance from federal and large metropolitan sites of policy innovation. In this setting, the odds of reform are low, making it a "least likely" kind of crucial case. Thus, if we do see reform here—and especially if the process tracing method connects reform outcomes to the progressive ideational pressures—then we can place greater analytic weight on the causal claim.

Acre reflects local political conditions that suggest a strong role for progressive-programmatic commitments. Acre is a leftist stronghold in that the PT has governed the state capital of Rio Branco since 1992 and has held the governor's office for three consecutive administrations since 1998. How has the dominant presence of the political left in Acre influenced judicial effectiveness and representativeness?

COURTS IN LEFTIST STRONGHOLDS: THE CASE OF ACRE

Interviews identified two key judicial moments in Acre: (1) the creation of Citizen Project (*Projeto Cidadão*) in 1995–1996, which was initiated during the PT's first municipal administration in the state capital (1993–1996); and (2) judicial lobbying and labor actions in 2000–2001, which overlapped with the court presidency of Desembargador (Des.)[3] Arquilau de Castro Melo (2001–2003). The following discussion examines each moment in greater detail, tracing the process of judicial change.

Projeto Cidadão (1995–1996)

A major change occurred in Acre's judiciary in 1995–1996—a judicial outreach program was created called the Citizen Project. The project was originally inspired by the experience of the local city government with public education in the state capital, Rio Branco, and a study of the national statistics office (Instituto Brasileiro de Geografia e Estatistica, IBGE). According to one senior judge, the Rio Branco municipal government was trying to increase the rate at which children finished primary and secondary school, and found that they could barely track the children over the years because of the absence of basic legal documents. Since school officials could not properly identify school children, they could not tell which students finished one year and entered the next (Interview 127). Further, the IBGE study found that nearly 80% of Acre's population did not have any official government identification (Interview 159).[4] Obtaining official documents, therefore, became the necessary first step towards a fuller, more effective and inclusive sense of citizenship, including legal or "civil" citizenship (see Marshall 1965; O'Donnell 1993; UNDP 2004). By targeting this problem, the Citizen Project was extraordinarily popular and received many awards nationally and internationally.

The program was designed by the PT's municipal administration in Rio Branco under mayor Jorge Viana (later elected governor in 1998). Specifically, Viana's secretary of education, Arnobio "Binho" Marques (Interview 127), who later succeeded Viana by becoming governor in 2006, spearheaded the design. The program originated with Marques and the PT, and the courts only came on later as partners in its funding and execution (Interview 127, 159). Importantly, while the IBGE study drew attention to the problem of legal documentation, access to education and effective citizenship, it was the PT and not another party or entity that designed this program specifically to resolve the problem. In doing so, the PT was motivated by the incorporation of large, marginalized sectors into Acrean society, but the inclusionary mission of the project is also consistent with the PT's programmatic preferences and its strong foundations in social movements and activist networks in the state, dating back to the early 1980s (Keck 1995).

The role of the courts, however, was and remains meaningful as the judiciary provided funding and lent its full institutional support to the program, bringing judges, the extended geographic network of the judiciary throughout the state, and the judicial process to neighborhoods. Eventually, the program moved beyond the state capital to carry basic legal proceedings, including marriages and other legal certificates as well as small claims resolution to cities in the state's interior.

The program received support from within the judiciary, especially from a crucial ally, Des. Arquilau de Castro Melo. Melo was sympathetic and effective for several reasons. First, with a background in journalism and rights advocacy in the state in the 1970s during the period of military censorship,[5] Melo had then gone to law school. At the time, following the teaching of liberation theology, the local church began defending "moradores" (informal residents on large, inactive landholdings) and rural workers, and unions started to form among these workers. Melo felt called to these movements and was both a founder of the PT in Acre and later a lawyer for the PT and the National Association of Agricultural Workers (*Confederação Nacional dos Trabalhadores na Agricultura*, CONTAG) and was attorney for Chico Mendes, including a case in which Mendes and Lula were charged with national security violations under the military regime (Interviews 127, 140). At the time, doing this kind of activity carried the risk of being labeled "subversive" and "communist" just for representing such figures, quite separate from any of Melo's other activities. Melo persisted despite these risks. Thus, after the transition to democracy, Melo had very deep and strong roots in local social movements and enjoyed an aura of legitimacy and moral authority (Interviews 127, 140).

From the judiciary's perspective, Des. Arquilau recalled Projeto Cidadão as an important program for the substantive benefits it brought to ordinary citizens; that is, it brought real services to individual citizens. However, he also valued Projeto Cidadão because it transformed the image of the judiciary, both externally and internally. Externally, judges realized they needed to conduct the business of the courts in a different manner, and started traveling out from the courtrooms in the state capital to conduct hearings and procedures in communities. The fact that judges traveled out to where people lived, even very remote communities, and settled legal issues helped citizens see justice and the courts as not something passive, distant and inaccessible that they had to struggle to reach, but rather as something close and accessible that actively took steps to reach them and represent them. Des. Arquilau personally described the law and the legal profession as a public service, and that "public service aims to make life easier, not to make it more difficult or arduous ... the goal of justice is to promote happiness." For him, the off-the-bench process of bringing judges down from their distant perches of authority to be closer to ordinary citizens was as valuable as the substance of actual legal services that judges would then provide. By taking the administration of justice out from the courthouse and into communities, judges interacted more informally and also had to adapt to conditions in the community, working in some places quite literally on the ground. In terms of the effectiveness of courts, this was a mighty step, essentially aiming to transform the poor image of the judiciary in popular attitudes by promoting a view of judges as accessible and helpful problem solvers. However, it also reflects an effort to make the form and content of court services representative of a community's needs.

Des. Arquilau stated as much, articulating a *cultural-ideational change* he hoped to provoke with Projeto Cidadão. Further, he hoped this cultural change would be internal to the courts as much as external. Externally, he sought a cultural transformation in the public's perception of the role of judges and the law in the lives of ordinary citizens, even citizens in the poorest and most remote parts of this Amazonian state. Internally, by forcing judges out of their chambers, out of their courtrooms, and into the city and the countryside, he hoped judges would interact with and see who they were working for. He believed this kind of activity "changes judges ... improves them—as a person, as a citizen." Given his origins in the labor movement and the PT, Melo promoted these ideas among judges, "marketing a justice closer to citizens, less in the office and with more of a view from the ground, *marketing that idea*—'hey, you need to be a different kind of judge' " (emphasis added). Thus, the PT's Projeto Cidadão complemented Melo's goal of transforming legal culture in Acre—in society and within the judiciary itself.

Melo's articulation of his goals and motivations resonate with a broader progressive current in Brazilian law and legal practice in the 1980s and 1990s—the alternative law movement (*direito alternativo*). Coinciding closely with Melo's own words, advocates of alternative law sought to humanize law, bring it down from the courts and law schools and into the streets, where rights and justice are least effective (e.g., Engelmann 2004, 2007). Emerging during the dictatorship—when judges resorted to fundamental principles of human dignity to override positive laws issued by the military regime but viewed as undemocratic by these judges—alternative law gained organizational momentum in 1990–1991 in the southern states of Rio Grande do Sul and Santa Catarina, and increasingly stood for a rights-protective, socially conscious, progressive legal movement among both academics and practitioners (Engelmann 2007, 54–58). At its core, the alternative law principles are consonant with representativeness as reconceptualized previuosly. Indeed, Melo's expressions of these principles, and the fact that his support of Projeto Cidadão was grounded in these principles, show how progressive ideational frameworks can shape a more representative judiciary.

Lobbying and Labor Actions by Judges (2000–2001)

Alongside *Projeto Cidadão*, a second key moment in Acre occurred between 2000 and 2001. On December 4, 2000, first-instance judges and local court staff (*servidores*) went on strike in Acre, asking primarily for a larger budget for the judiciary, an increased number of judges and support staff throughout the state and improvements to the physical infrastructure of the courts. During the previous week, work stoppages and slowdowns (*paralizações*, or *operações tartarugas*—literally "operation turtle"), as well as intentionally minimal staffing (*atendimento plantonista*) prefaced the strike. In other words, a week of labor-related disruptions led up to the strike as judges and court staff lobbied the judicial leadership and made their demands known (*Página 20* 2000, 1, 4). As these actions did not have any effect, the full strike ensued and first-instance courts shut down. Adair Longuini, then president of the state judges' association (*Associacão dos Magistrados do Acre*, or ASMAC),[6] noted that the governor was offering the judiciary a budget of R$29 million for 2001, but that the courts required a budget of R$72 million, more than twice the amount proposed by the executive (*Página 20*).

Longuini's leadership of the 2000 strike was important because he had a level of respect and legitimacy among judges, similar to—and for similar reasons as—Arquilau de Castro Melo. Longuini had been the judge who presided over the trial of the murderer of the land-rights activist Chico Mendes, doing so despite the politically charged environment and at personal risk. For this, he was a highly regarded public figure in the state with near folk-hero status, especially among his judicial colleagues (Interview 140, 178). In making ASMAC's case during the labor disruptions in late 2000, Longuini stressed that Acre was in dire need of more judges to staff courtrooms, that the physical structures of the judiciary were in need of repair and deteriorating rapidly, and that the judiciary required a greater number of support personnel to attend to the daily business of the courts. To address these needs and become a more effective judiciary, ASMAC proposed two new civil service exams (*concursos*)—one for judges and one for court staff—and the upgrading of numerous court buildings and facilities. Quoting Longuini, "We only want them [politicians and judicial leaders] to do something to stop the impending failure of the judiciary. The situation has become unbearable, to the point that we cannot do our work. We can no longer merely depend on budgetary supplements" (*Página 20*). Longuini was calling for a budget that would be sufficient to put an end to this practice of stop-gap funding that creates a chronic condition of institutional weakness and vulnerability.[7] Thus, ASMAC's argument was for a new, more adequate judicial budget aimed to strengthen the staffing, supplies and physical infrastructure of the judiciary, but these administrative improvements would also yield interinstitutional, political gains, strengthening the practice of separation of powers outlined in the Constitution. In short, Longuini was charting a path to judicial effectiveness.

On December 5, after a week of stoppages and slowdowns and only one full day of striking, the judges obtained a partial success and returned to work. The entire process lasted one week, and the gains included: (1) a new judicial budget of R$37 million, which, although it was not the full budget the judges were requesting did amount to an increase of over 27% from the governor's initial offer, and an increase over the 2000 budget of 50% (the 2002 budget increased further, adding another 49% from 2001 to 2002 (TJAC Informe 2002 and 2005); (2) a new civil service exam (*concurso*) to hire judges starting in May 2001; and (3) a commitment to hire 20 new judges by November 2001 (Batista 2000). By most accounts, the 2000 strike was a successful labor action.[8] Though all demands were not met, a reasonable compromise was achieved and the courthouse doors were closed for only one day.

In late 2000, Francisco das Chagas Praça had just a couple of months left in his two-year term as TJ president, which was scheduled to end in February of 2001. Praça was unpopular and the source of much dissatisfaction in the judiciary. Some judges referred to his administration as a "valley" (*vale*) in the recent history of the judiciary, also describing him as "*inviável*," translated literally as "not viable" (Interview 136, 140). Indeed, Praça likely contributed to the strike not only because he was perceived as a poor leader of the judiciary, but also because of an inability to negotiate

with the judges. Arquilau de Castro Melo, the same judge that had supported the PT's *Citizen Project* in 1995, had just been selected to become
the next president for the 2001–2003 term. Despite the fact he was not
scheduled to take the leadership position for nearly two more months (on
February 1, 2001), Melo negotiated the resolution of the strike with judges
and court staff in the first week of December 2000 (Batista 2000). Several
judges identify Melo as not only being pivotal in the strike's resolution, but
also credit his two-year administration of the judiciary as a positive *marco*
or reference point in the trajectory of the state judiciary (Interview 140, 148,
192; *Página 20* 2000).

Given Melo's background in local social movements and his roots in the
PT, he supported the judges' right to strike. That is, even as the institutional
leader of the judiciary, he thought that the judges he supervised *should* strike
if they thought they had a grievance against his office (Interview 127). Beyond his reputation, interviewed judges said this perspective endeared him
to many of their colleagues and court staff, facilitating the resolution of the
strike (Interview 148; 192). After only one day of striking, and two months
before he was supposed to take office as court president, Melo resolved the
strike for the sitting court president on December 5, 2000.

CONCLUSIONS

In Acre, the Citizen Project was an instance of positive institutional change
drawing on principled-ideological motivations outside and inside the judiciary—originating in the municipal government's strategy towards improving
education, which was motivated and shaped by political ideology, and finding
a key, ideologically sympathetic advocate within the courts. Further changes
were promoted by institutional pressures from below—lobbying and labor
actions by judges, led by a principled judge—and encouraged and ultimately
approved by the same actors and ideas that were behind the Citizen Project.

To be sure, ideas explain only a portion of the final outcomes in Acre,
and I do not claim that other, nonideational factors do not play meaningful
roles. As stated previously, I also do not claim that the programmatic right
is incapable of motivating reform. However, the present analysis finds that
crucial episodes of reform in Acre cannot be understood without attention
to ideas, and that programmatic commitments on the left have been crucial.
Highlighting ideas is also important due to the extent to which they help
us understand otherwise puzzling instances of reform. Further, this analysis
helps us understand the content of ideas, how they work to shape reform
and how they are acquired by or spread among actors. Regarding this last
point on the spread of ideas, the transition to democracy, the 1988 Constitution and resulting changes in the content of legal education after the
transition, the *direito alternativo* movement, and experience with labor and
human rights movements all suggest factors that influence the spread of

progressive ideas about the role of courts in democracies. Against conventional understandings of representativeness, I argue that these ideational concerns with making the law socially relevant to broad sectors of the population, especially marginalized sectors, justify thinking of the judiciary in terms of its representativeness.

Beyond the role of ideas, I emphasize the role of judges in justice sector reform. The prominence of judges has two salient features with implications for future research: (1) judges play a strong political-institutional role, not just a jurisprudential one; that is, they act politically "beyond the bench," not just "on the bench"; and (2) the influence of judges highlights the role of actors internal to institutions. Here, these internal actors are judges within courts, but elsewhere could be bureaucrats within agencies, or legislators within parliaments. In the law and courts literature, studies of judicial behavior must pay greater attention to "off-bench" behavior and the nonlegal preferences that motivate this institution-building behavior. More generally, studies of institutional change and development must account for the role of internal actors. In this regard, the politician-centered character of much existing research overlooks these features of institutional change.

NOTES

I am grateful to the National Science Foundation's Law and Social Science Program (Grant No. SES-067767) and to the Fulbright Commission for funding research in Brazil. I also thank Maria Tereza Sadek and the Centro Brasileiro de Estudos e Pesquisas Judicias (CEBEPEJ), and the FGV law school in São Paulo (Direito-GV)—especially Luciana Gross Cunha, Rafael Alves and Gustavo Alves Pinto—for providing institutional homes in São Paulo. I am further grateful to William Stanley, Kenneth Roberts, Wendy Hansen, Benjamin Goldfrank and Jeffrey Staton, as well as Rogerio Arantes, Ernani Carvalho, Javier Couso, Ludovico Feoli, David Fleischer, Diana Kapiszewski, Moira MacKinnon, Julio Rios-Figueroa, Daniel Sabsay, Celina Souza and Matthew Taylor for helpful comments at various stages of this research. Presentations at two research seminars in Brazil—at the FGV in São Paulo and at Ernani Carvalho's judicial politics seminar at UFPE—proved very productive. I am particularly indebted to Lisa Hilbink for helping me think through the role of ideas in shaping judicial behavior, both on and off the bench. Last but not least, I thank all the interviewees for participating in this study. Any errors are my own.

1. Some readers may object to a basic difference between qualifiers of dispute resolution (accessibility, efficiency and independence) and the more remote, causal relationship between these qualifiers and public trust. That is, accessibility, efficiency and independence are qualifiers of dispute resolution, and it is only when these three conditions are present that we expect to see public trust in justice institutions.

2. I spent a total of one month in Acre at two different times during a longer research stay in Brazil in 2007. I visited courthouses and courtrooms, as well as the official judicial archive. Archival sources consisted of state constitutions, legislation, annual reports on the "state of the judiciary," newspaper articles and litigation documents. The interviews were primarily with second- and

first-instance judges, including current and past court presidents, but also included current and former legislators. Direct observation also took place during participation in official dinners, ceremonies and associational gatherings of the judiciary.

3. *Desembargador* is the title of judges on the state Supreme Court, which are all second-instance or appellate judges in the state's judicial structure.

4. The lack of official documents is a major obstacle to citizenship in bureaucratic Brazil, where any interaction with the state requires the presentation of proper documents and identification. In the judicial arena, the lack of documents translated into an access to justice issue. Without the right documents, individuals could not file legal claims, request government services, legally marry, register the birth of a child, obtain work permits or initiate a host of other procedures.

5. Melo described his journalistic activities as exposing abuses under the dictatorship ("denunciando a ditadura ... e abusos") (personal interview with the author).

6. In 2007, Judge Adair Longuini became *desembargador*, promoted to the state Supreme Court (TJAC), and as of February 1, 2011, he had ascended to the presidency of the TJ for the 2011–2013 term.

7. Judges frequently used the phrase "com o pires na mão" (beggarly) to describe the chronic poverty of the judiciary vis-à-vis the other branches. This is largely no longer the case in Brazil, but there are still states that struggle to fund the courts appropriately.

8. Court staff remained on strike for an extra day and were not fully satisfied with the outcome (Batista 2000).

9 Judiciary and Democracy in Argentina

Daniel Alberto Sabsay

Since Spanish colonial rule, Argentine institutional history has been characterized by a general tendency towards hegemony both in the office of the president and in the democratic regime as a whole. Hegemony denotes concentration of power; thus, any governmental regime in which power is centered in one person or institution is hegemonic. In a presidential democratic system, this occurs in flagrant contradiction with the principles stated by the Constitution, favoring the president. Argentina, like other Latin American countries, has experienced a series of *coups d'etat*, which have affected the development of power-sharing mechanisms, promoting and exacerbating the hegemonic model. Undoubtedly, in Argentina (and many Latin American countries), the judiciary has tended to uncritically follow the will of the executive power.

The next section focuses on two sets of issues. First, it considers who embodies the law, who exercises the governing power and enacts the law and who is regarded as the authority by the citizens, regardless of what the Constitution states. Most people consider the president to be this person, not taking into account the two other powers of the state: the judiciary and the legislative. The second issue is the cultural context according to which law enforcement depends on the political convenience of the situation to which it will be applied and not on the respect for the supremacy of the Constitution. In other words, this second issue is driven by the so-called "*posibilismo*": justifying action only when it is in line with the government's objectives or when certain exceptional circumstances authorize the enactment of emergency legislation. To consider these issues, I examine constitutionalism and the rule of law, the "emergency," judicial review and supervisory functions, and the 1994 constitutional reform and the restoration of democracy. The section refers to the effectiveness and, to a lesser extent, the representativeness of the Argentine judicial system.

The third section looks briefly at the reforms that have been carried out in Argentina, mainly in order to strengthen the independence of the judiciary and to provide citizens with access to impartial justice systems. In the fourth section I analyze the various factors that conspire against the judiciary's independence. Thus, I try to find the reasons that lie behind the weak representativeness of the judiciary. Traditionally, according to the first period of constitutionalism, the concept of representativeness is understood as based on elections, following the influential Hamiltonian perspective, as Rios (this volume) reminds us. However, the emergence of "civil society" introduced new mechanisms of representativeness mainly through the institutions that characterize so-called participatory democracy. But the judiciary can also be considered representative in terms of accessibility; that is, when accessibility is guaranteed to every citizen, especially the most vulnerable minorities. The underlying concern is that the justice system should not be available only to wealthy elites, nor be viewed as perpetuating the dominance of one group over the other. The more representative the system, the more those who do not belong to an elite have access to it and fall under its protection.

Finally in the conclusion, I argue that the cultural institutional tradition that started in the colonial period has a lot to do with the weakness of the Argentine judicial system. The reforms that have taken place since the beginning of the period of transition to democracy have not produced the expected results. The boost given by civil society to justice in its search for the protection of collective rights and interests has been more important in the effort to build a participatory democracy. Nevertheless, an independent judiciary will only be achieved in Argentina when all the members of society consider that this is a crucial condition needed to improve their quality of life.

THE ARGENTINE JUDICIAL SYSTEM AND ITS EFFECTIVENESS

Constitutionalism and the Rule of Law

In order to speak of the judiciary as a state power it is necessary to recall several notions previously associated to the foundations of the political regime in which it is rooted; namely, the rule of law and the main elements and principles that underlie it. This helps us understand the role of justice in shoring up those notions in order to limit power, due to the more correct interpretation of legal rules that predetermine the actions of rulers. Montesquieu considered that the effective limitation of power rested on the effectiveness of reciprocal mechanisms of control (Montesquieu [1748] 1989).

The fundamental thread that runs through the political history of Argentina (and Latin America) is an institutional design derived from constitutional thought. As indicated above, if the judiciary is examined as a branch of government, several concepts associated with the basis of the political regime of which the judiciary is a part are relevant to the analysis; in particular the rule of law and the main elements and principles that underlie this legal maxim, referred to below. The rule of law is a creation of constitutionalism. The main objective of the rule of law is to apply a conception of limited power through an institutional framework, the elements of which are organized in a systemic manner. The concept of constitutionalism means that the government will adjust its behavior to a law higher than ordinary legislation and that this body of higher law is set out in a document called the constitution or some other form of fundamental law. One of the key elements is the principle of separation of powers. Montesquieu considered that this principle should be used primarily to control the operation of the system as a whole. This is the reason the structure of government is divided into three branches—legislative, executive and judicial—each of which receives its own sphere of competence based on the performance of a particular function. However, a number of powers related to the supervision of the other two powers are added to each of the branches, ensuring the checks and balances by the three branches. In the words of the author of *The Spirit of the Laws*, this model of governance is defined as "the power to stop the power" with regard to their jurisdictions, prerogatives, their domain of activity and their control over each other. The democratic system of government is based on a particular relationship between power and law, so as to construct the rule of law. The law is of the utmost importance for democracy since all the elements and relationships established under a democratic structure are based on subordination to a legal framework. Undoubtedly, judges have a challenging task to perform, as they must guarantee that the rule of law governs under all circumstances, ensuring that the provisions of the current constitutional and legal framework of the country are enforced and complied with. This should be the case in all decisions taken by the authorities, as well as in the contracts that govern the relationships between individuals.

The Argentine constitutional framer Juan Bautista Alberdi[1] was very clear about the significant role that justice played in the process of building democracy in Argentina. Thus, in line with his ideas, the preamble states that the government will "ensure justice" as one of the fundamental objectives of the nation. The concern for the independence of the judiciary is also reflected in various constitutional provisions, such as the one that mandates that the provincial constitutions organize a system of justice, or the one that prevents the nation's president from exercising judicial functions (Alberdi 1913). Only when the country has built prompt, objective and impartial justice has it achieved the goal set forth in the preamble. Impartiality is a principle of justice holding that decisions must be based on objective criteria, devoid of any particular interest, unbiased and unprejudiced. Therefore, impartial justice must disapprove of all kinds of disregard for the Constitution and the laws enacted pursuant to it. This significant achievement entails full democracy, along with the existence of other democratic principles such as legal security; separation of powers; control and transparency in the operation of political state powers; independence from the executive, legislative and judicial branches; and the unrestricted validity of human rights and the values of freedom and equality on which they feed. Democracies in Latin American latitudes present a serious deficit in this area. If there really is a pending issue in the democracies of Latin America, it certainly is the establishment of a genuine, impartial, properly institutionalized judiciary consistent with the principles of constitutionalism.

However, the lax controls exerted over our institutions, the helplessness of any ordinary citizen faced by a growing level of impunity, the lack of independence of the courts, the poor training of civil servants and the fact that some positions are filled by arbitrary methods of appointment (i.e., professionals running for elected offices or winning appointments to government positions through political influence), and the lack of access to the courtroom by the most disadvantaged sectors of society are some of the serious shortcomings of the organization of justice, both in our country and in much of the subcontinent.

At this point it may be useful to identify the basic conditions necessary to ensure judicial oversight to prevent the judiciary from using its broad powers for improper purposes. Thus, the need of a judiciary independent from political powers and private or corporate interests, capable of ensuring legal and constitutional continuity is soon evident. Besides, the judiciary must adequately fulfill the role of controlling the constitutionality of laws and governmental acts while ensuring respect for international agreements undertaken by the states, particularly those dealing with human rights, which have constitutional status. For instance, in their judgments judges should apply the *pro homine* principle, under which in case of doubt, they should seek solutions that are more conducive to the full enjoyment of human rights, freedom and equality within an environment that ensures the quality of life.[2] Judges should also put an end to all circumstances that generate any kind of discrimination against persons or groups of persons and continue their efforts to guarantee the human rights and freedoms enshrined in the Constitution, international treaties and laws. At all costs, they should avoid the existence of impunity since it generates an immediate violation of the principle of equality and prevents judges from fighting against corruption and organized crime.

The Emergency—An Argentine Syndrome

In Argentina, "the emergency" has been and is one of the key elements of its fluctuating institutional life. This phenomenon has its precedents in colonial times and, as in modern times, it seems to have been the cause of the abolition of the laws enacted by the Council of the Indies. The influence of the colonial period is central to current institutions and practices, such as the current lack of compliance with the law.

Whenever a so-called "emergency" is claimed to exist, almost all the institutions provided for in the Constitution are distorted: every time an emergency is invoked by the authorities, a part of the Constitution becomes temporarily void and the mandatory nature of public law is denied. In fact, the "rule of emergency" is inversely proportional to the rule of law. The alleged emergency, considered as such by those in power, cannot be an excuse for the abolition of all constitutional content, not even when such cases are stipulated by the Constitution. There are clear restrictions and limits on the scope of an emergency on the basis of definitions in both national and international sources. Nevertheless, the recurrence of this phenomenon in Argentina (and various countries in Latin America), where there seems to be frequent support for any departure from the rules set forth in constitutional norms, is a serious concern.

The result of this practice is that two Constitutions coexist permanently side by side; one is applied to regular times and the other to exceptional circumstances. Clearly, the analysis of our reality makes it difficult to determine which achieves more effectiveness. The development of the use of the emergency has been the result of many factors such as the existence of a culture originating primarily in those who rule the country, who are unwilling to submit their decisions to the rule of law. This attitude is combined with a disproportionate emphasis on the notions of order and efficiency and the claim that, to achieve them, it is necessary to deviate from the "formalities" established in the Constitution and laws. This leads to an ongoing confrontation between *de jure* legitimacy and *de facto* legitimacy as sources of rulers' authority, and of course, to the lack of an effective enforcement of the principle of separation of powers.

Undoubtedly, the inability to have controlling bodies, especially courts, capable of putting an end to this situation has led to a gradual erosion of many of the elements of the rule of law, since it has not been possible to avoid such deviations. All the above-mentioned circumstances have contributed to the weakening of the democratic system as a whole, with the corresponding increase in citizens' disbelief in the goodness of a system that proclaims the full force of the notions of limited power and recognition of human rights. For this system seems not to match word to action, since such notions are not translated into facts, limiting their scope just to what is set forth in the Constitution and the law.

Judicial Review—Supervisory Function

Very often the pretext of an "emergency" has served as a disguise for an underlying ultimate objective pursued by authorities at the head of the state. Indeed, this expression represents a sort of talisman at the service of autocrats to ignore any rule that may imply a limit to the exercise of their powers. This is not the way constitutionalism is supposed to evolve in democracies. On the contrary, in consolidated systems, the institutional framework shows a trend towards a progressive increase in supervisory functions. The role of the courts in ensuring the vitality and effective functioning of the Constitution has been critical. As early as 1803, the seminal case decided by the U.S. Supreme Court, *Marbury vs. Madison*, established the mechanism of judicial review, which entails the judicial control of the constitutionality of laws and acts of government. This mechanism entitled every person to appear before a judge pursuing a declaration of unconstitutionality of a law if they believed it infringed the exercise of a right. The power of judicial review implies that all courts are expected to determine the constitutionality of laws or decrees whenever such an issue is presented before them. This is a demonstration that the judiciary holds the function of power controller *par excellence*. Moreover, for the constitutional scheme to be successfully applied, it was necessary to create specific monitoring bodies to strengthen the tools that were already rooted in the three branches of government. Thus, the Ombudsman, the Auditor and Comptroller General's Office, the Office of Administrative Investigations and the Anti-Corruption Bureau are some of the bodies that have been incorporated to the Argentine system.

Notwithstanding the rules of judicial review, political authority has managed to place its actions out of the range of judicial eyes. Remarkably, this has been possible due to theories that have emerged within the judiciary itself. Among them, the doctrine of "nonjusticiable" political questions has been the most frequently invoked (Black 1927, 89). Fortunately, the evolution of constitutionalism has tended to dismiss such a position. This is what the Argentine Supreme Court decided in its ruling in *Verbitsky, Horacio s/ Habeas Corpus*, which carefully delimits the Court's powers against those of the administration.[3] The ruling establishes that courts are not competent to make valid assessments of public policies regarding prisons. According to this ruling, the judiciary must ensure the effectiveness of rights, and that is a clearly nonactionable issue. It is undoubtedly true that the judiciary must prevent rights from being violated—this constitutes their fundamental objective at the time of deciding a dispute. Policies have a constitutional framework that cannot go against what is enshrined in the Constitution.

Furthermore, the Inter-American Court of Human Rights, responsible for enforcing the jurisdiction of the American Convention on Human Rights, has taken sides. Again, it seems important to draw attention to one of the central paragraphs of its most emblematic statements, according to which "this obligation" refers to controlling the observance of the rights it contains. It also implies that member states are responsible for organizing governmental institutions and, in general, all the structures through which public power is exercised, so that they are capable of juridical protection, thus ensuring the free and full exercise of human rights. Because of this obligation, the state must prevent, investigate and punish any violation of the rights recognized by the convention. If possible, it must restore the right violated and, if necessary, repair the damage caused by the violation of human rights.[4]

Judges, of course, are the guarantors of the effective application of the fundamental law and, therefore, must prevent the violation of the fundamental rights it provides and those arising from the federal block of constitutionality as a whole, composed of the Constitution, international treaties and federal laws. Judges must not turn a blind eye to violations of this kind when they are the product of the action of government officials. Judges must enforce the accountability of government officials for acts and behavior that violate or undermine any fundamental rights. The judiciary has to take immediate, effective action to put an end to such abuse and monitor, investigate and, where appropriate, punish the offenders by annulling acts and restoring rights.

Judicial review of executive powers should be guaranteed in order to prevent any usurpation by the executive of the powers of other authorities. Indeed, there are actions requiring the intervention of Congress, for instance the appointment and removal of certain officials under the constitutional text. The executive has repeatedly infringed these mechanisms.

Judges must limit executive decision-making capacity according to the regulatory frameworks that make decisions predictable in order to ensure equality and transparency and, above all, that government acts are reasonable and pursuant to law. In short, any act of authority issued under the rule of law must conform to the principle of legality. However, this does not involve the annulment of the will of the president in the exercise of specific authority, considering the possibility and merit of each decision. The president is held responsible for a wide range of functions related to the subject of each decision he/she makes. However, every decision should be framed within the limits set by the respective rules governing the president's competence. Judges should restrict the arbitrary exercise of government powers so that the principle of supremacy of the Constitution is observed.[5]

Transition to Democracy—The Effects of the 1994 Constitutional Amendment

The transition to democracy that began in Argentina in 1983 has allowed the enjoyment of individual rights, but has not yet produced an adequate balance of powers. Especially important is the fact that the judiciary has been relatively restrained in the exercise of its power due to low independence (or, in some cases, even to the lack of it), from the executive and the legislative powers. In addition, there has been constant overlapping of jurisdictions between Congress and the executive. The current administration, far from rebuilding the controls, has insisted on opposing the return of powers to the legislature. Indeed, the executive continues to regularly enact necessity and urgency decrees exercising a number of legislative faculties delegated to it by Congress.[6] This has happened since the "Economic Emergency Act" in 2002,[7] reconfirmed every year by the Congress.

Issues arising from electoral life require thorough control to prevent the violation of equality among the contestants, provide for the proper use of funds and highlight the relevance of the provisions under the Constitution, laws and regulations. It is at this point that equality shows a serious deficit. The elections of 2009 and 2011 revealed serious breaches of both the Constitution and electoral laws that apply to political parties. Judicial review was delayed and ineffective and certain important attributions still remain in the hands of the Ministry of Interior, the last body that should possess them due to its institutional nature. Therefore, different mechanisms must be implemented in order to control election processes, seeking inspiration in the evolution of this issue in the more consolidated democracies of the world.

The so-called *amparo colectivo*, or collective injunction (Section 43 Argentine Constitution),[8] incorporated into the Constitution in the last amendment in 1994, has proved to constitute an appropriate tool for the defense of collective rights and public interests. Of course, there are significant shortcomings with regard to discrimination, the environment, consumer rights and the right to health, among many other legal rights. The amparo colectivo is a constructive institutional development that has become particularly evident in the Argentine Supreme Court ruling *"Matanza-Riachuelo."*[9]

The amendment of the chapter of the Constitution devoted to the judiciary was based mainly on that power's lack of prestige and independence. The reforms in 1994 tended to make the judiciary stronger after its loss of independence from political powers, particularly the executive. This amendment also comprised issues relating to the appointment and removal of judges and their training, as well as the administration of the judiciary and its budget, as well as its disciplinary power over its members. Therefore, it is noteworthy that the need to make a clear reference to a crucial aspect of the democratic transition underlies the reform in the matter at hand. For the above-mentioned reasons, within that context of transition, it seems clear that the decision of devising a constitutional reform aimed at achieving the strength and independence of the judiciary.

The Council of the National Judicature, an organ basically inspired by its Italian namesake, was created as a result of the amendment in 1994. However, the powers granted to the Argentine Council go beyond those conferred to the Italian body since the former is also responsible for selecting candidates for the lower federal courts (first instance justices and chambers of appeal), as well as for the administration of the judiciary and the exercise of disciplinary authority over members of the justice system, among other attributions. The Argentine Council of the National Judicature also incorporated a jury responsible for the removal of judges. It should be noted that the Argentine Constitution of 1853 took the U.S. Constitution as a model for developing its organic part. Thus, in the judicial field, the provisions were almost identical to those written in Philadelphia in 1787. However, in the United States, the system has worked significantly better, particularly in areas such as the independence of the judiciary. Such a significant distance between the source system and its "copy" forces us to conclude that the operational aspects in the former were different from those in the latter. What becomes evident as a problem in Argentina is related to the publicity surrounding the momentous events of appointment and removal of judges. In a longstanding custom in the United States, these processes take place in the public eye. In particular, all the work of the Senate, prior to the granting of the agreement to the candidate proposed by the executive, occurs in public hearings open to both the citizenry and the media. Therefore, the actions unfolding first in the committee, and then on the Senate floor, are broadcast on television and radio. Undoubtedly this public quality operates as an instrument of control that forces an institutional rationale to take precedence over a political-partisan one.

In light of this scenario, one could ask why the 1994 Argentine Convention preferred the adoption of institutions taken from European parliamentary systems, rather than introducing the abovementioned innovations of the evolution of the nomination of judges in the United States. A case in point: in Argentina, the current reform establishes the participation of politicians—legislators and an executive delegate—as members of both the council and the jury. The proportion of politicians versus lawyers as regards the composition of political powers (legislators and executive representatives) has become more unbalanced with the 2006 reform of the corresponding law,[10] which established that the political sector would constitute the majority in the council's composition, while the first minority would be composed of representatives of the ruling party. To submit three candidates to be considered for the appointment of a judge or to request the prosecution to initiate a process of removal requires two-thirds of the 13 members. Therefore, it is necessary that at least part of that minority be involved. Judges are under severe pressure from the executive. Due to the decisive presence of the government in the council, elections within are intimately connected with the duties of the judges and their performance. Therefore, there is always a threat that those who do not fulfill the political power's expectations might be punished, which undoubtedly implies a serious threat to the independence of the judiciary. Judges, then, have to face serious problems when they must act independently in cases that might affect the interests of the incumbent government.

REFORMS TO THE JUDICIARY

One of the most relevant issues in discussion during the transition to democracy was the need for an independent judicial system. The critical factors behind judicial reform in the region are "the need to provide citizens with access to impartial justice systems, and the recognition that the judicial systems in these countries need to be strengthened in order to promote investment and growth. Judicial reform efforts are alive and well" (Hall et al. 1996, 5). More specifically, the reform process was motivated by the weakness of the judiciary within the institutional framework; the need for a solution to the existing problem of the politically influenced appointment of judges; the need for more effective and dynamic mechanisms for the removal of judges; the lack of professionals qualified in management skills including administrative networks, such as human resources (discipline measures, hiring, promotion systems, etc.), budget administration and allocation of resources and organization of venues and jurisdictions; the appointment and removal of judges and finally, the creation of new federal organisms such as the Council of the National Judicature in Argentina and Venezuela.

As of 1998, 19 Latin American countries were moving from inquisitorial judicial systems to accusatory or mixed systems. Effective reforms were carried out in the following areas: (1) improving judicial administration, (2) strengthening judicial independence, (3) developing alternative forms of dispute resolution, (4) improving judicial education and (5) improving access to justice. The key factors in determining how successful this reform has been are the degree of institutionalization and the judicial budget. It has been stated that

> while increasing judicial budgets is seen as essential for judicial independence, that step alone will prove insufficient either to ensure independence or to produce a system that will satisfy both independence and accountability. To attain both these ends, expenditures must be made in a transparent and accountable manner ... In order to win public confidence there is a need to improve court administration and the day-to-day management of cases and enhance judicial independence by establishing procedural and budgetary autonomy. (Hall, Stromsen and Hoffman 1996, 7)

In Argentina, with the incorporation of the Council of the Judiciary, the 1994 constitutional reform aimed to limit the discretion and arbitrariness that had characterized the selection process for judges, and to provide a more technical and apolitical mechanism for removal. Thus, it was established that the council would fulfill the former role of the Chamber of Deputies as the prosecuting body in cases of impeachment and a special jury of judges who would assume the role of the Senate as chamber judge was created.

Before this amendment, the Constitution followed the Philadelphia model; that is, judges were elected by the president, with agreement of a majority in the Senate.[11] This choice was left to the discretion of the president and his occasional parliamentary majority in the Senate. Thus, there was no control over the technical and moral suitability of the candidates, a situation further affected by the fact that these Senate sessions were secret. Therefore, the representativeness and credibility of the judiciary[12] were questioned and this generated, first in academic circles and eventually throughout the legal environment,[13] the idea that it was necessary to create a new system for appointing judges which would ensure not only the suitability of the candidates, but also greater transparency and independence.[14]

Regarding the amendments of the system of constitutional control—judicial review—the model for establishing new organisms was taken from the European system (e.g., constitutional council). Furthermore, amendments to the effects of sentences regulating constitutional checks were also included, enabling them to have an *erga omnes* effect, not only restricted to the parties involved.

REPRESENTATIVENESS OF THE JUDICIARY

The above description of the operation of the judicial branch leads us to conclude that the evolution of institutions in Argentina (and probably in other parts of Latin America) underscores the role of the executive at the expense of the other powers. This situation is rooted, I argue, in the colonial period. Curiously, in most Latin American countries, the excessive power of the executive persists and leads to the so-called "hyperpresidentialism," an expression that describes a system in which the president plays a hegemonic role that considerably weakens the role of the legislative and judiciary, unlike what happens in the United States (Constitutional Reform 1986; Nohlen and Fernandez 1998; Ferrreira and Goretti 1994; Linz and Valenzuela 1994; Laría 2008; Peltzer 2006).

The fragility of the independence of the judiciary in relation to the other two powers is the result of various factors. One of them is related to the non-elective nature of judges in comparison to the occupants of other powers who are elected by vote; they are not representative, because they are not elected. In this regard, the criticism is connected with the so-called "countermajoritarian" argument that politicians often use whenever a sentence imposes a limitation on the exercise of state power. The argument aims to prove that, due to their lack of representativeness, judges are not entitled to oppose the decisions of those who are the true representatives of the sovereignty of the people—the president and the lawmakers. In fact, this argument is contrary to what the Constitution states. However, it reveals the existence of a culture opposed to controls, in which the powers of elected officials are considered to be absolute. Thus, the voter would be the only one entitled to control the political power through the vote. This situation would take place when the citizens choose not to reappoint an officer or to switch the majority of the representation in Congress from the ruling political party to another one (Tribe 1988; Bickel 1978; Ely 1980)

Judges generally come from the higher social classes. Although this feature has been somewhat limited since the democratic transition, it is still true in general terms. Some authors maintain that judges act according to a culture representative of what is considered the "family court," given the level of close bonds between them. Judges seem to have a tendency to act as a sort of elite. As a result, there are certain surnames that endure throughout the years and lead to the fact that the same families play key roles in the judiciary. In addition, judges have close relatives who very often fill vacancies in the judiciary due to the lack of transparency in the process of appointment of such officials.

Judges are considered state officials distant from the concerns of the community, unable in many cases to satisfy citizens' essential needs. The high cost of what we might call "legal services" together with attorney fees contribute to this idea. Citizens in Argentina can obtain what is called "benefit at no cost to litigate," but in any case, this also needs to be brought before the courts by a lawyer. Therefore, professional, appropriate, efficient and effective legal services free of charge, and legal counseling of people about their rights and how to uphold them is still a complex, difficult to realize objective. Citizens have free access to counseling and defense attorneys. However, this legal counseling is insufficient in view of the huge potential demand from the most vulnerable individuals in society.

All these factors support the idea that justice is not really representative. People are not aware that the judiciary is part of the government of the country the same way and together with the executive and legislative branches. In fact, the vast majority of the population, when asked about the government, thinks of the president's office. Despite this, I hold the view that popular elections are not convenient to appoint judges, as judges perform duties of a technical nature.

The emergence of nongovernmental organizations (NGOs) as new actors on the political scene, however, has made previously unknown judicial actions public. The phenomenon first appeared in the field of human rights during periods of dictatorship in various Latin American countries (Peru, Chile, Argentina, Brazil, El Salvador, Guatemala). The actions taken by these organizations created some awareness regarding the rights that deserve protection. With the return to democracy, NGOs became key players in the pursuit of truth and the punishment of those guilty of crimes against humanity.

As a result, the new concept of "civil society" appeared, referring to a militant stance in the defense of public issues, and fostering the development of advocacy work in several areas. NGOs were created to fight against discrimination, to uphold gender equality, protect the environment, the rights of consumers and users and institutional quality, among many other issues. The new Constitutions of redemocratized countries like Argentina left authoritarian systems behind by incorporating these new collective rights and certain legal tools aimed at their defense and protection, such as collective defense, prosecution to the defense of collective interests, class action, public hearings and right of free access to public information (Ryan 2001; Morello, Flah and Smayevsky 1993; Sabsay 1998).

The governments of new democracies ratified the international and regional treaties that make up the so-called International Law of Human Rights, which has had great influence on the evolution of institutions, particularly in strengthening the role of the judiciary. The American Convention on Human Rights, in particular, provides a supranational jurisdiction, and most members consider that the American Commission and Court's decisions supersede national judgments.

These new institutions have helped to obtain victories in the courts in environmental matters, defense of indigenous peoples and free market competition, among many other areas. Regarding the environment, NGOs have filed lawsuits to protect watersheds and required the completion of the environmental impact assessments when opposing a mining project. Furthermore, due to the importance, complexity and political sensitivity of the issues, these profound changes have promoted the mandatory holding of public hearings.

Another example of wider access to justice took place during the economic crisis in Argentina in 2001–2002, which spurred a set of regressive government interventions. The freezing of savers' bank deposits sought to avoid a dramatic reduction in international reserves and the beginning of a hyperinflation period. Nevertheless, this policy measure weakened the financial system's credibility and produced an avalanche of appeals, a phenomenon that produced the collapse of courts, as they were not able to deal with so many simultaneous claims. These new realities have helped to confer greater representativeness on judges who, in the eyes of the community and in contrast to previous years, are now considered more capable of resolving claims than the other powers, and more effective too. On the other hand, "judicial activism" or "guarantor judges" are expressions that hold a pejorative connotation for conservatives.

Another cause to bear in mind in terms of the lack of independence of the judiciary lies in the lack of constitutional continuity as a result of the military coups that have plagued most Latin American countries. Thus, after the collapse of the constitutional government in Argentina, the military government that followed each coup appointed new members of the judiciary. This did not happen after the first coup in 1930, since the Supreme Court declared through a statement that the new authorities were legitimate.[15] Therefore, the Supreme Court (whose members were appointed, or at least most of them, by that same government) had to seek pragmatic arguments to support the government of the moment, which necessarily influenced the other spheres of justice.

The 2010 Human Rights Watch (HRW) Annual Report noted some difficulties in the implementation of judgments of the Argentine Supreme Court. An example is the Sosa case, which aroused a strong reaction from most Argentine citizens. The Supreme Court decision in *Sosa* upheld that the former attorney general to the Superior Court of the Province of Santa Cruz, who had been unconstitutionally dismissed by former President Nestor Kirchner while he was the governor of that province in 1995, had to be reinstated in his position. Eduardo Sosa's claim reached the Supreme Court after 12 years of judicial proceedings and obtained a favorable judgment. Nevertheless, the governor of Santa Cruz has not complied with the ruling. The HRW's report states, "President Fernandez expressed her support for the governor, who refused to reinstate the Attorney General, noting that the ruling was unconstitutional" (192). The report also draws attention to the current situation in prisons, asserting that "overcrowding, abuse by guards and inmate violence continue to pose serious problems in detention centers." According to the report, "although in 2005, the Court [in *Verbitsky*, mentioned above] ordered that all prisons must comply with the UN Standard Minimum Rules for the Treatment of Prisoners," they are still held under extremely dangerous and "inhumane conditions."

CONCLUSIONS

It is necessary to go back to Argentina's colonial past in order to understand the difficulties for the establishment of a full democracy and the subsequent lack of a consistent collective institutional culture based on constitutional principles. That past, marked by the autocratic power embodied in the personal representatives of the Spanish crown in America, bore all the features of absolute power. In this context, a tradition in favor of organizing an independent judiciary becomes a difficult task.

I argue that the influence of the colonial period survives and is still central to the subject at hand, the fragility of the judiciary, due mainly to the disproportionate size of the executive branch. The practices of colonial government are reflected, above all, in an authoritarian way of ruling, even during democratic periods, which have been characterized by a hegemonic executive performance and very low enforcement levels of the law.

Spain's system of royal absolutism lasted nearly four centuries, beginning in the 15th century, and its rules were imposed on the colonies. It was based on the supremacy of the crown and the divine authority of the King, marking the supernatural origin of government. The autocratic power embodied in the personal representatives of the Spanish crown in America, bore all the features of absolute power. The Council of the Indies was the most important ruling institution, its competence extending to every sphere of government: legislative, financial, judicial, military, ecclesiastical and commercial. The King was the absolute Lord of the Indies and the council his mouthpiece. All laws and decrees relating to the administration, taxation and police of the American dominions were prepared and dispatched by the council, with the approval of the King and in his name. The decisions of the authorities established in the colonies had to be based on the laws and resolutions issued by the Council of the Indies, but when these arrived they were often not observed, either because they took eight months to arrive and were therefore outdated, or because they were not considered appropriate according to the criteria of the local ruler. In these cases, the latter attached the following text to the resolutions and laws: "the law is adhered to but not obeyed" (*la ley se acata pero no se cumple*). This is a very important feature of the institutional culture at that time that surprisingly still survives.

The presidential practice of legislating by decree under an alleged state of emergency is the typical present expression of the personal authority we are referring to. The lack of effective supervisory powers to counterbalance this phenomenon and the indifference of public opinion makes the principle of the separation of powers of a democratic system very difficult to fulfill. As this shows, the personal power of the ruler whose will was not limited by any legal framework prevailed, and survives even now in spite of the fact that a democratic Constitution should be an obstacle against the authoritarian behavior of the president.

The independence of the ancient colonies did not bring democracy to their societies; in most countries, the path to democracy has been slow and laborious and often punctuated by dictatorships. This was the case of Argentina through a long period that started in 1930 with the first *coup d'état*, which was followed by five more and ended in 1983 with the first elected government after nearly a decade of the most cruel military regime that Argentines had ever experienced.

The transition to democracy in Latin America that began in the 1980s was accompanied by important institutional reforms, starting with new Constitutions or at least far-reaching reforms to existing ones. Among them were proposals aimed at modifying the judiciary in order to overcome its shortcomings. The main objective was to increase its independence, and to that end amendments were made ranging from a system of appointment and removal of judges, and the administration of justice to the system of judicial review. However, many of these objectives have not yet been achieved.

The boost given by civil society to justice in its search for the protection of collective rights and interests is particularly important. It has been accompanied by the introduction of third generation rights and guarantees to the text of the Constitutions for their protection, with adherence to the core treaties that make up the International Law of Human Rights. These developments have facilitated access to justice and outstanding rulings in areas such as protection of the environment, consumer rights and discrimination, among others. As a consequence, the judiciary has acquired a reputation for greater effectiveness. Despite this progress, much remains to be done to ensure that Argentina possesses an independent and effective judiciary. For that to happen, it is necessary for society as a whole to perceive that its achievement is a crucial condition to improve the quality of life. To achieve this goal, other far-reaching institutional reforms should also take place, such as the amendment of procedural codes, the technical modernization of courts, a broadening of who has standing to sue thus providing better access to justice and the creation of institutional tools to facilitate citizen participation. I believe that only when that empowerment is experienced will the judiciary become more representative, opening the way for the consolidation of Latin American democracies.

NOTES

1. Argentine legal expert, scholar and politician, whose work inspired the drafting of the Argentine Constitution.
2. "The *pro homine* postulate represents an hermeneutical criterion that informs the whole system of human rights. According to it, the broader law should be used, or the more extensive interpretation, when recognizing protected rights and, inversely, the more restrictive law or interpretation when trying to set up permanent restrictions to exercising the rights or trying to suspend them extraordinarily" (Pinto 1997, 163).

3. Argentine Supreme Court, *Verbitsky, Horacio s/ hábeas corpus* (2005, vol. 328, 1146). The ruling analyzes the reality of prisons in the province of Buenos Aires, where the bad conditions in which inmates live imply a serious violation of the fundamental rights enshrined in international treaties.

4. Inter-American Commission on Human Rights, Velásquez Rodríguez Case, Decision of 29 July 1988, Inter-Am Court of Human Rights, Series C, N° 4, para. 166 (1988).

5. Argentine Supreme Court, *Itzcovich Mabel vs. National Administration of Social Security*, March 29, 2005, (Vol. 328 566).

6. Article 99.3 of the Argentine Constitution determines that the executive power is not allowed to legislate. Only when exceptional circumstances prevent Parliament from creating laws and when the matter does not involve penal sanctions, taxes, political parties or electoral issues can the executive power dictate decrees of a legislative nature.

7. Act 25.561, January 7, 2002.

8. A kind of injunction (*amparo*) devised to protect collective rights and a tool against discrimination.

9. Argentine Supreme Court, *Mendoza*, June 20, 2006 (Vol. 329, 2316). The case was an environmental suit for collective environmental damages by a group of neighbors in Cuenca Matanza-Riachuelo.

10. Act 24.937 of the National Council of Magistrates was amended in 2006 by Act 26.080.

11. The essence of this system, at least in the United States, was to limit—whenever possible—the excesses committed by representatives by making the Senate and the executive, the "weakest" powers, participate in the appointment process. It is worth reading Gargarella (1996, 29–34) for a description of the deliberate intention of the American constituent members to limit the excesses of the "irrational" performance of majorities, through their representatives.

12. For a description of the feeling of skepticism towards the judicial system, see Chapter I from *Verbitsky* (1993, 15–30).

13. From doctrine, Néstor Sagués may have been one of the most enthusiastic advocates and promoters of the Council. See "El Consejo de la Magistratura y su inserción en el régimen de reclutamiento de jueces," *Jurisprudencia Argentina* (1989, Vol. 4, 890) and "El Consejo de la Magistratura," *El Derecho* (113–851), where he promoted the incorporation of this body to our system long before the idea appeared in the minds of the most critical politicians.

14. Mario A. Midón states, for example, that in the 1994 reform, the framers of the Constitution came to a political agreement, a partisan one in the first place, and then a legislative one, Núcleo de Coincidencias Básicas, section H, part of Act 24.309, which declared the need for constitutional reform with the aim of limiting the executive's and Congress's intervention in the appointment and removal of judges that were not members of the Supreme Court; this was a way of counterbalancing the presidential government in Argentina and the concentration of constitutional power that it has.

15. These kinds of decisions of the Court are known as *acordadas*, to distinguish them from the judgments. Their main feature is the *erga omnes* effect.

Part IV
Civil Society

10 Meanings and Challenges of Representativeness in Brazilian Civil Society

Evelina Dagnino

The title of this chapter states the need to recognize that representativeness—and this is my main argument—is far from being univocal. Its different meanings within the Brazilian political debate, in its intellectual and academic versions, express a dispute between different views of civil society, of participation and even of wider conceptions of democracy itself. This dispute between different political projects pervades both civil society and the state, in their mutually constitutive relationships. Such a dispute cannot be understood without reference to the historical context in which it takes place, and I begin by briefly presenting it.

In Brazil today most of the political activity of civil society sectors takes place embedded in relationships with the state, at its various levels and sectors. Since the 1970s, a significant part of civil society has been deeply involved in the struggles for the reestablishment of democracy and also for its deepening and the extension of citizenship in the country. As Brazilian political elites and institutions, organized through liberal representative democracy, have been historically unable or unwilling to confront the striking levels of inequality and exclusion, civil society participation has been seen as a political tool to address these problems. Accordingly, that participation has been predominantly defined by a large part of its defenders as aiming at sharing decision-making power with respect to public policies related to inequality and exclusion. Sustained by defenders of participatory democracy, this definition translated a concern with the quality of representation, given the enormous distance between political society and the great mass of Brazil's population.

As a result, the 1988 Constitution, known as the Citizen Constitution, established the principle of civil society participation in decision-making processes. After it, a large number of public spaces were implemented in order to ensure this participation, conceived to share the decisional power of the state with respect to public policies. From management councils (*Conselhos Gestores*), in several areas of public policy, such as health, social assistance, housing, education, children and adolescence, women, and so on, which are mandatory at city, state and federal levels, to participatory budgeting, conferences, forums, and so forth, there is a multitude of spaces where concerned sectors of both civil society and the state must be represented, most of them on a quantitatively equal basis, in a parity relationship.[1] Although some of these spaces, such as participatory budgeting, include some mechanisms of direct democracy, all of them rely basically on representation. It is important thus to point out that, although participatory democracy has been introduced as an attempt to counter the vices and malfunctioning of a representative democracy recognized as ineffective to face the pervasive inequalities of Brazilian society, some of the challenges it confronts are related to representation, sharing therefore some of the same problems. As a consequence, representation and representativeness are crucial questions when we talk about civil society participation.

It must be clear that, although predominant today, representation within formalized public spaces does not exhaust the repertoires of action of civil society, that include public demonstrations, protests and other forms of addressing both state agencies and the society as a whole.

As it becomes clear from the nature of the 1988 Constitution, it is fair to say that political forces oriented towards the deepening of democracy have been able to assert some basic principles of a democratic participatory project that had articulated a significant part of civil society along the 1980s. A variety of social movements organized around the struggle for rights have been a key element in this articulation. The struggle for rights, the main reference to citizenship, included a range that runs from the "right to have rights" to the right to participate actively in power, thus transcending not only electoral participation and representation but also the idea of a mere passive "inclusion" (Dagnino 1994, 1998, 2005).

With the implementation of the neoliberal project in 1989, a year after the 1988 Constitution was approved, with the election of Collor de Mello and, later, with the eight years of Cardoso's government, from 1995 to 2002, other modalities of civil society participation have been defended and promoted. A focus on the transfer of public responsibilities from the state to civil society, formalized in the 1998 state reform led by the then Minister Bresser Pereira, and a conception of social policies as duties to be shared with civil society through the so-called partnerships (*"parcerias"*),[2] embodied in Brazil the neoliberal principles adopted at the global level. In addition to the privatization of state enterprises, the transfer of the state's social responsibilities to individuals, civil society and the private sector are considered fundamental for the paring down and reduction of the state's inefficiency.

Along the process, the previous meanings attributed to civil society and participation have been redefined accordingly. Thus, civil society began to designate increasingly—and almost exclusively—nongovernmental organizations (NGOs); that is, those organizations of civil society able to carry the new functions envisaged for them by dominant forces in the new correlation of forces. In this sense, the neoliberal project adopted by most governments in Latin America ended up by being a powerful force in shaping the so-called civic domain and its subjects. The reconfiguration of civil society is reflected in the accelerated growth and the new role that has been taken on by nongovernmental organizations (NGOs), often referred to as the NGO-ization of civil society (Alvarez, 1999). It is also seen in the emergence of the so-called Third Sector and of entrepreneurial foundations, with a strong emphasis on a redefined form of philanthropy, and the marginalization (what some authors have referred to as the "criminalization") of social movements (Oliveira 1997). Governments fear the politicization of their engagement with social movements and workers' organizations, and seek reliable partners who can effectively respond to their demands while minimizing spaces of conflict. The configuration of a new relationship between state and society, expressed in the neoliberal project, is determined (particularly in Latin America) by an assessment of the characteristics of the state that make it inadequate in the context of a new reality. Thus, a state that was seen as characterized by huge size, inefficiency, excessive bureaucracy and corruption would encounter in this new relationship a route toward more efficient forms of action.

In addition, the preeminence of the market as a reorganizing axis of the economy is seen as worthy of extension to the rest of society. The search for efficiency and modernization thus works to legitimate the adoption of the market as the organizing principle of social, political and cultural life. The transfer of market logic to the state arena transforms governments into "service providers" and citizens into "clients" and "users." Sensitivity toward their demands and efficiency in attending to them become institutional imperatives. Hence, the participation of civil society from the neoliberal perspective is conceived as two-fold. On the one hand, it should supply state and market with qualified information on social demands. On the other, it is seen as providing those organizations with the ability to efficiently assume the execution of public policies oriented toward the satisfaction of these demands. In this view, participation means taking on the efficient execution of social policies, though the definition of the latter remains under exclusive state control. Participation is thus concentrated in management functions and policy implementation yet does not include decision-making power in relation to them.[3]

My central argument is that, as the dispute between these different projects has characterized the Brazilian political scenario for the last two decades, different modalities of civil society participation—that have emerged, as mentioned, under different force correlations—coexist as well as different understandings and meanings attributed to them.[4] Along the same lines and heavily impacted by them, different meanings of representation and representativeness have emerged in this scenario. These different meanings are thus connected to different political projects as well as to the different existing spaces of interaction between the state and civil society and to the different actors that compose, as we know, the great heterogeneity that characterizes civil society.

Recent literature on civil society and participation is unanimous in emphasizing issues of representation as constituting a crucial problem among the many faced by the Brazilian experiments in participatory democracy.[5] At the same time, there have been a number of efforts directed towards theorizing about the new forms of representation that emerged along with participatory and deliberative democracy, not only in Brazil but also elsewhere.

NEW FORMS OF REPRESENTATION, NEW ANALYTICAL CATEGORIES

The theoretical debate about new forms of representation is obviously not restricted to Brazilian analysts and there has been a fruitful exchange with the growing international literature on the subject. From classical notions such as Burke's "virtual" representation to the already consolidated notion of representation by "advocacy" (Urbinati 2000), among many others, there is an abundant collection of available notions of representation that have informed the Brazilian debate on the subject. They include Young's (2000) "representation of social perspectives," "discursive representation (Drysek 2000), "self-authorized" representation (Montanaro 2008) and even the profuse classification of "promissory," "anticipatory," "gyroscopic" and "surrogate" forms of representation catalogued by Mansbridge (2003).

However, it is worth noting that the Brazilian debate faces a major challenge, which is accounting for the specificities of our own civil society participation and representation. Therefore, concepts of representation that may seem appropriate to other contexts still leave room for dissatisfaction with respect to their analytical usefulness in a context where the main locus for the representation of civil society is a direct relationship with the state especially in the (formalized, to a greater or lesser degree) public spaces where decisions about public policies are to be made.[6] In addition, the great diversity of civil society, where highly professionalized NGOs coexist with combative social movements such as the Landless Movement (MST), adds to the complexity of representation and the challenge of producing analytical tools to understand it.

Theoretical efforts in the recent Brazilian literature concerned with representation have a common point of departure: the recognition of the "pluralization" (Lavalle et al. 2006) of representation brought about by the participation of civil society, and the assertion of the need to formulate new analytical categories capable of contributing to the understanding of the new forms taken by representation. New characteristics presented by civil society participation include the emergence of collective as distinct from individual representation (Lüchmann 2007); of legitimacy criteria no longer reduced to election or to explicit authorization as expressed by voting; of the impact of the different spaces where representation takes place (Moura 2011); and of the different levels of mobilization and organization of represented sectors upon the different emerging modalities, among others.

The notions of representation that emerge from that literature express, fundamentally, an effort to recognize as legitimate the forms of representation adopted by civil society, in spite of the fact that they do not usually rely on formal authorization and accountability, like the traditional forms of representation based on elections. For obvious reasons, the assertion from Urbinati that "different theories of representation are possible, depending on the relations between state and civil society" (Urbinati 2006, 194), as well as her disassociation between representative democracy and electoral democracy, have been inspirational elements in those efforts.

Thus, Avritzer's "representation by affinity," considered to be the typical representation of civil society, would be legitimated by the existence of "an identity or partial solidarity that occurred previously" (Avritzer 2007, 458). In addition, "[p]revious experience and sharing aims gives legitimacy to the process of choosing a civil society representative"(Avritzer 2008, 12).

Along similar lines, Lavalle and others (2006) rescued from Burke the notion of "virtual representation," emphasizing the subjective component, the sentiment of "commitment with the interests represented" (Lavalle et al. 2006, 89) and the purpose of political inclusion implicit in the notion, making it relevant in the recent process of expanding democracy. In addition, the authors call attention to the links between virtual representation and the generalized notion of "advocacy" and those defended by an "identity politics." Recognizing the limits of this notion of representation with respect to consecrated democratic requirements such as responsiveness, accountability and sanctions, the authors point out the novelty and the experimentation that characterizes civil society's representation and the already existing pressures toward the institutionalization of those requirements.

Such a concern with the legitimacy of representation does not seem to be shared by Avritzer, who is more interested in the relationship and balance between the different forms of representation:

> "In this sense, the question posed by contemporary politics should be one of a reduced concern about the legitimacy of these new forms of representation and one of an increased concern about the way in which they should apply to a political system governed by multiple sovereignties. The future of electoral representation seems to be increasingly tied to its overlapping with the forms of representation that have their origin in the participation of civil society." (Avritzer 2008, 14)

In a later formulation, Houtzager and Lavalle redefine the notion of virtual representation as "assumed representation" as "the assumption of representative roles without authorization or accountability from the relevant constituency through politically sanctioned methods" (Houtzager and Lavalle 2010, 10). Based on a survey of a sample of 229 organizations of civil society of different kinds in São Paulo, they found, among the 73% that consider themselves to be representative, six different kinds of "representative claims":

electoral, membership, mediation, service, proximity and identity. Inspired by the assertion by Saward (2006) that "representation is, in its essence, a claim about a relationship," thus keeping the emphasis on the subjective commitment of representatives, these claims are presented as existing competing notions of representation. Hence, temporarily putting aside the field of abstract theory, the authors focus on the concrete arenas where different actors hold different arguments to legitimize their representativeness. Moreover, they correctly stress the fact that all notions of representation are a historical product, resulting from successive political struggles in different contexts. For them, the mediation argument, which is predominant among the organizations of civil society although co-existing with the other arguments, express the changes in Brazilian society brought about by the advances of participatory democracy (or participatory governance, as they say): "Tellingly, the notions with the deepest historical roots, the outcomes of earlier political battles by a different cast of social forces—voluntary membership, electing leaders, and also identity—are the least common" (24).

This recognition of the connections between different notions of representation and the political struggles and their different correlations of force comes somehow closer to my central argument. However, such recognition in Houtzager and Lavalle is restricted to the historical process and is not carried further into the analysis of new emerging notions of representation themselves. Thus, representation conceived as "mediation" is seen as a rather homogenous notion, when a coherent implication of recognizing the importance of political struggles and contestations would require acknowledging the different meanings this "mediation" assumes in the continuing dispute over democratic building in Brazil. In addition, a crucial question would be to examine, in the relationships between state and civil society, who defines the practices and contents of such "mediation."

NEW CONCEPTIONS AND PRACTICES OF REPRESENTATIVENESS: WHO DEFINES THEM?

Recent developments in that dispute, as I pointed out previously, have been marked by a confluence of distinct projects that, placing themselves within the democratic domain, have promoted distinct conceptions of representation and representativeness. Differently from past political contexts, these projects do share a perception of the importance of civil society and the need to redefine its relationship with the state, opening it up to new voices and their claims. However, beyond this general perception, distinct views on the relationship between state and society, particularly with civil society—ultimately, the core of representation and of democracy itself—have been at stake. The notion of representation as mediation describes the role of the representation of civil society as enforcing that general perception, ensuring channels of access to the state. But it remains far from accounting for the conflictive diversity of forms and contents assumed by the relationship between state and civil society. Conflicts between different conceptions and practices of representation and representativeness are obscured under the homogenizing category of "mediation."

Neoliberal innovations, introduced especially during Cardoso's years (1995–2002), produced an important and lasting impact on the reconfiguration of that relationship and on the ways of conceiving it. Results of a research project[7] conducted in 2000–2001 through case studies on what we then called various "encounters" between the state and civil society in Brazil provide some empirical basis for a preliminary attempt to analyze that impact and to observe the variety of conceptions of representativeness that emerge from concrete political practices. The diversity of actors and of the spaces of interaction between them and the state that we studied revealed the diversity of meanings attributed to representativeness and the emergence of particular notions of it, but also noting more complex aspects of representativeness.

Those results obviously cannot be generalized but they are suggestive of the consequences of a decade of neoliberal rule. What becomes particularly evident from them is how the neoliberal state not only reconfigures its relationship with civil society, and contributes to shape the latter in the process, but also introduces new practices of representation and, as a consequence, of representativeness. Such process shows a specific dimension of the representation of civil society where, in the absence of consolidated, formal rules, power relations play a crucial role in defining, ad hoc, so to speak, who are and who are not legitimate representatives. It is important to mention that the variety of conceptions and practices of representation also derive, on the one hand, from the diversity of actors, in a civil society that becomes increasingly heterogeneous and complex. On the other hand, it is also connected to the various spaces of participation and relationship with the state opened up by the process of democratization.

Research results showed that the question of representation assumes varied facets and/or is understood in different ways by various actors. On the one hand, the MST's capacity to pressure, for example, is evident in its undertaking of protests and mass demonstrations which, like the number of participants in the participatory budgeting process and its capacity for mobilization, attest to their respective capacity of being representative.[8] In this case, this capacity is understood along the lines of the "classic" sense of representativeness: the link between represented and representatives is clearly demonstrated, unequivocally proved by the convoking (assembling) capacity of the representatives made possible, in turn, by the existence of that link. It is important to emphasize that the conception of representativeness based on the existence of this organic link expresses the option of those sectors of civil society, usually popular social movements, following a classic tradition, now coupled with participation in the new spaces of formal relationships with the state.[9] The visibility of the represented, either in marches and demonstrations in the streets or in packing the rooms where priorities in government investments are chosen, in order to participate in decisions to be made, as in the case of the participatory budgeting (PB), is the crucial factor in the effectiveness of their representatives. Tellingly, the reaction of different sectors of the state to this conception of representativeness was very different. While the federal government of Cardoso systematically tried, heavily supported by the media, to disqualify the MST as a legitimate representative of civil society, the main argument being that "the movement is political," the city government of Porto Alegre, occupied by the Workers' Party, not only praised but also stimulated popular participation in the PB process.

The autonomy of those sectors to decide about strategies for political action and conceptions of representativeness is at stake here: To what extent can it be sustained in a context where governmental political projects occupying the state promote other conceptions of representativeness? Other empirical elements convey the centrality of power relations involved in the dispute about attributing legitimacy to different forms of representation and representativeness.

Because they are always connected to distinct political projects, displacements of the notion of representativeness are obviously not innocent, neither in their intentions nor in their political consequences. One interesting example is the composition of the Council of the *Comunidade Solidária* (Solidarity Community) already mentioned, created by the Cardoso government at the very beginning of his mandate to be the main agency in charge of social policies. The representation of civil society in it took place through invitations by the government to individuals with "high visibility" in society: artists, television performers, newspaper columnists, and so on. This particular understanding of the notion of representativeness reduces it to social visibility, understood in turn as the space occupied in the various types of media. Such "social visibility" would turn these individuals automatically into legitimate representatives of civil society or of society as a whole. Protests against this practice have not been able to counter it and eventually led other representatives, such as the President of the Brazilian Association of NGOs (ABONG), to withdraw from the council.

Another manifestation of displacement can be identified in the case of the CCDM: in the northeastern state of Ceará, the representatives of civil society in the council were named due to their connection, not with the women's movements, but with the political parties. Instances of representation and agglutination of interests traditionally privileged, in this case the parties managed to maintain this privilege and also to place under their control the representation of civil society in the CCDM. Considering that the emergence of public spaces where civil society could be represented and have a voice has been clearly linked to the deficiencies in the representativeness of Brazilian political parties, it is only ironic that its representatives should be chosen based on party membership criteria. Here, political parties have been able to supersede organizations of civil society linked to the women's movements thanks to their entrenched position as the "legitimate" representatives of society but also to their strong links with the leadership of women's groups, a non isolated phenomenon as we see similar occurrences in other countries of Latin America (Panfichi 2003).

The most outstanding (and successful) case of emerging practices of representation and representativeness has been the one that erected NGOs as the representatives of civil society *par excellence*, when not the exclusive one. As in the other cases, this one is closely connected with different views of participation and of the role of civil society itself embodied in different political projects.

REPRESENTATION, REPRESENTATIVENESS AND NGOS

As civil society became, in Brazil and elsewhere, overpopulated by NGOs, their role as representatives of its different sectors also proliferated. For this reason, but also because the analysis of their capacity as representatives sheds light on important challenges for civil society participation, we shall examine it more closely.

An initial consideration is that, in spite of the impact of the neoliberal project, the field of NGOs (as that of civil society) in Brazil is very heterogeneous. Thus, it would be unfair to homogenize their role and ignore the diversity of NGOs, not only in terms of their political projects but also, particularly, in terms of their specific relationships with the state and with social movements. The state-influenced multiplication of NGOs after the introduction of the neoliberal project cannot obscure that the origin of many of these organizations in the 1980s was very much rooted in their close relations with social movements of various kinds. Their activities then included consultancies and support to the specific needs of these movements: political formation, technical support, information and communication resources and functions of articulation. Such relations were based on political convictions about the importance of supporting and facilitating the mobilization and organization of civic agents excluded from political power. As the state looked for reliable partners, NGOs became a favorite target and most of them could refuse neither the resources that came with the so-called "partnerships" (*parcerias*) nor the opportunities for participation (Teixeira 2002, 2003). Very often, during the Cardoso years, the partnerships to develop specific projects were announced as pilot experiments, to be later incorporated into universal social policies, in which NGOs could grasp the opportunity to influence state policies. Nevertheless, since resources were scarce, such interaction simply never happened. Hence, it seems that World Bank recommendations played a more important role in the neoliberal approach to NGOs' participation, praised by their potential to "reach poor communities and remote areas at low cost," as well as "the skills and resources they bring to emergency relief and development activities" (Gibbs, Kuby and Fumo 1999, 10).

In the case of NGOs, the capacity to represent seems to be, in the first place, based on the kind of competence they have: the state sees them as representative interlocutors in so far as they have specific knowledge that comes from their connection (past or present) with certain social sectors: youth, blacks, women, carriers of HIV, environmental movements, and so on, plus their technical competence and institutionalized format.

As a result of the opportunities opened up by the neoliberal conception of transferring social policies to NGOs through "partnerships" with governments, there has been a geometric growth of NGOs, accompanied, as mentioned, by the increasing tendency to reduce the notion of civil society to this type of actor. Additionally, the new requirements posed by the new formal spaces of participation, particularly the management councils in charge of formulating public policies, also contributed to the expansion of the role of technically equipped NGOs as representatives. These two factors will be examined in more detail below, but their consequence has been that NGOs' own definitions of representativeness increased in legitimacy. Hence, their belief and assertion that their capacity to represent derives from the fact that they express diffuse interests in society, to which they "would give voice," coupled with their technical and institutional capacities, became largely accepted. Bearers of these specific capacities, many NGOs come to see themselves as "representatives of civil society," in a particular understanding of the notion of representativeness.

However, it should be pointed out that this particular view of representativeness would follow then, in most cases, much more from a coincidence among these interests and those defended by the NGOs than from any explicit articulation or organic relationship between them and the bearers of these interests, a constitutive component of a classic view of representativeness. Moreover, as the new role of NGOs also imposed new requirements, the relationships with social movements became less and less important, even for those NGOs that continue to share a more egalitarian, participatory democratic project. Instead, an emphasis was put on complying with the new requirements: institutional and professional consolidation, technical competence and pragmatism. A conception of efficacy as the production of measurable results increasingly replaces the previous emphasis on the process of stimulating and supporting popular organization.

With the increasing professionalization and a growing abandonment of the organic links to the social movements, which had characterized them in former periods, the political autonomization of the NGOs creates a peculiar situation. Thus, these organizations are responsible to the international agencies that finance them and to the state, which contracts them as service providers, but not to civil society, whose representatives they claim to be, nor to the social sectors whose interests they bear, nor to any other organ of a truly public character. For as well intentioned as they might be, their activities express, fundamentally, the desires of their directors (Dagnino 2002).

Most of the concepts of representation discussed in the literature, as shown before, mostly reflect that view of representation. "Virtual representation," "assumed representation," "representation by affinity," "surrogate representation" and the wider concept of "advocacy" are basically founded on that coincidence. The possibility that such coincidence can come to produce an articulation and organic links with the represented is real but it is not a constitutive element of those concepts of representation.

Within the field of NGOs, and given its heterogeneity, that predominant conception has been intensely discussed. There have been reactions against it. Acknowledging the misrepresentation (here in its two different senses) that it may carry, a former president of the National Association of NGOs (ABONG) reacted, stating: "We don't represent anybody, we represent ourselves, period" (Interview with the author, 2001). In addition, some NGOs, as a result of political choices, have maintained or developed their links with social movements, which legitimize them as "authorized" representatives of their claims.

REPRESENTATION, REPRESENTATIVENESS AND SOCIAL MOVEMENTS

The need for technical competence is not restricted to NGOs and has been a huge challenge to social movements that search for representation in the new public spaces of participation. As the formulation of public policies constitute the main objective of these spaces, representatives of social movements must have the technical and political qualifications required by these new settings. The so-called "institutional insertion" of social movements represented a deep inflection with respect to their previous practices and required a difficult learning process in multiple directions. But it also has crucial consequences for representativeness and effectiveness in their representation. In assessing the significance of this challenge, the multiplication of participatory spaces has to be taken into consideration: 75% of the 5,500 Brazilian cities adopt some modality of civil society participation in the formulation of social policies; only in the city of São Paulo are there 35 municipal councils with representation from civil society. At the national level, from 2003 to 2010, during Lula's governments, there were 74 civil society national conferences on several sectors of public policy. It is not by chance then that more recent studies of those spaces have focused on the so-called "quality of participation and representation," emphasizing the existing limits and difficulties.

The intensity and the novelty of the demands posed by those spaces of representation require a learning process for the different sectors of civil society, particularly for popular social movements that is far from easy. The recognition of the different interests present and the ability to negotiate without losing autonomy, the construction of the public interest, the participation in the formulation of public policies that can effectively express this interest, are some of the challenges faced. The central feature of most of those spaces—their involvement with public policy, whether in its formulation, discussion, deliberation or execution—almost always demands a command over specialized technical knowledge, which representatives of civil society, especially from subaltern sectors, generally do not have. This knowledge includes the ability to understand a budget, a disbursement plan, options for medical treatment, different construction materials and techniques for depolluting rivers—there is an endless list of specific types of knowledge required in the different spaces of participation. In addition, another type of qualification is required: knowledge of the functioning of the state, the administrative machinery and the procedures involved.

This need for special technical qualifications has revealed itself to be one of the most important challenges for the representation of civil society, not just because it is a necessary condition for more effective participation, but also due to the implications it has taken on in practice. In the first place, the lack of this qualifications is not just an absolute deficiency, it is also a relative deficiency with respect to government officials and representatives of other, more privileged sectors of civil society, such as, for example, the hospital owners in the health councils. In this sense, it transfers an additional inequality to the public spaces, which can end up reproducing precisely what is its objective to eliminate: the privileged access to state resources, which engenders broader social inequality. In situations of open conflict with governmental representatives in the councils, for example, this deficiency on the part of civil society's representatives has been used not just to politically disqualify the latter, but has also cultivated and reinforced by its opponents as a way of exercising control over the decisions. On the other hand, for the representatives of popular movements, the sense of empowerment and the strengthening of their self-recognition as subjects that the acquisition of these qualifications brings contribute decisively to confronting the weight of a hierarchical cultural matrix that favors submission in relation to the state and dominant sectors, in addition to asserting politics as an elite-exclusive activity.

Furthermore, because of its centrality with respect to the effectiveness of representation, the acquisition of technical competence on the part of the leadership representing the subaltern sectors has often demanded a considerable investment of time and energy, where these are of limited availability. This ends up by taking time and energy from the leadership, which could be otherwise dedicated to maintaining more effective connections with the bases to be represented. Thus, research has shown that emphasis on the organic links between representatives and represented have been replaced by a focus on other requirements of representation.[10] Most importantly here, an additional implication is that the rotation of representation in these spaces becomes restricted: given the difficulties of acquiring that competence, those who acquire it tend to be perpetuated as representatives.

Here we find again "technical competence" replacing organic and effective links with the represented as a basis for representation. The relations between represented and representatives become diluted, with important implications for the political mobilization, organization and cohesion of the represented.

In this sense, the need for "professionalization" that has determined the multiplication of NGOs also affects social movements and their representatives. It implies a radical change in the repertoires of collective action and, to some extent, problematizes not only the very meaning of "collective action" and the distinction between social movements and NGOs,[11] but also notions of representativeness.

Along with technical qualifications, the political qualifications required in those spaces have also brought dilemmas of their own, with implications for representativeness. The previous trajectory of social movements, since the late 1970s, has been deeply marked by a concern with their autonomy. Historically, both state and political parties, including those on the left, had submitted the political organization of popular sectors in Brazil to control and use for instrumental purposes. The authoritarian regime provided a context where a rupture with this tradition could be envisioned, and the struggle against it included a rejection and a distance of any kind of relations with the state and political parties, in the name of autonomy.

Democratic developments engendered a different context where, in the 1990s, proximity and joint action between political society (both state and political parties) and civil society became, as we have seen, regular practices. The creation of the Workers' Party (*Partido dos Trabalhadores*, or PT) in 1980 has obviously been a central ingredient in these changes. In this new context, particularly in the public spaces of participation, where emphasis on the production of possible consensuses, the diversity of interests present and the face-to-face dialogue with government representatives represent new challenges, the capacity of negotiation and of establishing alliances becomes a challenge for the maintenance of autonomy.[12] Thus, it has been not unusual that the identity of the movement becomes defined "much more on the basis of its relationships with the state and political parties than on its societal localization" (Munck 1997).

This has been true especially when this autonomy—conceived as a crucial basis for representativeness—becomes contradictorily entangled with effectiveness. Tatagiba (forthcoming) considers that there is an "intrinsic tension between the principles of autonomy and of political effectiveness." That is to say, political effectiveness as the capacity to affect the political game and the production of decisions in directions favorable to their interests often requires from social movements specific actions that "are not always compatible with the principle of autonomy." Emphasis on strategic, instrumental dimensions may end up by subordinating the relations between representatives and represented. We could add, however, that sometimes effectiveness conceived as the production of immediate concrete results can be prioritized by those represented, even if the autonomy of the movement is to be compromised in the long run. Thus, in some cases and for some actors, representativeness can mean effectiveness and the concern with autonomy may become secondary. A good representative would then be one who can ensure immediate positive results. The major challenge is precisely the maintenance of that tension in the relationship between autonomy and effectiveness, without which social movements would become mere "clients" of the state, demanders of goods and services, losing their radical democratic potential.

In addition to the complex contexts provided by the public spaces of civil society participation, the presence of left-inclined governments at the various levels of the state has presented additional dilemmas that are related to this set of questions (political effectiveness, autonomy and representativeness).

REPRESENTATIVENESS AND EFFECTIVENESS AND THE RELATIONS BETWEEN CIVIL SOCIETY AND GOVERNMENTS

From 1982, when the PT obtained its first electoral victory, a gradual and steady ascent to governments at various levels took place, until Lula's election as president in 2002, followed by his reelection in 2006 and that of his successor, PT's Dilma Roussef, in 2010. Given the historically strong connections of the party with sectors of civil society, especially social movements, the electoral growth of the PT has transformed these connections into relationships between these sectors and the state, creating situations with important and ambiguous consequences to their autonomous representation.

If the public spaces of participation had created proximity between state and civil society representatives, governments led by the PT installed another kind of proximity with those social movements sympathetic to the party. The party heavily recruited leaderships of social movements to occupy positions within the state apparatuses. These transits between civil society and the state[13] have a double dimension: on the one hand, they intend to strengthen the representation of the party's political project within the state bureaucracy; on the other hand, they mean to commit the loyalty and support of social bases sharing that political project. For social movements, consequences have been ambiguous. They have been negative to the extent that social movements lost their most experienced representatives. However, on the other hand, these leaderships continue to be perceived as bearers of social movements' demands, and thus are expected to act as their representatives within the state apparatus. The ambiguity of such situations has caused tensions as both the representativeness of these leaderships and the autonomy of the movements have been affected.

In these contexts, part of the social movements becomes divided between guaranteeing their demands and preserving the governability of a leftist agenda. It is not unusual that they "tend to orient their action in a less conflictive, more conciliatory disposition, sometimes avoiding pressing governments and decreasing protest as a form of negotiation" (Tatagiba forthcoming). The inherent ambiguities of these situations are exemplarily shown in the disturbing formulation of a leader from the São Paulo Union of Housing Movements (*União dos Movimentos de Moradia do Estado de São Paulo*, or UMM). Referring to the relations established between the movement, the PT and the city administration during the government of PT's Marta Suplicy (2001–2004), this leader stated: "We ended up by sinning, perhaps, for not having demanded more from Marta, pressing more. And, on the other hand, we also sinned for not being able to re-elect her."[14]

What is evident here is the complex context in which part of social movements in Brazil situate themselves and their modalities of informal representation. Handling multiple allegiances—to the party, to sympathetic or "allied" governments and to the movement itself—they face relations of representation that are not always compatible, entailing contradictions and difficult choices. These choices slide between different logics of representation according to specific contexts and their dynamics and implications for the representativeness and the autonomy of these sectors of civil society is one example of the complex and difficult relations between the latter and the political society.

A FINAL NOTE

The discussion above intended to show the diversity of conceptions and practices of representation and representativeness of civil society and their connection to different political projects in dispute, active both in political sphere and in civil society itself. In the absence of formal, consolidated and consensual rules for representation and of criteria for representativeness, different criteria operate in different spaces of representation. Parameters of legitimacy also vary depending on the different actors and their beliefs about, ultimately, what a democratic polity is. However, such variation is not free from constraints and power relations play a crucial role in defining these criteria.

Participatory democracy and the representation of civil society it entails is a recent development beginning to be implemented in many parts of the world. When compared to other countries, Brazil has an exceptional array of participatory institutions, installed in the structure of the state. Although this has produced a significant experience of experimentation and an ongoing learning process of the challenges involved, the diversity of the spaces, actors and themes that constitute those institutions and of the different political projects that orient political practices in these spaces, seem to prevent univocal understandings of representation and representativeness.

Differently from other countries, the main challenge for civil society is not the creation of spaces for representation but how to occupy them in legitimate and effective ways. If the failure of the institutions of traditional representative democracy that led to the emergence of those new spaces is to be taken seriously, the distance between representatives and represented cannot be reproduced. Thus, the existence of consistent organic links between them still seems to be a crucial element of the route to follow.

224   *Evelina Dagnino*

NOTES

I want to thank the research support from the *Conselho Nacional de Pesquisas* (CNPq) in Brazil.

1. If we take representation at the city level, in Brazil there are more representatives in councils than *"vereadores"* (members of legislative bodies elected through universal vote) (Avritzer 2007).
2. Partnerships with NGOs and the private sector to develop specific projects were formulated and practiced by the Solidarity Council (*Conselho da Comunidade Solidária*) (Silva 2006), the agency created by Cardoso at the very beginning of his government.
3. See Teixeira (2003). The reform of the state that was implemented in Brazil in 1998 under the influence of Minister Bresser Pereira (who introduced the principles of "New Public Management") is very clear in relation to the different roles of what is referred to as the "strategic nucleus of the state" and of social organizations. The former retains a clear monopoly over decision-making (Bresser Pereira 1996).
4. The fact that, in this conflictive coexistence, a common political vocabulary is used by divergent and even antagonist projects with different meanings produced what I have called a "perverse confluence," through which difference and conflict becomes obscured and apparently diluted (Dagnino 2002, 2004, 2006).
5. See, for example, several articles in Dagnino and Tatagiba's edited volume (2007), and Lavalle et al. (2006, 2007), Avritzer (2006) and Lüchmann (2007).
6. One example can be found in Avritzer's (2007, 424) critique of Urbinati's lack of concern with new institutional settings of representation, which is precisely the main characteristic (and a key novelty) of the Brazilian context. The same author, discussing Dryzek's proposition, within the framework of deliberative democracy, about a sphere for the representation of discourses as distinct from representing people or interests, points out the difficulties in making this distinction in the Brazilian context—as in any context, we may add.
7. The project was part of the Civil Society and Governance Project, financed by the Ford Foundation in 21 countries. In Brazil it was called Civil Society and Public Spaces. Case studies include formal spaces such as the Council for Women's Rights in the state of Ceará (*Conselho Cearense de Direitos da Mulher*, orCCDM) and the Porto Alegre Participatory Budgeting (*Orçamento Participativo*, orPB), but also specific localized "partnerships" between NGOs and the state and between the Landless Movement (*Movimento Sem Terra*, or MST) and the state. An additional case study analyzed a societal public space, the National Forum of Urban Reform (*Forum Nacional da Reforma Urbana*, or FNRU). For the complete project results, see Dagnino (2002).
8. Interestingly, when we first published the results of this project in English in 2002, we were told that the word "representativeness" did not exist in English. The "capacity of being representative" was recommended instead. Why and how representativeness became an acceptable word (judging from this book's subject) would be an interesting theme for discussion.
9. As an example of the adoption of multiple forms of representation, the MST created its own NGO, the *Associação Nacional de Cooperação Agrícola* (ANCA), in order to make possible the establishment of "partnerships" with governments, which require a formal organization as a civil society partner. A literacy project for youngsters and adults living in MST's settlements (*acampamentos*) is an instance of such a partnership and one of the cases researched.

10. This dilemma is central to an enduring debate within civil society, which is discussing the option for institutional struggle versus going back to previous strategies for social mobilization and organization.
11. See L. Thompson and C. Tappscott, "Introduction: Mobilization and Social Movements in the South: The Struggle for Rights and Substantive Citizenship," in L. Thompson and C. Tappscott (eds.), *Citizenship and Social Movements: Perspectives from the Global South* (London: Zed Books, 2010).
12. Autonomy is defined here as "the actor's capacity of establishing relationships with other actors (allied, supporters and antagonists) based on a moral freedom or independence that allows the co-definition of forms, rules and objectives of the interaction, based on his own interests and values" (Tatagiba forthcoming).
13. For an analysis of these transits in Brazil and in Chile, see, respectively, Feltran (2006) and Delamaza and Ochsenius (2006).
14. In Cavalcanti (2006).

11 Reflections on the "Representativeness" of Civil Society Organizations

An Analysis of Recent Latin American Trends

Enrique Peruzzotti

CIVIL SOCIETY AND THE QUALITY OF DEMOCRACY IN LATIN AMERICA

Since the return to democracy, the field of civil society in Latin America has been a very active one, promoting new forms of organizations, of politics and of civic forms of engagement. Processes of social innovation contributed to renew and expand the practice of democratic representation in various and original ways, from the emergence of rights and accountability politics to the establishment of different forms of policy councils that promote the active participation of civil society organizations (CSOs) in policy-making. Traditional ways of understanding civil society's contribution to democratic politics were challenged by the rise of those novel forms of citizen participation, forcing political scientists and sociologists to reflect on the particular contribution that new forms of collective action made to the political process. On several occasions, innovative forms of intervention have questioned the standard frame for analyzing the role of civil society under democracy and called for an expansion of the conceptual toolbox for thinking about the role of CSOs in contemporary Latin America.

The growing role played by civil society in areas that in the past seemed to be the monopoly of state institutions or of political parties have spawned a wave of questioning over the alleged legitimacy of new developments and the way they seem to be redefining traditional understandings of the democratic political process. As civic actors all over the region gain greater visibility and assume new responsibilities, concerns have been raised around the contribution of civil society organizations to the practice of democratic representation. It is common to hear objections from elected officials concerning the unrepresentative and unaccountable status of CSOs as well as skepticism about the alleged contributions that civil society actors truly make to the agenda of democratization.

The goal of this chapter is to address some of the criticism that civil society actors are confronting by focusing on one specific set of arguments: those that question the legitimacy of CSOs by raising doubts about their representative status. Elected officials usually challenge the claims of CSOs to represent the interest of the poor, women, indigenous populations, and so on, by arguing that they were chosen in free and competitive elections in which all citizens were able to participate under the equalitarian principle of one citizen, one vote, while CSOs lack such democratic credentials—in many instances representing a cadre of self-appointed leaders and activists. As it will argue below, such arguments are predicated on a very narrow understanding of what democratic representation means, an understanding that collapses democratic with electoral representation. Yet, the practice of democratic representation is a much more complex business than that of electoral politics and involves a wide variety of actors and arenas beyond that of parliament, parties and elected officials. Thus the role of civil society in democratic politics, and particularly its contribution to the practice of democratic representation, cannot be disregarded by just referring to their unelected nature.

The question of the "representativeness" of nonelected organizations has become a thorny issue in recent debates on democratic representation (Saward 2011; Montanaro 2008; Warren and Urbinati 2008). The increasingly important role played by civil society in different sorts of political processes—from acting as an informal oversight mechanism to directly participating in the formulation of public policies—has generated a series of questions regarding the proper role of civil society under representative democracy. What are the representative claims of civil society organizations? Why should legislatures and elected administrations that were appointed in competitive elections and are accountable to voters take into account the claims of self-organized and self-appointed entities?

To properly tackle the issue of the representativeness of civil society organizations it is necessary first to establish some analytical distinctions between various forms of civil society politics and their contribution to the practice of democratic representation. Civil society plays diverse roles in the democratic process so it is important to specifically analyze the particular problems that each form of intervention opens up for a theory of democratic representation. While there is a plurality of different forms of civil society participation, this chapter will largely focus on three distinctive types of civic politics. Each of the types of citizen politics that will be analyzed illustrates particular ways in which civil society contributes to the practice of democratic representation in contemporary Latin America. Each of them also poses a different set of challenges to the "representativeness" argument.

The three forms of civil society participation that will be the subject of analysis of this chapter are the politics of influence and identity, the politics of social accountability, and the role of civil society organizations in arenas of institutionalized participation. Each form of politicization serves to illustrate alternative ways in which different forms of civic participation confront the different accountability deficits that had been highlighted by the "quality of democracy" literature. In recent years, there has been a very interesting debate in Latin America over the need to democratize existing democracies by promoting processes of political innovation that could strengthen the different dimensions of democratic accountability.[1] Each particular form of civil engagement is guided by specific goals and poses quite distinctive sets of challenges to the theory of democratic representation, illustrating original ways in which civil society actors can contribute to the agenda of legal and political accountability in contemporary Latin American democracies. Social accountability initiatives are fundamentally concerned with strengthening the legal dimension of the concept of accountability while the politics of influence and mechanisms of institutionalized participation aim at improving the political receptiveness of representative institutions.

CIVIL SOCIETY AND REPRESENTATIVE DEMOCRACY

A central agreement of all theories of civil society is that in contemporary democracies an effective citizen is an associated one. The effective citizen, to borrow Philippe Schmitter's expression, is the one that joins an association that promotes the specific claims of different constituencies (Schmitter 2008). All theories of civil society share this belief in the indispensability of social groups to democratic agency. Civic participation is considered a vital complement to electoral politics, which helps to realize the citizenship principle in contemporary mass democracies. While the emphasis of various strands of civil society theory might be different, they all focus on particular associational formats and the role they play in social, cultural, economic and political life.

So while classical analyses of representation focus on the role of the individual citizen as voter and on political parties (Przeworksi et al. 1999; Manin 1997), civil society theories prefer to emphasize the role played by social movements, voluntary associations, advocacy organizations, NGOs, or informal publics in political and social life. Moving away from an individualist and election-anchored model of representation, theories of civil society concentrate on the self-constituting politics of *associated citizens* in civil society, for they consider that it is in that arena where a plurality of constituencies take form and exert voice throughout the duration of a representative tenure.

In Latin America, numerous authors focus on the contribution that different civil society actors are making to the agenda of democratization, and more specifically, they stress innovative ways in which CSOs are addressing the deficits of democratic accountability that have been a major topic of concern for the quality of democracy debates.[2] In which particular ways can civil society promote the agenda of more accountable government? Civil society can contribute in three different ways to the strengthening of democratic accountability. First, civil society enhances representative government by creating new constituencies, adding new voices and bringing novel concerns into the political agenda. Many of the social movements that have emerged in the region in recent years (human rights movements, indigenous movements, environmental movements, women's organizations, etc.) express identities and claims that were not properly represented or adequately processed by the existing mediating structures of representative government.[3] The monopoly of legislatures and parties on political representation is being challenged by a plurality of movements that engage in campaigns to broaden the existing political agenda to include issues and voices that had been largely overlooked by the "screening" structures of interest pluralism and competitive party politics. A salient example is the rise of indigenous movements and their efforts to redefine the boundaries and content of a notion of citizenship that was generally blind to the demands for recognition and autonomy of the diverse ethnic communities that existed within the boundaries of nation-states (Yashar 2005). By developing campaigns to draw the attention of decision-making authorities to a previously ignored voice, indigenous social movements in the public sphere forced the political system to address the concerns of a sector of the citizenry that had been historically neglected by traditional political institutions.[4] Social movements also contribute to collective learning introducing new discourses and identities in civil society that challenged the dominant interpretative frame in a society. In the case of indigenous movements in countries like Bolivia or Ecuador, their discourses and politics challenge the predominant forms of self-understanding that had historically shaped those societies' views of citizenship and the nation-state, calling instead for the establishment of a multinational state respectful of the different ethno-national identities that are present in their respective national territories (Yashar 2005, 5).

Second, there is the participation of civil society in formal arenas of decision-making, a trend that has become one of the most interesting democratic innovations in the region since the transitions from authoritarian rule. Brazil is perhaps the country that has most extensively experimented with these sort of participatory structures, which aim at promoting the participation of specific types of civil society organizations in various areas and aspects of the policy-making process. For instance, participatory arenas such as participatory budgeting, participatory urban planning and health or educational councils are understood as spaces that bring together state and social actors to discuss, decide and implement policies on particular policy areas. The incorporation of civil society actors into structures of institutionalized participation implies a redefinition of the classical political role attributed to civil society—the already mentioned "indirect politics of influence"—for these structures promote the direct participation of specific sectors of civil society in the process of decision-making and policy implementation. This is particularly the case of the different policy councils that had been created (such as the health and educational councils in Brazil) in which "representatives" of civil society directly engage in policy-making alongside public officials.[5] In contrast with actors attempting to influence politics from the "outside" as in the politics of influence, the councils provide an formal institutional space that grants civic organizations the prerogative to debate, make decisions and monitor the implementation of social policies in their respective communities alongside public officials and other stakeholders.[6]

Third and lastly, civil society politics can also revolve around issues of legal accountability. By denouncing violations of rights or breaches of law and due process by public officials as well as by efforts to develop strategies oriented to improve the workings of the mechanisms and agencies that regulate and frame the behavior of political representatives, civil society complements and many times activates mechanisms of legal accountability. This sort of demand has been analyzed by the literature on social accountability that focuses on a wide array of civic initiatives oriented to denounce breaches of law by public authorities, from human rights violations to corruption. Watchdog organizations such as *Poder Ciudadano* (Citizen Power) in Argentina that keep track of the evolution of assets of public officials, or the *veedurías ciudadanas* (Civic Audits) in Colombia, which monitor public bids and works to increase governmental transparency and prevent the misallocation of public funds by corrupted officials, are paradigmatic cases of a new social concern with the rule of law and legal accountability.[7]

The following section briefly describes the main characteristics of each form of politicization and the challenges they create for a theory of democratic representation. While each form of politics has generated ample debate on the nature and democratic consequences of such interventions, the focus of this chapter will focus on the "representativeness" issue; that is, it will address the question of whether such forms of participation undermine, strengthen or redefine our traditional electoral understanding of democratic representation.

THE DIFFERENT FORMS OF CIVIL SOCIETY POLITICS AND THE QUESTION OF DEMOCRATIC REPRESENTATIVENESS

Social Accountability Politics

The question of legal accountability has emerged as a central area of concern of Latin American democratization studies (Mendez et al. 1999; Uildriks and Peon 2010; Brinks 2008). Influential authors like Guillermo O'Donnell have made the issue of the deficits of legal accountability exhibited by some of the new democracies of the region a defining feature of such regimes (O'Donnell 1999, 2007). For O'Donnell, there is a specific pattern to democratization that has led to the establishment of a particular form of polyarchy where electoral mechanisms of political accountability function rather well yet the regime exhibits serious deficits of legal accountability. The end result is the absence of institutional checks on the executive (O'Donnell 1994). O'Donnell calls for the need to strengthen mechanisms of horizontal accountability and his analysis opened up a productive regional debate on the role that different mechanisms and agencies play in the control of illegal encroachments and other forms of unlawful state behavior.

Initially, the debate on legal accountability focused exclusively on the interrelationships that the network of state agencies of control established with one another without granting any meaningful role to social actors. The concept of social accountability attempted to broaden the debate on legal accountability by calling attention to the role that informal, nonstate mechanisms play in the promotion of more transparent and accountable democratic government. Citizens, the media and civil society organizations in the public sphere, many argued, can contest governmental decisions and denounce the unlawful actions of public officials, acting as informal watchdogs over public authorities. Repeated media exposes of official corruption by investigative journalism, for instance, serve to bring attention to the inadequacies of existing oversight mechanisms in preventing or detecting acts of corruption, particularly when they involve powerful governmental figures.[8] Similarly, watchdog organizations such as CORREPI in Argentina that monitor and publicly expose cases of police violence provide a valuable source of independent information on activities that otherwise would remain unreported and thus unpunished.[9]

In various articles I argued that an important novelty of the last democratizing wave was precisely that civic struggles for more accountable government and media exposés of governmental wrongdoing have become an established feature of the political landscape of the continent (Peruzzotti 2002, 2001). Those developments were indicative of the emergence of a new brand of citizen politics whose goal is to ensure the subordination of elected officials to legal and constitutional norms. The term *social accountability* attempted to provide a conceptualization of such politics on the ground that such set of actions and relationships represent an informal mechanism of vertical accountability that needs to be incorporated into analysis of governmental accountability. The politics of social accountability serves to raise social awareness about existing deficits of legal accountability, expressing a social cry for more effective mechanisms of horizontal oversight (Peruzzotti and Smulovitz 2002, 2006, 2003; Peruzzotti 2002; Fox 2008).

Social accountability politics involve civic efforts whose goals are to (1) monitor the behavior of public officials and agencies to ensure that they abide by the law; (2) expose cases of governmental wrongdoing involving corruption and human rights violations; and (3) activate, in many instances, the operation of horizontal agencies, such as the judiciary or legislative investigation commissions, that would otherwise not act or would act in a biased manner. In exposing cases of governmental wrongdoing, activating reluctant state agencies of accountability and monitoring the operation of those agencies, civic actors make a crucial contribution to the enforcement of the rule of law. Eventually, initiatives of social accountability could stimulate a virtuous circle of "stimulation" of horizontal agencies and "induction" of new social accountability agencies that could result in more effective controls on government (O'Donnell 2006, 337).

The politics of social accountability—being exclusively focused on denouncing unlawful state behavior and/or activating horizontal agencies—poses little difficulties for a theory of democratic representation. In this respect, it makes no difference what the "representative status" of the actors that motorized specific initiatives of social accountability is; what matters is whether the wrongful state behavior that is being exposed is effectively sanctioned or not. As long as initiatives of social accountability are oriented to denounce and expose state unlawfulness, it makes no difference whether such acts are promoted by quite "unrepresentative" and socially isolated civic actors—like a cadre of self-appointed advocacy NGOs or by the family and friends of victims of human rights violations—or by actors that are backed by the massive social support of the population. Their actions in search of legal accountability do not interfere with the political dimension of the concept for they are not guided by a logic of consequences but by a procedural one: they are not questioning the specific content of public policies but rather calling attention to breaches of due process or acts of blatant illegality. It consequently does not matter whether such actions are carried out by politically representative or unrepresentative civic actors.

The Politics of Identity and Influence in the Public Sphere

Civil society actors usually engage in a dualistic politics of identity and influence aimed both at civil society and the polity (Cohen and Arato 1992). The decentralized and pluralistic structure of civil society encourages efforts to influence sectors of public opinion as well as persuading political elites in government. The analysis of the *politics of influence* and of *identity* of social movements, advocacy NGOs, and publics is consequently crucial for understanding the role of civil society under representative democracy. By *politics of identity* Cohen and Arato refer to a politics that aims at questioning dominant identities, practices and institutions by bringing new discourses, meanings and interpretative frames that challenge existing social norms and democratize social relations outside the polity. In recent years, for instance, many Latin American societies have experienced the rise of gay, transsexual and lesbian organizations to fight social and legal discrimination on the basis of a person's sexual orientation. The *politics of influence* also refers to the transformation of a political culture, although in this case, it aims at altering the discursive universe of political society, at which collective action is predominantly directed. Following from the previous example, in some instances the efforts of gay, transsexual and lesbian organizations result in the passing of new legislation and the recognition of new rights (for example, gay marriage). The achievements of a politics of identity will be measured by the extent to which a certain social movement is able to reshape the forms of organization and self-understanding of civil society. A politics of influence will be successful not just by keeping political society open to social demands but also due to its ability to introduce new interpretive frameworks into the discourses and behavior of representative institutions (Cohen and Arato 1992, ch. 10).

The politics of influence and identity, Cohen and Arato argue, is the "recourse par excellence of those who are relatively powerless, political outsiders, and those without economic clout" who largely draw on autonomous networks that want to influence public opinion and thereby, indirectly, political elites, challenging the existing boundaries of the social and political sphere. Both forms of politics point to the creative dimension of democratic representation.

What do we mean by the creative dimension of democratic representation? Representative politics can be understood as an ongoing, multifaceted and complex economy of claim-making (Saward 2009). There are however two different sorts of "representative claims" (Peruzzotti 2010). There are claims to express or reflect an already existing or constituted interest or identity. This dimension of representation is guided by a mirror-logic: in this understanding, good representation entails properly reflecting the structure of interests and opinions that prevails in society at a certain time. This is the logic that generally guides private interest bargaining and electoral competition. There are, however, claims that do not seek to reflect an existing or already organized constituency but promote the formation of new ones. As Warren Nyamugasira argues, the role of many advocacy NGOs is not reflecting an already organized constituency but rather creating a new one (Nyamugasira 1998, 303). In this particular case, the success of a claimant can only be properly evaluated over a certain time span, for it usually requires a sustained campaign or struggle to bring awareness regarding new concerns, identities or interests. This is the creative side of the practice of democratic representation and expresses itself in initiatives that challenge a dominant configuration of interests and identities, hoping to bring about new ones. The politics of identity and influence distinguished by Cohen and Arato express such a transformative impulse of the practice of democratic representation. According to Cohen and Arato (1992), such a creative impulse is the *differentia specifica* of contemporary social movements, advocacy NGOs and publics in relation to other forms of politics such as electoral and pressure group politics. In the words of Kenneth Anderson (2009, 11), "The glory of civil society institutions ought to be that they are not representative, and because they are not, are free to argue and shout their visions of social justice, seek to persuade, offer alternatives that representative institutions cannot."

Democratic representation lives off this tension between mirroring and transformation. As Michael Saward (2009, 22) eloquently put it,

> Electoral politics requires non-electoral action to shake up and re-set its agenda on a regular basis—as new claims to authenticity challenge the

products of established processes of authorization. We might say that democracies need a series of mini refounding ... and that some of the re-funding need the relative absence of constraint that some non-electoral modes of representation foster.

A proper understanding of representation cannot ignore the creative dimension of democratic politics for if it only focuses on the activities of electoral and classical pressure groups politics it will inevitably turn a blind eye to the idealizing and judgmental nature of politics: "political representation transforms and expands politics insofar as it does not simply allow the social to be translated into the political, but also facilitates the formation of political groups and identities ..." (Urbinati 2006, 37).

Standard electoral notions of political accountability are consequently inadequate to evaluate the democratic status of advocacy NGOs or of social movements. It would be erroneous to force all social movements or advocacy organizations to be politically accountable to existing constituencies, or to grant democratic legitimacy only to those groups who fit the electoral authorization model. If we were to pursue such strategy, then the creative edge of the practice of democratic representation would be lost. For instance, initially the discourse and politics of human rights meet important resistance not only from military dictators but also from wide sectors of society as well. Yet, it was the "unrepresentative" nature of such movements what would latter (and after sustained efforts and campaigns) bring into the attention of society a question that was going to radically redefine the political culture of most of the region. The value of those initiatives during such a hostile time was precisely to call attention over a question that large sectors of society preferred to ignore or saw as unproblematic (Peruzzotti 2002).

Institutionalized Participation

Another important trend in civil society politics is the creation of arenas of institutionalized participation. Many Latin American democracies are engaging in interesting processes of institutional experimentation that lead to the establishment of arenas of encounter between state and society, like participatory budgeting, different sort of citizens' councils, oversight boards, participatory urban planning, neighborhood committees, national public policy conferences, national public policy councils, public hearings, and so on, which are meant to complement classic representative mediating mechanisms like local legislatures. These arenas establish permanent and institutionalized spaces for the participation of civil society actors, where public officials and civil society gather to jointly deliberate and decide on specific policies or issues.[10]

Arenas of institutionalized participation grant decision-making prerogatives to civil actors. The latter supposes a major break with what was considered the prototypical way in which civil society exerted influence on representative institutions: indirectly, through its capacity to mobilize citizens in the public sphere. The previously analyzed forms of civil society politics (social accountability and of influence and identity) represent what was traditionally considered the idiosyncratic form of civil society politics where external social actors attempt to indirectly influence the dynamics of the political system (either by activating mechanisms of legal accountability or by influencing the decisions of legislatures). By contrast, these novel participatory mechanisms promote the direct involvement of sectors of civil society in the policy-making process: neighborhood organizations, unions, parent-teacher associations, NGOs and other types of voluntary organizations engage in public and deliberative policy negotiations alongside state officials, deciding upon budgetary and policy priorities over a wide variety of issues from health or educational service provision to access to basic urban infrastructure.

Such an invasion of what traditionally was considered the exclusive terrain of representative institutions opens up difficult questions, particularly in relation with the "representativeness question" (Nylen 2003, 151). For scholars like Leonardo Avritzer, those structures should be understood as a hybrid that combines in an original way the principles of representation and participation, helping to connect the poor and marginalized with the political system (Avritzer 2009, 9). Many authors share Avritzer's opinion, arguing that mechanisms of institutionalized participation positively impact on democratic representation for they make possible the involvement of sectors of the population that generally lack the organizational resources to voice their claims to the political system via the indirect politics of influence. By gaining leverage through their involvement in institutionalized arenas of participation they access information and institutional resources to engage with (as well as control) state bureaucracies and elected representatives. They consequently produce an expansion of democracy for they make institutions more politically accountable to the demands of previously marginalized sectors of the population.

The truth is that arenas of institutionalized participation are not an alternative to representative institutions but a complement to them. In a way, they expand the repertoire of political mediations between society and state by adding new arenas besides political parties, classical pressure groups and legislatures. Furthermore, arenas of institutionalized participation are usually the product of an initiative of representative institutions and it is usually the executive branch that summons, convenes, and organizes them. This is the case, for example, of national public policy conferences in Brazil, which are convened by the executive power, and once they conclude their deliberations and formulate a set of guidelines for policy making, they engage with the legislature to turn those suggestions into legislation and policies to be applied at the federal level. As with other participatory mechanisms, national public policy conferences are alternative venues for the poor to have their interests politically represented in the legislative and the executive branches of government.

In the end, those structures are promoting an alternative form of "civil society representation" that is built on different grounds than electoral forms of representation. A large number of participatory arenas have mechanisms for selecting "civil society representatives" that will have the authority to decide on specific issues (for they are considered true expressions of the constituencies they claim to represent). These representatives are not individual citizens but collective actors that engage alongside public officials in the deliberation, design and implementation of public policies. The question of "representativeness" should lead to a debate over the institutional design and characteristics of those novel mediating mechanisms, which should be designed around the principles of publicity, inclusiveness, public deliberation and equality. Finally, those spaces can always become (if the need arises) the target for social accountability initiatives if sectors of society perceive that the interactions within them are not being regulated by norms of transparency, publicity, deliberation and equity.

CONCLUDING REMARKS

The chapter presented some innovative trends in civil society politics that are taking place in several Latin American democracies. Civil society has become an important protagonist of political processes in the region. Through different forms of intervention, it has sought to reduce many of the accountability deficits that have troubled analysts and advocates of stronger forms of democracy. Some of those types of civic intervention offer inventive responses, answering existing problems in an original way. They also defy traditional understandings of representative government.

There have been concerns over the legitimacy of some of those forms of civic politics. For some, many of those initiatives are overstepping the roles that had traditionally been the exclusive prerogative of electoral representative institutions. Those criticisms are predicated on a rather standard (and narrow) understanding of democratic representation that reduces the latter to its electoral rendering. Representative democracy, however, cannot be equated to electoral democracy but refers to a form of regime that relies on a wide variety of mediating structures to link society with the political system. The described participatory developments in Latin America have undoubtedly established a more complex topography for the practice of democratic representation, adding novel informal and formal mediating structures that seek to increase the political receptiveness of representative institutions to the demands of the citizenry and the effectiveness of mechanisms of legal oversight.

Each of the forms of civil society politics that were analyzed in this chapter emerged as a specific response to some of the accountability deficits that were present in the democratic regimes of the region. At the same time, they help to broaden the notion of democratic accountability by expanding the traditional repertoire of mechanisms of political mediation and legal oversight. The reviewed participatory innovations force us to go beyond inherited notions about democratic representation to be able to understand the manifold ways in which citizens and representatives connect with one another to promote more accountable democratic regimes in the complex political scenario of contemporary Latin America. Better representation will generate more responsive and responsible regimes and thus result in governments that can more effectively respond to citizens' demands.

NOTES

1. For some of the most relevant contributions to the quality of democracy debates see Levine (2011); Diamond and Morlino (2005); Mainwaring et al. (1992); O'Donnell (1996); Schmitter (2009, 19–35); O'Donnell et al. (2004).
2. The analysis of the contribution of civil society to the agenda of democratic accountability represents only a subset of participation studies. There are many forms of civic participation that are not directly related to the agenda of governmental accountability. To begin with, not all forms of participation are explicitly politically oriented; many of them refer to forms of participation that unfold in a prepolitical associative stratum of primary and secondary groups of voluntary associations such as choral groups, bowling leagues, social clubs, etc. And even within those forms of participation that are openly political, not all of them have as their main target representative institutions. In brief, only a subset of participation studies focus on initiatives that are specifically geared to promote greater governmental accountability by either trying to force governments to rectify policies/legislation or by denouncing breaches of legality. For a discussion of different models of civil society participation see Peruzzotti (2008).
3. For some of the most relevant literature on the role of new social movements under democracy see Alvarez, Dagnino and Escobar (1998); Yashar (2005); Mayer and Lebon (2010); Hochstleter and Keck (2007); and Brysk (1994).
4. For the notion of informal societal sensors see Habermas (1998, 359).
5. In Brazil there are around 28,000 policy councils throughout the country. Specific types of social councils have been established to respectively address social policies in the areas of health, education, social services and children and adolescent rights. See Avritzer (2009).
6. In the case of health councils, the process involves not only grass roots civil society organizations, but also trade unions, professional organizations and private companies operating within the health sector.
7. For an analysis of different initiatives of social accountability see Peruzzotti and Smulovitz (2006).
8. For an analysis of the accountability role of watchdog journalism in South America, see Waisbord (2000).
9. For an analysis of the struggle against police violence in Argentina, see Denissen (2008).
10. For some of the most relevant works on arenas of institutionalized participation in Latin America, see Avritzer (2009); Nylen (2003); Abers (2000); Wampler (2009); Baiocchi (2005); Cornwall and Schattan Coelho (2007); and Baiochi, Heller and Silva (2011). For a review of some of the debates that these participatory structures have generated, see Fung (2011).

12 Democratic Institutions and Public Effectiveness of Chilean Civil Society after 1990

Gonzalo Delamaza

This chapter argues that the political and social changes that took place during the Chilean transition to democracy after 1990 have altered the effectiveness and the representativeness of democracy in the domain of the relationship between the state and civil society. In the past, effectiveness was related to representativeness because the latter depended on the increasing capacity of the state to include social demands. The process was conducted mainly by the political system; the more pluralistic it was, the more effective democracy was, too. At the same time, political parties were strongly linked to civil society institutions and associations: universities, labor movement, churches, and so on. During the 1960s, new social movements give birth to new political expressions that expanded the political system.

The political model prevalent until the 1973 military coup has been replaced by depoliticized forms of mediation between civil society and the state that have a limited ability to drive transformations. As a result, civil society is now more autonomous but also more fragmented, diminishing the representativeness of democracy. This decrease in representativeness was justified by political elites as a requirement for the effectiveness of governability and the implementation of public policies. For all practical purposes this meant only economic growth and political stability. The need to strengthen civil society and foster its role in public affairs was not taken into account in this model. The data I provide herein reveal that society's capacity for collective action has been affected: it has become disassociated from the channels of democratic representation, intensifying the problem of representativeness and legitimacy of democracy.

I argue that a strong civil society is a necessary condition for democracy that is not restricted to the rules of competition between political parties (Avrtitzer 2002). A strong civil society is characterized by its capacity for autonomous action, a significant degree of organization (at different levels), internal diversity (that makes it inclusive) and its public voice; that is, the capacity to develop an interest in public affairs and to influence them through participation. This study approaches civil society as a factor of democracy and therefore considers public influence a central component of the analysis.

I consider an effective democracy to be one that increases the strength of civil society and generates channels of participation that expand the public space. In unequal societies like those in Latin America, this also implies challenges in terms of social inclusion since it means that currently excluded sectors should begin to participate and extreme inequalities be reduced. Representativeness will be analyzed in terms of electoral participation and citizen support of democracy.

In the first section, I develop my approach to democratic construction and justify relating the dimensions of representativeness and effectiveness to strengthening civil society and its capacity for public influence. The second section reviews the political representativeness and effectiveness of the democratic Chilean state before the 1973 military coup from a historical perspective. The third section examines the features of the transition pact, on the basis of which present-day democracy was built after General Pinochet's long dictatorship. The empirical analysis of primary and secondary sources follows: electoral participation, citizen support for democratic institutions, and the new participative mechanisms originated in the realm of public politics and their capacity for mediating between civil society and the state. I then present three cases that reveal the unequal distribution of public influence: expert knowledge networks, public-private strategic alliances and the urban citizen movements. The conclusions review the main points and examine some of the main challenges of Chile's democracy.

THE CONSTRUCTION OF DEMOCRACY, EFFECTIVENESS AND REPRESENTATIVENESS

The problems of effectiveness and representativeness of democracy in Latin America occur in the context of the challenges experienced by the construction of democracy following the cycle of dictatorships, military coups and crises that characterized the region during the 20th century.

The current democratic context has generated debate on inclusion in democracies, the quality of democratic institutions and the promotion of alternatives to the prevalent neoliberal model. The concept of governability, frequently used to assess democracy, has questionable value because, in its most frequent usage, it has preserved the basic, original definition provided by the Trilateral Commission in the 1970s; that is, how to reduce social conflict and ensure at any given moment that it does not impact politics and the state and, as a result, generate "ungovernability." Furthermore, there exists a limited or "minimalist" conception of democracy as a political electoral regime, which makes no reference to the process of democratization beyond the political regime and the social conditions that would make it viable (Nun 2002; Vargas 2008).

Nonetheless, theory has failed to respond to the challenges imposed by historical and political reality. Thus, although

...the historical experience of living in democracy has exceeded the boundaries of the political regime, comparative theories on democracy have had serious difficulties not only in trying to explain this phenomenon, but also in proposing conceptual and methodological innovations to identify and interpret democratic developments beyond the regime. . . .The rest—democratic rule of law, new mechanisms for citizen participation in public management, amongst others—are at best acknowledged as facilitating conditions of democratic regimes. (Vargas 2008, 12)

More recently, the relationship between democracy and public policies has gained importance within the context of a state that has become progressively weaker since the 1980s. The problems affecting governance are closely related to the inability of policies to generate inclusion and social citizenship. Economic and social crises no longer give way to military coups and interventions. Nevertheless, institutional stability "on repeated occasions has been affected by social protests that have exceeded the capacity of the system's institutional channels, revealing clear deficiencies in the representative institutions" (Varas 2006, 25). Although these crises have been solved enabling democracy to function, the challenges to improve the quality of democracy include new policies and perspectives aimed at broadening socioeconomic inclusion and participation. As Hagopian (2005, 126) points out, democracy in different countries of Latin America has had improvements, but "from different starting points and by different routes." During the last 30 years, democratic regimes have advanced throughout Latin America. The problem—or paradox—in this context, is that these regimes have revealed poor standards as regards the construction of the state and the incorporation and participation of social actors. They also demonstrate little capacity to process the most important issues and conflicts in Latin American society. These are the underlying factors that generate new conflicts in governability and increase uncertainty (Domínguez 2005). The theories (and practices) of participative democracy generate further debate, shedding doubts on representative political regimes. In specific contexts, the practices and the actors engaged in the construction of democracy seek to deepen the exercise of democracy, including new means of linking the state, politics and civil society (Dagnino, Olvera and Panfichi 2006).

Regardless of the different approaches, the exercise and deepening of democracy require certain social conditions. This is still true when we define democracy only in terms of the procedures used for the selection of authorities (Nun 2002). Even if we define democracy strictly as a political regime, the problems refer to the conditions necessary for that regime to carry out its functions. However, political regimes are not just about issues of electoral procedures; they should also act as "institutional mediators between the state and citizens that resolve the issues of how and who should govern society, how citizens define themselves and how conflicts and social demands are met" (Garretón 1994, 64).

Although the approaches that reduce democracy to a limited set of instruments identify the procedures that provide optimum stability, they do not consider its capacities for inclusion or social transformation. In the case of Chile, there is a tendency towards a type of hypergovernability where the main objective of the political system is to ensure its own stability (De la Cuadra 2006). In Hagopian's terms (2005, 127) "Chilean elites restricted the scope of competition and maintained the authoritarian era's economic reforms, institutional constraints on accountability, and citizen demobilization." This, in effect, influences the design of policies and determines their implementation. Meeting the objective is the proof of success. As a result, a series of objectives aimed at transformation have been postponed and left aside since they pose a threat to this model of governability. This design has generated a lack of representativeness and effectiveness in Chilean democracy as regards the reconstruction of better links between the state and civil society after the long military government to ensure that civil society has a bearing on public affairs. This chapter argues that this phenomenon explains the difference between democracy after 1990 and political development before 1973.

POLITICAL REPRESENTATIVENESS AND STATE EFFECTIVENESS IN DEMOCRACY BEFORE 1973

At the beginning of the 20th century, social conflict escalated in Chile, challenging the predominant models of "private" integration whereby the rich gave charity and the excluded sectors sought self-organization, both without state participation. This marked the origin of the "social question" (Morris 1968; Romero 1997); that is, the debate on whether or not social and economic fragmentation existed in the country, and its origins and consequences. At the same time, there was a violent rupture between social elites and popular classes, with the latter leading violent "urban riots" that were strongly repressed with the support of the army on repeated occasions during the first decades of the 1900s (Garcés 1992).

Although this political instability lasted until 1938, the regulatory function of the state as regards social conflicts began with the pronouncement of labor laws under military pressure (1924) and of the labor code at the end of that decade. During this period, forms of political representation of the popular sectors emerged—such as the Communist party in 1921 and the Socialist party in 1933—that not only led and channeled popular protests, but also began to participate in the political system. This process became consolidated in 1938 with the Popular Front government and lasted until 1973. An institutionalized system of labor relations and a pluralist political system with relatively high inclusion marked the relationship between society and the state for various decades, linking both representativeness and effectiveness in Chilean democracy. This explains why the Chilean political system is often described as the "vertebral column" that articulated the relationship between social actors and the state for 40 years until 1973 (Garretón 2000). During that period, electoral participation was permanently broadened within the context of political pluralism, and in 1949 women were granted the vote. In the mid-1950s the electoral law was reformed, which in practice meant an end to bribery, and finally the illiterate were given the right to vote and the voting age was set at 18 in 1970. All this significantly increased the capacity to channel the demands of the Chilean population through elections (Portales 2004).

Chilean civil society also developed within this framework. It tended to oscillate between a more autonomous constitution through urban and rural trade unions, and later through urban settler organizations, and its permanent link with the political system that channeled its demands to the state. This also increased the state's capacity to respond to these demands and, at different stages, to establish the structures necessary to address the problems emanating from society. Thus begins the institutionalization of social policies in Chile: education in the 1930s, health in the 1950s and housing and the Agrarian Reform in the 1960s (Arellano 1985). At the same time, electoral participation and the representativeness of democracy expanded.

As regards social movements, their structure was not entirely autonomous since they were partially included in the legal framework that maintained strong exclusions and limits; they channeled their demands through the state and were led by national political parties. In spite of this, popular organizations were powerful, and won important victories that broadened the political agenda. Nonetheless, this constant expansion of the political system did not manage to avoid significant social exclusions, such as peasants and the masses of rural migrants that increased the size of cities from the 1950s onwards (Moulian 2006; Collier and Collier 1991).

The distinctiveness of the Chilean case lies in the importance of the role that the institutionalized political parties played as mediators and representatives of a wide range of social issues, while they successfully processed the demands of the people they represented within the state. The results of their actions were visible in both Parliament and government as a whole, and in the galvanization of the diverse expressions of civil society. This distinctive feature, which various studies consider unique to Chile within the region, established the guidelines for action for civil society to date (Valenzuela 1977; Mainwaring and Scully 1995; Garretón 2006). Just as all political parties had a "strong social constitution," so they all governed during at least one period in the years between 1925 and 1973. The relationship that existed between political parties and social movements cannot be qualified simply as political clientelism, given its association with transformatory political projects. As Arturo Valenzuela (1977) points out, in contrast to other countries in the region such as Brazil and Colombia, political clientelism was not the distinctive characteristic of this relationship in Chile. When it was, it tended to be so at the local rather than the national level.

The dynamics of 20th century Chilean politics was also marked by successive political projects that emerged from and were imposed by politicians at the top. This situation was caused in part by the country's presidentialist system and the ever-increasing importance of technical and professional bodies. The 1925 Constitution recovered the *Portalian* (that is, authoritarian approach of minister Diego Portales) spirit of the 1833 Constitution, which strengthened presidential authority and limited the intervention of political parties. From then on, at least three presidents governed on the basis of their authority or personal charisma rather than that of political coalitions: Arturo Alessandri (1920–1925 and 1932–1938), Carlos Ibáñez (1927–1931 and 1952–1958) and Jorge Alessandri (1958–1964). Moreover, the last two also used a strong antipolitical discourse. Both the empowerment of the president and the rhetoric against politics and political parties were intensified and taken to an extreme during the military regime of Augusto Pinochet (1973–1990).

Organized civil society made its presence felt through its participation in different modes of cooperation with and cocreation of institutions. Examples abound of state financing, regulation, exceptions and benefits aimed at supporting initiatives established by civil society. This was especially so in the case of sectors whose power enabled them to open spaces for cooperation and convert them, through legislation and political initiative from the executive, into new institutions. Good examples are six of the eight universities that existed in 1973, and the Chilean Bar Association, which was created, financed and structured as a public institution and included in the nation's budget in order to supervise the profession, precisely due to the public character of lawyers' activities (Ibáñez 2003, 300).[1]

It is not, therefore, correct to claim that the state played a completely autonomous and unilateral role. Nor is it fair to state that this type of institution building was purely corporatist, or that its corporations were intent on "capturing" the state. With hindsight, they appear to be a form of cooperation between the state and civil society, characteristic of a period when the state had a more pivotal role and civil society had more power, especially within the upper middle class.

In this context, the state developed as public bureaucracy grew and a body of "developmental professionals" rose within it and gained increasing importance as the century wore on, regardless of social changes. The power of this sector has had significant influence in various circumstances although it has not been studied adequately, especially from those perspectives that place emphasis on the more political aspects of the process. Where there are conflicting alternatives and projects in the political realm, the continuity of the technical-bureaucratic body is far greater. As an example, let us take the Production Development Corporation, CORFO, regarded as the emblematic project of the Pedro Aguirre Cerda administration (1938–1941) and a symbol of state interventionism. To an important degree, its creation involved a group of conservative technical experts trained by the Ministry of Economy led by Gustavo Ross, the opposition candidate that ran against Aguirre Cerda (Ibáñez 2003; Correa 2004; Silva 2009). These technical experts and professionals had gained standing during the first government of General Ibáñez (1927–1931), and would continue to do so during the second half of his second government (1952–1958). The Jorge Alessandri administration (1958–1964) became known as "the government of the executives" because of the significant participation of high executives from the private sector. A similar situation had occurred during the Ibáñez government.

During the Eduardo Frei Montalva government (1964–1970) the management of the state was modernized and took a big leap forward, although this time it served a much broader social planning and engineering program. Not only did the model require the hiring of "consultants," but it also increased the number of government agencies that took over functions that had traditionally been carried out by political parties, this time under the executive. This was the case, for example, of the National Council for Social Promotion, which addressed the organization of slum dwellers by creating neighborhood committees and centers for mothers, inspired by the Belgian Jesuit Roger Vekemans and his theories to combat marginalization, and by the agencies in charge of the Agrarian Reform (Silva 2009).[2]

The power of technocracy was also decisive during the military dictatorship, once the military had controlled power and suppressed the restrictions emanating from political intermediation. This technocracy was given the privilege of controlling Chile's economic policies and the ensuing social policies. The process gave way to the influence of a group of economists from Catholic University, most of them with postgraduate degrees from the University of Chicago. Showing strong cohesion and political determination, this group led the country's economic and social policies during various periods of the administration, with the backing of Pinochet. Their approach continues to influence public management and, with increasing force, the exercise of politics (Valdés 1995; Silva 1991).

A STABLE, LOW-INTENSITY POLITICAL TRANSITION

The distinctive and original feature of the Chilean transition that began in 1989 was that it was carried out within a framework that was established by the dictatorship. This fact enabled the economic, political and social forces that supported it to retain a high level of influence and power in the economic, political and cultural spheres. In this context, the main transformations were the reinstatement of institutional democratic processes—albeit with restrictions—the incorporation of a new political elite into the state administration and, later, the dynamic revitalization of public policies by the new government, especially in the social sphere. This explains why the new political system—an incomplete democracy—lost its capacity to interpret and channel the demands of civil society, thus consolidating the change of the sociopolitical matrix that had existed in the past.

When democracy returned, there was no major constitutional change, no significant economic transformation. On the contrary, the political strategy was based on defeating Pinochet in a plebiscite that he himself had mandated and later, on negotiations with his representatives. Since the Constitution included institutional safeguards for the structure established during the military regime, the proposals for change were restricted. The economic strategy continued to focus on an open marketplace that operated under the hegemony of private foreign capital.

In view of the fact that there was no institutional discontinuity, the legal framework following the military regime was subordinated to the 1980 Constitution and restricted by military pressure, which gave the pro-Pinochet political block power to veto the government"(Moulian 1997). The 1980 Constitution underwent a partial reform in 1989 through a plebiscite agreed upon by the outgoing government and the opposition at the time. Reforms to what were known as the authoritarian enclaves of the Constitution were not included (Hagopian 2005). The consequences of this clearly antidemocratic tendency were felt during the next 15 years as they affected the composition of Parliament and presidential attributions. This situation persisted until March 2006, when the legislative power was democratically elected in full for the first time since the military dictatorship and the executive recovered the faculty to remove the institutional heads of the armed forces.

Political parties were reestablished once the transition began, but at this time they lacked the institutional and political conditions to perform as intermediaries, a role that had been traditional in Chile during the preceding 40 years (Fuentes 1999; Siavelis 1999). Moreover, within the new public space the political parties were relatively isolated, given that the universities, labor unions, media and even the church did not recover their previous roles. On one hand, the political system had been designed to "depoliticize" the country and on the other hand, both Pinochet and those later in charge of the transition opted for a model of reinforced presidentialism, under the criteria that it offered better control over the state and the existing social demands (Hagopian 2005). The great social mobilizations that developed with the explicitly political aim of recovering democracy suddenly ended, as was graphically described by the journalist Rafael Otano, "in a *coitus interruptus*, in the beginning of civil absence" (1995, 69).

The reconstruction of the political party system following the 1983 protests, was carried out in total compliance with the democratic-institutional tradition, given that it prioritized the creation of the political system. In other words, "the identification between democracy and the political system reached its maximum expression" (Valenzuela 1993, 119). Yet this political and institutional reconstruction did not have the same effectiveness as in the previous stage because of the effects of the economic restructuring, the reduction of the role of the state, and the narrow scope of the institutional reforms negotiated with the armed forces. The complex web of relationships between political institutions and society was destroyed by dictatorial action and could not be properly reconstructed. On analyzing this period, Edgardo Boeninger, a political actor of the transition, refers to this feature:

> The end of the social mobilizations, marked by the failure of the populist "Demanda de Chile" formulated by the Assembly of Civility (1986), unquestionably placed the leadership of the opposition in the hands of the political parties. The social organizations recognized the supremacy of politics and supported the new political electoral strategy, which was primordially conciliatory in the social sphere. (1997, 370)[3]

As a consequence, Chilean democracy post-1990 has been characterized by low social participation and the ensuing difficulties to transform itself and complete usual democratic procedures in place, even after more than two decades of development.[4] Moreover, the concentration of power in the groups that inherited a privileged position from the military government survives to date. The military were displaced from political power following the detention of Pinochet in 1998, and an important number of those responsible of violations to human rights have been tried and condemned (Lira 2009). However, there has been no similar action for civilians and many of them have retained important quotas of political, economic, academic and institutional power.

SUPPORT FOR DEMOCRACY AND EFFECTIVENESS IN THE RECONSTRUCTION OF CIVIL SOCIETY

As its links to politics have decreased in number and intensity, civil society has become more autonomous. Yet it has been unable to solve its internal fragmentation and the weakness of its organizations. Despite having staked everything on politics, as is the tradition in Chile, civil society has not been able to create its own projects or modify its subordination to the new institutional arrangement. The current attitude of society towards its democratic institutions, or what we could call civic commitment, is on the decline. The political process of the transition has spawned growing political disaffiliation, particularly among the youth. It has also generated mistrust of parliamentary institutions, a negative opinion of the country's representative political institutions, and a general decline in the support of democracy as revealed by opinion polls. Finally, the vigorous social mobilization that began in 2011 was made from the outside of the political system, with strong trends against political parties and electoral democracy.

The electoral population has risen in age due to the low percentage of young people that register even though they have the right to vote (if older than 18 years) (Luna and Seligson 2007). In 2008, only 62% of adults registered to vote, and voters under 30 represented only 6.7% of this group. Electoral participation has systematically decreased. Today Chile ranks in seventh place in Latin America, out of a total of 17 countries, in a ranking that measures low participation in presidential elections (Luna and Seligson 2007, 132).

The public opinion polls carried out periodically in Chile show that there is a permanent tendency to discredit political parties and the Parliament, which share the lowest levels of acceptance and the highest of rejection (Table 12.1).[5]

According to *Latinobarómetro*, Chile went from being one the countries with the highest levels of trust in political parties to ranking just over the Latin American average, in the context of a strong decline in the levels of trust in these institutions in the region. Also, in spite of the stability of the political party system, only a quarter of Chileans express sympathy for a given political party, and of these, 8% support political parties with no parliamentary representation. In other words, nearly 20% of Chileans support one of the six political parties that control parliament and political power (Luna and Seligson 2007, 150). Only the judicial courts in Chile have such a low level of acceptance by the population. The democratic system also lost support during the transition, and is significantly lower than in countries with a long tradition of democracy with which Chile tends to compare itself (Uruguay and Costa Rica).[6]

As regards the social and political movements, it is possible to appreciate a strong crisis in the institutions that traditionally served as intermediaries for social demands. It appears that political parties are no longer able to act as intermediaries or represent demands satisfactorily. Furthermore, they have distanced themselves from traditional social organizations. The latter have also lost part of their role as intermediaries. Labor unions, for example, have less social importance today; they maintain a conflictive relationship with the political parties, and their agendas make them look more like a group with limited interests rather than a social movement with broad projections.

Until 2011, this social disarticulation had not been broadly transformed into collective mobilizations or political demands. Instead, it has expressed

Table 12.1 Confidence in Political Parties in Latin America (Percentage)

	1996–1997	2001–2002	2003–2004
Chile	31.1	17.3	16.6
Country with most trust	Uruguay 38.1	Uruguay 33.0	Uruguay 23.9
Country with least trust	Colombia 16.1 Venezuela 16.1	Ecuador 7.9	Ecuador 5.4
Average of 18 countries	24.5	16.5	14.2

Source: Reelaborated from *Latinobarómetro* in Welp (2009, 30)

itself mainly as fear and insecurity, political disaffiliation and a weakening of the collective and communal links. UNDP data show weak sociability in Chile, and a "high degree of mistrust, a precarious capacity to associate, a growing instrumentalization of social relations and even a certain weakening of the intergenerational cohesion in families" (UNDP 1998, 216). Social mobilization decreased substantially during the governments of the Concertación (1990–2010) although it started to increase following this period. Yet in this new cycle, it has become evident already that social protest is not channeled by political parties, proving that there is a clear break between representative politics and the new forms of social mobilization.[7]

All this takes place within a political regime that does not stimulate participation and that is becoming increasingly elitist. The conditions of the Chilean transition show the paradox of a society that was mobilized under much more restrictive conditions, but that is demobilized and apolitical under democracy (Silva 2004). It is important to be aware of certain differences with countries such as Brazil, which also experienced transitions from military governments to democracy. Paul Posner, who studied the differences in the Brazilian case, shows that the legacy of the Chilean regime was different because the Chilean military achieved a much greater consolidation of their reforms. Posner points out that "for ideological, political and pragmatic reasons, the Brazilian military left behind a legacy of state reform which was a far cry from the highly market-oriented model that the military rulers bequeathed to their democratic counterparts in Chile" (2003, 55). Hagopian (2005, 124) also shows that democracy in Brazil advances on a much more representative and substantive path than Chile, which has more effective institutional procedures but does not advance in terms of representativeness. The disenchantment with politics and the depoliticization evinced in Chile has been dealt with through a series of political reforms, such as the direct election of mayors, and especially through the deepening of social reforms. The latter were the hallmark of the last two Concertación governments (Lagos and Bachelet) and, in line with the model established at the beginning of the 1990s, were designed and managed from above. This approach enabled both Lagos and Bachelet to end their terms with exceptionally high levels of public approval, close to 70% in the case of Lagos and more than 80% for Bachelet.

PUBLIC POLICIES, PARTICIPATION AND NEW FORMS OF MEDIATION

Has the role of civil society in the public space and its civic orientations changed? Statistics show a consistent decline in electoral participation, a development interpreted as a weakening of the public space. Given the current laws, which make voting compulsory once electors voluntarily register as such, this decline is more evident amongst the younger segments of the population, most of which choose not to register in the electoral rolls. This trend, which has persisted throughout the 20 years since the beginning of the transition, has reduced the size of the electoral universe in comparison to the total number of possible voters. If we include the voters that opt for none of the candidates available in this breakdown, by 2001 "electoral disaffection" was greater than the number of voters that chose one of the options competing in the electoral political system.[8]

As regards social participation, not everybody places trust on it. A 2005 survey of six regions in Chile identified three main tendencies distributed unevenly amongst the population. The largest group, almost 37%, could be defined as reluctant or having a low desire to participate, choosing not to do so, believing that collaborating with others is not a priority, and tending to be more critical of social leaders. Of those surveyed, 33% stated that they understood participation to be a relationship with the authorities, a tendency described as instrumental, and eventually clientelist participation. Finally, 25% of those surveyed expressed a consistently positive attitude towards participation, an expression of trust that matters to participation and democracy (Más Voces 2005).

Because there are no previous data on the scale and distribution of attitudes towards participation, any analysis of the data gathered since is merely hypothetical. However, it could feasibly be argued that the depoliticization and repression of participation instigated by the military government is a factor that helps to explain the attitudes of those reluctant to participate. This is probably intensified by the current cultural tendencies in Chile, which lean toward individual or strongly instrumental actions. Finally, these data should be analyzed in light of the weakness of the channels or instruments that enable citizens' participation during the post-1990 period.

Although overall direct and massive social mobilization has been relatively scarce during the political transition years, there have been two periods in which it increased substantially. In 2006, Chile's high school students led two months of massive demonstrations throughout the country that compelled the political system to reform the law on education promulgated by Pinochet on his last day in office, March 10, 1990. But the political elite's agreement on education was completely ineffective at satisfying the students' demands and they took to the streets again in 2011 and 2012, this time accompanied by teachers, university students and university deans, demanding more radical reforms aimed at doing away with the structures created by the dictatorship and consolidated in the democracy that followed. Furthermore, there have been major demonstrations against the construction of large-scale infrastructure works (hydroelectric power stations) and in defense of the environment as well as strong regional movements in Calama, Punta Arenas and Aysén. The common denominator in these mobilizations is that they take place with almost no participation of political parties. The Communist party is the only one that has some relationship with student and teachers' leaders. This is the first time in Chile that political mobilizations have taken place on a massive scale at the same time conveying strong criticism and disdain for institutionalized political parties and the representative system.[9]

In more general terms, the great problem at stake is the contrast between the very real economic and social advances that Chile has accomplished and the concrete evidence of the disenchantment or disaffection of the population with public issues and with engaging in political participation. If the different variables of democratic governability in Latin America are compared, Chile shows high performance as regards the control of corruption, the rule of law and the quality of regulations pertaining to citizens' freedoms. In all the international rankings, Chile occupies the top two places amongst a score of countries (Mainwaring and Scully 2008, 118). Nonetheless, as regards the "satisfaction with democracy" variable, Chile ranks markedly below countries such as Venezuela, Bolivia, Uruguay and Costa Rica, as well as below other countries in Central America and the Caribbean. A similar pattern is evinced as regards the preference of democracy over other models. Only 46% prefers democracy in any given circumstance. In other countries such as Argentina, Venezuela or Uruguay, this figure is as high as 75%, while the Latin American average stands at 56% (Mainwaring and Scully 2008, 124).

Patricio Silva has highlighted the importance of the cultural impact of neoliberalism as a result of its continuity along different periods. This should be viewed in conjunction with the political decision of the country's elites to deactivate the mass movements that emerged in the 1980s in order to create a space for more moderate forces (Silva 2004, 91–93). This generates the prevalence of an individualist approach to doing politics—detached from political parties—over the collective action that existed in the past. Lucy Taylor (1996) emphasizes the redefinition of civil society towards a depoliticized notion of the new social policies of the 1990s. This would reflect a change in the modes of representation in society, which would also be true of other countries, but that can have different expressions, some more participative than others depending on the contexts and circumstances. As regards these changes, Laura Tedesco (2004, 38–39) makes reference to the experiences in Argentina in 2001, when a sudden reactivation of citizens' actions occurred, and in Porto Alegre, Brazil, where most participatory activity takes place at the local level.

The state has promoted various initiatives aimed at fostering citizen participation and the incorporation of civil society in public policies. The first two Concertación governments stimulated participation mainly as part of the design of social programs. Thus, they sought to incorporate nongovernmental organizations and grass roots organizations into differing stages of execution of these programs, placing an emphasis on cofinancing and implementation. The issue of participation became part of the political agenda only after changes occurred in the political electoral context in 1997.[10]

Nevertheless Ricardo Lagos, the ruling coalition's presidential candidate, won by a narrow margin in 2000. Lagos proposed strengthening the role of the public sector as regards social protection, reflected in a bid to reform the healthcare system. He also addressed the issue of citizen participation and the need to strengthen civil society, as well as to deepen state reforms. This greater political priority granted to citizen participation expressed itself in a government plan that incorporated the ideas put forth by the Citizen Council created for that effect. In 2002, the government decreed a Presidential Instructive for Citizen Participation that compelled the ministries to commit to specific goals aimed at incorporating participation in the policies and programs they were implementing. An appraisal of the incorporation of citizen participation into public policies and programs shows a remarkable 305 mechanisms for participation as part of 155 commitments to citizen participation created by the 18 central government ministries (Fernández and Ordóñez 2007, 32). Nonetheless, the same study shows the scant potential effectiveness of promoting citizen participation.

An analysis of this government-led initiative confirms the absence of significant advances in its results, six years after the presidential plan. On one hand, it revealed that 37% of what is defined as participation by the ministries and agencies—and published as such as an official document—is not in actual fact participation but pertains mainly to improvements in attention to the user in public offices, and in the use of information and communication technologies. This demonstrates the lack of comprehension, clarity and standards regarding the topic. The participation tools employed are mostly instrumental (44%), principally in the most basic form, that is, information, which represented 26% of all the mechanisms. The participation defined as "empowering" by the authors—because of its capacity to strengthen state management and civil society participants—represents only 19% of all tools (Fernández and Ordóñez 2007). In sum, the state sought an appropriate opening for a weakened democracy but it has not been capable of fulfilling the commitment.

Similar problems have been experienced by the principal legislative initiative presented: the Citizens' Associations and Participation in Public Management Bill, submitted to Parliament in June 2004, following a process of prelegislative debate of more than three years. This bill established the right to citizen participation in public management, as well as the mandate to create civil society organization committees of an advisory nature for predetermined matters in the various government divisions, among other issues. More than six years later, in February 2011, the bill was finally approved.

In spite of this, all the proposals related to mechanisms of direct democracy in the first versions of the bill were excluded from the draft sent to Parliament. Apparently, this was as a result of agreements made by the Concertación decisionmakers. This is in stark contrast with citizen support for the introduction of mechanisms of direct democracy such as recall, plebiscites and the law of people's initiative, which stands at around 80% (Recabarren and Aubry 2005, 79).

The government initiative was strained by different opinions regarding citizens' participation. This was evident in the speech given by Bachelet in

September 2006 on the inauguration of the Pro Participation Agenda. The basis of the agenda included political reforms related to the binominal system, automatic registration of voters, the political participation of women, vote for Chileans living abroad, the election of regional authorities, municipal reform to create local governments and the law of people's initiative, amongst others. The agenda, however, was much more limited. It proposed the creation of civil society organization committees of an advisory nature at different levels, an increase in the competitive fund supporting social organizations, projects for the construction of infrastructure in Chile's regions for the use of organizations, improved access to information on public policies and the promotion of measures against discrimination and in favor of tolerance.[11]

HOW MUCH DOES CIVIL SOCIETY INFLUENCE CHILE'S DEMOCRACY?

I have stated that as depoliticization grows, the state has promoted initiatives that incorporate citizen participation in public policies. Through these, it creates new interactions with society that partially replace those that politics provided in the past. These new interactions, however, are far removed from public deliberation; they strengthen a kind of "statization" of diverse forms of organized social action and strengthen the role of the techno-bureaucratic elites.

In previous research we analyzed the action of local networks that coordinate social organizations and the entities in charge of public programs on the ground (Delamaza and Ochsenius 2010). An analysis of a selected sample of 129 initiatives on the linkages between civil society and the state shows that these processes have an impact on the approaches and methods adopted in several realms, from the exercise of citizenship to public management. The range of issues and methodologies of the initiatives analyzed could be a consequence of social policies that incorporate participative methodologies and diverse modes of interaction with civil society. It could also be an indicator of the vitality with which civil organizations address issues of public interest and establish different forms of interaction with the public sector. In short, it constitutes a new way of mediating with the state, outside of institutionalized democratic politics.

In the past, that relationship linked national social actors with expanding public policies through political actors who would mediate in parliament via the expansion of the state. Parliamentary groups did not only reflect the interests of specific sectors, they were also structured according to political parties with strong social roots that linked them organically and permanently to certain social sectors, and enabled them to coordinate long-term political projects. This political process was strongly linked to the development of the type of state and its linkages with collective interests (Abal Medina 2005).

The current panorama is very different. First, social actors are no longer coordinated in national organizations. They act at the local level and lack entities that represent their broader interests (UNDP 2000; Varas 2012). Moreover, their relationship with the state occurs through municipalities or through social programs at the local level. There are so many linkages that the implementation of the various policies presupposes that the beneficiaries are actively organized and participating. The participatory framework is imposed from outside and via the objectives established by the policies and programs themselves. This promotes the creation of local organizations and groups that make their contribution through various organizational structures. In other words, the relationship grows and deepens within a framework of policies and programs implemented and established by the state, rather than as a response to conflicting political claims made by different groups in civil society.

However, this participatory dynamics related to social programs is weakened principally by the fact that it occurs more or less on the margins of the public space, and thus fails to empower social organizations to influence public policies from said space. The relationship becomes instrumental or functional to previously designed policies, and to predefined regulatory and budgetary frameworks. And yet citizens' capabilities are strengthened by the initiatives generated by civil society as well as those promoted by the state. This suggests the presence of potentially democratizing actors in both these spheres of public action. Finally, in the realm of public administration, the influence of groups in civil society is lower and lies mainly within initiatives promoted by the state.

These are relatively isolated networks functioning separately, linking specific organizations with single state agencies. They are not part of one or several macro-networks, or blocks of actors linked by dense networks, but rather as multiple weak and scarcely interconnected ones. This analysis corroborates the diagnosis of Chilean civil society as an archipelago of small and isolated units. But it also reflects the internal diversity of the state. The convergence established at the intermediate levels and points of implementation lacks fluid channels towards the decision-making levels: there is no upward flow from the lower layers.

The low possibility for influencing public policies, despite their numbers and variety, is made evident by the analysis of this selected sample of initiatives with an organized participatory content. Organized civil society, acting in conjunction with local governments and services, and using all the relevant channels available, does not have the capacity to create sustainable and autonomous networks of public policies. Furthermore, there are no adequate institutions to promote such action.

This situation contrasts with other forms of linkage implemented, mainly in relation to social policies, which engage with civil society but are not channeled through the established entities. These arrangements take place at the national level or inhabit the public stage in such a way that they become relevant for political and institutional actors with national influence. In general, other sectors of civil society with more power or influence engage in them. Otherwise, they generate different strategies of linkage with the state that mobilize political or organizational resources that subnational initiatives do not have access to. Again, these are noninstitutionalized arrangements that replace more stable mechanisms. Designed *ad hoc* or simply as the result of the political dynamic between state and civil society actors, they are the expert knowledge networks (Varas 2006), public-private strategic alliances (Blanco and Vargas 2006) and the urban citizens' movements (Poduje 2008).

These arrangements differ from the previous samples in that they have a greater capacity to influence change in public policies, but in this case "from above" and engaging other types of organizations and actors from civil society. The three key factors that enable this capacity are technical knowledge, positions of power and the place occupied by the actors in the socioeconomic structure. The patterns of concentration of these resources in specific groups and places explain the greater influence that these social actors exercise in public policy decisions, and deepen elitism instead of decreasing it.

The case of the institutionalization of gender politics was analyzed by Augusto Varas (2006). Although this process has its origins in a social movement and has a political leaders participating in it, it does not strategically depend on either of them. A political agreement provided the framework for action, but from there onward the process is relatively autonomous from social dynamics. In essence, it depends on the strength of *think tanks*, international cooperation resources, and the opportunities available to women experts that pass from feminist civil society to government positions. As long as the communication channels between both sectors are open, influence can be exercised in different spheres of public policy. Rather than determine the process, the strictly political dynamic—parliamentary representation—lends support and reacts to what is generated by these expert networks.

This progressive modification of the political agenda—as exemplified here by the case of gender equality—is no different to what happens in other areas, such as citizens' security, higher education or the regulation of economic sectors. In these cases, the technical or specialized discourse plays a less progressive role. It uses its dense institutional networks to encourage the continuation of the public policies focuses adopted in the 1980s, rather than to promote their modification.

In the case of the penal reform process—one of the most important reforms carried out during the administration of Eduardo Frei (1994–2000)—a different type of network, coined as the "public-private strategic partnership" by Blanco and Vargas (2006), was established. This sectoral reform was also guided by the government, but did not come from the government since it was not included in its agenda. Its formulation and design was the result of a concerted effort between academic centers and civil society institutions, plus substantial support from the press. There were no previous social movements or demands for more or improved justice. Rather, there was a political decision that encompassed the dominant political elite (the government and the opposition). The cause can be found in the agendas of international organizations such as the IDB and the World Bank, concerned about the modernization of the justice sector in Chile in the context of the second generation of reforms.

Who are the actors capable of occupying the space and achieving broad political influence? In a sector as important as the justice system, the initiative and the agenda were the consequence of a strategic combination of actors, a new type of "public policy network."[12] In effect, the issue was firmly placed on the agenda of social actors with the power and capability to sustain, finance and disseminate the activities carried out by the network, and which eventually became far-reaching public policy. This brings in another factor usually considered important in a social actor's capacity to influence: the resources they can access and mobilize (Fuentes and Heiss 2006, 363).

Expert knowledge surfaces again. Conceptualized as the reverse of discourse and political knowledge, expert knowledge enables a fluid dialogue between the public and private sectors. But we also see the presence of sectors with resources and power. These manifest themselves in the financing of the initiatives, and rather than depend on the state, they are backed by academic institutions, companies and international cooperation. The question that arises is why this case, unlike so many others, is successful to the point of generating a key reform. It even manages to obtain the commitment of a substantial amount of public resources, paradoxically supported by champions of the "minimum state."

To answer to these questions, let us compare these last examples with the Presidential Advisory Council on Education in 2006. Educational reform was not included in the government's agenda either. As regards participation, this initiative was much broader (more than 90 people from very different groups). Both the social movement that instigated it and the council itself engaged significantly more sectors and people than the penal reform process. The expert knowledge available in Chile and public-private leadership were also present. Nevertheless, the council did not manage to formulate a consensual vision nor did it engage the political elites. The latter eventually settled on a reform that was substantially more restricted, and that did not adequately consider the results presented by the council or by the high school student movement. It came as no surprise, therefore, that five years later, in 2011, student demands for improvements to the education system resurfaced. Again, they received broad popular support, but this time the possibility of settlement through institutional channels was much lower. The diminishing effectiveness results in the lower representativeness of democratic procedures.

The issue of public education does not generate a consensus, rendering it unable to find "technical" solutions, while the entity created was unable to politically process the problem. One explanatory factor could be the broad range of participation. While in the case of penal reform participation was limited to the experts, the education process engaged social movements and organizations whose demands went beyond the model of governance as they sought to modify some key reforms dating back to the period of the dictatorship. Moreover, as Jorge Correa described, civil society engagement in the penal reform process was limited to just three academic centers closely associated with important political forces and the hegemonic Fundación Paz Ciudadana, and the ensuing support of the *El Mercurio* newspaper, a de facto power during the transition. In education, in contrast, the conflict was much broader (Aguilera and Fuentes 2011).

A final example is provided by citizens' movements seeking to solve urban issues. Emerging from 2003 onward, these movements have been highly successful and influential in achieving change as regards urban regulatory plans, urban mitigation works or simply the cancellation of urban megaprojects. Their composition evidences a strong socioeconomic bias: out of a total of 32 citizens organizations that emerged in the metropolitan region beginning in 2003, 18 (56%) are from Santiago's traditional upper-class district. If we include the organizations from recent housing developments in the wealthier boroughs and from high-income neighborhoods built in the popular boroughs, "the proportion of 'ABC1' movements increases to 66 percent. Another 16 percent comes from middle class neighborhoods [...] Only 19 percent of citizens' movements are from low-income neighborhoods" (Poduje 2008, 7). In this case, the organizational and participatory dynamic generates political influence. However, this influence is related to the socioeconomic characteristics described above, and tends to reproduce inequality in the realm of social participation.

CONCLUSIONS

The spaces and mechanisms of mediation between society and the state have changed significantly in Chile from the period of democracy that existed before the 1973 military coup to the democracy that emerged as a result of the negotiated political transition that began in 1990. The predominant role played by national level political parties, in conjunction with social movements that were also coordinated at the national level, has given way to the implementation of multiple sectoral policies with functional and micro-local participation, decreased voter participation, and social movements whose structures have become weaker.

These phenomena, together with the reinforced presidentialism that is part of Chile's political structure, have modified the space for political mediation. The national-level political parties and social movements that once occupied this space have been partially replaced by the relatively technocratic administration of social projects, mainly on the margins of public deliberation. The historical role played by political parties has lost importance. As a result, a vacuum has been created in the spaces used for the deliberation and formulation of political projects, and political parties today limit themselves to selecting personnel to fill positions at the executive and legislative branches.

At first, this change increased the effectiveness of the state apparatus to streamline public policies, especially in the social sphere. This mitigated some of the more severe impacts and discriminatory effects of the neoliberal economic model as individual incomes and social services improved. Additionally, this situation played a key role in securing political stability in the face of threats of a return to authoritarian rule, resting as it did on the control and negotiation of the political process by the two main coalitions. Yet it did not enable democracy to effectively administrate the reconstruction of mediation with a civil society undergoing transformation. Nor did it empower democracy to address the socioeconomic changes required to reduce inequity and exclusion and control and check the overwhelming dominance of market regulations in several spheres of society.

At the same time, Chile's transition pact had a serious effect on the representativeness of the democratic system. The majority rule law was curtailed by constitutional resolutions designed to prevent the transformation of the authoritarian rule model, and reinforced by an electoral system that privileges the first minority, and by the influence of the so-called *de facto* powers in decision-making. Indeed, over the past two decades there have been no significant advances on various fronts, including political decentralization, democratization of political parties, adaptation of the electoral rolls to Chile's demographic reality, and the financing of political activity. The one thing that was accomplished was the modification of the "authoritarian enclaves" such as the National Security Council, designated senators, the composition of the Constitutional Tribunal, and restoring the president's faculty to remove the higher layers of the armed forces. But the main consequences of this dynamic have been a reduction in the electoral universe, an increased disaffection among voters, and the lack of mechanisms promoting participation and deliberation in order to complement and enrich political representation.

The absence of institutionalized participatory mechanisms reproduces the inequity that prevails in Chilean society. The groups that own the most social capital and relative power enjoy much greater influence and power in political decision-making. In contrast, the local networks that the state uses as a link with popular communities have little capacity to influence the administration and implementation of predefined programs, and are, in effect, unable to intervene in the root causes of their problems. Thus, participation has not yet become a public issue susceptible to real accountability, decreasing at the same time the effectiveness of the democratic system and its policies.

This analysis has placed emphasis on the changes generated in Chilean society. It questions the validity of commonplace diagnoses that present a totally fragmented society penetrated by the individualistic logic of the neoliberal model. Even though the available empirical data are not enough, the analysis reveals an active but fragmented civil society. Besides lacking the broad networks necessary to create internal links, Chilean civil society has weak organic channels connecting it to politics. The analysis shows that the influence of local participatory initiatives is relatively low because they have no bearing on the orientation of policies and do not became institutionalized. This is not just a result of the fragmentation of civil society. It is also due to the fact that the spaces for the participation of civil society hardly receive regulatory or technical support, and are disconnected from public policy cycles. They are usually nonbinding spaces, frequently functional to the implementation of specific government programs. At the same time, citizens' participatory politics have not sought to significantly change this situation, although they did manage to get a law passed that establishes the right to participate in public administration, and broadens and strengthens civil society's advisory organizations.

Throughout 2011 there was a surge in social mobilization, with strong support from citizens, particularly as regards educational reform, the protection of the environment from destructive mega-projects, labor rights, and against the poor distribution of income. These mobilizations tend to have no political connections and do not want to form part of institutionalized political forces. This trend reveals a relative corrosion of the democratic model implemented since 1990. It also reveals a need for change as regards the effectiveness of public action and the capacity to represent the country's citizens. Chile's democracy is basically facing a challenge that will require future reforms to political institutions, as well as new spaces capable of projecting and channeling the new forms of collective action.

NOTES

A preliminary version of this chapter was presented at the Symposium on Representativeness and Effectiveness in Latin American Institutions and Democracy, held March 24, 2011, at Tulane University, New Orleans, LA.

1. Another example is the Junta de Adelanto de Arica, created to promote development in the Northern province of Arica, Chile. It was administrated by the Business Council and received funding from the global sales in the region, by law (González 2006, 315).
2. With support of the Jesuit Order, Vekemans also founded the School of Sociology of the Universidad Católica and the DESAL Center for the Economic and Social Development of Latin America. Both entities became centers for the study and development of ideas, proposing change for new generations of Catholic professionals. From then on, a wave of young Christian Democrat professionals implemented social reforms from the state, thus creating a professional technical body with increasing political importance (Beigel 2011).
3. The Assembly of Civility was the major coordination form that has been developed by the organizations that are fighting against Pinochet at the time. All its leaders are members of political parties. The "Demanda de Chile" was the platform for the transition to democracy.

4. The first legislature completely elected was appointed only in 2006; there is no election of regional governments, the electoral system overrepresented the first minority (i.e., the right-wing parties), among other issues.
5. According to data from a study on political culture under democracy in Chile in 2006, the level of trust in political parties stood at 39.6%; in the Supreme Court 48.6%; and in Parliament 51%, constituting the three least trusted institutions amongst the population polled (Luna and Seligson 2007, 47).
6. "Whilst in Costa Rica (the most stable democracy of the countries included in the study) 87.7% of those polled sustained that this form of government is 'always preferable to any other political regime,' in Chile a significantly lower percentage (although also a majority) agree with this affirmation." In fact, support stood at 70.5% in 2006. We can also say that "when compared with Costa Rica it also becomes manifest that 20% less of Chileans show a 'favorable' attitude with respects to a stable democracy" (Luna and Seligson 2007, 63). In relation to diminishing electoral participation some political scientists have criticized aspects of the electoral mechanisms, such as the obligatory nature of the vote and the voluntary character of registration in the electoral rolls, the lack of overlap between the presidential and parliamentary elections until 2006, the lack of attributions of Parliament, the binominal system, and the lack of financing of politics, among others (Navia 2009; Campos 2009).
7. Data from polls carried out in 2011 show that 34% of those interviewed felt identified with the government and 34% with the opposition; the approval of the work carried out by the Coalición por el Cambio reached 24% and by the Concertación 18%; approval of the work carried out by the members of Parliament reached 22% and of the Senate 25% (www.adimark.cl poll, consulted on December 10, 2011).
8. The population registered dropped from 89% of the total population with the right to vote in 1989 to 68% in 2008 (Saldaña 2009, 61). In December 2011, Parliament passed a law establishing an automatic system for electoral registration and voluntary voting. In the 2012 municipal election, only 39% of the population voted.
9. The education demonstrations have received constant support from citizens, and ranged between 60% and 80% (www.adimark.cl). Trust in representative institutions—Parliament and parties—has decreased continuously. Other economic and political institutions are also affected by diminishing trust (www.adimark.cl; http://www.encuesta.udp.cl/, accessed December 20, 2011).
10. In the parliamentary elections carried out towards the end of 1997, the ruling coalition lost around a million votes.
11. See http://www.prensapresidencia.cl/view/viewFrameComunicado.asp? codigo = 5262. Accessed April 10, 2009.
12. Jorge Correa, a key player in the reform, describes this network:

> The government's main agenda was not the brainchild of a political coalition's program, nor was it initiated within the Ministry. It was the product of the effort made by two NGOs. ...Paz Ciudadana...was associated with the *El Mercurio* newspaper....Paz Ciudadana partnered with the Corporación de Promoción Universitaria, a corporation with links to the Christian Democrats that had received funds from USAID to develop this area. They were joined by academics concerned about issues of due process and human rights, from Diego Portales University Law School. . ..[B]ut without a doubt, *El Mercurio* newspaper, through numerous editorials and its news coverage, gave the idea its final impulse. (1999, 308)

Part V
Conclusion

13 Conclusion

Ludovico Feoli

This volume has sought to broaden the discussion about representation and effectiveness by looking below the regime level, at the legislature, the judiciary and civil society, while drawing on cases from four key Latin American countries. The analyses presented wrestle, explicitly and implicitly, with some of the central questions of democratic representation: legitimacy, accountability, responsiveness and effectiveness. They also advance the discussion of how government structure impinges upon representation. This section briefly reviews these aspects, bringing the volume to a close. It also assesses the picture that emerges of the state of representation and effectiveness in the countries analyzed.

A central question of representation is who can legitimately represent. This in turn raises the question of how representation takes place, and since representation is seldom a "blank check," how representatives are held accountable and responsive to the interests of the represented (Pitkin 1967; Rehfeld 2006). In essence, the latter amounts to how the legitimacy of representativeness is maintained. As pointed out in the introduction to this volume, the traditional answers to these questions have focused on explicit electoral delegation: legitimate representatives are chosen and held accountable by periodic elections (Manin, Przeworski et al. 1999, 3; Urbinati and Warren 2008, 389). But the scope of representation that takes place in a democracy is much broader. As Pettit (2009) has stated, "any public authorities, and any citizens who assume a legitimate role in public discourse, may make a legitimate claim to represent the people" (61). This volume has shown how this occurs in the legislature but also in two other spheres, unmediated by elections—civil society and the judiciary—which are in turn interrelated with, and complement the actions of, elected representatives. The book has also shown that the extent of representation that takes place in these spheres has implications for how well they manage to exercise their given function. Table 13.1 summarizes the findings. This framework will be employed to discuss the contributions of the authors.

THE LEGISLATURE

The legislature is, by definition, the representative branch of government—its members are elected to serve as representatives of the citizenry in all public

Table 13.1   Questions of Representation and Effectiveness in Democratic Regimes

	Legislative	Judiciary	Civil Society
Why can it represent?	Popular mandate	Constitutional mandate	Self-authorization
			Institutionalized participation
How can it represent?	"Standing for"	Access to justice	Social accountability
	"Acting for"	"Standing for"	Identity politics
		Interpretation	Institutionalized participation
		Judicial review	
Accountability	Elections	Civic action	State recognition
	Lobbying	Public opinion	International recognition
	Public opinion	Checks and balances	Competition
	Checks and balances		
Responsiveness	Explicit	Explicit	Explicit
	Implicit	Implicit	Implicit
Effectiveness	Enactments	Rule of law	Influence on public policy
	Capabilities	Independence	State oversight
	Consensus	Protection of rights	
		Checks and balances	

Source: Author's creation

matters. The electoral system determines how representation reflects the population in the makeup of the legislature. Proportional representation systems foster greater inclusiveness and deliberation than single-member plurality systems, though the latter are probably better at generating accountability (Urbinati and Warren 2008, 399). Elections are the primary source of accountability for legislators, whether they act in anticipation of what voters will approve at the next election, or on the basis of campaign promises or internalized principles.[1] Legislators may also be subject to direct forms of pressure from interest groups and to public opinion. The form that representation takes in the legislature has been characterized in many ways by the literature (see the Introduction to this volume). For analytical purposes, it might be said that many of those forms fall within the categories of "standing for" or "acting for" a particular constituency. The issue of responsiveness, whether and to what extent policies correspond to the interests of voters, can also take many forms. Considered by Rehfeld (2009, 214) to be the "central normative problem" of democracy, it has an explicit dimension, where representatives act in accordance with the public opinion of constituents, and an implicit dimension, where representatives act in accordance with (their own) broader principles of right or justice, in the best interest of the represented (Pitkin 1967) and less responsive to electoral sanction (Mansbridge 2003; Rehfeld 2009).[2] Finally, the effectiveness of the legislature is typically expressed in terms of its productivity, but also its capacity to include multiple viewpoints in deliberations and procure the formation of societal consensus.

The contributors to this volume take up many of these elements. Jones and Micozzi focus on accountability, showing how party system denationalization in Argentina during the Kirchner-Fernández era has negatively impacted representation. Provincial parties form transient alliances for electoral purposes, with changing names and composition, even incorporating ideological opposites. Once elected, deputies join (national) congressional delegations with little or no resemblance "in name or programmatic goals to the electoral alliances supported by voters at the ballot box in congressional elections." This makes the link between voting and postelection actions by deputies increasingly tenuous, severing the electoral sanction and therefore encumbering accountability. Interestingly, the internal rules of the Argentine legislature, by delegating power on a majoritarian basis, provide incentives for deputies to join coalitions with the two dominant national parties. While this "compression" fosters effectiveness, in the sense that it helps the legislature to function, it does so by obfuscating who stands and/or acts for the citizenry, compromising representation. Representation suffers in degree as the judgment of citizens regarding the aims of legislation becomes marginalized. And it suffers in quality, as provincial-level politics are particularistic, based on patronage, pork barrel and clientelism.

In their examination of accountability Renno and Pereira arrive at a different conclusion when comparing subnational cases in Brazil. They find that federal deputies tend to be rewarded by voters for holding party leadership roles and for providing locally based assets, via budgetary allocations, much more than for performance in the lawmaking process at the national level. Rather than dismissing this practice as a simple type of clientelism, they see it as "a form of action oriented to solving immediate and pressing needs of local electorates ... to fund infrastructure, public health and education projects in localities that would not have access to these funds from other sources." This analysis suggests a level of explicit responsiveness on the part of the Brazilian Congress, which is often rewarded with reelection, although factors like campaign finance also play an important role. The authors highlight that such effectiveness on the part of Congress is an indication of its power, especially in comparison to other Latin American legislatures.

The tradeoff between national and local orientation on the part of legislators also surfaces in Alemán's study of the Chilean Congress. He finds that, attitudinally, Chilean legislators express greater interest in local/partisan issues than in more general, national issues. Yet their actual behavior is more congruent with national goals than district-oriented ones. This suggests that, while legislators see themselves as "standing for" the locality, there are other incentives at work that drive them towards a more general, implicit type of representation. The "institutional context in Chile facilitates the assignment of responsibility for governmental decisions, and party and coalition labels matter to voters and legislators—voters can discern among candidates in terms of policy and can expect candidates for the legislature to act in a rather coherent fashion." In this regard, the findings for Chile are the exact mirror image of those for Argentina. Alemán notes, however, that the Chilean electoral system limits the sanctioning power of elections. This is because the only way one of the two dominant coalitions can be excluded from a district is if the other one doubles its vote-share, a high order given their similar popularity across districts. Nonetheless, he finds that the Chilean Congress, while far from perfect, is "a rather effective institution," whether measured in terms of its output, its level of professionalization, or public perceptions.

In her analysis of Mexico, Casar questions whether the country's avowed lack of effectiveness in processing key policy reforms can be attributed to the broadening of representation brought about by the advent of full democratization. Key institutional reforms in the 1990s significantly improved representation, increasing the number and assertiveness of political parties in Congress and veto players in the policy process. Yet Casar observes empirical levels of effectiveness that belie the view (advanced by politicians and academics) that the Mexican Congress is in persistent gridlock: high success rates for bills; floor coalitions formed by the three main parties; frequent passage of constitutional reforms (which require supermajorities in both houses); and passage of key legislation (in energy, pensions, electoral law, banking, human rights, and others). She explains the apparent paradox by pointing to interest group organizations and "de facto powers" and the diffuse assignment of responsibility inherent to presidentialism: opposition parties and the president blame each other for the persistence of economic stagnation and the deterioration of public safety, creating a perception of stasis. These are, in effect, competing representational claims as both state powers contend to be "acting for" the citizenry. Much like the United States, the Mexican presidential system is designed to be permeable to societal interests at multiple levels—federal, state, local, bicameral chambers, and so on. This enables those interests to bear upon their representatives, to pass or obstruct policy reforms as the case may be, depending on the relative balance of forces.

At issue is whether increasing representation implies a tradeoff in legislative effectiveness. Casar reminds us that the broadening of representation she examines is part of a regional Latin American trend, so her study has broader implications. This trend has opened greater access to power. That is, it has enabled representatives to "stand for" more social groups with representational claims. But, as in the Mexican case, such broadening has not always been accompanied by other institutional reforms that, in the ensuing plurality and complexity, could foster coalition formation and executive-legislative cooperation, attenuating the impacts on effectiveness. The result has been a legislative process that is *perceived* as messy and ineffective, irresponsive to most needs of the citizenry, although the reality in terms of actual policy making is more complex. At the same time, if congressional effectiveness depends on the competence of Congress, as both Casar and Alemán suggest, the professionalization of its membership will also be a crucial factor. This is an area where Mexico and, possibly others, lag. In sum, Casar shows that the tradeoff between representation and effectiveness is contingent on institutional structures, congressional capabilities, and the balance of political forces.

The tradeoff between representativeness and effectiveness is analyzed further in MacKinnon's historical comparative study of the Chilean and Argentine early 20th-century Congresses. As with Casar, the impact of institutional structure, congressional capabilities, and the balance of political forces are central. The Chilean Congress was characterized by a concentration of power with complex and institutionalized rules and the capacity to deal with intractable conflict and "get things done." The Argentine Congress was characterized by a diffusion of power and an absence of strict procedural rules or specific conflict solving mechanisms, lacking the capacity to avoid "stalling and delay." While such characteristics made the Chilean Congress more effective, in the sense of its ability to enact key laws, they also limited its representativeness: the degree to which diverse voices, views and interests could be incorporated into its lawmaking process, and the ensuing laws. For similar, but converse, reasons, the Argentine Congress was more representative, in the sense of including more voices, views and interests into debates and their outputs, but limited in its ability to avoid getting mired in the process. In MacKinnon's terms, Congress was either an important public forum in the public sphere, as in Argentina, or a powerful lawmaker, as in Chile.

Yet the balance of political forces also plays an important role in MacKinnon's argument. The ability of Chilean elites to retain control of the agenda and push decisions up an "ascending spiral" towards more exclusive arenas, due to a concentration of power, goes a long way towards explaining the effectiveness of their Congress. Such control did not seem possible in Argentina, where power among the elites appeared to be much more fragmented and where the engine of congressional decision-making was the Lower Chamber, which was more socially diverse than the senate. This reaffirms the conclusion about the contingency of the tradeoff between congressional representativeness and effectiveness in the Chilean case, but not in the Argentine case, suggesting that, while it may occur, it is not inherently necessary. The key challenge, then, is how to advance both of them in balance. As Hagopian (2005, 125) has argued, a high-quality democracy is one where effective governance and political stability advance in tandem with political representation.

THE JUDICIARY

The representative role of the judiciary is perhaps the least intuitive, as judges tend to be thought of as accountable to the law, not to the people. In fact, the judiciary is often thought of as an unrepresentative power, given its obligation to uphold the law even when it is unpopular to do so (Rios-Figueroa, Ingram, Couso). Even in the few cases where judges are elected, their independence in office is paramount and higher courts are always free from direct representative accountability (Urbinati and Warren 2008, 398). While the constitutional mandate to apply the laws created by popular representatives endows judiciary representation with the mantle of democratic legitimacy, the extent to which it allows for interpretation of the law, aside from its strict application, is a matter of continuous debate. However, as the contributions to this volume show, there are multiple ways in which the judiciary serves a representative function, including the interpretation of laws to determine their original meaning, or giving new interpretation to existing legislation. When the judiciary interprets its constitutionally assigned role to protect minorities and rectify social injustices, becoming a voice for the marginalized groups of society, it exercises the role of an alternative societal representative (De Sousa 2010, 88). Such a role guarantees popular access to justice and representation to the disenfranchised. Judges can also bee seen as "standing for" all views in a society, balancing as full a range of principles and values as possible. The constitutional power of judicial review can also be used towards this purpose, guaranteeing the protection of rights. And while the judiciary is not electorally accountable, it is susceptible to public opinion (Kuklinski and Stanga 1979) and is responsive to civil society organizations (Sabsay, in this volume). This responsiveness should be implicit, as the judiciary acts to uphold general principles through the enforcement and/or interpretation of the law, but should not necessarily reflect the popular will.[3] However, from an administrative perspective the judiciary can respond explicitly to demands for inclusion by offering services that enhance accessibility to the community. The judiciary is held accountable by checks and balances exercised by other state powers—as in the appointment and removal of judges, for example—but also by the actions of civil society and public opinion (including the media). The effectiveness of the judiciary is captured by the concept of rule of law, meaning (at a minimum) the implementation of the law with equality and impartiality for all citizens, without consideration of class, status or power differentials, through the application of known and preestablished procedures, which no one is above (O'Donnell 2004, 33). It is also manifested in an independent judiciary, whose rulings are respected and enforced by all branches, that receives appropriate funding, and that is not compromised by political interference (De Sousa 2010, 92). Finally, it is measured by the exercise of the function of institutional checks and balances and the adjudication of disputes among powers.

Couso takes up the question of representation in the context of the judiciary's constitutional role. The legitimacy of judicial institutions, he asserts, depends on their being regarded as impartial adjudicators. The need for impartiality therefore rules out representation as explicit responsiveness to majority preferences. At the same time, however, a defense of the Constitution and the law, especially when unpopular, can trigger intervention from opportunistic executives claiming to embody the people's true representation. Representation as an implicit form of responsiveness involving interpretation of the law requires an ingrained culture of legality that accepts the judiciary as the ultimate arbiter of the Constitution and the law and respects its independence, submitting to its decisions. Otherwise, judicial action in general, and constitutional adjudication in particular, can be cast as an illegitimate constraint on democracy, implying "the nullification of democratically enacted law by non-elected judges." Such "constitutionalism" is also a precondition for the effectiveness of the judiciary because in its absence its institutions would be severely compromised and constrained. At the same time, it highlights that legitimacy must be constantly renewed through careful adherence to legality, professionalism and the exercise of restraint. As Sabsay argues in this volume, "judicial activism" and "guarantor judge" often carry pejorative connotations.

Couso's analysis of the Supreme Court's role in Chile's democratic consolidation raises an interesting paradox. Rather than expanding constitutional adjudication to contribute to the democratic transition, as most other Latin American countries, Chile's system of constitutional adjudication was established by the Pinochet regime to protect its political and economic constitutional design from change. Yet, the strict adherence to the Constitution by Supreme Court justices following a tradition of independence and respect for the law opened the way for the collapse of the regime, by forcing it into a clean plebiscite. Despite this, the Constitutional Court was subsequently deferential towards the government and Congress and did not play a substantial role in the democratic transition, remaining rather passive until 2005, when a constitutional reform drastically altered its structure. The reform increased the court's independence from the Supreme Court and drastically increased access by opening it up to ordinary citizens and lower court judges. The ensuing explosion of caseloads led the court to take a more activist stance and to become a major player in the policy-making process through the constitutional review of legislation. This increased role also increased the visibility of the court, subjecting it to public criticism and a greater level of accountability. The court has so far managed to maintain its legitimacy before the public, but not without controversy, and Couso warns that its activism will remain subject to scrutiny. It also remains to be seen if its increased caseload will hinder its effectiveness. For now, the court has "increased its representativeness, allowing broader sectors of the citizenry to have recourse to constitutional adjudication and thus, the protection of their constitutional rights."

Rios also views access as a measure of judicial representativeness. To the extent that it can bring judicial institutions closer to citizens, greater access can make the judiciary more permeable to ordinary concerns and societal values. Tracing the evolution of the Mexican Supreme Court and Public Prosecutor's Office from the late 1920s to the present, he shows they have fallen short of this objective. Despite successive reforms, access to justice has remained at low levels for ordinary citizens. Partly due to the institutional structures and power dynamics inherited from a long authoritarian past, compounded by a protracted and negotiated democratic transition, entrenched interests within the judiciary have managed to resist a dilution of their power. In fact, since 1999 the justice system has increased the Supreme Court's concentration of power. The Public Prosecutor's Office remains subordinated to the executive, and therefore loyal to that power instead of the citizens or the law. Outside of the executive it would appear that the judiciary has not been subject to societal accountability mechanisms and has remained unrepresentative, that is, inaccessible to the people. It has been responsive to the needs of the political elite while remaining unresponsive to broader social needs, neglecting the protection of individual rights. The Supreme Court, for example, has been capable of solving political disputes but not protecting individual rights. The Public Prosecutor's Office has been efficient at "getting things done for political bosses" but has a poor record of prosecuting the vast majority of criminal offences that affect common citizens. While a host of recent changes, all focused on citizen access, could revolutionize the representativeness of the judiciary, Rios argues that the fate of these reforms depends on their adoption by litigants and judges, and perhaps more importantly, further changes in police and prosecutorial practices. This suggests that a strong advocacy role on the part of civil society organizations could favor the implementation of these reforms, a point that surfaces in Ingram's analysis, as well as Sabsay's, and that will also be explored in the civil society section.

To Ingram, the judiciary is representative to the extent that it meets the needs and reflects the interests of democratic society as a whole, "balancing as full a range of principles and values as possible." This implies that courts should be protective of democratic values and human rights, representing "not just what is legal, but also what is just, fair, and equitable." Looking at the local level in Brazil, Ingram shows how activist judges organized themselves and capitalized on ties to local social movements to implement a judicial outreach program and to improve the strength and transparency of the judiciary. This can be seen as a complex accountability mechanism combining the actions of nongovernmental and state actors animated by progressive reform ideas in a mutually reinforcing relationship, resulting in both explicit and implicit forms of responsiveness. The outreach program implemented brought judges and the judicial process to neighborhoods, moving basic legal proceedings and small claims resolution to cities in the interior. An explicit response to community needs, it transformed the judiciary from a passive, remote and inaccessible entity into one that was accessible and willing to represent the citizenry. Judges also organized lobbying and labor actions, including strikes, to secure larger and independent budgets, improved physical infrastructure and increased support staff. Their success in this area strengthened the judiciary and improved its capacity to serve the community and enforce the law—an implicit response to community needs. By asserting its financial and administrative independence with regard to the executive, these changes also enabled the judiciary to conduct its role of institutional checks and balances. All of these changes advanced the effectiveness of the judiciary. At the same time, by "making the law socially relevant to broad sectors of the population" they also fostered representativeness.

Sabsay echoes Couso's preoccupation with constitutionalism and judicial independence as strong preconditions for judicial effectiveness, both of which he finds insufficient in contemporary Argentina despite a spate of reforms dating back to 1994. Independence of the judiciary is essential for the exercise of its function of horizontal accountability and guarantor of the rule of law, limiting the power of the state and guaranteeing adherence to the institutional framework provided by the Constitution, ensuring the absence of impunity and preserving its own legitimacy. Like the other authors in this section, Sabsay sees representativeness in terms of access, but also responsiveness to social organization. The judiciary can be regarded as representative "when accessibility is granted to every citizen, especially the most vulnerable minorities." He notes barriers to this objective ranging from the high cost of litigation and legal services, which exclude the poor, to the elitist structure of the judicature, which stems from nepotism and lack of transparency in judicial appointments. However, in the advent of democratization, the actions of civil society have increased access, making previously unknown judicial actions possible. He credits the advocacy work of nongovernmental organizations in areas of human rights, gender equality, consumer rights, the environment, indigenous rights and others, for the emergence of new collective rights and legal tools aimed at their defense and protection, including collective defense, class action, public hearings and access to information. This highlights the key accountability role that civic society can play in the judicial sphere through mobilization, advocacy and legal action. Civil society actors have also benefited from the ratification of treaties in the international and regional human rights regime, which has created a supranational jurisdiction in which they may bring suit to counter the ineffectiveness of the national judiciary. However, as the author notes, the implementation of these judgments, as well as those of the Supreme Court, can be slow to materialize, making questions about effectiveness linger.

CIVIL SOCIETY

Civil society has acquired growing relevance in contemporary democracy through a proliferation of representative claims that do not have an electoral basis. Party-mediated structures for popular interest articulation and inter-est intermediation have been challenged by new structures of representa-tion based on urban popular associations (Collier and Handlin 2009, 6). As described by Urbinati and Warren (2008, 403), these claims come from at least two classes of representatives, those who self-authorize and those des-ignated by governments and others as citizen representatives in new forms of institutionalized participation. Self-authorized representatives include ad-vocacy organizations, interest groups, international nongovernmental orga-nizations, philanthropic foundations and journalists. Citizen representatives are those participating in citizen panels, polls, participatory budgeting and multiple other deliberative forums. In the absence of elections, self-authorized representatives must look elsewhere for a source of their legitimacy as repre-sentatives, and this is a persistent challenge. Some groups find validation in their capacity for mobilization, which demonstrates a support base. Others rely on their institutional and technical capabilities, which make them valid interlocutors between the state and certain social sectors. Still others appeal to the inherent sense of justice underlying the claims they represent, as in the case of civil or human rights, for example. There are also many forms in which civil society actors represent. Peruzzotti groups them in three cat-egories (to be developed further on): social accountability, identity politics and institutional participation. However, questions often emerge about the legitimacy of these representational claims, particularly whether they are accountable and to whom. To the extent that they contribute to mobilize and validate the representational claims of civil society groups, the state and international nongovernmental organizations exert some level of account-ability upon them. Some could argue that this is not strictly speaking a form of democratic accountability, since it is not exerted by those social sectors that are the object of representation. At the same time, to the extent that the field for civic organization is open, civil society organizations are always accountable to competition, in the sense that alternative groups can contest their representational claims through mobilization. Civil society organiza-tions may be responsive to explicit claims grounded in the interests of a par-ticular constituency; but they can be responsive to implicit claims, as when groups monitor, expose, and denounce situations that if corrected impact the rule of law and democratic quality in general, benefiting all. Finally, the effectiveness of civil society is measured in terms of its ability to influence public policy, but also in terms of its ability to activate and/or complement the state's mechanisms of horizontal accountability.

As the authors in this section remind us, civil society is a vast and diverse universe, and so are the ways in which it represents. In turn, the different forms in which representation is expressed have different justifications and, therefore, different sources of legitimacy. Peruzzotti classifies the representa-tive roles of Latin American civil society into three types: social accountability, influence and identity movements and institutionalized participation. Orga-nizations focused on social accountability play an oversight role to "ensure the subordination of elected officials to legal constitutional norms." They are watchdogs over state policies and actions. Through the denunciation of abuses they increase public awareness, leading to action through outcry. Such actors are legitimated by their actions, which by improving the rule of law are implicitly responsive to general social needs and thus representative. Their composition or whom they "stand for" is unimportant. That is not the case with influence and identity movements. They represent minority or subaltern groups, advocating for their inclusion into the political mainstream by changing the dominant discourses, identities, practices and institutions. Such actions not only fall outside of electoral channels and classical pressure groups, they also challenge them. Examples include the human rights and gender equality movements. The legitimacy of these groups is based on the inherent justice of their claims, and the measure of their effectiveness is the degree to which they gain legislation of new rights and recognition from broader segments of society.

The third representative role assumed by civil society is that of institutionalized participation. Civil society actors represent various social sectors in "arenas of encounter" with the state. Their role is permanent and formally institutionalized, often constitutionally. It directly involves them in the policymaking process in such areas as municipal budgets, health and urban planning. Their effectiveness is given by their ability to incorporate community perspectives in the formulation of public policies. As these representatives are selected, not elected, they are sometimes questioned in terms of their representativeness. But because they help connect the poor and marginalized with a political system that often excludes them, granting access to "sectors of the population that often lack the organizational resources to voice their claims," they can be seen as leveling the playing field and advancing the democratic project. As long as the selection of civil society representatives is transparent, civil society itself may exert social accountability to ensure its inclusivity and fairness.

Dagnino picks up the discussion of institutionalized participation in her analysis of Brazil, where most of the political activity of civil society takes place embedded in relationships with the state. While intended to fill the representational gaps of irresponsive political elites and representative institutions, such activity poses new questions about representation and representativeness, especially given the varying levels of sophistication, professionalization and combativeness that exist among civil society organizations. Dagnino shows that representation in civil society can take many forms, but that in its most general sense it is a claim about a relationship of mediation between state and society. As civil society organizations assume this role, how the practices and contents of such mediation are defined is an open question, and in the absence of formal rules, power relations, typically dominated by the state, have an outsized role in the selection of representatives. This means that who is in power at a particular point in time matters greatly. During the Cardoso years, social policies were conceived as duties to be shared between state and civil society, and a policy of "partnerships" favored the strong growth of nongovernmental organizations (NGOs). The administration regularly rejected the more radical social movements (like the *Movimento dos Trabalhadores Rurais Sem Terra*, or MST) as valid interlocutors. Under the Workers' Party, the MST was readily embraced and the government recruited heavily from social movements for key cabinet positions, blurring the separation between state and society.

Social movements may have an autonomous source of legitimacy in their capacity to mobilize constituents. However, most NGOs qualify as representatives on the basis of their technical competence in the policy areas subject to institutionalized participation (budgeting, health, urban planning, etc.). Technical skills and organizational competence are thus increasingly held at a premium over organic representational links. And civil society representatives are accountable to the international organizations and state agencies that fund them, but not necessarily to the civil society whose representatives they claim to be, nor the social sectors whose interests they claim to bear.

Dagnino, like Peruzzotti, argues that the inclusion of popular sectors in institutionalized participatory mechanisms grants them voice in the policy-making process, contributes to their empowerment, and has the potential to serve as an equalizing factor. However, given the importance of technical acumen for effective participation, social inequalities may be reproduced in these participatory structures. Technical capacity is an absolute barrier to entry for some social movements and the more modest sectors. It may also act as a relative barrier, when social representatives are pitched against actors from more privileged sectors—employers, specialists—in the institutionalized participatory process. At the same time, social leaders investing their time and energy acquiring skills may be hindered from maintaining organic links to their sectors. And, given the costs, those who specialize become perpetuated as representatives, and there is little or no rotation.

A central problem of institutionalized participation is that when social groups become entangled with the state they sacrifice their autonomy, potentially compromising their ability to represent the social sectors from which they originate their representational claims. This suggests that when it comes to state-society relations, civil society groups face a tradeoff between access and autonomy: while access is fundamental given that the state remains the locus of policy-making authority, state resources can be used to control popular organizations or mobilize popular support (Collier and Handlin 2009, 82). Dagnino shows that representativeness and effectiveness are closely interrelated. To be representative, civil society must be able to channel the interests of a particular group or sector to the institutionalized arenas in which they act. It is effective to the degree that those interests are in fact reflected in public policies. However, if representatives compromise their autonomy in order to privilege effectiveness in the short term, they might end up sacrificing their long-term representativeness. As Dagnino puts it, representativeness requires autonomy, otherwise groups become mere clients of the state, "losing their radical democratic potential."

Delamaza sees post-Pinochet Chile as representing the inverse of this phenomenon. To him, civil society has becomes more autonomous, not less, as it has become disconnected from national networks and political parties. However, this has not increased its political relevance in a system dominated by a strong executive and the power of "groups that inherited a privileged position from the military government." Nor has it enabled it to play a role in, much less capitalize from, the vigorous social mobilization that began in 2011 outside of the representative political system. Delamaza argues that the strong collective action of pre-coup years, characterized by national parties with strong organic links to social sectors, has been replaced with a demobilized and apolitical civil society. Partly as a response, the state has promoted civil society involvement in the formulation of public policies through institutionalized participation. Most of the participatory mechanisms adopted, however, have been shallow, and only a few have involved meaningful deliberation and decision-making in relevant areas. With no organic social forces to back it, this spur to action from the state has only elicited responses from local groups, insulated from broader national networks. The result has been a Chilean civil society that is "an archipelago of small and isolated units," incapable of meaningfully influencing public policies. Such units are not responsive, implicitly or explicitly, to the representational needs of their constituents. They simply adapt to the requirements defined by the state as preconditions for participation. Delamaza contrasts these participatory programs with other top-down, ad hoc and noninstitutional networks that have been very effective at influencing public policies: expert knowledge networks, public-private alliances and urban citizens' movements. These groups are conformed by influential NGOs backed by—and accountable to—academic institutions, corporations and international organizations. Echoing Dagnino, Delamaza argues that the technical and organizational expertise required by these mechanisms can end up reproducing the exclusiveness and inequality of traditional representative mechanisms in the realm of social participation.

To conclude, this book grapples with a dilemma between representativeness and effectiveness. Similarly, Dahl (1998, 110) refers to a "dilemma of citizen participation versus system effectiveness": the larger the democratic unit, the greater its capacity to deal with problems important to citizens and the greater the need for citizens to delegate decisions to representatives. While this dilemma cannot be escaped Dahl argues that it can be confronted, which means striking as best a balance as possible between the benefits of participation and representation. It is achieved through a combination of national government with smaller units at the state and local level, and with a rich array of independent associations and organizations in civil society. This book shows how four Latin American countries have attempted to strike this balance and how it has impacted three key spheres of democratic government. By focusing the analysis on how the authors apply the key questions of representation and effectiveness to the different spheres, this chapter has uncovered several conclusions, of which we may highlight a few.

First, the accountability imposed by electoral mechanisms plays a key role in representation, but is influenced by other factors, such as the overall health of the party system. In Argentina, party denationalization has weakened the links between voting and the postelection actions of party coalitions, severing the electoral sanction, damaging representativeness in degree and quality. Conversely, in Brazil voters have been able to reward federal deputies with reelection for leadership roles and effective stewardship of local needs. Second, as we know, institutions matter: in Chile they have allowed voters to discern between candidates in terms of policy, while in Mexico they have allowed opposition parties and the president to blame each other for persistent problems. At the same time, the importance of an engrained respect for the Constitution as a prerequisite for judicial independence, highlighted in several of the cases, shows that the functioning of institutions depends on context and social practices. Third, as the historical analyses of Argentina and Mexico show, the tradeoff between representation and effectiveness in the legislature is contingent on institutional structures, congressional capabilities, and the balance of political forces. Fourth, social mechanisms or civil society organizations can have important effects in making state powers more representative and effective. The inclusion of popular sectors in the policy process can help level the playing field and improve democracy, while social mobilization can help activate the mechanisms of horizontal accountability and incorporate new discourses and rights into the mainstream. However, the need for technical skills and organizational competence required by some institutionalized participatory mechanisms can generate new forms of inequality in civil society representation. And popular organizations may often have to sacrifice their autonomy in order to gain access to a policy space controlled by the state. The case of Brazil shows how this can result in a loss of organic links between civil society organizations and underlying social sectors, while Chile illustrates how this can in turn lead to a loss of social trust, disenchantment with political participation, and higher levels of social conflict.

This chapter has also shown that the state of representation and effectiveness in Argentina, Chile, Mexico and Brazil is multifaceted and complex. For most of the cases, assessments vary across spheres. For example, while Casar finds that representativeness and effectiveness have evolved positively in Mexico's legislative sphere, Rios finds this only with effectiveness in the judiciary sphere, while representativeness remains constrained. Aleman finds the Chilean Congress to be representative and effective, and Couso argues that the country's Constitutional Court has increased its representativeness, but Delamaza argues that civil society has become depoliticized and fragmented, diminishing its effectiveness and representativeness. In Argentina, Jones and Micozzi note the negative effect of party denationalization on the representativeness of the legislature, but not its effectiveness, while Sabsay identifies low levels of representativeness in the judiciary. However, he also notes the positive influence of civil society organizations on both dimensions, a point also highlighted by the *Matanza-Riachuelo* case cited in the Introduction and also by Peruzzotti. Brazil seems to be the only case analyzed that is advancing both democratic dimensions simultaneously in all spheres: Renno and Pereira argue that the legislature is effective at improving the life of communities and this increases its representativeness; Ingram argues that activist judges have broadened access to justice and improved the effectiveness of the courts; and Dagnino shows the degree to which a large variety of participatory mechanisms has improved the representation of civil society, although the effectiveness of these organizations varies, and some face questions regarding the legitimacy of their representative claims.

This book shows that focusing on the dimensions of representativeness and effectiveness can reveal important aspects about democratic regimes, the functioning of their component parts, and their interactions. The chapters illustrate how applying these dimensions can yield important insights, especially in spheres where they are not typically employed. They also suggest the existence of a worthwhile research agenda for all scholars of democracy and its institutions.

NOTES

I would like to thank Moira B. MacKinnon for comments on preliminary versions of this chapter.

1. Respectively, anticipatory, promisory and gyroscopic representation, according to Mansbridge (2003).
2. These categories assimilate Carey's (2009) distinction between individual and collective responsibility described in the Introduction.
3. See Ingram (this volume) for a discussion of how the judiciary is more representative of majoritarian interests than is usually assumed.

References

Abal Medina, Juan. "La tensión entre participación y representación: repensando el vínculo entre gestión pública participativa y los fines político-partidarios." In *Fortaleciendo la relación Estado-Sociedad Civil para el desarrollo local*. Edited by Inés González Bombal. Buenos Aires: CENOC, 2005.

Abers, Rebecca. *Inventing Local Democracy: Grassroots Politics in Brazil*. Boulder, CO: Lynne Rienner, 2000.

Abrucio, Fernando. *Os Barões da Federação*. São Paulo: Hucitec Press, 1998.

Acemoglu, Daron, and James A. Robinson. *Economic Origins of Dictatorship and Democracy*. Cambridge, UK: Cambridge University Press, 2006.

Adelman, Jeremy, and Miguel Centeno. "Between Liberalism and New-Liberalism: Law's Dilemma in Latin America." In *Global Prescriptions: The Production, Exportation, and Importation of a New Legal Orthodoxy*. Edited by Yves Dezalay and Bryant Garth. Ann Arbor: University of Michigan Press, 2002.

Agor, Weston H. "The Decisional Role of the Senate in the Chilean Political System." In *Latin American Legislatures: Their Role and Influence. Analysis of Nine Countries*. Edited by Weston H. Agor. New York: Praeger, 1971.

Aguilera, Carolina, and Claudio Fuentes. "Elites y asesoría experta en Chile: comisiones y políticas públicas en el gobierno de Bachelet." In *Notables, tecnócratas y mandarines: Elementos de sociología de las elites en Chile (1990–2010)*. Edited by A. Joignant and P. Güell. Santiago: Ediciones de la Universidad Diego Portales, 2011.

Alberdi, Juan Bautista. *Bases y puntos de partida para la organización política de la República Argentina*. Vol 1. Buenos Aires: El Ateneo, 1913.

Alemán, Eduardo, and Ernesto Calvo. "Unified Government, Bill Approval, and the Legislative Weight of the President." *Comparative Political Studies* 43 (2010): 511–34.

Alemán, Eduardo, and Marisa Kellam. "The Nationalization of Electoral Change in the Americas." *Electoral Studies* 27 (2008): 193–212.

Alemán, Eduardo, and George Tsebelis. "Political Parties and Government Coalitions in the Americas." *Journal of Politics in Latin America* 3, no. 1 (2011): 3–28.

Almeida, Carla. "El marco discursivo de la 'participación solidaria' y la nueva agenda de formulación y implementación de las acciones sociales en Brasil." In *La Disputa por la Construcción Democrática en América Latina*. Edited by E. Dagnino, Alberto Olvera, and Aldo Panfichi. Mexico City: Fondo de Cultura Económica, 2006.

Alvarez, Sonia E. "Advocating Feminism: The Latin American Feminist NGO 'Boom.'" International Feminist Journal of Politics 1, no. 2 (1999): 181–209.

Alvarez, Sonia E., Evelina Dagnino, and Arturo Escobar, eds. *Cultures of Politics, Politics of Culture: Re-visioning Latin American Social Movements*. Boulder, CO: Westview Press, 1998.

Ames, Barry. *The Deadlock of Democracy in Brazil.* Ann Arbor: The University of Michigan Press, 2001.

———. "Electoral Rules, Constituencies Pressures, and Pork Barrel: Bases of Voting in the Brazilian Congress." *The Journal of Politics* 57, no. 2 (1995): 324–43.

———. "Electoral Strategy under Open-List Proportional Representation." *American Journal of Political Science* 39 (1995): 406–33.

AMMA Noticias. "AMMA pede o Tribunal a suspensão do concurso de juiz substitute." *Associação dos Magistrados do Maranhão (AMMA) Newsletter.* São Luis, MA. April 2, 2009. www.amma.com.br.

———. "Assembléia aprova projeto que cria vagas de juiz auxiliar da capital." *Associação dos Magistrados do Maranhão (AMMA) Newsletter.* São Luis, MA. March 25, 2009. www.amma.com.br.

———. "Diretores da AMMA pedem apoio a deputados para aprovação de projeto." *Associação dos Magistrados do Maranhão (AMMA) Newsletter.* São Luis, MA. March 24, 2009. www.amma.com.br.

———. "Juíza relata invasão do alojamento de Codó ao Conselho da AMMA." *Associação dos Magistrados do Maranhão (AMMA) Newsletter.* São Luis, MA. March 10, 2008. www.amma.com.br.

———. "Posse concorrida demonstra força da AMMA." *Associação dos Magistrados do Maranhão (AMMA) Newsletter.* São Luis, MA. January 12, 2007. www.amma.com.br.

Amorim Neto, Octavio, Gary Cox, and Mathew McCubbins. "Agenda Power in Brazil's Camara dos Deputados, 1989 to 1998." *World Politics* 55, no. 4 (2003): 550–78.

Anderson, Kenneth. "What NGO Accountability Means—and Does Not Mean." *American Journal of International Law* 103, no. 1 (2009): 170–78.

Angell, Alan. *Politics and the Labour Movement in Chile.* London: Oxford University Press, 1972.

Ansolabehere, Karina. "More Power ... More Rights? Mexico and Colombia: A Comparative Analysis of the Judicial Treatment of Abortion." Unpublished manuscript, 2009.

Argentine Supreme Court. *Itzcovich Mabel vs. National Administration of Social Security.* Vol. 328. March 29, 2005.

Argentine Supreme Court. *Mendoza.* Vol. 329. June 20, 2006.

Argentine Supreme Court. 2005. *Verbitsky, Horacio s/ hábeas corpus.* Vol. 328. May 3, 2005.

Arellano, José. *Políticas sociales y desarrollo. Chile 1924–1984.* Buenos Aires: Siglo XXI, 1985.

Assembleia Legislativa do Estado do Maranhão (ALMA). [n.d.] Deputada Helena Barros Heluy—Biografia. http://www.al.ma.gov.br/helena/paginas/biografia.php. Accessed April 12, 2009.

Associação dos Magistrados Brasileiros (AMB). "Aprovado reajuste de magistrados no Acre." *AMB Informa* (Brasilia) 51 (December 25, 2003): 6.

Avritzer, Leonard. "Civil Society, Participatory Institutions and Representation: From Authorization to the Legitimacy of Action." Paper presented at the Rethinking Representation: A North-South Dialogue Conference, Minas Gerais, Brazil, 2008. http://www.democraciaparticipativa.org/bellagio/bellagio.html. Accessed May 20, 2012.

———. *Democracy and the Public Space in Latin America.* Princeton: Princeton University Press, 2002.

———. *Participatory Institutions in Democratic Brazil.* Washington, D.C.: Woodrow Wilson Center/John Hopkins University Press, 2009.

———. "Sociedade Civil, Instituições Participativas e Representação: da autorização à legitimidade da ação." *Dados* 50, no. 3 (2007): 443–64.

Azaola Garrido, Elena, and Miquel Ángel Ruiz Torres. *Investigadores de papel. Poder y derechos humanos entre la Policía Judicial de la Ciudad de México*. Mexico City: Fontamara, 2009.

Baiocchi, Gianpaolo. *Militants and Citizens: The Politics of Participatory Budgeting in Porto Alegre*. Palo Alto: Stanford University Press, 2005.

Baiocchi, Gianpaolo, Patrick Heller, and Marcelo K. Silva. *Bootstrapping Democracy: Transforming Local Governance and Civil Society in Brazil*. Palo Alto: Stanford University Press, 2011.

Banco Central do Brasil. "A Synthesis of Brazilian Monetary Standards." Brasilia: Museum of Money of Banco Central do Brasil. May 2007. http://www.bcb.gov.br/?REFSISMON.

Barros, Robert. *Constitutionalism and Dictatorship: Pinochet, the Junta, and the 1980 Constitution*. Cambridge, UK: Cambridge University Press, 2002.

Batista, Josafá. 2000. "Magistrados se dizem otimistas com acordo feito com o governo." *Página 20* (Rio Branco). December 6, 2000: 1, 6–7.

Beigel, Fernanda. *Misión Santiago. El mundo académico jesutia y los inicios de la cooperación internacional católica*. Santiago: LOM Ediciones, 2011.

Bell, Charles G., and Charles M. Price. *The First Term*. Beverly Hills, CA: Sage, 1975.

Bergman, Marcelo. *Seguridad Pública y Estado en México. Análisis de algunas iniciativas*. Mexico City: Fontamara, 2007.

Bickel, Alexander M. *The Least Dangerous Branch: The Supreme Court at the Bar of Politics*. Indianapolis: Bobbs-Merrill, 1962.

Bickers, Kenneth, and Robert Stein. "The Electoral Dynamics of the Federal Pork Barrel." *American Journal of Political Science* 40, no. 4 (1996): 1300–26.

Black, Henry Campbell. "Political questions. Questions which are of a political nature are not the subject of judicial cognizance; courts will leave the determination of them to the executive and legislative departments of the government." Vol. 1 of *Handbook of American Constitutional Law*. St. Paul, MN: West Publishing, 1927.

Blais, André, and Marc A. Bodet. "Does Proportional Representation Foster Closer Congruence Between Citizens and Policy Makers?" *Comparative Political Studies* 39, no. 10 (2006): 1243–62.

Blanco, Javiera, and Gonzalo Vargas. *Participación en políticas de seguridad ciudadana*. Serie en Foco no. 88. Santiago: Expansiva, 2006. http://www.expansiva.cl/en_foco/documentos/21082006094033.pdf. Accessed May 17, 2007.

Boeninger, Edgardo. *La democracia en Chile. Lecciones de gobernabilidad*. Santiago: Andrés Bello, 1997.

Bonneau, Chris, and Melinda Gann Hall. *In Defense of Judicial Elections*. New York: Routledge, 2009.

Bresser Pereira, L.C. "Da administração pública burocrática à gerencial." *Revista do Serviço Público* 47, no. 1 (1996): 7–40.

Brinks, Daniel M. *The Judicial Response to Police Killings in Latin America: Inequality and the Rule of Law*. Cambridge, UK: Cambridge University Press, 2008.

Brysk, Alison. *The Politics of Human Rights in Argentina: Protest, Change and Democratization*. Palo Alto: Stanford University Press, 1994.

Burbank, Stephen, and Barry Friedman. *Judicial Independence at the Crossroads: An Interdisciplinary Approach*. Beverly Hills: Sage, 2002.

Caballero, José Antonio. "Amparos y abogánsters. La justicia en México entre 1940 y 1968." In *Del Nacionalismo al Neoliberalismo (1940–1994)*. Edited by Elisa Servín. Mexico City: Fondo de Cultura Económica, 2010.

———. "De la marginalidad a los reflectors. El poder judicial." In *Historia Contempóranea de México*. Edited by Ilán Bizberg, Lorenzo Meyer, and Francisco Alba. Mexico City: Era, 2009.

Calvo, Ernesto. "The Responsive Legislature: Public Opinion and Law Making in a Highly Disciplined Legislature." *British Journal of Political Science* 37 (2007): 263–80.

———. *Legislator Success in Fragmented Congresses: Plurality Cartels, Minority Presidents, and Lawmaking in Argentina.* New York: Cambridge University Press, forthcoming 2013.

Calvo, Ernesto, and Juan Manuel Abal Medina, eds. *El Federalismo Electoral Argentino.* Buenos Aires: INAP/Eudeba, 2001.

Calvo, Ernesto, and Juan Pablo Micozzi. "The Governor's Backyard: A Seat-Vote Model of Electoral Reform for Subnational Multiparty Races." *Journal of Politics* 67 (2005): 1050–74.

Campos, José. "El Sistema binominal: duro de matar." In *El genoma electoral chileno. Dibujando el mapa genético de las preferencias políticas en Chile.* Edited by P. Navia et al. Santiago: Ediciones Universidad Diego Portales, 2009.

Cantón, Darío. *El Parlamento Argentino en Épocas de Cambio: 1890, 1916 y 1946.* Buenos Aires: Editorial del Instituto T. di Tella, 1966.

Carey, John M. *Legislative Voting and Accountability.* New York: Cambridge University Press, 2009.

Carpizo, Jorge. "Otra reforma constitucional: la subordinación del Consejo de la Judicatura Federal." *Cuestiones Constitucionales* 2 (January–July 2000): 209–18.

Carson, Jamie. "Strategy, Selection and Candidate Competition in House and Senate Elections." *The Journal of Politics* 67, no. 1 (2005): 1–28.

Carson, Jamie, and Jason Roberts. "Strategic Politicians and U.S. House Elections, 1874–1914." *The Journal of Politics* 67, no. 2 (2005): 474–96.

Casar, Maria Amparo. "Executive-Legislative Relations: Continuity or Change?" In *Mexico's Democratic Challenges.* Edited by Andrew Selee and Jacqueline Peschard. Palo Alto, CA: Stanford University Press, 2010.

———. "Executive-Legislative Relations: The Case of Mexico (1946–1997)." In *Legislative Politics in Latin America.* Edited by Benito Nacif and Scott Morgenstern. New York: Cambridge University Press, 2002.

———. "Los Gobiernos sin Mayoría en México: 1997–2006." In *Política y Gobierno* 15, no. 2, 2° semester: 221–70. Mexico City: CIDE, 2008.

Case, David W. "In Search of an Independent Judiciary: Alternatives to Judicial Elections in Mississippi." In *Mississippi College Law Review* 13 (1992–1993): 1–33.

Cavalcanti, G. C. V. "Uma concessão ao passado: trajetórias da União dos Movimentos de Moradia de São Paulo." MA thesis, FFLCH–Universidade de São Paulo.

Cheibub, Argelina, and Fernando Limongi. "Presidential Power, Legislative Organization and Party Behaviour in Brazil." *Comparative Politics* 32, no. 2 (January 2000): 151–70.

Cheibub, José Antonio, and Adam Przeworski. 1999. "Democracy, Elections and Accountability for Election Outcomes." In *Democracy, Accountability and Representation.* Edited by Adam Przeworski, Susan C. Stokes, and Bernard Manin. Cambridge, UK: Cambridge University Press.

Cohen, Jean L., and Andrew Arato. *Civil Society and Political Theory.* Cambridge, MA: MIT Press, 1992.

Collier, Ruth Berins, and David Collier. *Shaping the Political Arena, Critical Junctures, the Labor Movement and Regime Dynamics in Latin America.* Princeton: Princeton University Press, 1991.

Collier, Ruth Berins, and S. Handlin. *Reorganizing Popular Politics: Participation and the New Interest Regime in Latin America.* University Park: Pennsylvania State University Press, 2009.

Converse, Philip E., and Roy Pierce. "Representative Roles and Legislative Behavior in France." *Legislative Studies Quarterly* 4, no. 4 (1979): 525–62.

Cooper, Christopher A., and Lilliard E. Richardson. "Institutions and Representational Roles in American State Legislatures." *State Politics & Policy Quarterly* 6, no. 2 (2006): 174–94.

Cornwall, Andrea, and Vera Schattan Coelho. *Spaces for Change? The Politics of Citizen Participation in New Democratic Arenas.* London: Zed Books, 2007

Correa, Jorge. "Cenicienta se queda en la fiesta. El poder judicial chileno en la década de los 90." In *El modelo chileno. Democracia y desarrollo en Chile.* Edited by P. Drake and I. Jaksic, I. Santiago: LOM Ediciones, 1999.

Couso, Javier. "The Judicialization of Chilean Politics: The Rights Revolution That Never Was." In *The Judicialization of Politics in Latin America.* Edited by Alan Angell, Rachel Sieder, and Line Schjolden. New York: Palgrave-Macmillan, 2005.

———. "The Politics of Judicial Review in Chile in the Era of Democratic Transition, 1990–2002." *Democratization* 10, no. 4 (2003): 70–91.

Couso, Javier, and Alberto Coddou. "Las asignaturas pendientes de la reforma constitucional chilena." In *En nombre del Pueblo. Debate sobre el cambio constitucional en Chile.* Edited by Claudio Fuentes. Santiago: ICSO (Instituto de Investigación en Ciencias Sociales) –UDP (Universidad Diego Portales), 2010.

Couso, Javier, and Lisa Hilbink. "From Quietism to Incipient Activism: The Institutional and Ideological Roots of Rights Adjudication in Chile." In *Courts in Latin America.* Edited by Gretchen Helmke and Julio Rios-Figueroa. New York: Cambridge University Press, 2011.

Couso, Javier, Domingo Lovera, Matías Guiloff, and Alberto Coddou. *The Constitutional Law in Chile.* Alphen aan de Rijn, The Netherlands: Kluwer Law International, 2011.

Cox, Gary. "Centripetal and Centrifugal Incentives in Electoral Systems." *American Journal of Political Science* 34, no. 4 (November 1990): 903–35.

———. "The Organization of Democratic Legislatures." In *The Oxford Handbook of Political Economy.* Edited by B. Weingast and D. Wittman. Oxford: Oxford University Press, 2008.

Cox, Gary W., and Scott Morgenstern. "Epilogue: Latin America's Reactive Assemblies and Proactive Presidents." In *Legislative Politics in Latin America.* Edited by Scott Morgenstern and Benito Nacif. Cambridge, UK: Cambridge University Press, 2001.

Crisp, Brian F., and Rachel E. Ingall. "Institutional Engineering and the Nature of Representation: Mapping the Effects of Electoral Reform in Colombia." *American Journal of Political Science* 46, no. 4 (2002): 733–48.

Dagnino, Evelina. "Civic Driven Change and Political Projects." In *Civic Driven Change: Citizen's Imagination in Action.* Edited by Alan Fowler and Kiees Bierkhart. The Hague: Institute of Social Studies, 2008.

———. "Culture, Citizenship and Democracy: Changing Discourses and Practices of the Latin American Left." In *Cultures of Politics/Politics of Cultures: Revisioning Latin American Social Movements.* Edited by S. Alvarez, E. Dagnino, and A. Escobar. Boulder, CO: Westview Press, 1998.

———. "Meanings of Citizenship in Latin America." IDS Working Paper 258. Brighton, UK: University of Sussex, 2005.

———. "Os Movimentos sociais e a emergência de uma nova noção de cidadania." In *Anos 90: Política e Sociedade no Brasil.* Edited by Evelina Dagnino. São Paulo: Brasiliense, 1994.

———, ed. *Sociedade civil e espaços públicos no Brasil.* São Paulo: Paz e Terra, 2002.

———. "Sociedade civil, participação e cidadania: de que estamos falando?" In *Políticas de Ciudadanía y Sociedad Civil en tiempos de globalización.* Edited by Daniel Mato. Caracas, Venezuela: FaCES, Universidad Central de Venezuela, 2004.

Dagnino, Evelina, Alberto Olvera, and Aldo Panfichi. "Introducción: Para otra lectura de la disputa por la construcción democrática en América Latina." In *La Disputa por la Construcción Democrática en América Latina*. Edited by E. Dagnino, A. Olvera, and A. Panfichi. Mexico City: Fondo de Cultura Económica, 2006.

———. "Para uma outra leitura da disputa pela construcão democrática na América Latina." In *A disputa pela construção democrática na América Latina*. Edited by E. Dagnino, A. Olvera, and A. Panfichi. São Paulo: Paz e Terra, 2006.

Dahl, R. A. *On Democracy*. New Haven: Yale University Press, 1998.

Dahl, Robert. *How Democratic Is the American Constitution?* New Haven: Yale University Press, 2003.

Damaska, Mirjan R. *The Faces of Justice and State Authority: A Comparative Approach to the Legal Process*. New Haven: Yale University Press, 1986.

Danesi, Silvina. "The Institutional Choices of Politicians. How and Why Legislators Shape Lower Chambers: Argentina-Chile (1945–2001)." PhD diss., Université de Montreál, 2010.

De la Cuadra, Fernando. "Reestructuración capitalista, equidad y consolidación democrática en Chile." *Polis* 4 (2006). http://www.revistapolis.cl/polis%20final/4/dela.htm. Accessed September 2009.

De Luca, Miguel, Mark P. Jones, and María Inés Tula. "Back Rooms or Ballot Boxes?: Candidate Nomination in Argentina." *Comparative Political Studies* 35 (2002): 413–36.

De Shazo, Peter. *Urban Workers and Labor Unions in Chile, 1902–1927*. Madison: University of Wisconsin Press, 1983.

De Sousa, Mariana M. "How Courts Engage in the Policymaking Process in Latin America: The Different Functions of the Judiciary." In *How Democracy Works: Political Institutions, Actors, and Arenas in Latin American Policymaking*. Edited by C. G. Scartascini, E. Stein, and M. Tommasi. Washington, D.C.: Inter-American Development Bank and DRCLAS-Harvard University, 2010.

Delamaza, G., and Carlos Ochsenius. "Innovaciones en los Vínculos Locales entre Sociedad Civil y Estado en Chile: Su Incidencia en la construcción de Gobernabilidad Democrática." *Revista Política y Gestión* 12 (2010): 11–35.

———. "Trayectorias, redes y poder: sociedade civil y politica en la transición democrática chilena." In *La Disputa por la Construcción Democrática en América Latina*. Edited by E. Dagnino, A. Olvera, and A. Panfichi. Mexico City: Fondo de Cultura Económica, 2006.

Denissen, Marieke. *Winning Small Battles, Losing the War, Police Violence, the Movimiento del Dolor, and Democracy in Post-Authoritarian Argentina*. Amsterdam: Rozenberg, 2008.

Desposato, Scott. "Parties for Rent? Careerism, Ideology, and Party Switching in Brazil's Chamber of Deputies." *American Journal of Political Science* 50 (2006): 62–80.

Diamond, Larry, and Leonardo Morlino, eds. *Assessing the Quality of Democracy*. Baltimore: The John Hopkins University Press, 2005.

Disch, Lisa. "Democratic Representation and the Constituency Paradox." *Perspectives on Politics* 10, no. 3 (2012): 599–615.

Domínguez, Jorge. "Construcción de gobernabilidad democrática en América Latina. Una evaluación de la década del 90." In *Construcción de gobernabilidad democrática en América Latina*. Edited by J. Domínguez and M. Schifter. Mexico City: Fondo de Cultura Económica, 2005.

Drake, Paul. "Chile, 1930–1958." In *Latin America since 1930: Spanish South America*. Vol. VIII, *The Cambridge History of Latin America*. Cambridge History of Latin America, Edited by Leslie Bethell. Cambridge: Cambridge University Press, 1991.

————. "El Movimiento Obrero en Chile: de la Unidad Popular a la Concertación." *Revista de Ciencia Política* 23, no 2 (2003): 148–58.

Dryzek, John. *Deliberative Democracy and Beyond*. Oxford: Oxford University Press, 2000.

Duch, Raymond D., and Randolph T. Stevenson. *The Economic Vote: How Political and Economic Institutions Condition Election Results*. New York: Cambridge University Press, 2008.

Edwards, Michael. *The Oxford Handbook on Civil Society*. Oxford: Oxford University Press, 2011.

Ely, J. H. *Democracy and Distrust: A Theory of Judicial Review*. Cambridge, MA: Harvard University Press, 1980.

Engelmann, Fabiano. "Diversificação do espaço jurídico e lutas pela definição do direito no Rio Grande do Sul." PhD diss., Institute of Human Sciences, Graduate Program in Political Science, Federal University of Rio Grande do Sul (UFRGS), Porto Alegre, Brazil, 2004.

————. "Tradition and Diversification in the Uses and Definitions of the Law: A Proposed Analysis." *Brazilian Political Science Review* 1, no. 1 (2007): 53–70.

Epp, Charles R. *The Rights Revolution: Lawyers, Activists and Supreme Courts in Comparative Perspective*. Chicago: University of Chicago Press, 1998.

Eulau, Heinz, and Paul D. Karps. "The Puzzle of Representation: Specifying Components of Responsiveness." *Legislative Studies Quarterly* 2, no. 3 (1977): 233–54.

Eulau, Heinz, John C. Wahlke, William Buchanan, and LeRoy C. Ferguson. "The Role of the Representative: Some Empirical Observations on the Theory of Edmund Burke." *American Political Science Review* 53 (1959): 742–56.

Feltran, Gabriel, "Dislocaciones. Trayectorias individuales, relaciones entre sociedade civil y estado en Brasil." In *La Disputa por la Construcción Democrática en América Latina*. Edited by E. Dagnino, A. Olvera, and A. Panfichi. Mexico City: Fondo de Cultura Económica, 2006.

Fennell, Lee C. "Congress in the Argentine Political System: An Appraisal." In *Latin American Legislatures: Their Role and Influence. Analysis of Nine Countries*. Edited by W. H. Agor. New York: Praeger, 1971.

Fenno, Richard. *Home Style: House Members in Their Districts*. Boston: Little, Brown, 1978.

Fernández, Matías, and Martín Ordóñez. Participación ciudadana en la agenda gubernamental de 2007. Caracterización de los compromisos. Programa Ciudadanía y Gestión Pública, 2007. http://www.innovacionciudadana.cl/portal/imagen/File/barometro/Informe%20final%20S.E.pdf. Accessed September 10, 2008.

Ferreira Rubio, Delia, and Matteo Goretti. *Government by Decree in Argentina* (1983/1993). *El Derecho* 32, no. 8525 (June 27, 1994): 848.

Figueiredo, Argelina, and Fernando Limongi. *Executivo e Legislativo na Nova Ordem Constitucional*. São Paulo: FGV Press, 1999.

Figueiredo, Argelina Cheibub, and Fernando Limongi. "The Budget Process and Legislative Behavior Individual Amendments, Support for the Executive and Government Programs." *World Political Science Review* 3, no. 3 (2007): article 3. Berkeley Electronic Press.

Finkel, Jodi. *Judicial Reform as Political Insurance*. Notre Dame, IN: University of Notre Dame Press, 2008.

Fix-Fierro, Héctor. "La reforma judicial en México, ¿de dónde viene? ¿a dónde va?" *Reforma Judicial. Revista Mexicana de Justicia* 2 (July–December 2003): 251–324.

Flah, L., and M. Smayevsky. "The Regulation of American Environmental Law." *La Ley* (1993).

Folha de São Paulo. "Judiciário pede a Lula explicação de declarações." *Folha de São Paulo* (May 15, 2003).

———. "Thomaz Bastos é confirmado para a Justiça." December 18, 2002.

Fox, Jonathan. *Accountability Politics. Power and Voice in Rural Mexico*. Oxford: Oxford University Press, 2008.

Friesema, H. Paul, and Ronald D. Hedlund. 1974. "The Reality of Representational Roles." In *Public Opinion and Public Policy*, 2nd ed. Edited by Norman R. Luttbeg. Homewood, IL: Dorsey.

Frymer, Paul. "Acting When Elected Officials Won't: Federal Courts and Civil Rights Enforcement in U.S. Labor Unions, 1935–85." *American Political Science Review* 97, no. 3 (August 2003): 483–99.

Fuentes, Claudio. 1999. "A Matter of the Few: Dynamics of Constitutional Change in Chile, 1990–2010." *Texas Law Review* 89, no. 7 (June 2011): 1741–75.

———. "Partidos y coaliciones en el Chile de los 90. Entre pactos y proyectos." In *El Modelo Chileno. Democracia y Desarrollo en los Noventa*. Edited by P. Drake and I. Jacksic. Santiago: LOM Ediciones, 1999.

Fuentes, Claudio, and Claudia Heiss. "¿Qué podemos aprender de las experiencias de incidencia ciudadana?" In *La propuesta ciudadana. Una nueva relación sociedad civil—Estado*. Edited by A. Varas. Santiago: Catalonia, 2006.

Fung, Archon. "Reinventing Democracy in Latin America." *Perspectives in Politics* 9, no. 4 (December 2011): 857–71.

Garcés, Mario. *Crisis social y motines populares*. Santiago: ECO, Educación y Comunicaciones, 1992.

García Ramírez, Sergio. "Consideraciones sobre la reforma procesal penal en los últimos años." In *Las reformas penales de los últimos años en México (1995–2000)*. Edited by Sergio García Ramírez and Leticia Vargas Casillas. Mexico City: IIJ-UNAM, 2001.

Gargarella, Roberto. *La Justicia Frente al Gobierno*. Barcelona: Ariel, 1996.

Garretón, Manuel. "Redefinición de gobernabilidad y cambio político." In *¿Qué espera la sociedad del gobierno?* Edited by L. Tomassini. Santiago: Universidad de Chile, 1994.

———. "Sociedad civil y ciudadanía en la problemática latinoamericana actual." In *Ciudadanía, sociedad civil y participación política*. Edited by I. Cheresky. Buenos Aires: Miño y Dávila Editores, 2006.

———. *La sociedad en que vivi(re)mos. Introducción sociológica al cambio de siglo*. Santiago: LOM Ediciones, 2000.

Gellner, Ernst. *Conditions of Liberty*. London: Hamish Hamilton, 1994.

George, Alexander L., and Andrew Bennett. *Case Studies and Theory Development in the Social Sciences*. Cambridge, MA: MIT Press, 2005.

Gerring, John, Strom Thacker, and Carola Moreno. "Centripetal Democratic Governance: A Theory and Global Inquiry." *American Political Science Review* 99, no. 4 (2005): 567–81.

Gibson, Edward, and Julieta Suarez-Cao. "Federalized Party Systems and Sub-national Party Competition: Theory and an Empirical Application to Latin America." *Comparative Politics* 43 (2010): 21–39.

Ginsburg, Tom. *Judicial Review in New Democracies*. Cambridge, UK: Cambridge University Press, 2003.

Ginsburg, Tom, and Nuno Garoupa. "The Comparative Law and Economics of Judicial Councils." *Berkeley Journal of International Law* 27, no. 1 (2009): 52–82.

González, Raúl. *Agentes y dinámicas territoriales: ¿Quién produce lo local? Estudio de tres ciudades chilenas (Valdivia, Temuco, Arica)*. PhD dissertation, Faculté de Sciences Economiques, Sociales et Politiques. Université Catolique de Louvain, Louvain-la-Neuve, 2006.

González Compeán, Miguel, and Peter Bauer. *Jurisdicción y democracia. Los nuevos rumbos del Poder Judicial en México.* Mexico City: Cal y Arena, 2002.

Greenwood, Daniel J. H. "Beyond the Counter-Majoritarian Difficulty: Judicial Decision-Making in a Polynomic World." *Rutgers Law Review* 53, no. 4 (2001): 781–864.

Grez Toso, Sergio. 2002. "¿Autonomía o escudo protector? El movimiento obrero y popular y los mecanismos de conciliación y arbitraje (Chile, 1900–1924)." *Historia* 35 (2002): 91–150.

Gross, Donald A. "Representative Styles and Legislative Behavior." *Western Political Quarterly* 31 (1978): 359–71.

Guarnieri, Carlo, and Patrizia Pederzoli. *Los jueces y la política. Poder judicial y democracia.* España: Taurus, 1999.

Habermas, Jürgen. *Between Facts and Norms: Contributions to a Discourse Theory of Law and Democracy.* Translated by William Rehg. Cambridge, MA: MIT Press, 1994.

Haggard, Stephan, and Robert R. Kaufman. "The Political Economy of Democratic Transitions." *Comparative Politics* 29, no. 3 (April 1997): 263–83.

Haggard, Stephan, and Mathew D. McCubbins. *Presidents, Parliaments, and Policy: Political Economy of Institutions and Decisions.* Cambridge, UK: Cambridge University Press, 2001.

Hagopian, Frances. "Chile and Brazil." In *Assessing the Quality of Democracy.* Edited by Larry Diamond and Leonardo Morlino. Baltimore: The Johns Hopkins University Press, 2005. 123–62

——. "The Rising Quality of Democracy in Brazil and Chile." Paper presented at the "Quality of Democracy: Improvement or Subversion?" conference, Palo Alto, CA, Stanford University, October 10–11, 2003.

Hall, Daniel J., Jan M. Stromsen, and Richard B. Hoffman. "Professional Court Administration: The Key to Judicial Independence." *Sistemas Judiciales* 4 (2003): 5–15.

Hall, Peter A. "Aligning Ontology and Methodology in Comparative Research." In *Comparative Historical Analysis in the Social Sciences.* Edited by James Mahoney and Dietrich Rueschemeyer. Cambridge, UK: Cambridge University Press, 2003.

Hall, Richard. *Participation in Congress.* New Haven: Yale University Press, 1996.

Hall, Richard, and Robert Van Houweling. "Avarice and Ambition: Representatives' Decisions to Run for or Retire from the U.S. House." *American Political Science Review* 89, no. 1 (1994): 121–36.

Hamilton, Alexander, James Madison, and John Jay. *The Federalist. A Commentary on the Constitution of the United States.* New York: The Modern Library, [1787] 2001.

Helmke, Gretchen, and Julio Rios-Figueroa. *Congressional Careers.* Chapel Hill: University of North Carolina Press, 1991.

——. "Introduction: Courts in Latin America." In *Courts in Latin America.* Edited by Gretchen Helmke and Julio Rios-Figueroa. New York: Cambridge University Press, 2011.

Hibbing, John R. "Legislative Careers: Why and How We Should Study Them." *Legislative Studies Quarterly* 24, no. 2 (1999): 149–71.

Hilbink, Lisa. "Assessing the New Constitutionalism." *Comparative Politics* 40, no. 2 (2008): 227–45.

——. "The Constituted Nature of Constituents' Interests: Historical and Ideational Factors in Judicial Empowerment." *Political Research Quarterly* 62, no. 4 (December 2008): 781–97.

——. *Judges Beyond Politics in Democracy and Dictatorship.* Cambridge, UK: Cambridge University Press, 2007a.

——. "Politicising Law to Liberalise Politics: Anti-Francoist Judges and Prosecutors in Spain's Democratic Transition." In *Fighting for Political Freedom: Comparative Studies of the Legal Complex and Political Liberalism*. Edited by Terence C. Halliday, Lucien Karpik, and Malcolm M. Feeley. Portland, OR: Hart Publishing, 2007b.

Hirschl, Ran. *Towards Juristocracy*. Cambridge, MA: Harvard University Press, 2004.

Hochstleter, Kathryn, and Margaret Keck. *Greening Brazil: Environmental Activism in State and Society*. Durham: Duke University Press, 2007.

Houtzager, Peter, and Lavalle, Adrian Gurza. "Civil Society's Claims to Political Representation in Brazil." *Studies in Comparative International Development* 45 (2010): 1–29.

Huber, Gregory, and Sanford Gordon. 2004. "Accountability and Coercion: Is Justice Blind When It Runs for Office?" *American Journal of Political Science* 48, no. 2 (2004): 247–63.

Huneeus, Carlos. *The Pinochet Regime*. Boulder, CO: Lynne Rienner, 2006.

Ibáñez, Adolfo. *Herido en el ala. Estado oligarquías y subdesarrollo. Chile 1924–1960*. Santiago: Universidad Andrés Bello, 2003.

Inter-American Commission on Human Rights. Velázquez Rodríguez, Judgment of July 29, 1988, para. 166. Inter-Am Ct.H.R., Ser. C, no. 4 (1988).

Inter-American Development Bank. *The Politics of Policies: Economic and Social Progress in Latin America, 2006 Report*. Washington, D.C.: IADB, 2006.

Jacobsen, Gary C. *The Politics of Congressional Election*. Boston: Little, Brown, 1983.

James, T.M. "Law and Revolution in Mexico: A Constitutional History of the Amparo Suit and Social Reform in the Mexican Revolution." PhD diss., University of Chicago, 2006.

Jewell, Malcolm E. *Representation in State Legislatures*. Lexington, KY: University Press of Kentucky, 1982.

Johnson, Joel W., and Jessica S. Wallack. "Electoral Systems and the Personal Vote." 2007. http://polisci2.ucsd.edu/jwjohnson/espv.htm. Accessed October 27, 2012.

Jones, Mark P. "Beyond the Electoral Connection: The Effect of Political Parties on the Policymaking Process." In *How Democracy Works: Political Institutions, Actors and Arenas in Latin American Policymaking*. Edited by Carlos Scartascini, Ernesto Stein, and Mariano Tommasi. Washington, D.C.: Inter-American Dialogue Bank and the David Rockefeller Center for Latin American Studies, Harvard University, 2010.

Jones, Mark P., and Wonjae Hwang. "Party Government in Presidential Democracies: Extending Cartel Theory Beyond the U.S. Congress." *American Journal of Political Science* 49 (2005): 267–82.

Jones, Mark P., Wonjae Hwang, and Juan Pablo Micozzi. "Government and Opposition in the Argentine Congress: Understanding Inter-Party Dynamics through Roll Call Vote Analysis." *Journal of Politics in Latin America* 1 (2009): 67–96.

Jones, Mark P., Sebastian Saiegh, Pablo T. Spiller, and Mariano Tommasi. "Amateur-Legislators-Professional Politicians: The Consequences of Party-Centered Electoral Rules in a Federal System." *American Journal of Political Science* 46 (2002): 656–69.

Kapizsewski, Diana, and Matthew M. Taylor. "Compliance: Conceptualizing, Measuring, and Explaining Adherence to Judicial Rulings." *Law & Social Inquiry* (forthcoming).

——. "Doing Courts Justice: Studying Judicial Politics in Latin America." *Perspectives on Politics* 6, no. 4 (2008): 741–67.

Kapur, Devesh, and Mehta Pratap. "The Indian Parliament as an Institution of Accountability." United Nations Research Institute for Social Development, Programme Paper 23, 2006.

Kaufman, Daniel, Aart Kraay, and Pablo Zoido-Lobatón. "Governance Matters." Policy Research Working Paper 2196. Washington, D.C.: World Bank Development Research Group, 1999.

Keck, Margaret E. "Social Equity and Environmental Politics in Brazil: Lessons from the Rubber Tappers of Acre." *Comparative Politics* 27, no. 4 (1995): 409–24.

Kernell, Samuel. "To Stay, To Quit, or to Move Up: Explaining the Growth of Careerism in the House of Representatives, 1878–1940." Paper presented at the American Political Science Association Meeting, Philadelphia, PA, 2003.

Kiewiet, D. Roderick, and Langche Zeng. "An Analysis of Congressional Career Decision, 1947–1986." *The American Political Science Review* 87, no. 4 (1993): 928–41.

King, Gary, Michael Tomz, and Jason Wittenberg. "Making the Most of Statistical Analyses: Improving Interpretation and Presentation." *American Journal of Political Science* 44, no. 2 (April 2000): 347–61.

Kinzo, Maria D'Alva. "Partidos, Eleições e Democracia no Brasil pós-1985." *Revista Brasileira de Ciências Sociais* 19, no. 54 (2004): 23–40.

Knights, Mark. "Participation and Representation before Democracy: Petitions and Addresses in Premodern Britain." In *Political Representation*. Edited by Ian Shapiro and Susan Stokes. Cambridge: Cambridge University Press, 2009.

Kuklinski, James H., with Richard C. Elling. "Representational Role, Constituency Opinion, and Legislative Roll-Call Behavior." *American Journal of Political Science* 21 (1977): 135–47.

Kuklinski, James H., and J. E. Stanga. "Political Participation and Government Responsiveness: The Behavior of California Superior Courts." *American Political Science Review* 73, no. 4 (1979): 1090–99.

Kurtz, Karl, Bruce Cain, and Richard G. Niemi, eds. *Institutional Change in American Politics: The Case of Term Limits*. Ann Arbor: University of Michigan Press, 2007.

Langston, Joy. "Strong Parties in a Struggling Party System. Mexico in the Democratic Era." In *Party Politics in New Democracies*. Edited by Paul Webb and Stephen White. Oxford: Oxford University Press, 2009.

Laría, A. F. *Presidentialism and Institutional Quality*. Buenos Aires: Nuevo Hacer/Grupo Editor Latinoamericano, 2008.

Laserna, Roberto. "Mire, la democracia boliviana, en los hechos… " *Latin American Research Review* 45 (2010): 27–58.

Lavalle, Adrián Gurza, Peter P. Houtzager, and Graziela Castello. "Democracia, pluralização da representação e sociedade civil." *Lua Nova* 67 (2006a): 49–103.

———. "Representação Política e Organizações Civis: novas instâncias de mediação e os desafios da legitimidade." *Revista Brasileira de Ciências Sociais* 21, no. 60 (2006b): 42–66.

Leiras, Marcelo. "Los Procesos de Decentralización y la Nacionalización de los Sistemas de Partidos en América Latina." *Política y Gobierno* 17 (2010): 502–41.

Leoni, Eduardo, Carlos Pereira, and Lucio Renno. "Political Survival Strategies: Political Career Decisions in the Brazilian Chamber of Deputies." *Journal of Latin American Studies* 36, no. 1 (2004): 109–30.

Levine, Daniel, ed. *The Quality of Democracy in Latin America*. Boulder, CO: Lynne Rienner, 2011.

Lijphart, Arend. "Comparative Politics and the Comparative Method." *American Political Science Review* 65 (1971): 682–93.

———. *Patterns of Democracy, Government Forms and Performance in Thirty-Six Countries*. New Haven: Yale University Press, 1999.

Lima, Miguel Alves. "O Direito Alternativo e a Dogmática Jurídica." In *Lições de Direito Alternativo II*. Edited by Edmundo Lima Arruda Jr. São Paulo: Acadêmica, 1992.

Linz, Juan, and Alfred Stepan. "Toward Consolidated Democracies." *Journal of Democracy* 7, no. 2 (1996): 14–33.

Linz, Juan, and Arturo Valenzuela. *The Failure of Presidential Democracy*. 2 vols. Baltimore: The John Hopkins University Press, 1994.

Lodge, Milton, Kathleen McGraw, and Patrick Stroh. "An Impression-Driven Model of Candidate Evaluation." *American Political Science Review* 83 (1989): 399–419.

Lodge, Milton, Marco Steenbergen, and Shawn Brau. "The Responsive Voter: Campaign Information and the Dynamics of Candidate Evaluation." *American Political Science Review* 89 (1995): 309–26.

Longuini, Adair. "Dois pesos e duas medidas." *Página 20* (Rio Branco, Brazil), May 7, 2003.

López Ayllón, Sergio, and Héctor Fix-Fierro. "La modernización del sistema jurídico (1970–2000). In *Del Nacionalismo al Neoliberalismo (1940–1994)*. Edited by Elisa Servín. Mexico City: Fondo de Cultura Económica, 2010.

Loveman, Brian. *The Constitution of Tyranny: Regimes of Exception in Spanish America*. Pittsburgh: University of Pittsburgh Press, 1993.

Lowi, Theodore. "American Business and Public Policy, Case Studies and Political Theory." *World Politics* 16 (1964): 677–715.

Lüchmann, Ligia Helena. "A representação no interior das experiências de participação." *Lua Nova* 70 (2007): 139–70.

Luna, Juan, and Michael Seligson. *Cultura política de la democracia en Chile: 2006*. Santiago: Instituto de Ciencia Política Universidad Católica de Chile, 2007.

Lupia, Arthur. "Shortcuts versus Encyclopedias: Information and Voting Behavior in California Insurance Reform Elections." *American Political Science Review* 88, no. 1 (1994): 63–76.

Lupia, Arthur, and Matthew McCubbins. *The Democratic Dilemma: Can Citizens Learn What They Need to Know?* Cambridge, UK: Cambridge University Press, 1998.

MacKinnon, Moira B. *Los Años Formativos del Partido Peronista (1946-1950)*. Buenos Aires: Instituto Di Tella- Siglo Veintiuno de Argentina Editores, 2002.

MacIntyre, Andrew J. *The Power of Institutions: Political Architecture and Governance*. Ithaca: Cornell University Press, 2003.

Madrazo, Alejandro, and Estefanía Vela. "The Mexican Supreme Court (Sexual) Revolution." *Texas Law Review* 89, no. 7 (2011): 1863–93.

Magaloni Kerpel, Ana Laura. "El Ministerio Público desde adentro. Rutinas y métodos de trabajo en las agencias del MP." Documento de Trabajo 42, División de Estudios Jurídicos, CIDE, 2010.

———. "¿Por qué la Suprema Corte no ha sido un instrumento para la defensa de derechos fundamentales?" Documento de Trabajo 25, División de Estudios Jurídicos, CIDE, 2007.

Magaloni, Ana Laura, and Ana María Ibarra Olguín. "La configuración jurisprudencial de los derechos fundamentales. El caso del derecho constitutional a una defensa adecuada." *Cuestiones Constitucionales* 19 (July–December 2008): 107–47.

Magaloni, Beatriz. "Authoritarianism, Democracy and the Supreme Court: Horizontal Exchange and the Rule of Law in Mexico." In *Democratic Accountability in Latin America*. Edited by Scott Mainwaring and Christopher Welna. New York: Oxford University Press, 2003.

Maier, Elizabeth, and Natalie Lebon, eds. *Women's Activism in Latin America and the Caribbean: Engendering Social Justice, Democratizing Citizenship*. New Brunswick, NJ: Rutgers University Press, 2010.

Mainwaring, Scott P. *Rethinking Party Systems in the Third Wave of Democratization*. Palo Alto: Stanford University Press, 1999.

Mainwaring, Scott P., Rachel Meneguello, and Timothy Power. "Conservative Parties, Democracy, and Economic Reform in Contemporary Brazil." In *Conservative*

Parties, the Right, and Democracy in Latin America. Edited by Kevin J. Middlebrook. Baltimore: The Johns Hopkins University Press, 2000.

Mainwaring, Scott P., Guillermo O'Donnell, and Samuel J. Valenzuela, eds. *Issues in Democratic Consolidation: The New South American Democracies in Comparative Perspective*. Notre Dame, IN: University of Notre Dame Press, 1992.

Mainwaring, Scott P., and Timothy Scully, eds. *Building Democratic Institutions: Party Systems in Latin America*. Palo Alto: Stanford University Press, 1995.

———. "Latin America: Eight Lessons for Governance." *Journal of Democracy* 19, no. 3 (2008): 113–27.

Mainwaring, Scott, and Mathew Shugart, eds. *Presidentialism and Democracy in Latin America*. Cambridge, UK: Cambridge University Press, 1997.

Malleson, Kate, and Peter H. Russell, eds. *Appointing Judges in an Age of Judicial Power: Critical Perspectives from Around the World*. Toronto: University of Toronto Press, 2006.

Manin, Bernard. *The Principles of Representative Government*. Cambridge, UK: Cambridge University Press, 1997.

Manin, Bernard, Adam Przeworksi, and Susan Stokes, eds. *Democracy, Accountability, and Representation*. Cambridge, UK: Cambridge University Press, 1999.

Mansbridge, Jane. "Rethinking Representation." *American Political Science Review* 97, no. 4 (November 2003): 515–28.

———. "Clarifying the Concept of Representation." *American Political Science Review* 105, no. 3 (2011): 621–30.

———. "A Selection Model of Political Representation." *The Journal of Political Philosophy* 17, no. 4 (2009): 369–98.

———. "Should Blacks Represent Blacks and Women Represent Women? A Contingent 'Yes.'" *Journal of Politics* 61 (August 1999): 628–57.

Marbury vs. Madison. 5 U.S. 137 (1803).

Marenghi, Patricia R. "La representación territorial en los legisladores iberoamericanos: qué intereses defienden y qué políticas impulsan." PhD diss., Universidad de Salamanca, 2009.

Marenghi, Patricia R., and Mercedes García Montero. "El rompecabezas de la representación: qué intereses defienden y cómo se comportan los legisladores latinoamericanos." In *Políticos y política en América Latina*. Edited by M. Alcántara. Madrid: Siglo XXI, 2006.

Marshall, Pablo, ed. *Jurisprudencia Constitucional Destacada. Análisis Crítico*. Santiago: Legal Publishing, 2011.

Marshall, Thomas H. *Class, Citizenship, and Social Development: Essays*. Garden City, NY: Doubleday, 1965.

Martinez-Gallardo, Cecilia. "Out of the Cabinet: What Drives Defections from the Government in Presidential Systems?" *Comparative Political Studies* 45, no. 1 (2011): 62–90.

Marván Laborde, Ignacio. "La Revolución Mexicana y la organización política de México: la cuestión de la separación de poderes (1908–1932)." In *La Revolución Mexicana, 1908–1932*. Edited by Ignacio Marván Laborde. Mexico City: Fondo de Cultura Económica, 2010.

Más Voces. *Más voces para la democracia. Los desafíos de la sociedad civil*. Santiago: Más Voces, 2004.

Mayhew, David. *Congress: The Electoral Connection*. New Haven: Yale University Press, 1974.

Meckstroth, Theodore W. " 'Most Different Systems' and 'Most Similar Systems': A Study in the Logic of Comparative Inquiry." *Comparative Political Studies* 8, no. 2 (1975): 132–57.

Mendez, Juan E., Guillermo O'Donnell, and Paulo Sergio de Pinheiro, eds. *The (Un) rule of Law and the Underprivileged in Latin America*. Notre Dame, IN: University of Notre Dame Press, 1999.

Meneguello, Rachel. "Partidos e Tendências de Compartamento: O Cenário Político em 1994." In *Anos 90: Política e Sociedade no Brasil*. Edited by Evelina Dagnino. São Paulo: Brasiliense Press, 1994.

Mesquita, Lara. "Emendas ao Orçamento e Conexão Eleitoral na Câmara dos Deputados." Dissertação de Mestrado, Universidade de São Paulo, 2009.

Micozzi, Juan Pablo. "The Electoral Connection in Multilevel Systems with Non-Static Ambition: Linking Political Careers and Legislative Performance in Argentina." Ph.D. diss., Rice University, 2009.

Midón, Mario A. "Proyecto desequilibrado." *La Ley* (Buenos Aires), December 19, 2005.

Miguel, Luís Felipe. "Representação democrática: autonomia e interesse ou identidade e advocacy." *Lua Nova* 84 (2011): 353–64.

Miller, Warren E., and Donald E. Stokes. "Constituency Influence in Congress." *American Political Science Review* 57, no. 1 (1963): 45–56.

Ministério da Justiça. *Diagnóstico do Poder Judiciário*. Brasilia: Secretaria da Reforma do Judiciário, 2004.

Molinelli, Guillermo N. *Presidentes y Congresos en Argentina: Mitos y Realidades*. Buenos Aires: Grupo Editor Latinoamericano, 1991.

Molinelli, Guillermo, M. Palanzza, M. Valeria, and G. Sin. *Congreso, Presidencia y Justicia en Argentina, Materiales para su Estudio, CEDI—Fundación Gobierno y Sociedad*. Buenos Aires: Temas Grupo Editorial, 1999.

Moncrief, Gary F., Richard G. Niemi, and Lynda W. Powell. "Time, Term Limits, and Turnover: Membership Stability in U.S. State Legislatures." *Legislative Studies Quarterly* 29 (2004): 357–81.

Montanaro, Laura, 2008. "The Democratic Legitimacy of 'Self-Authorized' Representatives." Paper presented at the Rethinking Representation: A North-South Dialogue Conference, Minas Gerais, Brazil, 2008.

Monteón, Michael. *Chile in the Nitrate Era. The Evolution of Economic Dependence, 1880–1930*. Madison: University of Wisconsin Press, 1982.

Montesquieu, Charles de Secondat. *The Spirit of the Laws*. New York: Cambridge University Press, [1748](1989).

Morello, Augusto "The defense of diffuse interests and procedural law." *Jurisprudencia Argentina* 3 (1978): 321.

Moreno, Erika, Brian F. Crisp, and Mathew S. Shugart. "The Accountability Deficit in Latin America." In *Democratic Accountability in Latin America*. Edited by Scott Mainwaring and Christopher Welna. Oxford: Oxford University Press, 2003.

Morris, James. *Las elites, los intelectuales y el consenso*. Santiago: INSORA, 1967.

Morris, James O. *Elites, Intellectuals and Consensus: A Study of the Social Question and the Industrial Relations System in Chile*. Ithaca: Cornell University Press, 1966.

Moulian, Tomás. *Chile actual. Anatomía de un mito*. Santiago: LOM Ediciones, 1997.

———. *Fracturas. De Pedro Aguirre Cerda a Salvador Allende (1938–1973)*. Santiago: LOM Ediciones, 2006.

Moura, Joana Vaz de. "As relações entre arranjo institucional e representação política nos conselhos." *Ciências Sociais Unisinos* 47, no. 2 (2011): 101–7.

Munck, G. L. "Formação de atores, coordenação social e estratégia política: problemas conceituais do estudo dos movimentos sociais." *Dados* 40, no. 1 (1997).

Navia, Patricio et al., eds. *El genoma electoral chileno. Dibujando el mapa genético de las preferencias políticas en Chile*. Santiago: Ediciones Universidad Diego Portales, 2009.

Negretto, Gabriel, ed. *Debatiendo la Reforma Política. Claves del Cambio Institucional en México.* Mexico City: CIDE, 2010.

———. "Paradojas de la Reforma Constitucional de América Latina." *Journal of Democracy en español* 1 (July 2009): 38–54.

———. "Political Parties and Institutional Design: Explaining Constitutional Choice in Latin America." *British Journal of Political Science* 39 (2008): 117–39.

Nohlen, D., and M. Fernandez. *The Presidentialism Renewed—Institutions and Political Change in Latin America.* Caracas: Nueva Sociedad, 1998.

Nokken, Timothy P., and Keith T. Poole. "Congressional Party Defection in American History." *Legislative Studies Quarterly* 29 (2004): 545–68.

Nolte, Detlef. "Radiografía del Senado de Chile: informe de la encuesta 2002." Working Paper 8, Institute for Ibero-American Studies, Hamburg, Germany, 2002.

Nun, José. *La democracia. ¿Gobierno del pueblo o gobierno de los políticos?* Mexico City: Fondo de Cultura Económica, 2002.

Nunes, Rodrigo. "Politics without Insurance: Democratic Competition and Judicial Reform in Brazil." *Comparative Politics* 42, no. 3 (2010a): 313–31.

———. "Ideational Origins of Progressive Judicial Activism." *Latin American Politics and Society* 52, no. 3 (2010b): 67.

Nyamugasira, Warren. "NGOs and Advocacy: How Well Are the Poor Represented?" *Development in Practice* 8 (1998): 297–308.

Nylen, William R. *Participatory Democracy versus Elitist Democracy: Lessons from Brazil.* New York: Palgrave Macmillan, 2003.

O'Donnell, Guillermo. "Why the Rule of Law Matters." *Journal of Democracy* 15, no. 4 (2004): 32–46.

———. "Acerca del estado, la democratización, y algunos problemas conceptuales: una perspectiva latinoamericana con referencias a países poscomunistas." *Desarrollo Económico* 33, no. 130 (1993): 163–84.

———. "Delegative Democracy." *Journal of Democracy* 5, no. 1 (1994): 55–69.

———. *Dissonances: Democratic Critiques of Democracy.* Notre Dame, IN: University of Notre Dame Press, 2007.

———. "Horizontal Accountability in New Democracies." In *The Self-Restraining State: Power and Accountability in New Democracies.* Edited by Andreas Schedler, L. Diamond, and M. F. Plattner. Boulder, CO: Lynne Rienner, 1999.

———. "Illusions about Consolidation." *Journal of Democracy* 7, no. 2 (1996): 34–51.

———. "Notes on Various Accountabilities and Their Interrelations." In *Enforcing the Rule of Law.* Edited by Enrique Peruzzotti and Catalina Smulovitz. Pittsburgh, PA: Pittsburgh University Press, 2006.

O'Donnell, Guillermo, J. V. Cullell, and O. Iazzetta, eds. *The Quality of Democracy: Theory and Applications.* Notre Dame, IN: University of Notre Dame Press, 2004.

Oanda. *Oanda: The Currency Site, FX History,* n.d. www.oanda.com. Accessed April 14, 2009.

Oliveira, Francisco. "Privatização do público, destituição da fala e anulação da política: o totalitarismo neoliberal." In *Os sentidos da democracia. Políticas do dissenso e hegemonia.* Edited by F. Oliveira and M. C. Paoli. São Paulo: Vozes/NEDIC/FAPESP, 1999.

Página 20 (Rio Branco, Brazil). "Paro geral: Juízes radicalizam movimento e começam greve por tempo indeterminado." December 5, 2000.

Palanza, Valeria, and Gisela Sin. "Veto Bargaining and the Legislative Process in Multiparty Presidential Systems." *Comparative Political Studies* 47 (forthcoming 2014).

Panettieri, Jose. *Los Trabajadores.* Buenos Aires: Editorial Jorge Alvarez, 1967.

Pateman, Carole. "Participatory Democracy Revisited." *Perspectives on Politics* 10, no. 1 (2012): 7–19.

Patzelt, Werner. "Recruitment and Retention in Western European Parliaments." *Legislative Studies Quarterly* 24, no. 2 (1999): 239–79.

Peabody, Bruce, ed. *The Politics of Judicial Independence: Courts, Politics, and the Public*. Baltimore: The Johns Hopkins University Press, 2011.

Peltzer, Enrique. *Los Presidentes: Sus excesos, sus debilidades y el ocaso de la Argentina*. Buenos Aires: Nuevo Hacer/Grupo Editor Latinoamericano. 2006.

Peña, Carlos, Jorge Correa, Pablo Ruiz-Tagle, and Agustín Squella. *Evolución de la Cultura Jurídica Chilena*. Santiago: Corporación de Promoción Universitaria, 1994.

Pereira, Carlos, and Bernardo Muller. "Partidos Fracos na Arena Eleitoral e Partidos Fortes na Arena Legislativa: A Conexão Eleitoral no Brasil." *Dados* 46, no. 4 (2004): 735–71.

Pereira, Carlos, Timothy Power, and Lucio Renno. "Under What Conditions Do Presidents Resort to Decree Power? Theory and Evidence from the Brazilian Case." *The Journal of Politics* 67, no. 1 (2005): 178–200.

Pereira, Carlos, and Lucio Renno. "Successful Reelection Strategies in Brazil: The Electoral Impact of Distinct Institutional Incentives." *Electoral Studies* 22, no. 3 (2003): 425–48.

Pereira, Carlos, Lucio R. Renno, and David J. Samuels. "Corruption, Campaign Finance, and Reelection." In *Corruption and Democracy in Brazil: The Struggle for Accountability*. Edited by Timothy J. Power and Matthew M. Taylor. Notre Dame, IN: University of Notre Dame Press, 2011.

Perlin, Jan. "Rol del fiscal o ministerio public en la persecución penal: derechos de la víctima, el imputado y la sociedad. Tendencias en las reformas procesales latino-americanas." In *Instituciones, legalidad y estado de derecho en el México de la transición democrática*. Edited by Gustavo Fondevila. Mexico City: Fontamara, 2006.

Peruzzotti, Enrique. "Democratic Credentials or Bridging Mechanisms? Constituents, Representatives and the Dual Politics of Democratic Representation." In *Legitimacy Beyond the State? Re-examining the Democratic Credentials of Transnational Actors*. Edited by Eva Erman and Andres Uhlin. Houndmills, UK: Palgrave, 2010.

———. "The Nature of the New Argentine Democracy: The Delegative Democracy Argument Revisited." *Journal of Latin American Studies* 33, no. 1 (February 2001): 133–55.

———. "Representation as Mediated Politics." Centre for Civil Society, Non-Governmental Public Action Research Paper 26, London School of Economics, 2008.

———. "The Societalization of Horizontal Accountability: Rights Advocacy and the Defensoría del Pueblo de la Nación in Argentina." In *Human Rights, State Compliance and Social Change*. Edited by Ryan Goodman and Thomas Pegram. Cambridge, UK: Cambridge University Press, 2011.

———. "Towards a New Politics: Citizenship and Rights in Contemporary Argentina." *Citizenship Studies* 6, no. 1 (2002): 77–93.

Peruzzotti, Enrique, and Catalina Smulovitz. "Accountability Social, la otra cara del control." In *Controlando la política. Ciudadanos y Medios en las Nuevas Democracias Latinoamericanas*. Edited by Enrique Peruzzotti and Catalina Smulovitz. Buenos Aires: Editorial Temas, 2002.

———, eds. *Enforcing the Rule of Law: The Politics of Social Accountability in the New Latin American Democracies*. Pittsburgh: University of Pittsburgh Press, 2006.

Pettit, Philip. "Varieties of Public Representation." In *Political Representation*. Edited by Ian Shapiro, Susan C. Stokes, Elisabeth Jean Wood, and Alexander S. Kirshner. New York: Cambridge University Press, 2009.

Phillips, Anne. *The Politics of Presence*. New York: Oxford University Press, 1995.

Pinto, Mónica. "El principio pro homine. Criterios de hermenéutica y pautas para la regulación de los derechos humanos." In *La aplicación de los tratados sobre derechos humanos por los tribunales locales*. Edited by Martín Abregú and Christian Courtis. Buenos Aires: Editores del Puerto, 1997.

Pitkin, Hannah Fenichel. *The Concept of Representation*. Berkeley: University of California Press, 1967.

Pitkin, Hannah. *The Concept of Representation*. Berkeley: University of California Press, 1972.

Plato. *The Republic*. Translated by Desmond Lee. 1955. Reprint, New York: Penguin Classics, 2003.

PNUD. *Desarrollo humano en Chile 1998. Las paradojas de la modernización*. Santiago: PNUD, 1998.

———. *Más sociedad para gobernar el futuro*. Santiago: PNUD, 2000.

Poduje, Iván. *Participación ciudadana en proyectos de infraestructura y planes reguladores*. Temas de la Agenda Pública Año 3, no. 22. Santiago: Pontificia Universidad Católica de Chile, Vicerrectoría de Comunicaciones y Asuntos Públicos, 2008.

Polsby, Nelson W. "Legislatures." In *The Handbook of Political Science*. Vol. 5 of *Governmental Institutions and Processes*. Edited by Fred I. Greenstein and Nelson W. Polsby. Reading, MA: Addison-Wesley, 1975.

Poole, Keith T., and Howard Rosenthal. "D-NOMINATE after 10 Years: A Comparative Update to Congress: A Political-Economic History of Roll Call Voting." *Legislative Studies Quarterly* 26 (2001): 5–26.

Portales, Felipe. *Los mitos de la democracia chilena*. Santiago: Catalonia, 2004.

Posner, Paul. "Local Democracy and Popular Participation: Chile and Brazil in Comparative Perspective." *Democratization* 10, no. 3 (Autumn 2003): 39–67.

Powell, G. Bingham. "Citizens, Elected Policymakers, and Democratic Representation: Two Contributions from Comparative Politics." In *The Evolution of Political Knowledge: Democracy, Autonomy, and Conflict in Comparative and International Politics*. Edited by Edward D. Mansfield and Richard Sisson. Columbus: Ohio State University Press, 2004.

———. *Elections as Instruments of Democracy*. New Haven: Yale University Press, 2000.

Pozas Loyo, Andrea, and Julio Rios-Figueroa. "Enacting Constitutionalism: The Origins of Independent Judicial Institutions in Latin America." *Comparative Politics* 42, no. 3 (2010): 293–311.

———. "The Politics of Amendment Processes: Supreme Court Influence in the Design of Judicial Councils." *Texas Law Review* 89, no. 7 (2011): 1807–33.

Przeworski, Adam, and Susan C. Stokes, and Bernard Manin. *Democracy, Accountability and Representation*. Cambridge, UK: Cambridge University Press, 1999.

Przeworski, Adam, and Henry Teune. *The Logic of Comparative Social Inquiry*. New York: John Wiley, 1970.

Putnam, Robert D. *Making Democracy Work*. Princeton: Princeton University Press, 1993.

Ramseyer, Mark. "The Puzzling (In)Dependence of Courts: A Comparative Approach." *Journal of Legal Studies* 23 (1994): 721–47.

Recabarren, Lorena, and Marcel Aubry. "Resultados del estudio de asociatividad y participación ciudadana." In *Más democracia: Propuestas para la participación ciudadana*, various authors. Santiago: Más Voces, 2005.

Reforma Constitucional. Dictamen Preliminar del Consejo para la Consolidació de la Democracia. Buenos Aires: EUDEBA (Editorial de la Universidad de Buenos Aires), 1986.

Rehfeld, Andrew. "Representation Rethought: On Trustees, Delegates, and Gyroscopes in the Study of Political Representation and Democracy." *American Political Science Review* 103, vol. 2 (2009): 214–30.

———. "The Concepts of Representation." *American Political Science Review* 105, no. 3 (August 2011): 631–41.

————. "Towards a General Theory of Political Representation." *Journal of Politics* 68, no. 1 (2006): 1–21.

Remmer, Karen L. *Party Competition in Argentina and Chile: Political Recruitment and Public Policy, 1890–1930.* Lincoln: University of Nebraska Press, 1984.

Renno, Lucio. "Rewarding the Corrupt? Reelection and Scandal Involvement in the Brazilian 2006 Legislative Election." *Colombia Internacional* 68 (2008): 98–106.

Riker, William H. "Electoral Systems and Constitutional Restraints." In *Choosing an Electoral System: Issues and Alternatives.* Edited by A. Lijphart and B. Grofman. New York: Praeger, 1984.

Rios-Figueroa, Julio. "Fragmentation of Power and the Emergence of an Effective Judiciary in Mexico, 1994–2002." *Latin American Politics & Society* 49, no. 1 (2007): 31–57.

————. "Justice System Institutions and Corruption Control: Evidence from Latin America." *Justice System Journal* 33, no. 2 (2012): 196–214.

Rivas, Jose María. *Leyes de Trabajo Anotadas.* Buenos Aires: Editorial Victor P. de Zavalía, 1969.

Rocchi, Fernando. "Un largo camino a casa: empresarios, trabajadores e identidad industrial en Argentina, 1880–1930." In *La Cuestión Social en Argentina, 1870–1943.* Edited by Juan Suriano. Editorial La Colmena: Buenos Aires, 2000.

Rodriguez-Garavito, Cesar. "Toward a Sociology of the Global Rule of Law Field: Neoliberalism, Neoconstitutionalism, and the Contest over Judicial Reform in Latin America." In *Lawyers and the Rule of Law in an Era of Globalization.* Edited by Yves Dezalay and Bryant Garth. New York: Routledge, 2011.

Rohde, David. "Risk Bearing and Progressive Ambition: The Case of the Members of the United States House of Representatives." *American Journal of Political Science* 23, no. 1 (1979): 1–26.

Romero, J. *¿Qué hacer con los pobres? Elite y sectores populares en Santiago de Chile 1840–1895.* Buenos Aires: Editorial Sudamericana, 1997.

Rosenthal, Alan. "State Legislative Development: Observations from Three Perspectives." *Legislative Studies Quarterly* 21 (1996): 169–98.

Roxborough, Ian. "The Urban Working Class and Labour Movement in Latin America since 1930." In *Latin America since 1930, Economy, Society and Politics; Part 2, Politics and Society.* Vol. 6 of *The Cambridge History of Latin America.* Edited by Leslie Bethell. Cambridge, UK: Cambridge University Press, 1994.

Ryan, Daniel. "Democracia participativa, ambiente y sostenibilidad en Argentina." In *Ecología de la Información. Escenarios y actores para la participación ciudadana en asuntos ambientales.* Edited by Rodrigo Araya Dujisin. Santiago: FLACSO/Chile-Nueva Sociedad, 2000.

Sabato, Hilda. *La Política en las Calles. Entre el Voto y la Movilización. Buenos Aires 1862–1880.* Buenos Aires: Editorial Sudamericana, 1998.

Sabsay, Daniel A. "Environmental Issues and Sustainable Development within Participatory Democracy." *Aportes* 5, no. 12 (2008).

————. "El denominado 'amparo colectivo' consagrado por la reforma constitucional de 1994." In *Las Acciones de Interés Publico: Argentina, Chile, Colombia y Perú.* Edited by Felipe Gonzalez. Santiago: Ediciones de la Universidad Diego Portales, 1997.

Saiegh, Sebastian M. "Active Players or Rubber Stamps? An Evolution of the Policymaking Role of Latin American Legislatures." In *How Democracy Works: Political Institutions, Actors and Arenas in Latin American Policy Making.* Edited by Carlos Scartascini, Ernesto Stein, and Mariano Tommasi. Washington, D.C.: Inter-American Development Bank, 2010.

————. *Ruling by Statute: How Uncertainty and Vote-Buying Shape Lawmaking.* New York: Cambridge University Press, 2011.

Saldaña, Jorge. "Crisis en la participación electoral y debate sobre la obligatoriedad del voto en Chile." In *El genoma electoral chileno. Dibujando el mapa genético de las preferencias políticas en Chile.* Edited by P. Navia et al. Santiago: Ediciones Universidad Diego Portales, 2009.

Samuels, David. "Ambition and Competition: Explaining Legislative Turnover in Brazil." *Legislative Studies Quarterly* 15, no. 3 (2000): 481–97.

———. *Ambition, Federalism, and Legislative Politics in Brazil.* Cambridge, UK: Cambridge University Press, 2003.

———. "Incumbents and Challengers on a Level Playing Field: Assessing the Impact of Campaign Finance in Brazil." *The Journal of Politics* 63, no. 2 (2001): 569–84.

———. "Pork-Barreling Is Not Credit-Claiming or Advertising: Campaign Finance and the Sources of the Personal Vote in Brazil." *The Journal of Politics* 64, no. 3 (2002): 845–63.

Sánchez, Arianna, Beatriz Magloni, and Eric Magar. "Legalists vs. Interpretativist: The Supreme Court and Democratic Transition in Mexico." In *Courts in Latin America.* Edited by Gretchen Helmke and Julio Rios-Figueroa. New York: Cambridge University Press, 2011.

Santos, Fabiano. "Recruitment and Retention of Legislators in Brazil." *Legislative Studies Quarterly* 24, no. 2 (1999): 209–37.

Santos, Fabiano, and Lucio Renno. "The Selection of Committee Leadership in the Brazilian Chamber of Deputies." *The Journal of Legislative Studies* 10, no. 1 (2004): 50–70.

Santos, Wanderley G. *Sessenta e Quatro: Anatomia da Crise.* São Paulo: Vértice Press, 1986.

Saward, Michael. "Authorisation and Authenticity: Representation and the Unelected." *Journal of Political Philosophy* 17 (2009): 1–22.

———. "The Representative Claim." *Contemporary Political Theory* 5, no. 3 (2006): 297–318.

Scartascini, Carlos G., Ernesto Stein, and Mariano Tommasi, eds. *How Democracy Works: Political Institutions, Actors, and Arenas in Latin American Policymaking.* Washington, D.C.: Inter-American Development Bank and DRCLAS-Harvard University, 2012.

Schmitter, Philippe. "A Crisis of Real Existing Democracy or a Crisis of Representation? Or a Crisis of the Channels of Representation? Or a Crisis of One Channel of Representation?" Rethinking Representation: A North-South Dialogue Conference, Minas Gerais, Brazil, 2008.

Schmitter, Philippe C. "Defects and Deficits in the Quality of Neo-Democracy." In *Democratic Deficits: Addressing Challenges to Sustainability and Consolidation around the World.* Edited by Gary Bland and Cynthia J. Arnson. Washington, D.C.: Woodrow Wilson International Center for Scholars, 2009.

Schor, Miguel. "Constitutionalism through the Looking Glass of Latin America." *Texas International Law Journal* 41, no. 1 (2006).

Schumpeter, Joseph A. *Capitalism, Socialism, Democracy.* New York: Harper and Brothers, 1942.

Searing, Donald D. "Roles, Rules, and Rationality in the New Institutionalism." *American Political Science Review* 85, no. 4 (1991): 1239–60.

Selee, Andrew, and Enrique Peruzzotti, eds. *Participatory Innovation and Representative Democracy in Latin America.* Washington, D.C.: Woodrow Wilson Center/John Hopkins University Press, 2009.

Shapiro, Ian, Susan Stokes, Elisabeth Jean Wood, and Alexander Kirshner. *Political Representation.* Cambridge: Cambridge University Press, 2009.

Shepsle, Kenneth, and Barry Weingast. "The Institutional Foundations of Committee Power." *American Political Science Review* 81 (1987): 85–104.

Shirk, David. "Criminal Justice Reform in Mexico: An Overview." *Mexican Law Review* 3, no. 2 (2011): 1–38.

Shugart, Mathew S., and John M. Carey. *Presidents and Assemblies: Constitutional Design and Electoral Dynamics*. New York: Cambridge University Press, 1992.

Siavelis, Peter M. "Continuidad y transformación en el sistema de partidos en una transición 'modelo.'" In *El modelo chileno. Democracia y desarrollo en los noventa*. Edited by P. Drake and I. Jaksic. Santiago: LOM Ediciones, 1999.

———. "Elite-Mass Congruence, Partidocracia and the Quality of Chilean Democracy." *Journal of Politics in Latin America* 1, no. 3 (2009): 3–31.

Silva, Patricio. "Doing Politics in a Depoliticised Society: Social Change and Political Deactivation in Chile." *Bulletin of Latin American Research* 23, no. 1 (2004): 63–78.

———. "Technocrats and Politics in Chile: From the Chicago Boys to the CIEPLAN Monks." *Journal of Latin American Studies* 23, no. 2 (1991): 385–410.

Smith, Peter. *Argentina and the Failure of Democracy, Conflict among Political Elites 1904–1955*. Madison: University of Wisconsin Press, 1994.

Smith, Rogers M. "Historical Institutionalism and the Study of Law." In *The Oxford Handbook of Law and Politics*. Edited by Keith E. Whittington, R. Daniel Kelemen, and Gregory A. Caldeira. New York: Oxford University Press, 2008.

Smulovitz, Catalina, and Enrique Peruzzotti. "Societal and Horizontal Controls. Two Cases about a Fruitful Relationship." In *Accountability, Democratic Governance and Political Institutions in Latin America*. Edited by Scott Mainwaring and Christopher Welna. Oxford University Press, 2003.

Snyder, Richard. "After the State Withdraws: Neoliberalism and Subnational Authoritarian Regimes in Mexico." In *Subnational Politics and Democratization in Mexico*. Edited by Wayne Cornelius, Todd Eisenstadt, and Jane Hindley. La Jolla, CA: Center for U.S.-Mexican Studies at the University of California, San Diego, 1999.

Snyder, Richard. "Scaling Down: The Subnational Comparative Method." *Studies in Comparative International Development* 36, no. 1 (2001): 93–110.

Snyder, Richard, and David Samuels. "Devaluing the Vote in Latin America." *Journal of Democracy* 12, no. 1 (2001): 146–59.

Souraf, Frank. *Party and Representation*. New York: Atherton, 1963.

Spiller, Pablo T., and Mariano Tommasi. *The Institutional Foundations of Public Policy in Argentina: A Transactions Cost Approach*. New York: Cambridge University Press, 2007.

Squire, Peverill. "Member Career Opportunities and the Internal Organization of Legislatures." *The Journal of Politics* 50, no. 3 (1988): 726–44.

———. "Measuring State Legislative Professionalism: The Squire Index Revisited." *State Politics & Policy Quarterly* 7, no. 2 (2007): 211–27.

———. "Membership Turnover and the Efficient Processing of Legislation." *Legislative Studies Quarterly* 23, no. 1 (1998): 23–32.

Stein, Robert, and Kenneth Bickers. "Congressional Elections and the Pork Barrel." *The Journal of Politics* 56, no. 2 (1994).

Stokes, S. C. "What Do Policy Switches Tell Us about Democracy?" In *Democracy, Accountability, and Representation*. Edited by A. Przeworski, B. Manin, and S. Stokes. New York: Cambridge University Press, 1999.

Stone Sweet, Alec. *Governing with Judges: Constitutional Politics in Europe*. New York: Oxford University Press, 2000.

Strøm, Kaare. "Rules, Reasons and Routines: Legislative Roles in Parliamentary Democracies." *The Journal of Legislative Studies* 3, no. 1 (1997): 155–74.

Studlar, Donley T., and Ian McAllister. "Constituency Activity and Representational Roles among Australian Legislators." *Journal of Politics* 58 (1996): 69–90.

Suriano, Juan, ed. *La Cuestión Social en Argentina 1870–1943*. Buenos Aires: Editorial La Colmena, 2000.

Swift, Elaine. "The Electoral Connection Meets the Past: Lessons from Congressional History, 1789–1899." *Political Science Quarterly* 102, no. 4 (1987): 625–45.

Taagepera, Rein, and Mathew S. Shugart. *Seats and Votes: The Effects and Determinants of Electoral Systems.* New Haven: Yale University Press, 1989.

Tatagiba, Luciana. "Relação entre movimentos sociais e instituições políticas no cenário brasileiro recente. Reflexões em torno de uma agenda preliminar de pesquisa." In *Interrogating the Civil Society Agenda: Social Movements, Civil Society, and Democratic Innovation.* Edited by S. E. Alvarez, G. Baiocchi, A. Laó-Montez, and J. Rubin. Forthcoming.

Taylor, Lucy. "Civilising Civil Society: Distracting Popular Participation from Politics Itself." In *Contemporary Political Studies: Proceedings of the Conference of the Political Studies Association.* Edited by H. Monk and J. Stanyer. Glasgow: University of Glasgow, 1996.

Tedesco, Laura. "Democracy in Latin America: Issues of Governance in the Southern Cone." *Bulletin of Latin American Research* 23, no. 1 (2004): 30–42.

Teixeira, Ana Cláudia Chaves. "A Atuação das Organizações Não Governamentais: entre o Estado e o Conjunto da Sociedade." In *Sociedade civil e espaços públicos no Brasil.* Edited by E. Dagnino. São Paulo: Paz e Terra, 2002.

———. *Identidades em Construção: As Organizações Não Governamentais no Processo Brasileiro de Democratização.* São Paulo: Annablume/Fapesp, 2003.

Tendler, Judith. *Good Government in the Tropics.* Baltimore: The Johns Hopkins University Press, 1997.

Tocqueville, Alexis de. *Democracy in America.* New York: Anchor Books, [1835] 1969.

Tomz, Michael, Jason Wittenberg, and Gary King. Software for Interpreting and Presenting Statistical Results. Version 2.1. Stanford University, University of Wisconsin, and Harvard University. January 5, 2003. http://gking.harvard.edu/.

Torre, Juan Carlos, ed. *La Formación del Sindicalismo Peronista.* Buenos Aires, Editorial Legasa, 1988.

———. *La Vieja Guardia Sindical. Sobre los Orígenes del Peronismo.* Buenos Aires: Editorial Sudamericana-Instituto di Tella, 1990.

Tribe, L. *American Constitutional Law.* New York: The Foundation Press, 1988.

Tsebelis, George. *Veto Players: How Political Institutions Work.* Princeton: Princeton University Press, 2002.

Uildriks, Niels, and Nelia Tello Peon, eds. *Mexico's Unrule of Law: Implementing Human Rights in Police and Judicial Reform under Democratization.* Lanham, MD: Lexington Books, 2010.

United Nations Development Program (UNDP). "Democracy in Latin America: Toward a Citizens' Democracy." New York: United Nations, 2004.

Unsaín, Alejandro. *Ordenamiento de la Leyes Obreras Argentinas. IV Edición Actualizada.* Buenos Aires: Editorial El Ateneo, Academia de Ciencias Económicas, Ediciones Especiales, No. 2, 1952.

Urbinati, Nadia. "O Que Torna a Representação Democrática?" *Lua Nova* 67 (2006): 262–69.

———. "Representation as Advocacy: A Study of Democratic Deliberation." *Political Theory* 28, no. 6 (2000).

———. *Representative Democracy: Principles and Genealogy.* Chicago: University of Chicago Press, 2006.

Urbinati, Nadia, and Mark E. Warren. "The Concept of Representation in Contemporary Democratic Theory." *Annual Review of Political Science* 11 (2008): 387–412.

Valdés, Juan. *Pinochet's Economists: The Chicago School of Economics in Chile.* Cambridge, UK: Cambridge University Press, 1995.

Valenzuela, Arturo. *Political Brokers in Chile: Local Governments in a Centralized Polity.* Durham: Duke University Press, 1977.

Valenzuela, Eduardo "Sistema político y actores sociales en Chile." *Proposiciones* 22 (1993): 112–36.

Valenzuela, Samuel. *Democratización Vía Reforma, La Expansión del Sufragio en Chile.* Buenos Aires: Ediciones del IDES, 1985.

Valverde, Vanesa. "El Rol Representativo de los Legisladores Latinoamericanos." *Elites Parlamentarias Latinoamericanas.* Boletín de Opinión 3 (April 2009).

Varas, Augusto. "La (re)construcción democrática del espacio público." In *La propuesta ciudadana. Una nueva relación sociedad civil–Estado: Argentina, Colombia, Chile y Peru.* Edited by A. Varas. Santiago: Catalonia, 2006.

———. *La democracia frente al poder.* Santiago: Catalonia, 2012.

Vargas, José. "Democratización y calidad de la democracia." In *La reforma del Estado y la calidad de la democracia en México. Una reflexión sobre sus instituciones.* Edited by O. Ochoa. Mexico City: Miguel Angel Porrúa/EGAP, 2008.

Vázquez, Rodolfo, ed. *Corte, jueces y política.* Mexico City: Fontamara-Nexos, 2007.

Verbitsky, Horacio. *Hacer la Corte. La construcción de un poder absoluto sin justicia ni control.* Editorial Planeta-Espejo de la Argentina, Buenos Aires, 1993.

Waisbord, Silvio. *Watchdog Journalism in South America: News, Accountability, and Democracy.* New York: Columbia University Press, 2000.

Waisman, Carlos. "Autonomy, Self-Regulation and Democracy: Tocquevillean-Gellnerian Perspectives on Civil Society and the Bifurcated State in Latin America." In *Civil Society and Democracy in Latin America.* Edited by R. Feinberg, C. Waisman, and L. Zamosc. Basingstoke, UK: Palgrave MacMillan, 2006.

Waldron, Jeremy. "The Core of the Case against Judicial Review." *Yale Law Journal* 115 (2006): 1346–1406.

Wampler, Brian. *Participatory Budgeting in Brazil: Contestation, Cooperation and Accountability.* State College: Pennsylvania State University Press, 2009.

Warren, Mark, and Nadia Urbinati. "The Concept of Representation in Contemporary Democratic Theory." *Annual Review of Political Science* 11 (June 2008): 387–412.

Wehner, Joachim. *Legislatures and the Budget Process: The Myth of Fiscal Control.* New York: Palgrave Press, 2010.

Weldon, Jeffrey. "The Political Sources of Presidentialism in Mexico." In *Presidentialism and Democracy in Latin America.* Edited by Scott Mainwairing and Matthew Shugart. New York: Cambridge University Press, 1997.

Welp, Yanina. "La democracia insuficiente." In *Armas de doble filo. La participación ciudadana en la encrucijada.* Edited by Y. Welp and U. Serdült. Buenos Aires: Prometeo, 2009.

Whalke, John C., Heinz Eulau, William Buchanan, and LeRoy C. Ferguson. *The Legislative System.* New York: Wiley, 1962.

Wiarda, Howard, and Harvey F. Kline, eds. *Latin American Politics and Development,* 3rd ed. Boulder, CO: Westview Press, 1990.

Wilson, Bruce M., and Juan C. Rodríguez Cordero. "Legal Opportunity Structures and Social Movements: The Effects of Institutional Change on Costa Rican Politics." *Comparative Political Studies* 39, no. 3 (2006): 325–51.

Woods, Patricia. *Judicial Power and National Politics: Courts and Gender in the Religious-Secular Conflict in Israel.* Albany: SUNY Press, 2008.

Wynia, Gary W. "Argentina's New Democracy: Presidential Power and Legislative Limits." In *Legislatures and the New Democracies in Latin America.* Edited by David Close. Boulder, CO: Lynne Rienner Publishers, 1995.

Yashar, Deborah J. *Contesting Citizenship in Latin America. The Rise of Indigenous Movements and the Postliberal Challenge.* Cambridge: Cambridge University Press, 2005.

Young, I. M. *Inclusion and Democracy.* Oxford: Oxford University Press, 2000.

Zepeda Lecuona, Guillermo. *Crimen sin Castigo. Procuración de Justicia Penal y Ministerio.* Mexico City: F.C.E.-CIDAC, 2004.

———. "Evaluación de la reforma procesal penal en Chihuahua." Unpublished manuscript, 2011.

Zimmerman, Eduardo A. *Los Liberales Reformistas. La Cuestión Social en la Argentina, 1890–1916.* Buenos Aires: Editorial Sudamericana, 1995.

Zurn, Christopher F. "Judicial Review, Constitutional Juries and Civic Constitutional Fora: Rights, Democracy and Law." *Theoria: A Journal of Social and Political Theory* (2011): 63–94.

Index